3000 800012 18414

St. Louis Community College

C0-AKP-538

F V

WITHDRAWN

 St. Louis Community
College

Library

5801 Wilson Avenue
St. Louis, Missouri 63110

MICROCOMPUTERS IN READING AND LANGUAGE ARTS

MICROCOMPUTERS IN READING AND LANGUAGE ARTS

ERNEST BALAJTHY

State University of New York
College at Geneseo

PRENTICE-HALL, INC., *Englewood Cliffs, N.J. 07632*

Library of Congress Cataloging in Publication Data

Balajthy, Ernest (date)
Microcomputers in reading and language arts.

Bibliography: p.
Includes index.
1. Language arts—Computer-assisted instruction.
2. Reading—Computer-assisted instruction. I. Title.
LB1576.B259   1986   428'.007'8   85–9259
ISBN 0–13–580473–6

Cover photo by Laimute Druskis
Cover design: Photo Plus Art
Manufacturing buyer: Barbara Kelly Kittle

© 1986 by Prentice-Hall, Inc., Englewood Cliffs, New Jersey 07632

All rights reserved. No part of this book may be
reproduced, in any form or by any means,
without permission in writing from the publisher.

Printed in the United States of America

10   9   8   7   6   5   4   3   2   1

ISBN   0-13-580473-6   01

Prentice-Hall International (UK) Limited, *London*
Prentice-Hall of Australia Pty. Limited, *Sydney*
Prentice-Hall Canada Inc., *Toronto*
Prentice-Hall Hispanoamericana, S.A., *Mexico*
Prentice-Hall of India Private Limited, *New Delhi*
Prentice-Hall of Japan, Inc., *Tokyo*
Prentice-Hall of Southeast Asia Pte. Ltd., *Singapore*
Editora Prentice-Hall do Brasil, Ltda., *Rio de Janeiro*
Whitehall Books Limited, *Wellington, New Zealand*

To my family

CONTENTS

PREFACE

To as great an extent as possible in such a rapidly developing field, I've tried to make this book a comprehensive and timeless introduction to its topic of microcomputers in reading and language arts. "Timeless" in this area, however, means that some of its contents are out-of-date almost as soon as I send my final copy to the publisher. Computer instructional material is pouring onto the market in such quantities that it is a full-time job simply keeping track of the programs that are relevant to the reading and language arts teacher.

In this text, I deal with the broader issues involved in using computers and software in the classroom. I do not point to "the best" software on the market, simply because the market is constantly changing. Instead, I discuss general principles, then offer specific examples of these principles in operation, often referring to one or more published programs.

Bear in mind that the programs used as examples are not necessarily superior products. They are chosen *only* because they illustrate the principle under discussion. A word recognition program may have excellent graphics—and be cited accordingly—but may employ regrettable instructional techniques. Final evaluation of software is *your* responsibility as a professional educator, and the choice involves a wide range of criteria.

I hope to go beyond mere description to make positive statements about computer instruction and its relation to reading and language arts. Too often we accept as fact the general public's notion that no one knows what constitutes "good teaching." This is rubbish. A vast amount of research clearly shows the paths to effective instruction.

Our confusion arises from the complexity of the learning process, which in turn derives from the complexity of the human organism. We are all different. Therefore, we learn differently. These differences are not so enormous as to make effective instruction a hopeless goal, but they do make differentiated, individualized instruction a necessity.

It is impossible for any author—removed from the realities of your particular classroom and school—to pass final judgments on instructional techniques and material. The exceptions to most judgments would make them almost valueless. A certain program has excellent graphics, for example, which motivate many students but distract some learning disabled children. Another program uses a particularly effective technique, but it just doesn't fit well into your curriculum. Even if I were to limit my generalizations to a specifically defined group of students—the learning disabled, for example—the vast differences within even such a supposedly well-defined group would obviate many of the conclusions (Shepard, Smith, and Vojir, 1983).

The bottom line, then, is that *you must choose the software that best fits your students.*

Another policy carried out in this book is to avoid discussing materials that are useless to the classroom teacher. Specially funded research projects are not discussed here for several reasons: (1) They are often carried out under ideal laboratory settings and have little application to the classroom; (2) their materials are not available to teachers; and (3) their software is often user-unfriendly and amateurish, and many projects do not bother to debug their programs once they have gathered whatever research data they desire. These projects are often well publicized in the media and demonstrated at educational conferences. Careful examination, however, frequently brings out woeful shortcomings.

In addition, software that is limited to computers rarely found in the schools is not discussed. Publishers of such materials are usually given financial support by computer companies attempting to gain a foothold in the educational market. None show any potential for widespread success.

This book is not a wide-eyed prediction of the future. It deals with what is going on in *today's* classroom—with materials on the market *now*.

ACKNOWLEDGMENTS

Portions of Chapters 6, 7, and 8 are adapted, by permission of the International Reading Association, Newark, Delaware, from:

BALAJTHY, ERNEST. "Reinforcement and Drill by Microcomputer." *The Reading Teacher* 37, no. 6 (February 1984), 490–494.

BALAJTHY, ERNEST. "Computer Simulations and Reading." *The Reading Teacher* 37, no. 7 (March 1984), 590–593.

Screen page quotation on page 50 from *Alphabet Beasts & Co.* Used by permission of Software Productions, Columbus, Ohio.

Screen page quotations on pages 64 and 65 from *Cloze-Plus.* Used by permission of Milliken Publishing Company, St. Louis, Missouri, and Instructional/Communications Technology, Inc., Huntington Station, New York.

Screen page quotations on pages 70–71 from *Wordwright.* Used by permission of Encyclopaedia Britannica Educational Corporation, Chicago.

Screen page quotations on pages 81 and 86 from *Critical Reading.* Used by permission of Jostens Learning Systems, Arlington Heights, Illinois.

Screen page quotation on pages 92–93 from *How to Read in the Content Areas: Mathematics.* Used by permission of Educational Activities, Baldwin, New York.

Screen page quotation on page 140 from *Grammar Mastery.* Used by permission of The Regents/ALA Company, New York.

Quotation on page 143 from *Computer Power and Human Reason* by Joseph Weizenbaum. Used by permission of W. H. Freeman and Company, New York.

Figure 14–3 on page 178 used by permission of *Media and Methods*, Philadelphia.

Screen page quotation on page 201 from *MasterType*. Used by permission of Lightning Software.

1

INTRODUCTION: GETTING INTO MICROS

Once again high technology is redirecting the field of reading and language arts. Publisher after publisher produces instructional programs for use in classrooms. Computer manufacturers who once ignored the schools now hawk their wares, attempting to make a mark on the huge educational materials market.

The microcomputer "revolution" has hit the field of education. Large numbers of teachers have eagerly become involved. State and local educational agencies allot dollars for computers when every other aspect of their budgets is cut. The American educational system has been challenged to narrow the so-called technological gap in an effort to reverse the economic troubles plaguing the United States.

Where does this leave the reading and language arts teacher, who still may be having trouble threading movie projectors? How can the classroom teacher "get into" computers?

The first stage involves becoming acquainted with computers in a general way, to determine where and how they can fit into your classroom. Before dealing with this matter, however, let me offer three prefatory notes about the limitations of *computer-assisted instruction* (*CAI*), instruction provided with the aid of a computer:

1. Let's not greet the microcomputer blindly, uncritically accepting it into our classroom with open arms. Some computer material available today is second-rate or worse, prepared by enthusiasts eager to take advantage of this expanding market. Remember what we already know about language instruction and be prepared to reject any attempt (even by computers!) to degrade sound instruction.
2. Let's get our priorities straight. It is far more important to be aware of the latest developments in language learning theory and research—and

1

to incorporate them into our classroom instructional programs—than it is to jump on the computer bandwagon.

3. The suggestion that every teacher (or every student) must become *computer literate* (in the sense of learning how to program) is silly. It is akin to saying that every car driver must learn how to rebuild a carburetor or that everyone who wears clothing must be able to design and put together his or her own. Effective use of computers does not require any knowledge of programming at all. Using most software today requires as much technical expertise as using a cassette tape recorder.

The fact of the matter is that, while computers have already become an important part of all our lives, most people will be involved with them little more than inserting cartridges (as in home video games) or pushing a few simple buttons (as in programmable microwave ovens). Chapter 19 presents ideas for incorporating programming into a reading and language arts curriculum, increasing the value of the skill by relating it to the fundamental language skills.

DEVELOPING YOUR COMPUTER KNOWLEDGE

Or, How to Become a Microcomputer Expert in Eight Easy Steps

No, you don't need a B.S. in computer science to make microcomputers a part of your professional life, but you should become experienced with them. Here are eight suggestions for beginning, followed by a brief summary of research on the effectiveness of computerized instruction:

1. Overcome your fears. Most reading and language arts people begin their careers with studies in the humanities. They are insecure when dealing with technology.

There is nothing to fear. Little eight-year-olds readily adapt to using computers, and if they can do it, so can we! The basic ingredient in becoming familiar with computers, as with anything else, is time spent on the task.

Start out with computers by playing video games. Go to your nearest arcade with five or ten dollars worth of quarters. Choose a game. Watch an experienced ten-year-old for a few minutes; then try it yourself. Become an expert with it.

For a cheaper alternative, find a friend with a video game set hooked to a television. An even better idea is to find a friend who owns a microcomputer with game programs so that you can gain experience working the keyboard on an actual micro. Many teachers have found this to be the most successful method of introducing children to computer-assisted instruction. It connects CAI to something with which the child is already familiar. If it works for children, it will work for adults.

2. Allot time. Any skill requires time to develop. To become familiar with computers, one must spend time with them. You must work directly

with the machine, read books and periodicals, and listen to others who are interested and knowledgeable.

Frankly, I was dragged into working with microcomputers kicking and screaming. I knew that once they got into my blood, I wouldn't be able to drag myself away. After the first two-month high, during which I connived in every legal way (and maybe one or two mildly illegal ways) to spend time in front of various TRS–80s, I finally faced the fact that my life was being ruined by the darned things—physically (sleepless nights and no time for exercise), socially (who cares about humans when I can be with a computer?), and professionally (supervisors take a dim view of someone who ignores students in favor of the computer). It was time for withdrawal.

Since that time (except for occasional backsliding), I've organized my personal schedule in a more realistic fashion. If you are just starting with computers, such time management is necessary—one way or the other. That is, some people expect to gain expertise after just a few hours of study. With a topic as new and involved as microcomputers, this expectation is simply unrealistic. A very real commitment of time is necessary. Stories abound about micros gathering dust in schools where teachers and administrators have not made this commitment.

So much for the preliminaries. Let's get down to some serious matters:

3. Read your instruction manual or a good introductory book about your computer model. Remember Ausubel's (1960) work with advance organizers? He found that we learn faster and more efficiently when we start with background knowledge about the subject in the form of a well-developed schema (concept-network). Useful introductory books about each model of computer overflow the shelves at bookstores and libraries. The present book avoids duplication of them as much as possible. Choose a book to suit your own personality. Some are staid and scholarly, but many others are informal and generously illustrated with cartoons.

Be wary of the assumptions of the books' authors, however. A book written for hobbyists, programmers, or business executives will often contain advice inappropriate to instructional uses of computers. A book written for teachers who want to teach programming is not satisfactory for classroom teachers who wish to deal with language arts and reading.

4. Visit a classroom, school, or college that has microcomputers already in operation. As a matter of fact, visit several. Schools fortunate enough to have micros show them off eagerly. If the teachers have become true *hackers* (computer fanatics), you'll have a problem getting them to *stop* talking about their newfound hobby.

These experiences are invaluable. You will see the real thing, micros in use by live children. You will also get some feedback on what hardware to buy and what not to buy. You will examine commercial software programs and find out what the teachers and students think of them.

Finally, and perhaps most importantly, these visits give you the opportunity to establish relationships with fellow educational computer buffs, and someday you'll be able to trade programs and ideas with them. As more and more teachers become involved in use of computers, they will rely heavily on the expertise of experienced computer users.

5. Read monthly personal computing and educational computing journals. The field is expanding so rapidly that books on the subject simply do not keep up with new software and hardware developments. The time lag between writing a book and publishing it is too great. Journals and magazines such as *Creative Computing* or *Teaching and Computers* (see Appendix C) include such vital topics as software reviews—evaluations of how particular pieces of software perform in actual use. Some also publish sample programs that can be typed into your machine. Just as interesting are the advertisements for newly published software and hardware.

Obtain some of these periodicals through your local public library. Your school library may be willing to subscribe. Remember—computing is expensive. Always see if someone else is willing to spend money before you spend yours.

6. Begin collecting software catalogs and reviews. Computer journals and magazines carry advertisements from software manufacturers and distributors who send catalogs with descriptions of available software. Bear in mind, especially in the humanities and the language arts, that the description of the software may bear little resemblance to the actual package. Published reviews of software vary dramatically in quality, with unreliable mixtures of overly generous or unrealistically stringent evaluative criteria.

7. Visit professional educational conferences to see and use software that exists. Software distributors cannot send out a sample copy to each prospective buyer, because it can be illegally duplicated too easily. A few publishers offer demonstration diskettes with sample exercises of various programs. Distributors, especially the larger concerns that sell software from a variety of manufacturers, attend educational conferences and offer their wares for examination. These are the best places to review software.

Don't be timid. Push right on up to the front of the booth and ask the salespeople to demonstrate whatever they recommend for reading and language instruction. At general education conferences there might be little or nothing. Most educational software today is for computer literacy, mathematics, or school administration. At reading and language arts conferences, however, the salespeople will have their software ready and waiting for you.

Use it. Don't just look. Imagine yourself in the role of one of your students, left on his or her own to figure out what to do. Most programs should be completely self-explanatory. After all, CAI is supposed to enhance independent instruction. Press a few wrong keys. Find out what the program does when an incorrect answer is given.

As you use the program, keep in mind the checklists in this book, the Language Arts Software Evaluation Form (Chapter 4). Perhaps carry along a few copies to write quick notes after the demonstration. Also, be sure you get the exact name of the program and the name and address of the distributor.

8. Visit computer stores to see and use the hardware. As with all shopping, take everything the salesperson says with a grain of salt. Some stores sell only one brand and will push theirs as the best. Others sell several brands but will push the one from which they get the most profit. In addition, few salespeople really know very much about education and the specific needs of computer-using teachers. Let the buyer beware!

Ask to actually use educational programs with the hardware and to have a salesperson there to help you. If they aren't willing to cooperate with you before you buy, they certainly won't after they have your money. But be realistic—go to the store at off hours when there isn't a line of people waiting in front of every machine. Take notes. You won't remember everything afterward.

Many salespeople, by the way, really don't know very much about any brands other than their own, so general questions like, "Why is your computer better than Brand X?" won't get you very far. Be specific about your needs, and the salespeople will know what to show you.

RESEARCH ON COMPUTER EFFECTIVENESS

Are computers effective in improving instruction? It depends. It depends upon a wide variety of factors. A question phrased in this way has the same pertinence as the questions, "Are books effective in improving instruction?" or, "Are teachers effective in improving instruction?" Answers to our educational questions depend on far more than simply the medium of instruction. Future research must investigate specific aspects of various instructional media in order to determine how they differentially affect cognitive processing during learning (Reinking, 1984a).

While a good deal of research has been carried out on CAI, the fact of the matter is that this research is rendered undependable by a number of issues.

One is the so-called Hawthorne effect. New and innovative teaching techniques are often effective simply because they are new and innovative. Students like variety. They respond well to changes in their learning environments. It may be that positive effects of CAI research are due only to the fact that computers are new. When students become more accustomed to working on micros, this benefit will evaporate.

Almost all research to date has been carried out under very artificial learning conditions. The teacher-student ratio is invariably far better than the average classroom. Financial support from research grants greatly exceeds what would be expected in schools. Select groups of students are targeted.

Finally, each study focuses on a particular type of CAI in a particular content area. We have no reason to assume that all approaches to CAI are equally effective in all areas, any more than we can draw such sweeping generalizations about nonelectronic educational methods.

Chambers and Sprecher (1980) reviewed the research literature to draw three conclusions as to consistent findings:

1. CAI improves upon or equals the amount of learning from nonelectronic approaches.
2. Children learn faster through CAI.
3. Students' attitudes improve with CAI.

These researchers also have found evidence that the computer cannot replace the human teacher. Significant teacher involvement is necessary. Computerized instruction succeeds as long as there is human interaction to accompany it.

2

WHAT CAN A COMPUTER DO FOR ME?

A technical, machine-oriented answer to the question, "What is a micro-computer?" satisfies the average person about as much as a lecture on the internal combustion engine in answer to the question, "What is a car?" An automobile is defined according to its capabilities and functions, not its mechanical construction. A car takes us places, enables us to be independently mobile, and saves time.

Similarly, users of computers ought to feel no guilt about understanding electronic internal workings only vaguely. After all, how much do you really know about your car's engine, or the plumbing and electrical systems in your house for that matter? In our specialized society, we leave such matters to the specialists. Our concern in this chapter is about the role of the computer in reading and language arts instruction. We must examine the issue of just what we mean when we talk about "reading and language arts." Then we will look at the wide variety of computer applications in these fields, dividing them into two categories. First, some applications require language skills to use the computer to generate text or understand printed output. Second, other applications use the computer to improve language skills in ways that are directly instructional, such as tutorials and practice exercises. The two types of applications overlap to some degree. Each specific application is elaborated later in this book in the chapters listed in parentheses.

Interested readers can refer to the many good general introductions to the functioning of computers. Some have appeared on best-seller lists. Christopher Evans's *The Making of the Micro: A History of the Computer* (1981) is among the most complete and most readable about computers in general. Peter McWilliams's *The Personal Computer Book* (1983) offers a substantial amount of information about microcomputers in particular.

THE COMPUTER AND PRINT

Not too long ago, in the revolutionary days of the 1960s, some writers claimed that print was a dying medium. No longer would reading and writing be the key skills they once were. The electronic media offered more powerful and more direct lines of nonprint communication (McLuhan, 1964). The television screen, with its graphic visual images and auditory accompaniment, would be the medium of the future.

Has it happened? In classroom after classroom, home after home, business after business, television screens (*video monitors, video display terminals* [*VDTs*], or *cathode-ray tubes* [*CRTs*], in computer jargon) are appearing in droves. But we find that, instead of replacing print, the television screens themselves are full of print. From the typewriter-like word processors, which seem to have the effect of enormously multiplying the amount of printed verbiage flooding our "information society," to the complex business and mathematical programs such as *VisiCalc*, the computer has become devoted to the production and dissemination of printed material.

What then is the role of the language arts teacher in preparing students for this microcomputerized future? Have reading and writing become less important as electronics reform our society? Hardly. John Naisbitt notes in his best-selling *Megatrends* (1982) that reading and writing skills are all the more important today because of the changes brought about by microcomputers. "In this literacy-intensive society . . . we need basic reading and writing skills more than ever before" (p. 19).

THE COMPUTER AND LANGUAGE ARTS

Current theory and research support traditional approaches to the teaching of language that emphasize the interrelatedness of the varied language skills. The mind is at the core of the language program, in both its cognitive and its affective aspects. Attitudes, values, and motivations cannot be satisfactorily separated from cognition. Meaningfulness of activity in language arts curricula must be a central theme of each teacher's classroom planning in order to deal with both aspects of the mind's operation. Dull skill drills, centered on contentless reading or writing subskills and isolated from meaning, debase the language-learning process and inhibit children's conceptualizations about the true functions of language.

For purposes of analysis, the language arts curriculum is generally categorized into two major areas, receptive and expressive language. Teachers recognize, however, that both are interwoven in actual classroom practice, and they avoid the assumption that one is passive while the other is active: Both involve active construction of meaning, though in different forms.

The four basic emphases of receptive language are these:

Listening
Learning to read
Reading to learn
Literature

Listening skills are developed from the child's earliest years of instruction. Preschool and kindergarten teachers are aware of the vital importance of listening comprehension and oral vocabulary to future success in reading. Learning to read, which is of major importance in the primary years, involves word recognition skills (phonics, structural analysis, context, sight words), development of a meaning vocabulary, and comprehension skills. Older students, from the middle grades on, face the challenge of learning from text, of applying reading and study skills for efficient knowledge growth in the various content areas. Emphasis upon understanding and appreciation of good literature is characteristic of secondary English programs.

The four basic emphases of expressive language are the following:

Speaking
Learning to write
Writing to learn
Creative writing

Just as they do with listening skills, schools focus upon speaking skills from the earliest grades as the foundation for later expression. In the primary years, children are taught writing as an alternate form of expression, including the system of rules by which our language operates (grammar, spelling, punctuation). As the child grows older, writing is used increasingly as a particularly effective way to improve learning of content material (Emig, 1977). Creative writing for personal self-expression and enjoyment, as well as for appreciation of language, is an ongoing activity in the later years of student life.

It will be recognized at once that these skills are not completely hierarchical in nature. Creative writing and appreciation of stories are part of the elementary curriculum, just as college students learn speaking skills in their public speaking courses and listening skills in order to learn from lectures. This recognition creates the need for a "spiral curriculum" in the language arts, one in which the eight foundational elements are dealt with at each grade level, but in successively more complex ways.

The long-range goal, then, is to guide our students to be fully literate: not simply capable of carrying out basic listening, speaking, reading, and writing tasks but of going well beyond the performance-oriented basics in these language tasks. Huck (1979) describes the "fully literate" reader, a description which can be just as appropriately used to describe the "fully literate" listener, speaker, and writer:

the fully autonomous reader who reads widely on a variety of subjects; who makes rational decisions based upon an enlightened view of all sides of a controversy; the humane man or woman of letters who can entertain new ideas, accept different points of view and through reading can enter into the joys and hopes, the sorrow and despair of the world across time and space. (p. 26)

This view of language arts is not unique, nor will any of it come as a surprise to teachers. Balance and integration of the varied language skills has been the goal of teachers over the years. The unique goal of this book is to suggest ways in which the *computer* can be used as a teaching tool to further our traditional curricular goals. And the potential applications of the computer to language arts are virtually limitless.

Figure 2–1 offers a graphic view of the many ways in which the language arts relate to various aspects of the microcomputer. Far from having a diminished responsibility, language arts teachers at the elementary, secondary, and college levels now face additional demands in terms of preparing students to face the many language-oriented tasks that involve the use of microelectronics. In addition, the possibilities for instructional and classroom managerial use of microcomputers also expand the role of the reading and language arts teacher.

What are all these reading- and writing-centered applications? The list below is impressive in its dimensions and underscores the importance of the traditional language skills to the microcomputerization of society. Schools that are pouring thousands of dollars into teaching programming skills are really misunderstanding the major purpose of the computer literacy they think they are teaching. Our society will need few programmers. The great majority of our students will work with computers using ordinary language skills rather than BASIC or Pascal.

Applications in Which Language Skills Are Required

Information retrieval   (Chapter 20). Naisbitt's (1982) first chapter in his discussion of major trends in American society deals with the change from an industrial to an information society. Until 1956, blue-collar and agricultural workers outnumbered white-collar and office workers in the United States. Since that turning point, jobs in which workers deal with paper—with information rather than production of goods—have increased dramatically. Naisbitt notes that more people are employed in American colleges and universities than on farms, for example.

The handling of information by computers is called *data base management.* Typically, when the home computer user makes his or her first hardware purchase, a data base management package is one of the three software tools to be suggested by the computer store. (The other two are a *word processor*, which allows the computer to function like a typewriter, and a *spreadsheet* arithmetic calculator.) Data base packages (described in more detail in Chapter 20) function as electronic filing systems. Information is entered in labeled categories and can be sorted alphabetized, added to, subtracted from, or handled in a variety of other ways.

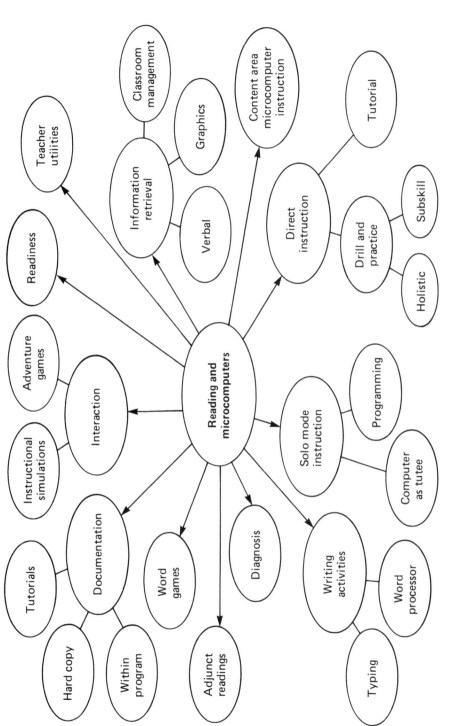

FIGURE 2–1. Model of microcomputers and reading

11

Teachers make use of these data base systems to manage the voluminous student records necessary to individualization. Software tools designed specifically for this purpose are called *computer-managed instruction* (*CMI*) programs. CMI programs make test results available for individual students, groups, or an entire class. Comprehensive CMI packages also include the actual testing of children and provision for prescriptions based upon that testing.

Businesses use data base management tools such as *PFS File* to control inventories and maintain customer files. Use of information stored in these systems requires knowledge of language and of organization, since much of the material is verbal in nature.

Charts and graphs   (Chapter 9). The vast increase in available information, coupled with the processing powers of the computer, has led to a new emphasis upon graphic presentation of information. A chart or graph can sum up huge amounts of information in a concise format. As a result, newspapers, newsmagazines, and television increasingly print charts and graphs. Many graphing programs are available for the microcomputer, for such visual presentations are readily adaptable to the computer, whether in printed format or on monitor display. Teachers need to pay special attention to teaching the use and construction of graphs and charts.

Programming   (Chapter 19). Development of programming skills requires great amounts of reading. While teachers can verbally pass on the major concepts, programming rules are so nit-picking as to be impossible to cover in reasonable amounts of classroom lecture time. Most programming is learned from books that present examples and explanations of each of the rules. Reading and ability to apply cognitive learning strategies are key skills.

Computer programming also involves problem solving. Programmers must develop the ability to think in an organized manner, reducing every problem to a series of subproblems to be solved in a step-by-step fashion. Papert (1980) labels this "machine thinking" and suggests that the development of these thinking patterns will dramatically improve students' general thinking ability. Bork (1981) agrees that programming "is a form of training for analytic thinking applicable to broad classes of problems" (p. 14). Largely as a result of such assertions, programming instruction is mushrooming as schools hope that the thinking skills used will transfer to general intellectual tasks, such as those involved in the language arts.

Word processing   (Chapters 10, 11, 17, and 20). Word processing has become an established part of the office routine. Everyone from company executives to the secretary communicates through word processors. Perhaps more than any other computer application, word processing will be used by students and office workers alike.

Documentation   (Chapter 21). While most computer users will never have to learn programming, all will be forced to deal with the *documentation*—written instructions—of various software packages. Such documentation may come in book form, in a computerized interactive tutorial program that leads the user through a sequenced process of learning, or in instructions that are available within the software program. Complex software requires complex abilities in following directions and in locational skills for finding needed instructions (that is, use of table of contents and index, skimming, and scanning). Documentation of some programs is hundreds of pages long.

Content area instruction by microcomputer (Chapter 9). Schools and corporations are making increasing use of computers for instructional purposes. Material is usually presented in print, requiring a student to learn from text. Text-learning strategies continue to be vitally important to efficiency of learning.

Interaction (Chapters 9 and 18). The computer's interactive qualities—its ability to respond to input—is of interest in two major areas. Computer simulations enable teachers to present scenarios requiring action on the student's part. The computer acts out the situation. Simulations can vary from running a neighborhood lemonade stand in order to learn about the capitalist system to flying an airplane or diagnosing and treating heart patients. Popular adventure game programs place players in far-off imaginary lands where they fight dragons or spies. Users of simulations must both read and write. Though some graphics are often used, the heart of the simulation is text based. Interaction is also a key feature of instructional tutorial programs.

Applications in Which Language Skills Are Taught

Readiness activities (Chapter 5). Simple programs to teach preschoolers important readiness skills are abundant. These range from drawing activities and video games to more closely reading-related programs that teach letter identifications and sight words. Color and animation possibilities in this software add tremendously to its appeal.

Direct instruction (Chapters 6, 7, and 8). An explosion in software availability enables teachers to offer instruction in virtually any reading or language arts skill. The term *computer-assisted instruction* is used for two kinds of teaching. *Drill and practice* programs do not teach, per se. They are designed to develop automaticity of performance by providing practice on skills, with feedback usually limited to whether answers are right or wrong.

Tutorials offer instruction. Simple-minded tutorials present pages of information on the screen, much like a printed textbook. They may include intermittent requests for a yes-no or multiple-choice answer. More effective tutorials create opportunities for active participation by the learner. The student engages in interactive dialogue as the computer guides the way through a series of carefully structured questions. The tutorial enables educators to create learning experiences similar to those carried out by Socrates. The Socratic method of teaching involved the asking of questions in a well-planned sequence. Rather than being lectured, the learner reacted to questions and was led to draw conclusions.

Writing activities   (Chapters 10, 11, and 12). The word processor has not only revolutionized the business office, but promises to revolutionize the classroom. The ability to compose and revise on computer offers teachers the opportunity to deal with writing processes in a way that emphasizes content and expression to a far greater extent than is possible with handwritten compositions.

Diagnosis   (Chapter 20). Diagnostic procedures can be carried out in an ongoing manner as students complete their work. Computerized reports on student progress can accurately pinpoint the skills that need further teaching or reinforcement.

Special diagnostic programs can also be used to test students' skill abilities. In addition, inexpensive test-scoring devices enable schools to grade standardized test answer sheets and obtain computer printouts of the results immediately.

Adjunct readings   (Chapter 21). Computer activities offer rich opportunities for supplementation with traditional print materials. A simulation program about pioneers crossing the western territories lends itself very well to reading a variety of stories and books.

Instructional games   (Chapter 18). Board games involving language activities have always been popular. Computerized versions can reinforce a variety of skills and enhance metacognitive abilities. The thinking required by such games as nim, backgammon, and chess can improve problem-solving abilities. Computer versions of *Scrabble,* crossword puzzles, and find-a-words can develop language abilities.

The microcomputer will greatly influence the teaching of language arts. Far from replacing language by some electronic hocus-pocus, the microcomputer has reemphasized the vital need for sophisticated language skills. In addition, it offers as much as it demands, for new and exciting instructional applications make possible the achievement of many objectives that lack of time and manpower once made impossible.

3

WHAT COMPUTER SHOULD I BUY? EVALUATING HARDWARE

This should be the last chapter you read. It is placed near the beginning of the book because most people expect it to be there. After all, they think to themselves, *hardware* is the key, isn't it? It's the nuts and bolts, the basics of your operation: the computer itself and all the peripheral devices such as disk drives, printers, and monitors. Isn't that supposed to come first?

No. The decision as to which microcomputer you buy should be your last decision in the process of computerizing your classroom.

First, decide exactly what you want to do with your microcomputers. This is a *software* decision, concerning the programs that will command the computer to do what you want. Decisions made at this point are irreversible in the future. Consider your needs both for today and for tomorrow. Once you've made the decision, you've committed your school to it for years to come. Only as a final step should you buy the computer hardware that will do what you want done.

CAN A "MERE" TEACHER EVALUATE HARDWARE?

As a matter of fact, teachers are best suited to perform evaluations of hardware, with some appropriate guidance. Many articles and checklists are available to aid in this task, but most miss the point. They ask technically complex questions about amount of available RAM, whether the computer is eight-bit or sixteen-bit, and so forth. These questions are not very important for the average user.

The *only* question of interest is, "Does this computer do what I want it to do, both now and during the next few years?" If the answer is yes, then no other questions need be asked.

This is not a technical question involving intricate knowledge of computer electronics. It *is* a technical question involving the very heart of language arts education. If the computer performs the functions you want in language arts instruction—in the ways you want—then buy it. You don't want "the best," "the newest," "the most innovative," "the simplest," or "the most powerful." You want the one that does the job.

A lot of half-truthful information is floating around about hardware. The rest of this chapter discusses the facts and fancies about computer hardware.

THE MYTHOLOGY OF COMPUTER HARDWARE

"Our Children Need Computer Literacy Today! And There's a Sale at Cheap Eddie's on the Model XTR–00!"

There's no rush. Our children don't need computer literacy today. As a matter of fact, most people will never have any need of much of the so-called "computer literacy" floating around today. Schools must take their time in purchasing hardware. Once thousands of dollars have been committed to a particular model, you can't turn back.

"Buy Cheap."

Arthur Luermann, one of the nation's leading experts on computer-assisted learning, advocates the teaching of BASIC to all children. Teachers can use the least expensive microcomputer available today to teach programming in BASIC. If that is your goal, it makes no sense to buy expensive models.

Inexpensive computers can be purchased for less than $100 these days. But do you want a computer for language arts instruction that cannot print lowercase letters on the monitor? Or, what will you do with a computer that has no software available for it? Such "good buys" are simply not acceptable in the teaching of language arts.

Computers that are powerful enough and flexible enough to meet meaningful needs cannot be purchased today for $300 or $400. The cheaper models are suitable for video game playing or programming in BASIC—not much more.

"Wait—Cheaper and Better Models Are Coming Out Next Month."

Prices of computers are declining. Newer and more powerful models arrive on the scene weekly. In this unstable environment, many are tempted to hold off until the choices become clearer.

However, the computer market is far more stable than most people believe. The major brands of computers suitable for classroom use, such as the Apple II and TRS–80, have been around for a number of years now, and software is widely available for them. Advanced models coming out aim at the business market (though they often don't state this in their advertisements) and have little or no application to the schools. It takes years to develop large amounts of software for new models, not to mention the time needed to iron the bugs out of the new products. Don't pay attention to salespeople who talk about future developments. Evaluate hardware based on what is available today. Michael Crichton (1983) compares this problem to the "Housewife's Fallacy: Don't clean the house, because it will only get dirty again anyway" (p. 104).

"This Micro Has 200 Cartridges to Choose From!"

A computer's "flexibility" is dependent upon the amount of software available for it. The Apple II (and its assorted descendants and "clones" such as the Franklin) is the most flexible computer on the market, by far. An estimated two to three times as many educational programs are available for the Apple II as for its nearest competitor in this area, the Radio Shack TRS–80. Atari, Commodore, and IBM computers, in turn, have less software than Radio Shack. Other computers are not in the running at all. Salespeople may tell you differently. Go to the software publishers' catalogs to prove it to yourself. It will take years for this situation to change significantly, if it ever does.

For most school systems, software availability should be the most important factor in choosing hardware. Most teachers will want to pick and choose different types of software in order to use their computers for word processing, for drill and practice in reading, for writing tutorials, and for the many other applications possible in the classroom. If they do not have tremendous flexibility, they will be forced into choosing from a surprisingly limited selection. I have seen many computers sitting unused in school closets because there is simply no suitable software available.

Keep in mind also that not all computers manufactured by the same company run compatible software. The Apple III and Apple's Lisa were designed for the business community and do not run the software for the less expensive Apple II, II+, and IIe computers. The latter three use the same software, for the most part. The Commodore PET, VIC, and 64 do not run the same software.

But should flexibility be the only factor in choosing a computer? What of the teacher who wishes to use her computers only for word processing? Every major computer model has word processing software available. *Bank Street Writer*, for example, is available for the Commodore, Atari, and Apple. If that is all you want, it makes no sense to buy the more expensive models. The cheaper computers perform the function just as well. If you wish to purchase a comprehensive skills management program that will use up most of your students' computer time, then flexibility in choosing other programs is not important. The school that uses the *CARD* series of reading programs from TRS–80 or Houghton Mifflin's *Microcourse* skill series can keep any number of their computers in constant use. Flexibility is a moot point.

In general, the more software the better. For teachers who know exactly what instructional software programs they want used, a less expensive system that can be dedicated to one use is satisfactory.

"There's More and More Software Coming Out for This Model."

Mr. Adams read in *Time Magazine* about the surprising growth in popularity of the IBM PC. First produced years after the Apple, it quickly outpaced Apple in sales. Many press reports predicted that it would be "the computer of the future" and that sooner or later all software would be compatible with it. He bought it for his school.

As he searched for software to use in the classroom, however, he found that almost all IBM software was for business use. Sure, he had plenty of accounting and data base programs to choose from, but there was precious little software for teaching reading. Yes, more and more programs might become available for the IBM, but he really hadn't expected to wait five or ten years before his teachers could use the machine. By that time, he agonized, the IBM will be out of date!

Beware of the promises of salespeople and manufacturers. No one knows what the future holds in store. A computer company might be sincerely planning to develop a version of LOGO for the computer, for example, but those plans have a way of falling through. "What you see is what you get."

"We'll Start with a Micro and Add the Peripherals When We Get Money."

Mrs. Bonnie, the PTA president, proudly presented two brand new microcomputers to the principal of Central Avenue School. A lot of bake sales had been held to purchase them, and the principal was suitably gracious.

Silently, however, he wondered just what he was expected to do with them. Each had a monitor, but there was no data storage device and no printer. Students couldn't load any programs into them. Even if he used up his entire discretionary fund to buy a disk drive, inability to print any output would severely limit the computer's usefulness.

"You Don't Have to Buy a $300 Disk Drive; This Works with a $30 Cassette Tape Recorder."

Some computers allow programs to be stored on cassette tapes in much the same way music is recorded on them, an inexpensive alternative to disk drives. Several years ago, use of cassettes was standard for personal computer owners, since disk drives were prohibitively expensive.

Use of tape recorders as data storage devices is impractical and results in a great waste of student time. Cassette programs take far longer to load into the computer than programs on disk. As a result, complex programs such as word processors cannot be stored on cassettes. A recorder runs at 1⅞ inches of tape per second. This translates into a load time of four to seven minutes (!!) for a tiny 16K program. Cassettes are simply not practical in the classroom.

Today's technology involves the use of *diskettes* (also called *disks, floppies,* and *floppy disks*). These are 5¼-inch circles of Mylar plastic, covered with a magnetic coating similar to that used on cassette tapes. They are encased in a stiff cardboard envelope that is never removed. A magnetic head (again similar to the head in a cassette recorder) reads magnetically encoded information through an oval hole in the protective envelope. Floppies are inserted into the slit on a disk drive. The latch is then flipped shut, and a red light goes on as the drive head begins to read whatever is on the disk. You can think of them as specialized records that are automatically played by the disk drive.

Dramatic reductions in prices of disk drives have brought them well within reach of school budgets. If a school can afford a computer, it can afford at least one disk drive to go with it, or else events similar to the following will be commonplace:

As Tommy sat waiting in front of a blank screen the five minutes necessary to load his vocabulary game program from the cassette tape, he idly jammed his pencil point between the computer's keys. . . .

"Waiting for your computer when it has to search for some information on a tape is like waiting for Godot" (Sandberg-Diment, 1983).

"A Printer Is Nice, but You Don't Need One."

If a teacher plans to restrict use of the microcomputer to tutorials and drills, a printer may not be necessary. A well-rounded language arts curriculum, however, requires a printer to put results on paper. Compositions completed on a word processor seem very incomplete unless the final draft can be printed out on paper. Printers also help in producing material for student use, as in preparing ditto or mimeograph masters for duplication.

Three types of printers are widely available. Most *letter quality* printers use a star-shaped *daisy wheel* that spins to the appropriate letter and is punched to print a character as clear as those printed on a typewriter. These are expensive. They also make so much noise that they will disrupt classrooms several doors down the hall, not to mention your own. While some are quieter than others, you will need a soundproofing box costing several hundred dollars to enclose the machine. Letter quality printers are unacceptable for classroom use. Don't buy one.

Dot matrix printers form characters from a pattern of tiny printed dots. Once so crude as to be almost unreadable, today's dot matrix printers can print almost as nicely as letter quality, and they are far more flexible for printing of graphics. By doublestriking, some are able to fill in the dots for a very attractive print quality. Though dot matrix printers are not as noisy as letter quality printers, it is generally best to restrict printing to times when other children are not concentrating on reading or other assignments. Dot matrix printers are much faster than letter quality printers, an important factor when using them to type out long essays. They are also less expensive.

Thermal printers are the least expensive and are completely silent, using heat-sensitive paper to form characters by burning them onto the page. The paper is ten to 20 times as expensive as normal paper and is not pleasant to touch. Since no printing head strikes the paper, teachers cannot use thermal printers directly to impress ditto or mimeograph masters. In terms of classroom use, however, their silence is indeed golden.

Some large computer centers, such as those at universities, use ink-jet printers or laser printers. Ink-jet printers spray ink onto the page, and laser printers burn the print onto paper. Both are very fast and usually cost upwards from $20,000, a bit steep for the average classroom. Ink-jet printers have recently become available at much reduced prices.

Only one printer is necessary for each classroom except in unusual circumstances. Schools often house letter quality and dot matrix printers in a central office or computer room where their noise will not be disruptive to classes. Students who wish to print out their compositions take their disks to this room.

"This Baby Has 256K RAM."

Random access memory (RAM) refers to the amount of memory available in a computer. Computers actually have two types of memory. RAM involves memory space into which software programs can be loaded. *Read only memory* (ROM) is memory space used by the internal workings of the computer. The user cannot change the contents of ROM, but every time someone loads a program into the computer, RAM contents are changed.

Memory is measured in *kilobytes* (K). The more kilobytes available in RAM, the larger and more complex the software can be. As microprocessors decline in price, newer computers are becoming available with more and more memory space. The old Apple II, for example, had 48K. A newer version of the Apple was produced in the early 1980s with 64K. Franklin, an Apple competitor, then played one-upmanship by producing a computer with 126K. Computers with very large memories are increasingly available.

For most instructional purposes, however, a massive memory is useless. Software producers realize that most schools are equipped with the less expensive 48K machines, so they have published programs that are small enough to fit that memory capability. Since 64K machines are rapidly becoming available, we will soon see larger, more complex programs designed for this memory capability. Money spent on buying hardware with greater memory size than 64K is wasted.

Monitor the market closely, however. Software producers are champing at the bit to produce programs that take advantage of greater memory capabilities. In years to come, as schools buy more powerful computers and a market develops for larger, more powerful programs, they will be produced.

Many computers can be upgraded to larger memory size at any time after purchase. A simple insertion of a single board with microchips into a slot at the back of the Apple increases its memory, for example.

"Children Are Motivated by Color Graphics; Don't Buy a Monochrome Monitor."

Clarity of screen presentation (called *resolution*) is key to the language arts. No one can read fuzzy letters on a screen without developing a headache. The ideal monitor for classroom use is a color high-resolution screen. *High resolution* indicates that the screen presentation is extremely detailed and clear. Even the very small print involved in using an 80-column word processor is clearly seen. (Letters are printed small enough so that 80 fit across the screen. Most microcomputers normally print larger letters, of 40-column size.) When using such small print, high resolution is necessary. Color high-resolution monitors, called *RGB* (for "red-green-blue") monitors, are expensive and often require a special piece of hardware called an "interface card" inside the computer to work properly.

Keep in mind that the size of print appearing on the screen is controlled primarily by the computer, not the monitor. The Apple II, for example, normally prints characters that are sized to yield 40 columns across the screen. The TRS–80 Model III displays smaller characters, fitting 64 across the screen. Special modifications, made in either the hardware or the software, can change print size. The monitor controls the print size only in terms of its own screen size. Larger monitors print the letters larger, of course, and smaller monitors print them smaller.

Choosing monitor size is not difficult. Simply avoid extremes. The tiny nine-inch screens on portable computers (measured diagonally as with television sets) are ridiculously small for children to use. Huge 19-inch monitors are more appropriate for whole-class instruction than for use at individual micro stations.

Most schools that want color buy *low-resolution* monitors, called *composite* monitors. The quality of letter production on these screens is less satisfactory. The colors that make up the white tend to be misregistered, and text gets fuzzy or spangled with random flecks of color. Again, however, availability of hardware has dictated what software publishers are producing. Most educational software avoids use of the smaller letter sizes so that their programs are presented acceptably on low-resolution screens. The original version of *Bank Street Writer*, designed for classroom use, used a 40-column display rather than the smaller 80-column print size used in most adult word processors. If you use a low-resolution color monitor, turn off the color by using the color control knob when children are dealing with large amounts of on-screen text. This helps a bit.

Consider an inexpensive alternative, however. In language arts, color is far less important than ability to read the screen presentation with ease. High-resolution monochrome (one-color) monitors are inexpensive and present very clear pictures. Such monitors come in black and white, black and green, and black and amber. Black-and-green monitors are most popular among office workers who deal with large amounts of text. Amber is very popular in Europe, and many users believe these monitors produce less eyestrain. Research has shown that white on black is the worst combination for the eyes (Gabel, 1982), even though computers such as the TRS–80 Model III offer it as standard.

Ordinary television sets may also be used as monitors when connected to the computer by way of a small device called a *modulator*. Some computer models have built-in modulators and others require an extra purchase. Resolution of television sets is poor, however, and they are unacceptable for use in language arts classrooms.

"Start with Inexpensive Computers Now; in a Few Years We'll Switch to the Better Models."

Mrs. Perretti wandered the aisles of publishers' displays at the annual state reading association conference. Time after time attractive microcomputer software caught her eye. "Is this available for the XLR Kumquat?" she inquired of the salesperson. Time after time the answer was the same: no. The Kumquats had seemed like such a great buy at three for the price of two, but the software available simply didn't meet the needs of Mrs. Perretti's eighth grade remedial readers. And the school system certainly was not going to scrap $10,000 worth of hardware and replace it with $20,000 worth of a better brand.

Inexpensive computers rarely have much educational software available. Avoid making hardware purchases on the basis of price alone.

"Leave the Choice Up to the Pros; Let the Computer Science Teachers Decide."

Joseph Olneski, superintendent of schools in Arlestown, had done his homework when the microcomputer issue first surfaced. He researched computer-assisted instructional issues, subscribed to the leading educational journals, and conferred with experts at the state university. The advice was pretty clear: Centralize decision-making power in the hands of the school system's computer experts. Follow the lead of such influential organizations as Minnesota Educational Computing Consortium to choose one brand of computer for greater consistency of software management and for easier maintenance.

The decision was made. The school district's specially appointed computer literacy committee had chosen the Orangepeel IIIA, a powerful and expensive computer. The computer programming courses were going full blast, from the teaching of LOGO in the kindergarten to Pascal in the senior high school.

But now the reading supervisor was complaining. The basal reading series used by the entire school system had microcomputerized its diagnostic/prescriptive management system on the XLR Kumquat. Hadn't the computer science experts taken this into account when they made their choice? And what about the language arts supervisor who wanted to start students studying the revising process in composition by using word processors? Why should she be allotted ten Orangepeels at $2,000 apiece when exactly the same word processing program would run on the Kumquat, twice as many of which could be purchased for the same price?

Different needs dictate different hardware. The teachers and supervisors who are involved in actual use of the machines must be involved in the decision-making process.

"The Software Situation Is Ridiculous; Let's Wait Until They Come Up with a Computer That Will Run All Different Types of Software."

An Apple cannot run TRS–80 software. Software designed for the Atari will not work in a Commodore. Marketing decisions and copyright laws have led different companies to produce different *configurations* (operational designs) that are incompatible with each other. If you decide to wait for some sort of standardization to occur, you've got a very long wait ahead of you.

What does the future hold in store? No one really knows, but two trends are evident.

First, there will be a general "shaking out" of the industry, to describe the phenomenon in business executives' terms. Computer companies that have not grabbed a significant part of the computer-market pie will drop out of the business. Osborne, maker of portable computers, and Texas Instruments were the first two major producers to stop production of their personal computers.

There is a moral to this story for school systems. Invest your money wisely, in a company that will be around for the foreseeable future. Once a hardware company goes out of business, no one will construct any more software for their computers.

Second, computers are already being developed that run more than one type of software. This is much more complex than most people imagine. Software of one type is intrinsically incompatible with other types. In order for a computer to run two different configurations of software, you actually need two different types of computers built into one console, with two different series of microprocessing chips. In essence, what you end up with is one keyboard and one monitor connected to the internal workings of two different computers inside one computer cabinet shell.

Quadram was one of the first to develop such a device, which enables an IBM PC to run Apple software. A plastic board, complete with all the microprocessing chips necessary to form the heart of an Apple computer, is inserted into a slot inside the IBM. Apple disks placed inside the IBM's disk drives are then read, and programs are run. While the Apple insert board is in operation, the central processing microcomputer chips of the actual IBM are inactive.

A standard joke among computer users is that the Quadram board is a $700 device capable of turning a $5,000 computer (the IBM) into a $2,000 computer (the Apple).

Other such devices, available for some time, enable various computers to run software constructed under the Control Program for Micro-computers (CP/M) operating system.

These conversion devices are quite expensive, because they are constructed of the most complex components of the computer they are designed to simulate, but they are certainly not as costly as buying a completely new computer with accompanying peripherals.

Many other hardware devices are available for use with microcomputers. Modems allow computers to communicate with one another over phone lines. Speech devices provide limited capabilities for the computer to produce and recognize speech. Light pens and touch-sensitive monitor screens and pads allow the user to point at the screen or at a tablet to communicate with the computer. These and other devices of interest in the teaching of reading and language arts are discussed elsewhere in this book.

Still other hardware devices are less applicable to educational situations but may be of interest to computer enthusiasts. Plotters allow the computer to print blueprints and charts using pens that move in all four directions. Graphics tablets enable users to create graphic designs by drawing on an electronic slate. A user can employ a printer buffer so that he or she can use the printer while the computer is being used for another purpose. Popular computing journals have regular columns reviewing such hardware developments.

4

EVALUATING LANGUAGE ARTS SOFTWARE

When a teacher first becomes interested in the possibility of using a microcomputer in the classroom, the first question asked is almost always, "What kind of computer should I buy?" The second question asked is, "What is some good software to use in my classroom?" These questions should be reversed in order. Often your choice of software will dictate which computer you should buy. Not all software runs on all computers.

Sadly, educators and publishers are not paying enough attention to software concerns. Schramm (1977) concluded his discussion of the various media with the following observation:

> A visitor from another planet, unfamiliar with the atmosphere in which educational development takes place here, might be astonished to see how much of the effort and resources of a typical project go into procuring and operating expensive hardware rather than into producing more effective software (preferably for less-expensive hardware). (p. 278)

How can we find good software? Everyone evaluates software these days. Software reviews appear in dozens of publications, as individuals and organizations jockey for a toehold in the computer field. Computer magazines and journals are proliferating. Mimeographed newsletters abound, their publishers hoping to graduate to the "big time" and establish themselves as nationally recognized computer authorities.

If this sounds cynical, there is good reason for it. Do schools and teachers choose their texts, their skill development systems, or their supplemental drill books on the basis of reviews? Do supervisors look through evaluations of reading basal series and choose one solely on the basis of what *Instructor* magazine or *The Reading Teacher* has to say about it? Of course not. Print materials are chosen by personal evaluation, carried out with the needs of particular classes or schools in mind.

Computer materials must be evaluated in exactly the same way. Teachers, supervisors, and administrators should personally choose software. Only they know what is best for their particular students. Published reviews give a useful head start, but they are only a beginning. Use reviews to narrow your choices, then personally evaluate the top few contenders.

PUBLISHED REVIEWS OF SOFTWARE

A list of selected sources for software reviews is in Appendix C. Let the buyer beware, however. The review process is unsatisfactory for a number of reasons, some of them insurmountable:

1. By their very nature reviews deal with general suitability. No reviewer knows what is needed by your students.
2. Reviews are written by computer enthusiasts, not by professionals who understand the functioning of the classroom.
3. Reviewers base their critiques on their own use of the program, not on watching children use it.
4. Reviewers have a hidden agenda—a purpose that they might not even recognize themselves. They operate under the assumptions that, first, the computer *must* be used in the classroom, and, second, that there *must* be some software out there that is worth using for every possible application. Neither assumption is true. We *don't* need to use computers. Many times other media suit our needs just fine, thank you.
5. A review gives just one person's opinion. Some reviews are constructed cooperatively by several people. These are just several people's opinions—no more than that.
6. Reviews offer vague summaries rather than exact blow-by-blow descriptions of software performance.
7. Reviewers are biased toward one particular instructional format or theory. Anything that doesn't fit that bias is denounced.
8. Reviews are outdated by time of publication. Revisions of software are carried out far easier than revisions of printed material. Publishers can and do modify programs frequently.

One important exception to a reluctance to rely on the review process involves programs such as data management systems, word processors, and calculation spreadsheets. Because of their extreme complexity, the average user cannot properly compare more than one or two without wasting enormous amounts of time. Decide which features you want, read the reviews carefully, then try out the one program you believe to be the best for your needs. If it lives up to expectations, buy it.

LANGUAGE ARTS SOFTWARE EVALUATION FORM

Michael Crichton's theme in his opening chapter of *Electronic Life* (1983) is that the computer does not give less individual control over our world. Instead, it gives more. Once upon a time we used human operators to place every telephone call. The change to automatic switching devices seemed at first to depersonalize the phone system. No longer could you hear operators talking to one another in their regional accents, routing calls through their switchboards.

After initial complaints, the public realized that automatic devices gave faster service and increased privacy. In similar fashion, teachers will understand the benefits that the computer offers in terms of personal control. Every aspect of instruction from content to method is increasingly under the control of teachers, depending upon their choice and use of software.

> It's at this point that the question of who's running the revolution becomes answered. You are. . . . Computers have become small, cheap, and widespread. . . . These . . . events put you firmly in charge. You're a general, not a private. In fact, there are no privates. Step to the mirror and salute yourself—then go carry out your own orders. (Crichton, 1983, p. 10)

The moral of our story is, *Evaluate software yourself*. The whole point of the microcomputer revolution is that *you* should be in charge of what goes on in your classroom.

The Language Arts Software Evaluation Form at the end of this chapter can be helpful. Keep in mind that this list is only a first step in the evaluation process. Your critique should continue with more in-depth analyses based on the particular type of software being reviewed. Later chapters on the various types suited to language arts instruction will help guide this process.

Do not use this checklist to rate software by any point system. Some items are far more important than others. Which is more important, for example, instructional quality or cute graphics? Both might be nice, but few teachers would have any trouble choosing. If you like the clean, decisive aspects of a point system, develop your own adaptation of this list, giving varying point values to each item depending on importance.

Some items must be considered on a relative basis. User-friendliness is one thing when playing an arcade vocabulary game. Such games should practically run themselves without instructions. Use of word processing software is considerably more complex. Even the most user-friendly word processor requires close study of detailed directions.

To summarize: The Software Evaluation Form provides a solid start for evaluation, once it has been modified to meet your needs. The chapters that follow give detailed evaluation criteria for particular types of software. The final and most important step involves classroom testing. If the software efficiently provides for the needs of your students, it has passed its most important test.

A. IS THE PROGRAM EDUCATIONALLY VALUABLE?

1. Is the Content Important to Learning Language?

Knowledge of research in language instruction helps in this decision. Do scrambled word lists such as *Magic Spells* really teach spelling skills? Do find-a-word puzzles such as *Wordsearch* help students in visual perception or word identification? Does the study of obscure Latin and Greek word parts improve vocabulary? Many teachers suspect that these activities tend to be meaningless busywork beyond having some motivational value.

Bork (1984) criticizes much educational software as placing the major emphasis on technology rather than pedagogy. The simple fact that we can accomplish a task with computers does not automatically confer educational justification on that accomplishment.

2. Do the Instructional Techniques Mesh with Current Trends in Education?

Learning should be an active, hands-on process. Some programs do not involve students in learning. Instead they present frame after frame of printed information to be read. The program consists of printed pages transferred to the video screen. The computer acts only to turn the pages. No interaction takes place between student and computer except for the press of the space bar when the frame has been read. Such programs miss the point of computerized instruction. They assume that learning is simply a matter of communicating information to students. Current theory in cognitive psychology suggests a radically different approach to learning, one involving personal responsibility for learning and active construction of personal meaning (Wittrock, 1979).

Well-designed instruction presents material in sequenced steps that are small enough to be integrated with past learning (O'Day, 1971). Presentation of too many ideas or skills at one time ends up confusing children. The behavioral psychologist B. F. Skinner (1953) noted that learning increments should be so small that correct responses to problems by children are almost certain.

3. Can the Same Work Be Done Just as Well with Nonelectronic Media?

Take advantage of the best media for your purpose. Controlled Readers (EDL/McGraw-Hill) or Guided Readers (Instructional/Communication Technologies) are superior to computers for the purpose of flashing lines of print at varying speeds. Electronic books, much touted in the media as the wave of the future, are still far in the future. More traditional media, including books, workbooks, and films, offer many advantages over computers for certain purposes.

4. Does the Program Involve Actual Experiences in Language or Writing, or Is All Work Isolated Drill Instruction?

In *Comprehension Power* students read stories about sailing or about American Indians. In *Getting the Main Idea* there is no unified passage but rather a series of unrelated paragraphs. Which approach is more valuable for students, both in terms of learning from text and in terms of actual reading experience?

5. Will the Skills Learned Have Value to Students in Your Classroom?

Do any of your students need to be taught the skill? One teacher uses the language experience program *Story Machine* with her sixth graders. Students type in THE BOY DANCES and watch an animation sequence of a boy dancing. While it's fun to type in sentences and see the actions performed, do sixth graders really benefit from working with a program which has a 40-word preprimer vocabulary? Do your second graders really need *Customized Alphabet Drill* to review their letters?

6. Will This Program Serve as a Useful Supplement to Your Classroom Language Arts Program?

Some programs require major changes in your teaching. Are you willing to revise your writing curriculum to center it on word processing technology? If not, a word processor will not fit into your classroom very well. On the other hand, many programs can fit very neatly into small niches in the overall classroom curriculum. If you are looking for some materials to correct deficiencies in homonym identification, *Homonyms in Context* may fit the bill.

Decide in advance the program's role in your classroom. Is the program intended to present initial instruction in a concept? Is it meant to act as an individualized device for remediating a specific skill? Is its role to review material already learned, or to provide extended drill and practice?

7. Do the Skills Involved in the Program Fit into the Scope and Sequence Chart That You Use as a Guide?

If the curriculum guide states that all fifth grade teachers are to introduce students to poetry writing by using Haiku, *Compupoem* can provide instruction, examples, and practice, fitting neatly into the established curriculum.

8. Is the Program of Use to Students with Special Educational Needs?

The value of keeping all students—including language-impaired children, special education students, those with low motivation, and those studying English as a second language—in the mainstream of the educational process is apparent. The problems with this approach are apparent as well. The ability of the computer to provide independent, individualized instruction to such students, to serve as a teacher's aide in this regard, is one of its most valuable assets to the classroom teacher. Programs may be procured to provide individualized attention to special students. A complete English as a Second Language series of tutorial programs, including *Grammar Mastery*, is available from Regents/ALA, for example. A secondary school teacher with mainstreamed special education students can provide instruction to them at almost any level, with the right software.

9. Does the Program Use Correct Standard English?

Faulty English (grammar, spelling, punctuation) is a problem especially with low-budget or public domain software (that is, material that is free, donated by its programmer to the public). Publishers of the less expensive materials often do not have the quality control resources necessary to do a top-notch job.

10. Are Instructional Objectives Stated, and Does the Program Fulfill Those Objectives?

Listening to publishers' claims about LOGO, *Delta Drawing*, and the like may give the impression that we should scrap the entire elementary curriculum in favor of having children draw pictures on video monitors. This software is all we need.

Few of these claims have been substantiated by research. Critical consideration must be given to whether programs actually fulfill their stated goals.

B. IS THE PROGRAM EASY TO USE (*USER-FRIENDLY*)?

1. Is the Level Appropriate for Students in Your Classroom?

Keep in mind that, unless you plan to work closely with students in explaining how to use the software, both the instructions and the content should be readable. Publishers often claim a very wide range of grade appropriateness for their software in order to increase its marketability. A readability analysis on the contents may be necessary.

2. Is There a Wrap-Around Problem?

Public domain software has traditionally had *wrap-around* problems because of lack of time and effort in its construction. A word may be split by the computer so that the first part of the word appears on one line and the second part appears on the following line. This usually occurs in two cases. First, the programmer may not have accurately counted the number of spaces required to print a line on the screen. With the Apple II, for instance, if a printed line is longer than 40 characters, the computer will split it after the 40th character. Second, sometimes programmers do not allow enough space on a line for a particularly long answer. If a question asks for a student's last name, for instance, and allows only ten spaces on the line for input, the last few letters of a long name will be wrapped around to the next line.

3. Are Screen Pages Easy to Read, with Appropriate Spacing Between Lines?

Some programs try to squeeze so much text on one screen page that it becomes very hard to read. Monitors are not well designed for display of large amounts of visual material. Plenty of space is required between lines of print for ease of reading.

Format of the screen page is a particular problem in language arts instruction, which involves large amounts of text. A monitor can clearly display only a fraction of the text displayed in a single book page. Low-resolution monitors add to the problem. Language arts teachers must recognize that printed books are often the superior medium for text presentation.

4. Is Print Size Appropriate?

A computer can generate a variety of print sizes using its graphics capability. Younger children function best with larger print sizes, as in printed primers. If you do not have high-resolution monitors, small print sizes can be disturbing.

5. Is the Student Able to Leave the Program at Any Point?

Computers in the classroom present a very real scheduling problem. The normal day involves dozens of interruptions. Student access to micro-computers must be severely rationed because of hardware shortages. A program that allows students to stop in the middle of a lesson and later pick up where they left off can be a real advantage, if not a necessity. No child should be forced to restart a lesson he had half-finished the day before but not had enough time to finish.

Users should be able to enter lessons in the middle, or to leaf through the frames quickly until they return to the spot where they left off. Even better, some software stores information as to student progress on disk and then automatically returns the student to the appropriate point when he or she signs on. *Cloze Plus* indicates "Started" in the management system when a child has partially completed a lesson, and it immediately starts the child at the point where he or she left off in the last session.

6. Does the Student Control the Rate of Presentation?

Many instructional frames print the words PRESS ANY KEY TO GO ON or PRESS RETURN. When the user hits the appropriate key, the input signals the computer that the frame has been completely read and that the next frame should be displayed.

Some early software did not include this feature. The programmer estimated how long it would take to read a frame and instructed the computer to display the frame for that length of time, then automatically move on to the next. This meant that faster readers were left waiting for the new frame to appear, and slower readers did not have enough time to finish.

Most publishers today place the user in control of rate of presentation. Some programs that are designed to provide practice in speeded reading allow the user to set the rate in words per minute prior to reading the stories. *Comprehension Power* allows a range of from 60 to 650 words per minute. It helps to allow the user to reset the speed in the middle of the story in case it has been set too fast or too slow.

Some programs provide a subtle feature to stimulate attention to instructional frames. The PRESS ANY KEY prompt does not appear for the first few seconds of frame display, forcing the reader to wait and, hopefully, read the content. This feature helps eliminate the possibility of rushing too quickly through the instruction.

7. Can the Student Return to Previous Screen Pages?

Another characteristic of good programming is the ability to return to material already read. Rather than marching inexorably on through the frames, a simple PRESS ← TO GO BACK prompt may be included at the bottom of frames. This feature enables readers to review material by paging backward through the frames. After all, learners can review when using books. The computer should offer more capabilities, not fewer.

8. Does the Computer Program Accept Abbreviations for Frequent Responses?

It has become a standard feature in computer programs of all types to allow Y or N to be entered instead of the complete YES or NO. While the time saved might seem to be insignificant, it adds up, especially for the hunt-and-peck typist. One-letter entries also help eliminate typing errors.

This practice has become common, but children must be informed about it, since they otherwise would not know.

9. Is the Dialogue Style Informal and Conversational, Addressing the Student Personally?

Apple Keyboard is an introduction to the keyboard functions of the computer such as the CONTROL key, the RETURN key, the BREAK key, and so forth. New computer users are invariably pleasantly surprised when, after being asked for their names, the computer addresses them as "Sue" or "George." A COMPUTER CAN USE WHAT YOU TYPED TO CALL YOU BY NAME, SUE!

An informal, personal style of presentation motivates both children and adults, humanizing the computer. The computer is, after all, only the electronic equivalent of a pile of nuts and bolts. Instructional software, however, ought to use a very human form of communication. The teacher communicates to the student, albeit through a machine. This communication can be as personalized as desired. Just as a good book comes alive when written by an author who can communicate effectively, a good software program can be an experience in communication rather than a lifeless bore.

10. Is There a HELP Command by Which the Student Can Return to the Instructions?

In a workbook the student can always page back to review the instructions. Computer programs often do not include this luxury. Apparently programmers assume that everyone memorizes the instructions at first glance. But the human tendency is, as the saying goes, to read the instructions when all else fails. If all else is failing in the middle of the program and the programmer has not allowed for movement back into the instructions, the student is stuck.

It helps if the instructions are on disk. While printed instruction booklets are invaluable, they are often lost, misplaced, or simply not available. If the student must interrupt the teacher to search for the instruction book, everyone is frustrated. Directions should be exact. Some programs open with a title page and expect students to know enough to hit the RETURN key to get things rolling. Such assumptions of competence cause problems. The bottom of the screen should display the exact prompt: PRESS RETURN TO GO ON.

On occasion the instructions are available on disk, but they require an inordinate amount of time to access. *Story Machine* has an on-disk dictionary that lists words children are allowed to use in the activities. A minimum of 40 seconds is required to access the dictionary and return to the program, because the dictionary must first be loaded from disk, and then the original program must be reloaded.

11. Is the Management System Easy to Use, Yet Safe from Student Penetration?

Government and corporations are increasingly aware of the problems of access to their computers. On the one hand, the heavier the security a system has, the better its protection against would-be saboteurs who could steal or destroy its contents. However, heavier security means greater difficulty of entry for everyone, including those who legitimately use the system.

Management systems have simple protection schemes, generally consisting of a particular combination of commands in conjunction with a special teacher password. The easier the commands, the easier it is for students to access the management system by guessing the combinations.

A management system accessed by typing in TEACHER when requested for a name entry is insufficient protection against any except the youngest students.

12. Does the Program Allow Input Mistakes to Be Corrected?

Many programs do not allow users to recheck their typed answers. As soon as the multiple-choice answer C is typed, the program moves on to the next step. An incorrect choice cannot be altered even if the user spots the error immediately.

For the most part, users should at least be given a display of the answer they type and the short time between typing the answer and pressing the RETURN key to spot errors. Many programs add an extra step, asking the user, ARE YOU SURE THIS IS THE ANSWER YOU WANT? This procedure slows down the process to allow time for greater reflection and accuracy on the part of the user. Many people type in answers and do not look at the screen to check typing accuracy before pressing the RETURN key. The follow-up question gives such users the opportunity to recheck their input. This is particularly important for children who do not know how to touch-type and stare at the keys instead of the screen.

13. Is the Program Bug-Free?

A program *bug* is an error in the construction of the program that causes it to perform unsatisfactorily. The list of possible bugs is infinite. A program that simply does not work correctly has probably not been field-tested sufficiently.

C. DOES THE PROGRAM MAKE MAXIMUM USE OF THE COMPUTER'S CAPABILITIES?

1. Are Students Motivated?

A wide variety of factors can influence motivational value of a program, including topics of reading material, graphics, frequency of feedback, variety, and interaction. Look for duration of motivation. Practically any program can hold a child's interest for a few minutes. If the child is asking, "How long till this is over?" after the first five minutes of an hour-long program, however, you are in trouble. If a teacher must stand over the child to force continued work, the usefulness of the computer as a tool for individualizing instruction is obviated. Children must function independently on computers, and the motivational techniques built into programs are one key to maintaining this independence. Research shows that well-designed programs are successful in engaging even highly distractable learners for long periods of time.

2. Are Attractive Graphics and Audio Included?

Children expect color graphics almost as a matter of course when working on computers. Graphics should ideally add something of substance to the program. They should not distract from the main purpose of the learning experience.

Audio effects can be important motivators as well, but the user must be able to turn off the audio to avoid distracting the class. Users of *Story Machine* are asked whether they want audio and respond with a Y or N. Some other programs silence their sound effects if CONTROL S is pressed at the beginning of the program.

A program that displays a rocket ship slowly crossing the screen or plays the theme song from a movie might be motivational at first. When the student has seen or heard it 20 times, it becomes a serious bore. Variety is important. Effects that are repeated frequently should be short, no more than two or three seconds in duration.

3. Does the Program Time Student Work?

Time on task can be an indication of student progress or lack of it. Many times the only difference in results between a student who is proficient at a task and one who is not is time needed to complete the task. Accuracy of performance may be identical. *Comprehension Power* keeps count of the number of passage rereadings necessary to answer questions correctly, an indirect measure of time on task.

4. Is a Score Kept of Student Achievement? Are These Scores Recorded on Disk for Teacher Monitoring?

Since the computer is a tool for independence and individualization, provision must be made for periodic monitoring of performance. One of the key differences between busywork and effective skill development involves teacher control. A management system built into a program is vital. The management system must be large enough to monitor all students. Comprehensive systems keep detailed information on number of incorrect responses, the actual incorrect responses, and time needed to complete the task.

5. Does the Program Provide for Individual Differences in Ability?

Courseware may cater to individual needs by offering different levels of difficulty, varying rates of presentation, and built-in branching. Programs should be flexible enough to allow teachers to assign specific lessons to specific children. In *Sentence Combining*, the teacher may assign lessons either to the whole class or to particular students.

Some programs provide a HINT option to help students who are having problems. *Micro Skillbuilders* gives a hint whenever a question is answered incorrectly and allows a second try.

6. Does the Program Branch in Some Way to Suit the Needs of Individual Students?

A *linear* program involves students in a set sequence of activities. Students' responses do not cause any variation. Those students who have mastered the activity are put through the same experiences as those who have not.

The computer has the capability of recognizing when students are having problems or have already mastered an activity. It can *branch* to a subprogram to meet the diagnosed needs. A simple command can be placed in the programming to branch when the student incorrectly answers three problems in a row, for example. Conversely, when a student demonstrates skill mastery by answering seven or eight problems in a row correctly, the computer can move on to another skill rather than wasting student time in drilling skills already mastered. The goal is to achieve the best path to learning.

To date, automatic branching is a feature rarely seen in instructional courseware. In order to provide branching, numerous subprograms must be available on disk, adding to the cost of courseware development. Most students will never even see most of these subprograms, since they will proceed through the main *trunk* of the program without demonstrating needs that require branching. As a result, courseware publishers have tended to produce materials that lack branching, forcing every student to proceed through the main trunk of the program in parallel fashion.

7. Does the Student Control Forward or Backward Movement through the Program?

If the student conceptualizes the inference-making process in the middle of the fourth problem, can he or she return to the first three problems to correct wrong answers? If not, the management system will report that those were incorrectly answered, and the teacher may be led to believe that further instruction in that skill is necessary.

8. Is Immediate Feedback Given?

One of the great advantages of the computer over drill books is that the student can receive an immediate indication of accuracy or inaccuracy of answers. Studies by Angell (1949) and Kaess and Zaeman (1960) indicate the importance of immediate feedback. Some programs wait until the end of a series of drills to give a report. Since the main function of feedback is to indicate errors and provide information to set them right (Hartley and Lovell, 1978), the greater the distance between the feedback and the teaching experience, the less power it has to reinforce.

Some programs provide explicit feedback only for incorrectly answered problems. When students choose the correct answer, the program simply goes to the next problem. Students understand that this is an implicit signal that their responses were correct. R. Anderson, Kulhavy, and Andre (1971) found that this technique was just about as effective as continuous explicit feedback.

9. Are Explanations of Incorrect Answers Provided?

Many programs give only CORRECT or INCORRECT feedback. Software publishers often take the lazy way out and fail to provide meaningful responses to incorrect answers. Simple responses might be appropriate for providing reinforcement or building performance speed in simple arithmetic problems or motor activities. They are not appropriate for many complex cognitive skills involved in language processing.

D. IS THE PROGRAM USER-PROOF?

Murphy's law states, "Anything that can go wrong will go wrong." A program that is *user-proof* eliminates the possibility of things going wrong. No matter what the user does, no matter how naive a computer user he or she may be, the program accomplishes its purpose.

Absolute protection from error is impossible, of course. Computers themselves are far from user-proof. Though it might be helpful to use the flat plastic keyboards that respond to finger pressure rather than the usual keyboards with separate keys, if a child dumps a jelly sandwich or a glass of milk onto the keyboard, there is going to be big trouble. Opening the back of the computer and wiggling the components while electricity is turned on could result in a shocking experience and almost certainly will destroy the computer's main board. Dropping the thing on the ground is another sure guarantee of trouble. Sticking pencils, gum, and other assorted objects into the disk drives means expensive trips to the repair shop.

Similarly, computer software is not completely user-proof, and cannot be. Cartridges are certainly more durable than floppy disks, but both can be ruined without much trouble.

Physical abuse of equipment and software aside, programs should be evaluated for ability to withstand user mistakes and naivete.

1. Does the Program Crash if an Inappropriate Key Is Pushed?

A *crash* occurs when the program stops operating. Computers were designed for use by programmers, not by children. As a result, several keys on the keyboard are liable to cause trouble if pushed in the middle of a program. As Murphy's law implies, some force beyond our ken makes fingers slip to press these keys at particularly inopportune moments.

The RESET key performs the most effective job of crashing a program. If it is pushed, no matter what the computer happens to be doing at the time, control of the computer is returned to the keyboard. In other words, the program is stopped dead and the user must start over from the beginning. Plenty of classroom demonstrations have been ruined by a finger slipping from the RETURN key to the RESET key on the old Apple II, which placed them side by side for some inexplicable reason. Many newer models place RESET in a spot off the keyboard, inaccessible to accidental slips of the finger. Poole (1981), in an authoritative manual on use of the Apple II, suggests prying off the RESET key to install a rubber washer between it and the console, making the key physically harder to press.

The BREAK key can be just as fatal to the smooth performance of a computer program. Pushing the BREAK key causes the program to stop running and, as with RESET, control of the computer returns to the keyboard. The program may be restarted by a RUN command, by a command to the disk controller to reload the program from disk, or by turning the computer off and on again, called a *cold start.*

Many novices worry about touching the wrong key and destroying the program. This cannot happen. No key press can erase information stored on a disk. I repeat: There is no key on the computer that will destroy that $50 computer disk you just bought. Just as turning a cassette recorder off and on or adjusting its tone controls never harms the cassette itself, using the various keys on the computer will not harm the information stored on the disk.

When evaluating software, always try typing input that differs radically from what the program expects. Type a question mark instead of a letter, for example. Some less sophisticated programs might become so confused they stop operating.

2. Does the Program Inform the User When an Inappropriate Key Is Pushed?

If the student pushes a 1 instead of an A, will the program ask her to PLEASE PRESS A, B, C, OR D? If she is asked to type in a number from 1 to 100, will the computer remind her of the parameters if she types 150?

Regrettably, many programmers appear to be following less specific policies in their program design. If an unacceptable key is pressed, the computer beeps and displays the question again, refusing to accept the input but not specifying why it hasn't been accepted. This procedure can confuse students. Directions must be as exact as possible.

3. If the RETURN Key Is Accidentally Pushed before Any Input Has Been Typed, Will the Program Give the User a Second Chance?

Computer programs often have students type in their responses, then input the responses to the computer by pressing the RETURN key. Sometimes in the rush of the moment, it is easy to hit the RETURN key before typing any response. The program should so inform the user, giving a second chance: PLEASE TYPE YOUR RESPONSE.

4. If the Space Bar Is Accidentally Pushed before or after an Input, Will the Computer Ignore It?

To our unpracticed eyes, a space is nothing. To our less intelligent companion the computer, however, the space is something. Each space typed into the computer is understood to be an input character, just as much as if you had typed in a G or a 9. As a result, hitting the space bar and then the B is quite a different response from simply hitting the B.

Since such slips of the typing fingers occur frequently, computers should be programmed to ignore inappropriate spaces. When the program asks for a child's name, for example, and the child accidentally presses the space bar, then types MARY, the program should recognize that the child's name is not spelled M-A-R-Y with a blank space before it.

5. If the Reader Cannot Figure Out the Answer, Will the Program Refuse to Go On?

Many tutorials are arranged so that the program will refuse to proceed until a correct answer is typed in. While this isn't too bad if the answer choices are as simple as ABCD, some very real frustration can set in if a more complex answer is required and the child has no idea what to type.

6. Will the Program Refuse to Accept Input of Inappropriate Length and Inform the User Why It Refuses?

If a child is requested to type in an ABCD multiple-choice answer, and she accidentally types two letters instead of one, the computer should recognize the answer as inappropriately long. Rather than counting it as incorrect, the child should be informed of the type of error and given a second chance.

7. Is the Program Reasonably Protected against Sabotage?

As noted earlier, it is virtually impossible to erase a disk accidentally except through physical damage to the disk. No key press will erase or harm a disk. Certain specific commands must be entered.

Unfortunately for teachers, there is a "whiz kid syndrome" going around these days. Adults read articles about how youngsters have tapped into Defense Department computers, about FBI raids on teenage microcomputer networks, and so forth. The too-common reaction is to chuckle with amusement and comment on how bright children are these days. This attitude implicitly communicates to children that they are free to do whatever they can do when it comes to computers. Ripping a book or scribbling on its pages is a crime. Erasing your $50-a-disk courseware and replacing it with a *pirated* (illegally copied) version of *Pacman* is ingenious.

It is possible to erase information on disks, of course, and it doesn't take a genius to know several ways of doing it. In the Apple, the command DELETE, coupled with the name of the program, will erase that program. The command DEL, with specified line numbers, will erase those lines in the program. DEL 100,150 will erase lines 100 to 150. An entire disk may be erased by reformatting it with a single command. If one disk is copied to another disk, the original contents of the second disk will be lost.

A well-designed program will disable most of these functions, however, making it almost impossible for students to destroy information except by damaging the disk physically. Programs on disk can be protected from erasure in a variety of ways. One simple method is to make the catalog of programs inaccessible. Users do not know the names of the programs and cannot erase them by DELETE.

Some disks are *write protected* and cannot be erased or changed. Disk drives are equipped with devices to determine whether there is a notch in the side of the plastic disk sleeve. If the notch has been covered with a piece of tape, or if it was never cut out to begin with, the disk cannot be *written to*. That is, additional material cannot be saved onto that disk, and nothing can be erased from it. Unfortunately, it is easy to defeat that protection scheme by simply removing the tape or using a hole puncher to cut a notch.

The best solution to this problem, if it is a problem for you, is to be aware of what is going on in your classroom and maintain an accurate list of who has what software when.

E. IS DOCUMENTATION PROVIDED IN PRINTED HARD COPY?

1. Are Objectives Listed?

The purpose of the software should be clearly stated. Vaguely defined objectives (for example, "to teach word recognition") can be misleading and are of little help to teachers.

2. Is There a Summary of the Program's Function?

It might be nice for every teacher to work through every computer program in its entirety, but it is impractical. Some programs require hours of student time, and to require that teachers spend hours completing punctuation or word attack exercises would be ridiculous. The documentation should include a detailed description of the program, with example exercises.

This summary can be invaluable when a student has a question about a program or when the teacher is analyzing results in the management system. With several dozen programs floating around the classroom, it is hard to keep them all straight.

3. Are Prerequisite Skills Listed?

Are students required to be familiar with underlying subskills? Does the program fit into a hierarchy of skill development? In a program designed to drill students on subordinate clauses, does the documentation note whether the teacher must first instruct students about subordinating conjunctions?

4. Is Grade-Level Suitability Given?

Has a readability analysis been completed on the material? Is the content best suited to particular ages? Computer materials are no more flexible than ordinary printed materials in this regard.

5. Does the Documentation Include Practical Suggestions for Use in the Classroom?

Some suggestions for use in the classroom are rather mundane. The documentation for one vocabulary program, for example, suggests that students use flash card drills for further practice with the vocabulary words. Ingenious.

Other documentation is invaluable. The ideas contained in the notebook-sized teacher's guide to *Bank Street Writer* increase the value of the word processor tremendously. Teachers need practical ideas for implementation of this new technology, and publishers should prepare software with specific ideas for that implementation in mind.

6. Are Suggested Supplemental or Elaborative Materials Listed?

References to materials available in other media can help the teacher to supplement instruction offered by the computer. Specific reference to pages in basal series, for example, can be invaluable.

7. Are Student Guides Provided, Written in Forms Understandable by Your Students?

Your students should be able to follow directions and learn how to use the program independently of teacher direction. In addition to a detailed explanation designed for adults, *Bank Street Writer* includes a student guide prepared for use by middle grade youngsters.

8. Are Supplemental Worksheets Provided?

9. Is the Teacher's Instruction Guide Clear and Adequate?

10. If the Program Is Modifiable, Are Suggestions Offered?

Courseware publishers are increasingly aware that some teachers wish to modify their courseware to fit it more exactly to the needs of students. *Teacher utility options* (see Chapter 17) allow the teacher to reprogram the courseware without any knowledge of programming skills. For a vocabulary game, for example, the teacher only has to type in the desired vocabulary words and their definitions.

F. WHAT ASSURANCE OF PROGRAM QUALITY IS THERE?

1. Is the Program Publisher Well Established with a Good Reputation?

The entry of such well-known educational publishers as Borg-Warner, Milleken, and Scott, Foresman into the software-publishing field has done much to raise the standards of computer instruction in language arts. These large corporations have the financial backing necessary for the development of top-quality products.

Keep in mind, however, that the software market is still at the stage where much of the most imaginative material is being published by newcomers to the educational publishing field.

2. Is There a 30-Day Return Guarantee?

The ultimate test of a program is its success in your classroom. The nature of the medium makes it difficult to fully evaluate software ahead of time. Never buy software that does not come with a 30-day money-back guarantee. You'll find that you will take advantage of that guarantee very frequently to send poorly designed or inappropriate materials back to publishers.

At one time software distributors were reluctant to allow free previews because of the ease with which programs can be copied. Some distributors have since realized that schools will simply not purchase expensive materials on blind faith. Knowledgeable teachers and administrators insist on examining the materials before committing hundreds of dollars to their purchase.

Some publishers provide demonstration disks that give a small sample of the program for examination. These demonstrations are often satisfactory for evaluation of simple game or drill programs. No one can determine the effectiveness of the more complex tutorial programs without testing the full program with actual students.

3. Are Sales Representatives Willing to Come to Demonstrate the Program?

Demonstrations by sales representatives are particularly necessary with complex programs such as word processors. If you ordered the program for a 30-day trial period, you would need many hours to learn the program well enough to evaluate it. A salesperson who is familiar with the product can save you a lot of time.

4. Are Published Reviews Available?

Publishers should make references to published reviews of their products available. Well-written reviews contain very specific references to the functioning of the courseware, with exemplary instructional and drill frames. Poorer reviews make sweeping generalizations about how good or how poor the courseware is.

5. Has the Program Been Classroom Tested?

6. Has the Program Been Recommended by Teachers Whose Judgments You Trust?

Teacher recommendations are often the best source of evaluative comment. Keep in mind that, while a teacher may be able to judge whether a program works or doesn't work satisfactorily, it is much harder to make comparative judgments between programs. That is, few teachers will be able to tell you what is the "best" program for teaching structural analysis skills, since they will have had experience with only one or two.

The best method of evaluating software, short of using it in your classroom for a trial period, is to visit colleagues' classrooms and see the material in use with their students.

LANGUAGE ARTS SOFTWARE EVALUATION FORM

A. Is the program educationally valuable?
1. Is the content important to learning language?
2. Do the instructional techniques mesh with current trends in education?
3. Can the same work be done just as well with nonelectronic media?
4. Does the program involve actual experiences in reading or writing, or is all work isolated drill instruction?
5. Will the skills learned have value to students in your classroom?
6. Will this program serve as a useful supplement to your classroom language arts program?
7. Do the skills involved in the program fit into the scope and sequence chart that you use as a guide?
8. Is the program of use to students with special educational needs?
9. Does the program use correct Standard English?
10. Are instructional objectives stated, and does the program fulfill those objectives?

B. Is the program easy to use (user-friendly)?
1. Is the level appropriate for students in your classroom?
2. Is there a wrap-around problem?
3. Are screen pages easy to read, with appropriate spacing between lines?
4. Is print size appropriate?
5. Is the student able to leave the program at any point?
6. Does the student control the rate of presentation?
7. Can the student return to previous screen pages?
8. Does the computer program accept abbreviations for frequent responses?
9. Is the dialogue style informal and conversational, addressing the student personally?
10. Is there a HELP command by which the student can return to the instructions?
11. Is the management system easy to use, yet safe from student penetration?
12. Does the program allow input mistakes to be corrected?
13. Is the program bug-free?

C. Does the program make maximum use of the computer's capabilities?
1. Are students motivated?
2. Are attractive graphics and audio included?
3. Does the program time student work?
4. Is a score kept of student achievement? Are these scores recorded on disk for teacher monitoring?
5. Does the program provide for individual differences in ability?
6. Does the program branch in some way to suit the needs of individual students?

   7. Does the student control forward or backward movement through the program?

   8. Is immediate feedback given?

   9. Are explanations of incorrect answers provided?

D. Is the program user-proof?

   1. Does the program crash if an inappropriate key is pushed?

   2. Does the program inform the user when an inappropriate key is pushed?

   3. If the RETURN key is accidentally pushed before any input has been typed, will the program give the user a second chance?

   4. If the space bar is accidentally typed before or after an input, will the computer ignore it?

   5. If the reader cannot figure out the answer, will the program refuse to go on?

   6. Will the program refuse to accept input of inappropriate length and inform the user why it refuses?

   7. Is the program reasonably protected against sabotage?

E. Is documentation provided in printed hard copy?

   1. Are objectives listed?

   2. Is there a summary of the program's function?

   3. Are prerequisite skills listed?

   4. Is grade-level suitability given?

   5. Does the documentation include practical suggestions for use in the classroom?

   6. Are suggested supplemental or elaborative materials listed?

   7. Are student guides provided, written in form understandable by your students?

   8. Are supplemental worksheets provided?

   9. Is the teacher's instruction guide clear and adequate?

  10. If the program is modifiable, are suggestions offered?

F. What assurance of program quality is there?

   1. Is the program publisher well-established with a good reputation?

   2. Is there a 30-day return guarantee?

   3. Are sales representatives willing to come to demonstrate the program?

   4. Are published reviews available?

   5. Has the program been classroom tested?

   6. Has the program been recommended by teachers whose judgments you trust?

Strengths of the Program:

Weaknesses of the Program:

Your Professional and Personal Reaction:

Student Reactions:

5

SOFTWARE: READINESS

Schools are on firm ground when dealing with the formal teaching of reading skills. Our methods "work." Thousands of children enter the first grade every September not knowing how to read and leave the following June with clearly developed reading ability.

Educators ought to be less secure when making declarations about reading readiness skill development. Early childhood is a new and unstudied branch of the formal educational enterprise. Much of what has been written about the development of readiness for schooling and for reading is what some have called "educational wisdom literature," the presentation of what seem to be good ideas, but without the necessary research backing for either the theory or the practice.

Many such marvelous, wide-sweeping claims have been made for the impact of the computer on preschool learning.

The computer is not a potion that will magically increase a four-year-old's attention span. Preschoolers are not geared to independent activities. Despite claims of news articles such as "My Four-Year-Old Can Program in BASIC," youngsters' work on computers requires close adult supervision. Left alone with a software program, they will not function for any length of time.

Software for readiness-level youngsters requires the teacher to show how to use it. Children cannot figure out the directions on their own, even for the simplest programs. Advertisements and reviews of readiness software give the impression that all the adult has to do is show the child how to turn on the computer. Teachers and parents are often surprised to find printed instructions for use of the program. "How can a four-year-old read this?" they ask. Of course the children can't read it. Adults must take the time to demonstrate and supervise use of the program.

EVALUATION OF READINESS SOFTWARE

In evaluating software for children at the preschool level, several factors are of particular importance.

Value of the Concept

How important is the concept being taught by the software? Lists of readiness skills are amazing. They include everything possible. From gross motor skills to fine motor skills, from perceptual skills to auditory discrimination, preschool teachers are supposed to deal with every imaginable skill.

Some are clearly more important than others, especially if the teacher's major concern is for *reading* readiness. Teaching a child to kick a ball or run in a circle will do little to improve reading. While these and other perceptual-motor activities may be of benefit for themselves, research shows that they do not develop the child's ability to begin reading in any demonstrable way (Robinson, 1972).

Is a computer program designed to teach the concepts of up and down worth the devotion of hours of individualized computer time for a class? Perhaps it is in some cases, but most teachers handle that concept quite well in whole-class activities and through informal discussion.

Transfer of the Concept

Will the concept under consideration be transferred to situations beyond the computer courseware itself? It is quite nice to tell up from down on the computer keyboard, but does it mean that children will be able to understand the concept "up in the tree" or "down on the ground"?

The imagined values of children's programming languages such as LOGO and Delta Drawing have been touted in newspapers and television. Children supposedly develop qualitatively different and superior forms of thinking and problem solving, but will this problem-solving ability be transferable to problems other than those in computer programming? It is dangerous to make the unproven assumption that it is transferable, especially if such programming languages are taught to children at the expense of skills of more proven value. One teacher has told the story of a child who could program the computer to draw a square in LOGO but could not draw one with a pencil.

Motivational Value

Are children motivated to spend time on the activity? Fortunately for software producers, the computer's graphic capabilities offer a display that is highly attractive to preschoolers. Monitors to be used with preschoolers should certainly be color.

Learning experiences for younger children should emphasize the natural relationships between play and discovery. As children play and experience their world, they create their own ideas about how the world works. This trial-and-error process is an ongoing cycle of hypothesis generation and refinement. Children revise their theories about how the world works as they discover new information that does not fit in with their old concepts.

Staples (1984) notes the difficulty of predicting which programs have the greatest "staying power." She suggests that the less elaborate programs often offer the greatest flexibility, so that children return to the games to try new strategies, create new creatures, or draw new pictures.

Simplicity of Use

Can children perform the activity independently, once it has been explained and demonstrated by an adult? A computer program that requires continuous adult aid is useless. The adult might just as well be working with the child on nonelectronic forms of readiness training.

It is too much to expect a program to be self-explanatory, however. Older students can read directions and use their knowledge of computers to figure out how to operate a program. Preschoolers must have adult supervision as they learn how to use the program.

Ease of Success

Does the child experience success with the program? Inability to deal with the concepts in a program or inability to operate the program both lead to frustration. This sense of failure can transfer to dislike of computers in general, especially with children who were insecure from the beginning with the devices.

Keyboarding Skills

Does the program demand keyboarding skills that are beyond the students' capabilities? Youngsters often have no trouble pressing a single key in response to a question. The tempo of the learning experience slows tremendously as greater amounts must be typed. Preschoolers have a great deal of trouble in using the standard typewriter keyboard. Modified and simplified versions are often used.

Voice Synthesis

Does the program include voice synthesis? The readiness child has a rich store of oral language knowledge. Readiness and beginning reading instruction traditionally build upon this knowledge in an attempt to link oral and printed language. Reading readiness software that does not take advantage of voice synthesis devices such as those discussed later in this chapter offers negligible advantages over printed media. If the parent or teacher needs to read a software program display that resembles an alphabet book to the child, why not use a printed alphabet book?

Preschool software is discussed below under two classifications. Reading readiness software deals with those skills specifically related to reading, such as letter, word, and concept development. As Durkin has stated,

"Readiness instruction [is] reading instruction in its early stages" (1970, p. 534). General preschool software includes a wide variety of skills traditionally associated with preparation of youngsters for formal instruction.

READING READINESS SOFTWARE

Letter Identification

An abundance of letter-identification programs are available. A letter is displayed. The child then types the matching key. While simple in design, these programs are just fine for the purpose of entertainment and education of preschoolers. Children gain experience in use of the keyboard as they practice their letters.

Display letters must be well drawn. Letters like W and M are hard to recognize when drawn using low-resolution graphics. The diagonal lines tend to look more like staircases of small blocks (called *pixels*) than straight lines.

Several variations of such programs are available for teaching alphabetical order. In one activity an A is displayed. The child responds with a B, and so forth. In *Early Games for Young Children* the progression of letters continues until the child makes a mistake. Then the entire preceding alphabet is displayed in order, giving the child a chance to sing the alphabet song and decide on the next letter. Only uppercase letters are available, a serious weakness.

Other similar activities list series of letters with an inserted blank. The child provides the missing letter, whether it be the first, the middle, or the last. *Customized Alphabet Drill* provides teachers the useful option of specifying letter combinations a particular child needs to drill.

Letter-identification and alphabet programs available include *Letters and Numbers*, *My First Alphabet*, *Alphabet Keyboard*, and *Early Learning Fun*. *Alphabet ID*, presented in Appendix A, reinforces alphabetical order and location of letter keys on the typewriter keyboard.

Alphabet Books

Alphabet Beasts & Co. provides an electronic version of the alphabet book. When a letter is typed, a little verse in which the letter appears and a high-resolution picture are displayed:

```
My new ROBOT, her name's Rose
     I taught her all
    The games she knows!
    R is for ROBOT.
```

The verse is to be read aloud to the child by an adult. The advantage of such programs over traditional printed alphabet books is doubtful. We must await the incorporation of voice synthesis devices in programs to make this software worthwhile.

Other alphabet book software includes *Stickybear ABC*. This program is accompanied by a little book and colorful alphabet stickers featuring the central character Stickybear.

Beginning Word Identification

These activities provide words to be copied by typing. An adult types a word into the computer, and the word is displayed on the monitor. The child keys in the appropriate letters and receives some form of reinforcement. Such programs can be used to complement Sylvia Ashton-Warner's approach, which allows children to choose those words they want to learn. She made the following argument: "First words must have intense meaning for a child. . . . They must be words organically tied up, organically born from the dynamic life itself. They must be words that are already part of the child's being" (Ashton-Warner, 1963, p. 30). Such intrinsically meaningful words always include the child's own name, so that the subprogram designed to serve this function on the *Early Games for Young Children* disk is called *Name*.

Specific Word and Concept Development

Juggle's Rainbow is a colorful collection of three programs. One teaches the words and concepts *above* and *below*. The game involves the child in pressing keys in the top rows of the keyboard when prompted with ABOVE and keys in the bottom rows when BELOW appears. Portions are added to a diagram on the monitor screen as the child responds.

Stickybear Shapes, one of the *Stickybear* series of programs, which use bears as characters in their graphics, teaches simple geometric forms: the circle, square, rectangle, triangle, and diamond. In one activity, the word RECTANGLE is printed at the bottom of the screen with a sample of the shape. The child uses the ARROW keys until a matching shape starts to flash in the picture at the top of the screen. A book is included with the disk to introduce the shapes, and a parent's guide gives suggestions for further related activities.

Puss in Boot teaches positional concepts, such as *off, over, above, on the right, in front of,* and *beside*. A cat is pictured in front of a boot, for example. The child chooses either PUSS IS IN FRONT OF HIS BOOT or PUSS IS BESIDE HIS BOOT. *Stickybear Opposites* teaches simple antonyms through use of high-resolution illustrations. UP is illustrated by a bear climbing up a stairway. The touch of the ARROW key changes the illustration to DOWN, with a bear climbing down the stairway.

GENERAL PRESCHOOL SOFTWARE

Piaget's observations of youngsters have noted the need for exploration and discovery, for experiencing the world rather than simply being told about it. As children play in their world, they conceptualize an increasingly complex personal reality. The best general readiness software allows children to play. As they engage in these structured play experiences, they are led to make important conceptualizations about their world.

Drawing Shapes and Pictures

Not all graphics construction programs need to be as complex as the popular *Turtlegraphics*, which is in LOGO, a powerful programming language requiring a time-consuming curricular emphasis. *Early Games for Young Children* offers a very simple drawing program that very young children can use to doodle. Pressing a key in the top center of the keyboard will draw a line up the monitor screen. Keys to the right of the keyboard will draw a line to the right. Keys in the upper left will draw a diagonal line to the upper left of the screen. Pressing the space bar changes the color of the line.

Delta Drawing is another drawing program for youngsters. It is one of a number of new graphics construction packages designed as simpler alternatives to LOGO *Turtlegraphics*. As with LOGO, children can create pictures by constructing programs, allowing them to experience trial-and-error problem-solving methods and develop the step-by-step procedural "machine" thinking (Papert, 1980) used in programming. Programs can be *nested*, that is, placed one inside another, to create whole pictures composed of discrete subprograms for each part.

One advantage of Delta Drawing is that there are two modes for the creation of pictures. The text mode, described above, allows creation of pictures through programming. The graphics mode allows children to draw pictures by simple key presses. When D is pressed several times, a straight line is drawn. An R pressed three times turns the triangular cursor 90 degrees, and more Ds start a new line perpendicular to the first.

Facemaker is an even simpler drawing program. Children use a succession of menu-driven (listed) graphics choices to construct humorous cartoon faces. First they choose from a menu of different mouths; then they choose a set of eyes; and so forth. As each choice is made, the new facial feature is added to the drawing.

In *Jeepers Creatures*, a similar game, the screen page is divided horizontally in thirds. Children mix and match body parts from several different animals to create their own unique species. A panda's head combined with the body of a kangaroo and feet of an octopus becomes a PANGAPUS.

Drawing programs can be used in conjunction with language experiences. Children love making up stories to fit the faces they've drawn in *Facemaker*. Since the program offers the ability to animate the faces—making them wink, cry, and smile—the animation can be arranged to fit events in the creative story.

Number Skills

As with letter-recognition and alphabet software, many number-identification and simple arithmetic programs are available. *Early Games for Young Children* has several number games on the disk. In one, a number is displayed, and the child must press the appropriate number key on the keyboard. In another, a group of blocks is displayed for the child to count. In yet another, one group of blocks must be added to or subtracted from another group of blocks.

Alphabet Beasts also includes a number-identification program. When the child presses a number key, the name of the number is printed with its Arabic equivalent. Then a group of dragons appear one by one until the appropriate total is reached. When a number key is pressed in *Sticky-bear Numbers*, a variety of animated shapes are placed on the screen one by one to reinforce counting. Stickybears emerge from airplanes, windows, spaceships, birds, and so forth.

Specific Concept Development

A variety of preschool programs have been targeted at skills more specific than that of general problem solving.

Gertrude's Puzzles is an adventure game in which children classify colors and geometric shapes. Children follow a map diagram to a puzzle display with several colored geometric pieces. By trial and error, rules are discovered as to which pieces fit the puzzle. For example, perhaps only blue pieces are allowed, or perhaps only the hexagons. The purpose is to give children experience in classification of objects. Adult supervision is required.

The scale of musical notes from A to G is the subject of *Early Games Music*. In one game on the disk, a note disappears and its tone is sounded on the computer speaker. The child then presses the matching letter key. Another game involves the child in pressing keys to imitate sample tunes, while the computer monitors for accuracy.

SPEAKING COMPUTERS

Artificial production of speech is of vital importance in readiness instruction because of the central task of integrating already developed oral language skills into reading and concept development curricula. Speaking computers will undoubtedly be of importance in other areas of language instruction as well.

The first major contribution of voice synthesis to education is used primarily by blind students. It is called the Kurzweil Reading Machine, manufactured by Kurzweil Computer Products of Cambridge, Massachusetts, a division of Xerox. The Kurzweil machine is designed to recognize standard print from any book and read the words aloud.

Its key feature is an optical recognition scanner, developed by Raymond Kurzweil in 1974, which recognizes virtually any typeface. Reading material is placed face down on the glass surface of the scanner. A scanning camera locates the first line and electronically transmits the visual information to a letter-recognition device. Letter order is then analyzed within the word to determine relevant phonics rules, including pitch and stress. A speech synthesizer then produces the word aloud.

This process may sound simple, but it is actually quite complex. Oddly printed letter shapes are analyzed for context, and then their shape is stored in memory. One thousand linguistic rules, with 1,500 exception words, are used for language recognition. Punctuation and phrase analysis rules enhance prosody (accurate oral production).

Users have a great deal of control over the process as well. Speed and tone of the voice can be adjusted. Other optional commands allow repetition of previous lines, spelling out a word, announcing punctuation or capitalization, and marking words or phrases for later reference.

With optional hardware the Kurzweil machine can also automatically produce Braille material and can recognize text output from computers and convert it to speech.

This machine is highly specialized, designed specifically for its task. General-purpose microcomputers are unable to perform its functions at present, but future trends will certainly lead in that direction. A variety of methods are used today for oral language production by computers.

Optical Code Readers

Texas Instruments has published a series of children's books called *Magic Wand Books* that allow for oral production of the text. A bar code similar to that used for pricing items in supermarkets is printed on each page below the picture and text. As the child moves an optical code-recognition device (the "magic wand") over the bar code, a speech synthesizer reads the words in the story aloud.

Tape Recorders

The tape recorder is an inexpensive device to add speech capability to computers. Hartley Courseware's Cassette Control Device (CCD) is connected by cable from the computer to the remote control input port of a tape player. The computer automatically turns the tape player off and on when needed. While somewhat cumbersome to use, the excellent quality of tape-recorded speech is superior to voice synthesis. Hartley has a wide selection of software available which uses the CCD.

Programmed Voice Synthesis

The ability of the computer to talk is of tremendous benefit to readiness-level children, as well as to the visually impaired, English as a second language, and English as a foreign language students. *Voice synthesis*, as it is called, is bringing a whole new meaning to the term *user-friendly*. Computers can now speak to us.

The 1980 development of Votrax Corporation's SC–01 speech synthesizer chip provided an integrated circuit capable of producing 64 phonemes, the minimal sound units of language. The chip produces speech by blending phonemes to form words. A speech synthesizer built around such chips can come in the form of an internal circuit board or an exterior device connected by cable to a slot at the back of the computer or under its cover.

Phoneme synthesizers interpret anything that is typed as instructions to speak. Words are formed by blending of the phonemes represented by the input symbols. Echo II (Votrax) is a phoneme synthesizer.

Digitized synthesizers produce better quality speech but use a great deal of computer memory. *Supertalker* (Mountain Computer) has a microphone into which the user speaks. Sounds are digitized, that is, translated into number code that is stored in memory. The device produces speech by retranslating the number code back into speech sounds. In order to conserve computer memory space, messages in software are stored on disk and must be loaded when required, slowing down operation of the program.

Mechanical production of speech is not at all new. Phonographs store speech in grooves on a plastic record. Computers store speech represented in numeric form, just as they store all other types of data. The voice synthesis device converts this numeric data into electrical signals that can be delivered to a loudspeaker.

Computer-synthesized speech drones mechanically. It takes some getting used to, but the results can be very recognizable. Clarity depends, first, upon the quality of the synthesizer and, second, upon the accuracy of the programming that is being synthesized.

The Echo II speech synthesizer illustrates the advantages and limitations typical of these devices. Echo will read anything programmed into it by PRINT statements. Type a program such as

```
10 PRINT "HELLO.  HOW ARE YOU TODAY?"
```

and Echo will pronounce the words in quotes, complete with a rise in inflection at the end of the question, a convention of English speech. There are problems to be aware of, however. Echo will be confused by exceptions to phonics rules. *Sweat* and *sweet* are pronounced identically with a long *e* sound. *Psychology* is pronounced with the first *y* as the short *i* sound and the medial *ch* as the *ch* sound in *church*. In order to obtain the correct pronunciations, words must be spelled according to regular graphophonemic rules. *Sweat* can be spelled *Swet* and *psychology* can be spelled *psykology*. Also, the programming language common in commercial programs (called *machine language*) will not be correctly read by Echo. The synthesizer works best with public domain programs written in BASIC.

Programs custom-designed for the Echo are available. The *Textalker* disk contains several programs of interest to reading and language arts teachers. *Sec Demo* allows users to type in words and sentences, then speaks them aloud. *Robot Demo* does much the same thing, but a high-resolution robot is displayed to do the talking. *Talking Typewriter* has the user type a letter or character, then says its name. Type a question mark, and the synthesizer will say, "Question mark."

Spelling Test is also on the *Textalker* disk. The teacher can provide spelling words by using the subprogram *List Builder*. First the teacher is asked to type the correct spelling of the new word. Then the program asks, NOW TYPE THE WORD SO I CAN PRONOUNCE IT. The teacher must type in the word according to regular phonics rules. The computer pronounces the word and asks, DID I PRONOUNCE THAT CORRECTLY? (Y/N). If so, the next word can be typed. If not, the computer gives the teacher as many chances as necessary to arrive at the correct pronunciation.

The actual spelling test gives each question aloud: "Okay, Paul, how do you spell menu?" When the child types it in, the computer reads each letter orally. It says, "Good work," if the answer is correct and spells the word aloud correctly if the answer is wrong. Each spelling test is followed by an evaluation of performance, such as "Needs work!"

When considering the purchase of a voice synthesizer, look both at the quality of the synthesizer itself and at the commercial software that can use that particular synthesizer. A synthesizer without appropriate software is not much use in the classroom.

6

SOFTWARE: WORD RECOGNITION

Word-recognition ability—the ability to recognize the printed form of a word and associate it with its oral equivalent—is crucially important to fluent reading. Students recognize words by using a wide repertoire of strategies. These are typically categorized in four ways: phonics, structural analysis, contextual analysis, and sight-word identification. Each of these skills is considered in its relation to computer instruction in the second half of this chapter.

First, however, we discuss the fundamental issue of how to go about teaching word identification (as well as other basic skills). What is the role of drill and practice in the teaching of language?

THE ROLE OF PRACTICE

The process of growing up, of becoming familiar with one's world, is one continuous vocabulary-learning experience. From the first utterance of "Mama" and "Dada," the child's increasing world knowledge is reflected by vocabulary knowledge. Indeed, our society measures what it means to know about our world—our concept of intelligence—by the depth and breadth of our knowledge of words.

Though every experience in school and in the outer world potentially builds vocabulary, most schools supplement this natural growth with a vocabulary development program. In the child's first years of schooling, a large part of this program is centered on the transfer of oral vocabulary knowledge to printed language. Controversy still rages among educators on how best to guide this transfer. Vocabulary can be taught in many ways.

The old adage "practice makes perfect" remains a source of heated debate among educators, debate which deals less with the actual importance of practicing important skills than with the usefulness of specific skills we require our students to practice.

Mathematics educators like Seymour Papert (1980), a developer and proponent of the discovery-learning programming language LOGO, avidly denounce traditional drill and practice approaches to education. Many teachers are entranced by the myriad possibilities offered by creative use of LOGO and are given widespread media coverage because of increased public interest in computerized education. They quote Papert's assertion that by using tutorial and drill programs our schools are allowing computers to program children. Instead, they assert, our children should be learning to program computers through discovery of the basic mathematical and computer concepts offered by using LOGO.

A parallel controversy has long existed in the language arts professions, in a division labeled the "holistic/subskill" controversy (Vacca, 1980; Downing, 1982). On the one hand, advocates of holistic approaches to teaching language insist that language is a "whole" process and that language instruction should not be fragmented into subskills. Researchers and theorists such as Frank Smith (1978) and Moffett and Wagner (1983) denounce the teaching and practicing of reading and writing subskills. Instead, they insist that children read complete stories and works of literature in order to learn how to read, and that they write essays and stories in order to learn how to write. Even more, reading and writing, as well as listening and speaking, should not be fragmented. Since all language skills are interrelated in real life, they should be closely interrelated in the classroom.

On the other hand, advocates of the subskill approach suggest that reading is actually a highly complex process composed of a multitude of underlying abilities (Davis, 1972; Samuels, 1976). They argue that these subskills must be practiced in order to develop the fluency needed for skilled reading.

LaBerge and Samuels (1974) offer an explanation to help resolve this controversy. Though couched in psychological terms, their ideas on automaticity and reading have great implications for the classroom use of microcomputers. They suggest that reading is indeed composed of a series of underlying processes and that the teaching of reading must deal with each of these processes in turn, especially for slower learners. Brighter children synthesize these varied strands so easily that they appear to be learning a single skill. Slower learners, however, show clear evidence of the many different skills involved in learning to read.

The goal of the teacher is to develop each of the important subskills to such an extent that it can be performed automatically, without requiring attention on the part of the student. "We can attend to one thing at a time, but we may be able to process many things at a time so long as no more than one requires attention" (LaBerge and Samuels, 1974, p. 295). For example, when phonics analysis is performed fluently and automatically, the reader's attention can be centered on comprehending the meaning of a passage. If sentence comprehension has developed to the point of automaticity, attention can be directed toward the meaning of the paragraph or of the entire reading selection. If attention must be directed to lower processes such as word recognition or meaning of individual words, other higher-order components of the reading process will suffer.

Drill and practice are central to the development of automatic performance of reading's component processes. Edmund Burke Huey, in *The Psychology and Pedagogy of Reading*, recognized this when he wrote, "Repetition progressively frees the mind from attention to details, makes facile the total act, shortens the time, and reduces the extent to which consciousness must concern itself with the process" (1908, p. 104).

The task of the teacher, then, is to help students achieve the automaticity necessary for the skills important to success in school and in life. Most educators recommend some use of drill work to help children achieve this automaticity.

Yet the criticisms of language drills cannot be simply cast aside. One universally held conclusion from this debate is that drill activities must be incorporated into the total language arts program. Isolated drill activities are of doubtful value. Outcomes of drill activities need to be immediately transferred to important language events. Students must apply their newly learned skills in meaningful and comprehensive reading and writing activities if this transfer is to occur.

Computer Advantages for Language Practice

Criticism of drill work often focuses on its monotony. Children are frequently assigned such activities simply to keep them busy rather than because needs have been diagnosed for which the drills can act as remedies. Lack of feedback for correct or incorrect answers may result in children actually gaining practice in doing things the wrong way. At best, feedback tends to be delayed, since the children are forced to wait until the teacher is able to correct or discuss the answers.

The microcomputer functions in a variety of helpful ways to assist teachers and students in language practice. In some ways the computer is superior to humans in providing this instruction. Human teachers quickly tire of the monotony of administering practice exercises. Computers are infinitely patient (though some software programs may not be) and allow students to take their time, providing as much practice as the students need. The advantages of patience may be most dramatically illustrated in working with special education children, who need much repetition to improve their skills.

Another benefit of computerized drill instruction is that there is little ego involvement on the part of children when being corrected by a computer. They don't need to worry about the teacher's frowns or the giggles of classmates—the computer simply tells them whether their answer is correct or incorrect. No personal judgments are made.

This advantage is clearly seen in the difference in children's responses to human and computer assessment of their work. The *Pygmalion in the Classroom* studies initiated by the work of Rosenthal and Jacobson

(1968) have shown that teachers' expectations of and responses to children can have unforeseen effects on children's performance, both positive and negative in nature. Very subtle responses of the teacher to the student, often not consciously recognized by either, can lead to increased or decreased achievement. Hints of negative expectations, for example, may lead the student to expect or even welcome failure.

Reaction to computer assessment of performance is apparently qualitatively different. "Even a daggot can shoot better than that," one video game claims after the player is shot down by an alien spacecraft. For a teacher to compare a student's performance to that of a dog on the science fiction show *Battlestar Galactica* would be unprofessional, but children find the computer insults to be amusing, and they are motivated to try harder. While few educational publishers go to such extremes for fear of teacher reaction, some teacher-programmers have found that children love to see the computer generate such responses as, "Try again, turkey!!" Rather than affecting self-concept, these pert evaluations apparently work to humanize the child's conception of the computer.

Schools instill too much fear of failure in children. If learning is to take place through discovery, and if children are to develop a love of learning, teachers must encourage exploration and experimentation. Occasional failure is a necessary corollary to such a style of learning. The acceptance of temporary setbacks, and the recognition of them as interesting discoveries rather than discouraging failures, is one of the key concepts realized by children involved in programming. In LOGO, for example, the child plans procedures, then experiments to find which commands work and which do not. This *debugging* (getting rid of the errors) approach to problem solving is perhaps the most important outcome from teaching programming to children. It also parallels Goodman's (1967) portrayal of reading as a process of trial and error. Reading is a "psycholinguistic guessing game" in which the mind makes use of its language knowledge to predict upcoming content, then checks those predictions as accurate or inaccurate. Efficient adult reading, far from being an exact word-by-word identification process, is a constant round of hypothesis generation and verification.

Criticisms of Computerized Practice Exercises: "Beyond Drill and Practice"

Almost every computer conference dealing with educational issues offers a lecture entitled "Beyond Drill and Practice." The speaker criticizes computer courseware because it "does not take full advantage of the computer's capabilities." Such critics of microcomputer instruction insist that available software is limited to "computerized flash cards" or "electronic workbooks."

Much of this criticism is justified. With an exploding demand for software, publishers are primarily concerned with producing material quickly so that they can establish themselves in the software market. One educational program was evaluated as being a workbook transferred to the video screen—and the contents were estimated as equivalent to only 12 workbook pages. All this sold for the nice sum of $40!

The use of such material cannot be blamed on either the publishers or on the computer itself. Schools buy software. Just as a school would not purchase inferior print materials, it is incumbent upon administrators and teachers to evaluate software before buying it. If a school is stuck with simple-minded electronic flash card programs, it has no one to blame but itself.

In a reply to critics who condemn all drill and practice software, Roblyer (1982) pointed out that they seem to be missing the point of instructional uses of computers. Rather than criticizing courseware simply because it does not "make best use of the medium," computer experts need to first examine the instructional problems to be solved.

> If the computer is the only device with the characteristics desired (such as immediate, responsive feedback and automatic data collection), and if only a few of all the computer's capabilities are required to solve the problem and meet the need, *why use more?* (p. 29)

In other words, our concern should be with the questions, "What do I need to teach?" and, "How can I use the computer to teach it?" rather than with an esoteric concern for creating an ultimate educational computer application as some perceive LOGO to be. Much of the criticism of LOGO has been directed at just that point. It seems to some that LOGO has put the cart before the horse, in that its development preceded the multitude of justifications for its existence.

Too many educators have a knee-jerk reaction against practice exercises. Yes, there undoubtedly is too much busywork going on in American classrooms. Yes, the majority of materials—both computerized and non-electronic—available to teachers are unimaginative drills. But the history of the educational enterprise has clearly shown that repetition and practice have a role to play in learning. Emotional reactions simply cloud the issues. Each teacher must make judgments regarding the emphasis upon drill for each student.

Again, there is a misconception on the part of some computer users that the tremendous flexibility of computer applications means that the computer is the best tool for every educational task. Roblyer notes that effective use of instructional technology begins with the task of establishing just what it is that students do in their reading or writing (or whatever the desired learning outcome may be). Instruction, practice, and evaluation activities must then be matched to these objectives. Only as a final stage does the selection of the most appropriate medium for instruction take place. Those computer advocates who begin with the assumption that "the computer can do it better" will be sorely frustrated, especially in the complex area of language arts instruction.

A wide variety of word-recognition practice software is available, even at this early stage in the use of microcomputers for the teaching of reading. Publishers are aware of the tremendous emphasis placed upon practice work in the teaching of beginning reading in many classrooms and see a large potential market. In addition, every child in the schools is taught to read, creating a market much larger than that for algebra programs, for example. Finally, word-recognition exercises do not require the careful forethought and planning necessary for the teaching of higher-level skills. Programs can be created quickly and placed on the market. Characteristics of practice programs are discussed in Chapter 7.

BEGINNING READING AND THE COMPUTER

Ultimately the question of how children should be taught to read will not be resolved by the computer. The computer is simply a tool to more efficiently provide the kind of instruction decided upon by educators. Microcomputer programs can emphasize whole-word methods or phonics-first methods. Some experimental programs are even employing alternative alphabet methodologies similar to the ITA (Shelton and Kleiman, 1983). Other teachers are using word processors to provide lessons in the language experience approach.

The key decision for the educator to make involves a philosophy of teaching reading rather than a technological issue. Nor is this decision of the "either-or" variety. In practice, every methodology in use today is eclectic to some degree. No classroom teacher completely ignores meaning in favor of isolated phonics drills or uses story material to the complete exclusion of practice in word identification strategies.

As more and more reading instructional software has appeared on the market, a wide variety of word recognition material has become available. The teacher is able to choose material to give students practice on virtually any of the major word-identification strategies, at every elementary level. The key word-recognition skills involve phonics, structural analysis, use of context, and sight word identification, each to be considered in turn in the remainder of the chapter.

Phonics

Word Families deals with three beginning reading skills: recognition of initial consonants, final consonants, and medial vowels. A word is displayed at the top of the screen with one letter underlined: BI<u>G</u>. Below it are four additional letters, such as S, H, D, and B. The child must choose the letters that form other words when substituted for the underlined letter in the target word. As the letters are chosen, BID and BIB appear at the bottom of the screen. A clown face appears after several correct responses.

Another slightly more advanced program, *Fundamental Word Focus*, calls for students to identify word endings to form complete words. The letters CE are given at the left of the screen and a listing of four choices at the right. The student must choose DAR to form the word CEDAR. *Fundamental Word Focus* deals with several other skill areas as well, including alphabetizing and syllabication.

Structural Analysis

Tank Tactics at first appears to be a game activity, but it soon reveals itself to be a multiple-choice drill with some simple graphics tacked on. Several different versions are available to teach compound words, prefixes, and suffixes. In the prefix drill, students are first presented with brief definitions of frequently used prefixes such as *pre, im, pro,* and, *com.* As the "game" begins, an enemy supertank appears, firing a word part such as *set* at four smaller friendly tanks, each of which is paired with one of the prefixes under study. If the student makes an incorrect match, one of the friendly tanks is destroyed. If the exercise is successfully completed, the enemy tank is blown up.

Tank Tactics illustrates the problem with many exercises dealing with structural analysis skills. While *precook, present,* and *predawn* are good choices to teach the meaning of *pre* in an applied sense, students will only be confused when they try to determine just what it is that such words as *present* and *pretense* have to do with "before." In an effort to work with a wide variety of words in these exercises, creators of such materials—whether computerized or not—often include words that add to the confusion rather than act as good examples of the use of structural analysis skills.

Vocabulary Skills: Prefixes, Suffixes, and Rootwords includes introductory lessons, a review, a word-building activity, and an arcade game called *Alien Rain.* Words are presented in sentence contexts. Students are motivated to learn so that they can earn points during the review quiz that enable them to play the game.

Compound words are the topic of *Word Mate,* a card game in which the user plays against the computer. At the beginning of a hand, the student is dealt ten cards with such words as *light, rain, nest,* and *pole* listed on the screen. The student must enter a compound word such as *lightpole* at each turn. About 100 words are stored on the disk, and a teacher utility option allows additional words to be added.

Word Division is a simple activity that engages students in dividing words into morphemes. A word is displayed that must be divided into its meaningful parts by positioning a cursor at the appropriate spot in the word. If the word is correctly divided, the next word appears. Four files of 400 words each deal with compounds, suffixes, and prefixes. A utility option can be used to add files of new words, and a management system monitors up to 30 students.

Context

One of the most powerful and popular devices for improving students' language skills has been the use of the cloze procedure. Named after the Gestalt psychological concept of *closure,* of filling in the blanks in one's view of the world to form a unified whole, this teaching exercise has been demonstrated to improve reading ability when used properly (Jongsma, 1980). The procedure is actually quite simple. A passage in which certain words have been deleted is given to the student, who must fill in the blanks, making use of meaning context clues (that is, semantics) and language-structure context clues (syntax or grammar). *Cloze-Plus* is a powerful instructional program equipped with a fine diagnostic and management system. Each set of exercises is centered on a unified passage, about modern-day sailing vessels, for example. Work is thereby put into meaningful context and interest is maintained as the student learns both from the content of the passage and from the cloze exercises.

The passage is presented paragraph by paragraph. Each frame includes a cloze problem.

```
The rebirth of sailing vessels was pio-
neered by a fisherman in the late 1960's
His _____ then was not fuel prices.
Rather, he was anxious about the supply
of fish.  He wanted to fish in far-off
waters where fish are plentiful.

5. Type a word that fits in the blank.
   _____
```

If a hint is required by the student, pressing the space bar causes "he was anxious" to be underlined.

Students must use their contextual skills to determine the correct answer. Context exercises are presented in a variety of ways in each lesson. Some problems require that a multiple-choice option be chosen. Others include an underlined word for which students must determine the meaning from context:

```
"Impressive" means about the same as
   a. slight        c. meaningless
   b. small         d. important
```

Of particular interest to the teacher is that this program analyzes responses according to subskill involved and makes this analysis available to the teacher in a management system (see Chapter 20). Level F–1 of the program maintains a file similar to that presented in Figure 6–1 for each exercise on the disk. The skills report for each student is accessible to the teacher at any time and can be invaluable for diagnostic purposes. A student showing consistent difficulty in time order, for example, could be individually assigned supplemental work in that skill. *Cloze-Plus* demonstrates the potential of the computer for constant, unobtrusive, time-efficient monitoring of student skill development.

While *Cloze-Plus* deals with context clues, it is designed more to reinforce already-learned skills than to teach new skills. It is, in computer parlance, a *drill and practice* program rather than a *tutorial*. *Context Clues*, on the other hand, is designed to teach students to use contextual analysis

```
                    ---BILL---

F-1   SAILING SHIPS              FINISHED
F-2   SEEING EYES                NOT STARTED
F-3   COME INTO MY PARLOR        NOT STARTED
F-4   FASHION                    NOT STARTED
F-5   HOW MUCH AND HOW MANY      NOT STARTED


                    F-1   F-2   F-3   F-4   F-5

SAME MEANING        2/2   ...   ...   ...   ...
OPPOSITE MEAN.      ...   ...   ...   ...   ...
ASSOC./SYNTH.       3/3   ...   ...   ...   ...
CATEGORIZATION      ...   ...   ...   ...   ...
TIME/ORDER          ...   ...   ...   ...   ...
SIGNALS             1/1   ...   ...   ...   ...
PRONOUN REFER.      ...   ...   ...   ...   ...
SIMIL./DIFF.        1/1   ...   ...   ...   ...
FORM/FUNCTION       ...   ...   ...   ...   ...
CONCLUSION          2/3   ...   ...   ...   ...
DEFINITION          1/1   ...   ...   ...   ...
     EXTRA TRIES     4    ...   ...   ...   ...
```

FIGURE 6–1. *Cloze-Plus* management report

when dealing with unfamiliar words. The first lesson is a general introduction to the importance of context. Following lessons deal with various context skills one by one. Use of *that is, or,* and *meaning* as devices to explain unfamiliar words is explained. Another lesson deals with inferring meaning from examples.

Each lesson includes the tutorial material, some examples, practice drills, and a final mastery test.

Sight-Word Identification

A wide variety of traditional sight-word identification activities have been transferred to the computer. Some offer significant advantages over their nonelectronic counterparts. The importance of other activities is sometimes questionable. In general, the further removed the activity is from meaning, the less important it is to children's language development.

Instant words. Teachers of beginning readers recognize the importance of teaching the most frequent words in the English language so that recognition of these words is immediate. Such words as *the, of,* and *and* must be recognized instantly for fluid reading. Edward Fry has called these words the "instant words" and has incorporated the 300 most frequent words in his *Fry Instant Words Program.* Children are presented a target word for study:

The word (COLOR is the 300th word) then appears repeatedly with missing letters for the child to type in a drill:

C_L_R   _O_O_

Picture-word matching.   One of the most frequent sight-word activities has children look at workbook pictures and match words to the pictures. *Word Wise* includes similar activities in which a high-resolution picture appears, for instance of a boy eating a chicken drumstick. Four words are listed:

1. the
2. eat
3. we
4. see

The student chooses the word to match the picture and receives immediate feedback as to accuracy of the response.

Matching words.   In *Word Radar* common sight words are presented at the bottom of the screen. Students use the ARROW keys to move a cursor and reveal hidden words, then press the space bar when a match is found. A timing device is pictured as a radar screen.

Scrambled words.   The importance of scrambled word exercises to word-identification and spelling skills is not established. Children seem to enjoy these problems, however, and that may be sufficient justification for their use. Even teachers unfamiliar with computer programming may be willing to invest a little time and effort into typing a simple scrambled word game into the computer. A number of these are available in text format and can be typed into the computer.

Magic Spells is one of many prepared scrambled word games in which students compete against each other or against the computer. Teachers may use an optional utility to add their own words to those on the disk.

Do such scrambled word games drive you batty? The computer can help! *Word Plus* is a program whose main function is to serve as a *spelling checker* for word-processing text files. It has a large internal dictionary of words that can also be accessed for use in solving scrambled word puzzles. Enter the letters LECUN and a subprogram called *Anagram* will search its memory for an actual word with the same letters: UNCLE.

Scrabble-type games.   *Pandemonium* displays a five-by-five grid with single, double, and triple value squares. Randomly generated letters are displayed that must be formed into words and placed on the grid. As in the board game *Scrabble,* word values vary according to length of word and placement on special-value squares. The computer checks each entry against an internal list of words to be sure it is an acceptable word.

Find-a-word puzzles. Few defend the frequent use of these puzzles for any reasons other than that some students find them motivational and that they may improve word perception. The *Wordsearch* game included in the *Wordwright* series of vocabulary programs involves students in solving a find-a-word puzzle through association of the target words with their definitions—an important component which gives value to the traditional find-a-word game. Students must use definitional and etymological hints given to recognize the word, since visual identification alone is almost impossible, the target words' letters being in scrambled order within the find-a-word grid.

Teacher utility programs that enable teachers to create these puzzles using words of their own choice are described in Chapter 17.

Crossword puzzles. *Crossword,* another game in the *Wordwright* series, involves players in a competitive crossword game. Utility programs designed to generate crossword puzzles from teacher-supplied words and clues are described in Chapter 17.

For serious crossword puzzle addicts, the spelling checker *Word Plus* includes two subprograms that can help. Type FIND H?T?O?S and *Word Plus* will search its internal dictionary for a word to fit the input: HOT-DOGS. The command FIND *HING will list all words in the dictionary that end in HING. Another program, *Anagram,* can be ordered to search for a five-letter word beginning with AA: ANAGRAM AA???.

Hangman games. Several varieties of prepared hangman games exist. Simple versions are available in print and can be typed into the computer and saved on disk.

The widely distributed *Don't Fall* is an adaptation of hangman differing only in terms of the graphics. The computer randomly chooses a word from its list, then generates a dash for each letter. Several categories of words are available, from American Indian tribes to cities. A low-resolution picture of a man takes a step closer to the edge of a cliff whenever a letter not in the target word is guessed. If too many wrong letters are guessed, he falls off and lands on his head. The game has three levels of difficulty, differing only in how many steps the animated figure can take before falling.

Word wheels. The computer offers a wide assortment of variations on the traditional word wheel. In *Wordman* a letter (for example, H) travels around a square track with groups of letters on it. When the individual letter matches the letter group (for example, EN) as an initial consonant to form a word, the player taps the space bar to earn a point.

7

SOFTWARE: VOCABULARY

As a child develops in reading ability through the primary grades, instructional emphasis shifts from word recognition to development of an extensive meaningful vocabulary. Growth in knowledge of word meaning has many levels, ranging from ability to recognize idiomatic expressions to application of multiple meanings and connotations. For success in speech and in writing, the student must also be able to recall the required word and use it correctly in the appropriate contexts.

Though extensive research has been carried out on the effectiveness of vocabulary instruction (Manzo and Sherk, 1972), vocabulary skills are often taught badly. Most adults remember the long lists of vocabulary words they had to memorize in their school years. Odds are that many recognize that these exercises did little to improve use of words. Once the weekly quiz was administered, all was forgotten. Despite this realization, some classrooms still include this dull, meaningless routine.

Preparation for effective teaching of vocabulary requires an analysis of teaching procedures in the light of research. Unfortunately, many software programs designed to teach vocabulary do little to go beyond the "weekly list of words" approach. We begin this chapter with some generally recognized principles that can lead to far more meaningful vocabulary growth in our students. Then, since one principle of vocabulary instruction is to give students plenty of exposure to new words, we describe and evaluate different designs for computer practice programs. Though vocabulary can be taught in many ways (see the chapters on writing and content areas for other ideas), practice formats give intensive, repeated experiences with words and their uses in many contexts. The chapter concludes with some ideas for using computer practice exercises in the classroom.

PRINCIPLES OF VOCABULARY INSTRUCTION

1. A vocabulary development program is important. Perhaps this statement seems obvious, but the fact is that vocabulary instruction is conspicuously absent in some classrooms. It is often assumed that vocabulary is learned through wide reading and through daily classroom activities. Research demonstrates, however, that wide reading, while unarguably a powerful language development tool over the years, does not provide rapid improvement over the short run (Manzo and Sherk, 1972).

2. Vocabulary is best learned in conjunction with experiences that are as direct as possible (Dale, 1969). If a child is to learn the names of animals, for example, a field trip to see the animals in their natural habitat would be most effective. A trip to the zoo might be next best. A film or video documentary might serve almost as well. The least effective, most abstract method of teaching vocabulary is to describe the meaning of the word orally.

Attempts to provide direct experience are often impossible. Field trips are expensive and time consuming. Although schools must provide a program for general knowledge development that includes field experiences, such trips are certainly not the answer to most of our concept-development concerns. A field trip to a factory, for example, will not provide much of a personal experience with the concept of business administration or supply and demand.

Computers can provide simulations of direct experience designed to improve understanding of key terms and concepts. It is one thing to list the definitions of "assets" and "deficits" on the chalkboard and use them in sample sentences. It is far more meaningful to use a simulation activity like *Lemonade Stand* to involve the students in a personal process of discovering the meaning of these concepts as they run a profit-making business simulated by the computer.

3. An effective vocabulary development program is part of the regular language development program. Too many schools see vocabulary as an add-on, a supplemental program to be thrown in on top of the basal reading series and the usual writing assignments. To be effective, vocabulary must receive systematic attention from all teachers as they incorporate word-meaning instruction into their daily teaching.

Sadly, the present state of microcomputer instruction tends to foster the teaching of vocabulary as distinct from the rest of the educational program, teaching lists of words unrelated to classroom activity. The economics of the marketplace have led most vocabulary drill programs to be designed for as wide a market as possible. As a result, the words drilled will have little or no relation to the words being taught in your reading series or in the thematic units your students are working with.

Two important trends are already beginning to provide solutions to this problem. One is the rapid development of microcomputer supplemental programs by basal series publishers. To a greater or lesser extent, these programs are designed to fit into the regular basal reading program, reinforcing vocabulary taught in the reader and in workbooks. A second trend, discussed later in this chapter, is to include teacher utility options in many vocabulary programs.

4. Targeted vocabulary must receive extensive attention. Superficial study of long lists of vocabulary words may result in good weekly quiz scores, but this method does not result in long-term vocabulary improvement. It is more effective to deal with a few words and provide the repeated exposure necessary to make those words part of the students' lives. Again, the teacher utility options and prepared programs integrated with basal series provide opportunity for repeated exposure to specific words. Supplemental software is of dubious value if it is unrelated to anything else going on in the classroom.

Wordwright is one of the few vocabulary development programs on the market today to offer extensive practice with lists of words prepared by the software developer. Teachers may choose from an assortment of *dictionary disks*, each of which contains 25 lessons with ten words each, targeted to a specific subject area (such as English or social studies) and to a specific secondary grade-level range. Each lesson's words may be practiced in a wide variety of practice and game activities.

Each lesson generally begins with a multiple-choice pretest. A concluding report page indicates which words were correctly defined by the student and which were not. The student is then presented with a frame for each of the unknown words with a definition, two example sentences, and a short etymology.

For example, a high-school-level English word:

```
            forensic
          1. DEFINITION
   Pertaining to legal proceedings
          or debates.
         2. SENTENCE I:
   The coroner was an expert at
        .... medicine.
         3. SENTENCE II:
   Investigators used a .... ap-
   proach to solving the mystery.
         4. WORD HISTORY
      From Latin meaning of a
            forum.
```

Students are then allowed to choose from a variety of optional strategies for studying the words. The "exercise option" presents sample sentences with blanks, with the correct vocabulary definition to be chosen from a multiple-choice listing. If the student's response is incorrect, the definition with sentences and word history is displayed for study.

ennui
The students' .... was obvious to the lecturing teacher.

Three game options are also available, all of which involve competition between two players. *Wordsearch* is a meaning-oriented find-a-word puzzle. Vocabulary words are scrambled and inserted in a wordsearch puzzle. Each player is allowed 35 seconds to move a cursor across the board. If the cursor crosses a word, a beep is sounded. The player must then determine which word is hidden. Since the word has scrambled letters and may be written vertically or horizontally, this is much harder than it sounds. The student must press a key for hints (for example, number of syllables, definition, word history, example sentence). Meanwhile the clock is going, and time is running out. When the 35 seconds are up, the second player can take over where the first left off.

Fragmentation, the second game option, involves making up words from syllables. Players must link word parts such as EMPTI with NESS or EMPLOY with MENT. In the third option, *Crossword*, players move a cursor to the beginning space of a word blank on a crossword puzzle and press a key to get clues.

By involving students in a variety of activities, this series of programs allows a vast amount of experience with each lesson's words, probably more than most students would need. By constant repetition the definitions and use of the words are taught to the students. Students are motivated to learn, as well, since they will be held accountable for the word identifications on the games. A final posttest determines how well the students have performed on the lesson's vocabulary.

Another vocabulary development program that offers a variety of activities is *Word Attack*. Though less comprehensive than *Wordwright*, it nonetheless goes well beyond most vocabulary software. Words are presented along with definitions and sentences. Once these words have been studied, students are quizzed by the presentation of words and four numbered definition options. The quiz is timed.

The sentence-completion exercise presents a sample sentence and the definition of the vocabulary word. If help is needed in recalling the word, the user can request a listing of four possible word choices. The last exercise is a video game multiple-choice drill. Four words are displayed at the top of the screen. At the bottom is a definition and a creature wearing a dunce cap. The student moves the creature under the word choice that matches the definition and fires the dunce cap at the word. Extra points are earned for quickness and for hitting bonus targets that appear occasionally.

5. Vocabulary must be taught in depth. It is more effective to study a few words closely than to skim over long lists. Herber's (1978) suggestions to content area teachers are appropriate to consider. He noted that it was impossible to spend sufficient teaching time to cover every technical

term encountered in such fields as economics, science, and social studies. Yet vocabulary must be taught. How can this conflict be resolved? Teach vocabulary so that there is transfer of skills. Choose a few words for each lesson and develop them through word analysis, word recognition, word meaning, and use of context. Instead of dealing with words as discrete entities, deal with generalizable skills that can be used by students to deal with unknown words they encounter in the future.

6. Vocabulary should be taught in meaningful context. Never simply list a word and its definition. Always provide at least one example sentence. Word-meaning exercises such as categorizing are helpful in providing cognitive organizational structures for some types of words.

TYPES OF COMPUTERIZED PRACTICE EXERCISES

Producers of software are making available a number of different types of drill activities. Keep in mind that many of these programs are combinations of two or more of the following categories.

Reinforcement versus Drill

Two stages of learning are apparent in the development of automaticity. The first stage involves the student in learning accuracy: knowing how to perform the skill in a functional manner. Only after accuracy has been established can the student gain automaticity, the second stage.

Reinforcement exercises are designed to promote the accuracy of performance. Such exercises are often limited in number, the goal being largely one of teaching as opposed to practice. Clear feedback, especially for incorrect answers, is essential. Drill exercises, on the other hand, provide large amounts of practice, emphasizing fluency (and perhaps speed) of performance. Drill programs may assume accuracy and provide only minimal feedback. In *Word Master* students are presented a sequence of words and must race the clock to shoot down synonyms, antonyms, or homonyms. Students who respond incorrectly are not provided with correct answers. The game simply goes on.

Randomly Generated Problems

Mathematics exercises are often composed of randomly generated numbers. The computer, for instance, chooses numbers to be multiplied or divided. Language arts exercises are not amenable to this procedure, since meaningful sentences cannot be constructed of randomly chosen words, and there is no such thing as a randomly spelled word except in scrambled word exercises.

Random generation in language arts usually involves the randomly ordered presentation of preconstructed problems. A series of exercises might be presented in a different order for each student in the class. Software such as PILOT and *E-Z Learner* allows teachers to construct their own problems for computer presentation to students. Randomized order of presentation can give some new life to old exercises. A student who is working through a series of exercises for the second time, in order to reinforce learning or to master skills inadequately learned the first time, benefits from this varying order of presentation.

Linear Programs

In most software available today, the program presents exercises in an unvarying order to each student. While such programs are often the result of poor design (and they may not deal with individual differences by branching; see Chapter 4), this is not always the case. There are situations in which a predetermined order is the best form of presentation, such as exercises that move from less complex to more complex problems and instructional situations that lend themselves to a high degree of structure.

Self-Paced versus Timed

Programs developed for instruction or reinforcement of accuracy are most flexible when designed to accommodate themselves to each student's learning rate. Certain situations lend themselves to timed practice. Programs can be timed in several ways. In courseware that includes an emphasis upon reading-rate improvement, students are able to choose a speed of presentation at the beginning of the presentation, then attempt to keep up with it. Another option is to request the student to press a key, usually the RETURN key or space bar, when he has finished reading the page. The computer then prints out the time on task.

Gamelike Exercises

Just as imaginative teachers have traditionally attempted to increase motivation by making drills into gamelike activities, the computer can be programmed to present exercises in game formats (see Chapter 18). Homonym baseball, morpheme concentration, computer-generated crossword puzzles, and the like are all available as software. Word games are intrinsically interesting, as shown by the popularity of such board games as *Scrabble*.

CHARACTERISTICS OF GOOD PRACTICE PROGRAMS

Since "drill and practice" exercises are helpful in supplying numerous exposures to the vocabulary words under study, their characteristics are discussed in this chapter. Most of the factors discussed are equally applicable to practice programs based on skills other than vocabulary as well.

Instructional value. Practice is vital for development of automatic processing. Some skills, however, are of dubious value in learning to read. Is it really necessary to drill students on each of Rudolf Flesch's (1981) 181 phonics skills? Most teachers would agree that it is not.

Computer management system. The diagnostic/prescriptive teacher uses exercises for more than simple busywork, closely reviewing student performance. A good management system (see Chapter 20) will allow the teacher to track students on the tasks assigned, individually and as a class. Specificity is vital. The management system in *Word Flip*, a *Concentration*-type game in which players match words and their endings (for example, LEARN and ED), simply informs that Johnny correctly answered 14 out of 20 vocabulary questions. This procedure is of limited value when planning remediation. It is important to know exactly which words are recognized regularly and which are not.

Immediate feedback. The ability of the computer to respond immediately to student performance is one of its most useful characteristics. It is hard to imagine why a software publisher would market a program that requires the student to wait until the end of a series of exercises before being told which answers were right or wrong. Some do, however.

LaBerge and Samuels (1974) emphasize the importance of continuous feedback to the student, especially during the stage of learning in which accuracy is developing. Once consistency of accurate response has been established, such feedback may become redundant, since the child knows whether the answer is right or wrong. In that case, however, important feedback can be given in the form of the time it took to complete the exercise, since automaticity and speed of execution are the goals.

Self-paced instruction. Unless there is some overriding reason to present material at an unvarying speed, the student should be able to control rate of presentation. The computer is ideally suited to match rate of learning to each individual student.

Varying levels of difficulty. Using a vocabulary program that presents material at a single level of difficulty is just as ineffective as buying a single vocabulary book to use with every student. Software needs to be matched to learners' needs just as printed material does. A fifth grade classroom in which all software is at the fifth grade level provides no challenge for superior readers and no adapted instruction for slower students. *Wordwright* provides disks of words varying in level from the junior through the senior high school.

Provision for changes in difficulty level. Some programs are designed to move students automatically to easier or more challenging problems when exercise results call for such an alteration in instructional level. For example, when a student scores 100% on fifth grade level material over a series of several exercises, the program may switch the student to the sixth grade material.

Less efficient options, whose advantages lie in greater teacher or student control over instruction, have the program generate reports that difficulty level should be changed. Still other programs require that the teacher recognize the need for a change when examining the management system report.

Repetition of incorrectly completed problems. The program should recirculate problems that were answered incorrectly for further practice and reinforcement. In *Homonyms in Context*, for example, students are presented a sentence and must choose the appropriate homonym to fit the blank. If an incorrect answer is given, the correct answer appears. The next frame repeats the presentation of the target sentence. New sentences are not given until the student correctly answers the first. When the lesson is concluded, the incorrectly answered sentences are repeated for review.

Interesting, gamelike activity. Unimaginative programs in which the problem is presented, the answer typed in, and the response given abound in the software marketplace. Practice activities are best presented in the form of games in order to maintain student interest in what is often a rather dull, repetitive function.

Recognizing the tremendous interest in video games and the motivational advantages that may be gained by using this format, publishers have made available a tremendous variety of computer vocabulary games. *Vocabulary Baseball*, for example, pits two players or teams against each other. Each batter has the option of trying for a single (easy words), double, or triple (very difficult). The ball is pitched by displaying the target vocabulary word and four possible definitions. A successful choice results in a hit and an advance to the appropriate base. Action is illustrated by high-resolution screen graphics of the baseball diamond.

Trickster Coyote, a *Frogger*-like game in which a character jumps from object to object to reach a goal, displays a definition at the top of the screen. An animated boy must chase a coyote by jumping across a row of floating logs, landing only on logs that have the correctly matching word written on them. *Pacman*, another popular video game, is the model upon which *Chambers of Vocab* is built. Players wend their ways through a maze in which "word beasts" slowly move around, their letters like parts of a caterpillar's body. When a definition is displayed, the player moves to the matching word beast to capture it. Play is timed. The quicker the word beasts are captured, the more points the player wins.

In *Snake-O-Nyms*, a fleet of about 20 words moves horizontally across the screen toward the user's playing piece, a smiling frog face. Among the words are snakes that plan to make the frog their lunch. The player guides his frog face to the word that is synonymous with the target word displayed at the bottom of the screen, simultaneously avoiding the snakes. As the game progresses, the words and snakes move faster and faster, increasing the challenge to maintain interest. Another optional version of the game uses antonym identification.

Word Flip, a game similar to the television show *Concentration*, requires students to match words and their endings. Blocks labeled A through X are displayed on the game board. If the player uncovers a word and an ending, she must decide whether or not the pair is a match and, if a match, whether it is misformed. For example, TEACH and ED is a match, but it should be spelled TAUGHT.

Interest-arousing graphics.   Lack of graphics may be an indication that publishers have not spent sufficient time and money on developing a program. Advances in graphics production in the past few years and the astonishing graphics capabilities of microcomputers add color and interest to the program.

Teacher utility for customizing.   Each classroom has its own unique vocabulary needs. Different stories require work with different vocabulary words. Different vocabulary workbooks use different words and, even when words are the same, arrange them in different order of presentation. A teacher customization utility allows each teacher to change the vocabulary drill program so that his or her own choice of words and definitions is used.

Programs that do not correspond to vocabulary activities in the classroom are of very limited usefulness. Recognition of this fact has led many software publishers to include customization utility options in their programs. These require some additional work on the part of teachers, since the vocabulary words and their definitions must be typed into the computer, but the final product can be well worth the effort. *Trickster Coyote, Word Attack, Antonyms/Synonyms, Homonyms,* and *Homonyms in Context* all contain utility options in which words and definitions can be easily entered by the teacher.

A more comprehensive program like *Wordwright* requires more comprehensive input. Teachers must first obtain information on the words' definitions, syllabication, meaningful word parts, etymology, and sample sentences, then type this information into the computer, which stores it on disk. A significant flaw in the design of *Wordwright's* utility is that the same information must be laboriously typed for each of its three game disks if students are to use the words with all three games.

Active thinking and involvement.   Thoughtless repetition is the foundation for too much vocabulary instruction. Students learn words better when led to think about them actively. A fine example of a vocabulary development program that goes well beyond the typical repetitive drill format and provides a teacher utility for customization is *Quizit.* Designed and programmed by Bill Wadlinger, an instructor of English as a second language using computer-assisted instruction, *Quizit* is well suited for all types of students in integrating vocabulary reinforcement with contextual analysis problem solving in a game format reminiscent of the old television show *Name That Tune.*

The game can be played by one or two players or teams. A sentence is displayed using the target vocabulary word in context, but representing it with a blank space.

```
THE ^^^^^^^^^^ OF CHURCH AND STATE IS AN
ESTABLISHED PRINCIPLE IN OUR COUNTRY.
```

Players are told how many letters are in the word and are given two hint options. They may request a definition or synonym.

```
A HINT:
    KEEPING THINGS APART
```

Or they may request as many initial letters of the word as they think they need. The more letters requested, the fewer points earned when they guess the word.

While *Quizit* is sold with some exercises already prepared for use, the real purpose of the program is to allow teachers to add their own words, definitions, and sentences. The utility option includes a mini–word processor to make typing easy. As many vocabulary exercises as desired can be created and stored on the disk to be used with the *Quizit* game.

Clue In is another vocabulary exercise that requires thoughtful analysis on the part of the students. A categorization exercise, the game offers up to four clues to players to help them make a choice. The more clues requested, the fewer the points won when the target word is guessed.

```
1. UP OR DOWN
2. MOVING
3. STEPS
4. ONE-WAY
```

When the players are ready to guess, they request the answer choices and choose one.

```
A. STAIRS
B. ESCALATOR
C. ELEVATOR
```

USING COMPUTER PRACTICE EXERCISES IN THE CLASSROOM

1. Use exercises in an individualized manner. Assign only the amount of drill needed to develop the accuracy and automaticity necessary for successful transfer of skills to whole reading and writing activities. Brighter students often are assigned far too much drill work. Drills should only be used until fluent transfer to meaningful tasks is possible.
2. Keep progress charts as motivational devices. *Reading Aids through the Grades*, a popular book of reading ideas (Mueser, 1981), offers many suggestions. Children like to see evidence of their own progress.
3. Intervene when necessary. No software is completely self-sufficient. At times it becomes apparent that the student needs teacher instruction or guidance. One of the key differences between assigning drills as busy-work and effective use is that the effective teacher monitors activities closely to recognize moments when intervention is required.
4. Become personally familiar with the program yourself before using it with students. It is often necessary to work through the entire set of

exercises. A program may be highly touted by its publishers and well reviewed in the journals, and yet be poorly suited to your students. Instructions may have to be posted or simplified for independent student use.

5. Transfer learning to holistic language exercises—reading and writing. Just as the better basal series lessons integrate skill work with stories, so should the teacher develop plans to transfer the skills learned on the computer to meaningful reading and writing activities. Without planned transfer, skills learned in isolation will not be applied in important language contexts. The advantages of a teacher utility option in vocabulary programs, which allows this integration, are clear.

One final note having to do with computerized practice work in general. Experience has shown that teachers are far more impressed by the computer's capability to present and manage drill work than they are by the many other types of software available. This preference is symptomatic of a key problem in many elementary classrooms—reliance upon unimaginative repetition for teaching of skills. It is a shame, because simulation and word processing software programs, for example, take far greater advantage of the computer's power to enhance language instruction.

Many writers have warned against overuse of worksheets in language instruction (for example, Aulls, 1982; Durkin, 1981; R. Smith and Johnson, 1980). Reinking (1984b) points out that simple transferral of this form of instruction to the computer may increase student motivation, but that increased motivation does not justify use of poor teaching methods.

> A student who would rebel at doing another irrelevant or inappropriate dittoed sheet may eagerly carry out the same activity when it means using a joystick to specify answers on the computer screen. The difference in the student's motivation in these two instances does not, however, validate the content or purpose of the instructional activity. (p. 11)

Selecting and using a variety of programs, rather than relying simply on drills, can only enhance the effects of computer use in the reading and language arts classroom.

8

SOFTWARE:
READING
COMPREHENSION

What is comprehension? How can computers help us teach it?

E. L. Thorndike once described the reading process as being as complex as any form of thought. "The act of answering simple questions about a simple paragraph . . . includes all the features characteristic of typical reasonings" (1917, p. 425). Comprehension, simultaneously a key component and the ultimate product of this complex process, must be just as mystifying. In order to deal with computer applications in comprehension instruction, we must first decide just what we mean by the term.

This chapter considers reading comprehension from the vantage points of two opposing "camps." Some teachers and researchers favor subskill instruction. They emphasize the various subskills thought to underlie the general comprehension process (see Chapter 6 for a more detailed discussion of the subskill approach). Others promote the use of holistic activities, which involve all the language arts in an integrated, meaningful way. This latter approach, at the forefront of contemporary research and theory, is discussed at length here and is elaborated upon in Chapters 10, 11, and 12.

Advocates of subskill instruction often use comprehensive skills management or mastery learning systems that deal with dozens of comprehension skills, as well as word-attack and study skills. These detailed learning packages involve pretesting students with a criterion-referenced test (a nonnormed test in which students are evaluated in terms of mastery of particular skills), the assignment of learning packages to particular students designed to shore up weaknesses diagnosed by the test, and posttests to evaluate whether skill deficits have been corrected.

On the other hand, those who favor holistic instruction have attempted to link reading and writing by such methods as the language experience approach. The student tells the teacher a story, the teacher writes it down, and the student reads the story (Allen and Allen, 1966; Allen, 1976). Another favored approach has been "individualized reading," in which the students are allowed to choose their own reading material and essentially teach themselves to read by actually reading (Barbe, 1961; Veatch, 1959). The emphasis is on performing "whole" language tasks rather than on breaking down the tasks into minor components.

Tovey (1976) represented such viewpoints when he claimed that "comprehension cannot be taught directly, but situations can be provided to facilitate and encourage the processing of print into meaning" (p. 289). He suggested that the reading teacher's most important task is that of "encouraging and guiding children to seek books they *can* read and *desire* to read" (p. 292).

Which approach is the best? As in so many areas of education, the research is not conclusive (Rosenshine, 1980). Instead of toeing a hard-line position, most teachers use a sensible, "middle of the road" (Niles, 1968) eclecticism, combining the two approaches to capitalize on strong points of each. An effective eclectic approach can be based on three principles:

1. Use meaningful, natural-language (holistic) activities unless the situation suggests otherwise. Many students learn to write by writing and to read by reading. Interminable subskill drills simply take time away from more motivational and integrative work.

2. Interweave comprehension subskill instruction with holistic activities. When students are reading a story, for instance, teach them to make inferences, to draw conclusions, and to find main ideas. Model and explain these skills. Isolated skill drill robs reading of its inherent motivational values. "Strong motivation, so necessary in learning any skill, springs from two main sources: Specific evidence of progress in learning the skill and proof of its practical application" (Niles, 1968, p. 130).

3. Monitor student progress in subskill areas. If particular students require corrective instruction in a skill, provide practice on a small-group or individualized basis.

EVALUATION OF COMPREHENSION SOFTWARE

The purpose of holistic software differs greatly from the purpose of subskill software. Evaluation must emphasize different factors in each. Be mindful, however, that software need not be (and often cannot be) neatly divided into holistic versus subskill. Evaluate all material using both criteria: The best software may fit both bills to greater or lesser extents.

The Holistic Approach: The Reading-Writing Connection

1. Is material presented in a way that emphasizes meaning?   Is the content of the reading material important to read? Can it be understood as a unified whole, or are short reading passages selected with no relation to each other? Much instructional material reads like a dictionary; it resembles collections of unrelated articles (or even unrelated sentences) that cannot be processed together into some meaningful whole.

Do you read the encyclopedia in your spare time, or lists of randomly chosen sentences? Neither do your students.

Many instructional materials use very short passages when longer passages are optimal for the skill to be taught. This is especially true in microcomputer programs, where screen space severely limits the amount of text that can be displayed. The following frame is offered in *MicroSystem 80 Critical Reading*.

```
     Carl looked at the cars in
  front of his house.  Every one
  was red.  Some had white-wall
  tires.  The big car belonged to
  Mr. Trent.  A small car was in
               the middle.

  (c) The small car was red.

     True   False   Unsure
```

While such an exercise helps clarify the meaning of "inferential reading" or "drawing a conclusion," it is not clear whether this skill would transfer to the reading of a complete story. Would the child recognize those points at which a conclusion must be drawn? In referring to this same problem in basal reading series curricula, Durkin (1981) concluded, "One possible consequence is that the children receiving the instruction never do see the relationship between what is done with reading in school and what they should do when they read on their own" (p. 542). When making use of such materials, teachers should show students how these skills can be transferred to larger selections.

2. Is the child given an important experience with language, in terms of his own life and background knowledge? Learning to read should not be separated from reading to learn. The chief purposes of reading in school and on the job are to learn and to act based on that learning (Mikulecky, 1982). Will your students learn from the material, or is the content used only as a meaningless tool for illustration of a skill?

Exercises involving use of the cloze procedure naturally lend themselves to use of unified reading selections. Cloze is a fill-in-the-blanks procedure (Bormuth, 1967) in which the student must make use of context clues from a passage to determine the appropriate word to fill each blank. One passage from *Cloze Plus*, for instance, offers an interesting account of life among the Plains Indians in the 1800s, inferentially pointing out the contrast between their customs and life in today's society. While fragmented into paragraphs because of screen-size limits, the paragraphs are tied together into an organized selection that encourages learning from text.

Several software utilities allow teachers to type their own choice of selections into the computer, then transform those selections into cloze passages that can be printed out in hard copy or displayed on the video screen for computer instruction. Again, such passages can simultaneously teach both skill and content if chosen appropriately (see Chapter 17).

3. Is it possible to interrelate varied language arts naturally into assignments associated with the software? A key concept for holistic language instruction involves the indivisible linkages between the varied language arts. Reading and writing, for example, are outgrowths of the same basic process. One deals with language in receptive form, the other in expressive form. Similarly, these two language skills are the print-oriented versions of listening and speaking.

This description paints perhaps a too simplistic picture of the interrelationships between the four skills. After all, reading does have qualitative differences from writing. However, it is undeniable that the two skills are closely related—and that this relationship should frequently be made apparent to students by directly tying them together in instruction.

A few software programs have attempted to tie reading and writing together. One of the first commercial ventures in this area is the popular *Story Machine*, a story creation program designed for primer-level students. *Story Machine* provides youngsters with the opportunity to create their own stories using the 40-word vocabulary understood by the software. As the child creates a story, characters are brought to life in graphic form on the monitor screen, performing actions matching those in the written story.

THE BOY GOES TO THE FLOWER, for instance, creates a cartoon-image boy walking to a flower. THE GIRL DANCES yields a picture of a girl dancing. Sentences can be strung together to form simple stories that are sequentially acted out on the screen. A variety of characters are allowed (boy, girl, flower, house, fence, rock, etc.), as well as a variety of playful, motivating verbs (jumps, runs, sings, dances).

This story construction provides language experiences that display the functions of reading and writing. Children conceptualize the purpose of these skills. The interrelationships of the two skills are also demonstrated. Children create their own stories, then reread them as they are acted out on the screen. These stories can be saved to disk and rerun at any time. Children enthusiastically swap disks to read each other's stories for amusement and to get ideas for their own creations.

Sadly, many teachers react negatively to *Story Machine*. Natural language experiences are not "neat." Drills are neat. The child is either right or wrong. All loose ends are tied up. There are loose ends in *Story Machine* that some teachers do not tolerate, though children do well enough. These loose ends illustrate the ambiguities that exist in holistic computer exercises (and, to a great degree, in all natural-language experiences that require something more than a yes-no, true-false, A, B, C, or D response).

First, *Story Machine* requires close adult supervision when used with the beginning readers for whom it was designed. In order to start writing, several steps must be completed. The child must boot the disk, answer several housekeeping questions (for example, "Do you want sound?"), then choose the correct option from the main menu. These tasks require someone who can read and understand the directions.

Second, the story options are severely limited. Only the 40 words in the software dictionary are understood by the computer. The child must keep a file card with the words for easy reference.

Third, some sentences just don't work, a frustrating experience for child and teacher alike. The computer is limited in terms of its under-standing of syntactic arrangements. For example, THE BOY EATS IN THE HOUSE uses allowable words, but the combination of the verb EATS with the prepositional phrase IN THE HOUSE does not fit the software's programming as an allowable grammar construction.

Fourth, the computer can mistake semantic content (meaning). One student typed THE BOY SINGS TO THE FLOWER. The animated boy moved away from the flower, sang a few notes (beeps from the com-puter's speaker illustrated by musical notes on the screen), then moved back. Apparently the software misinterprets TO THE FLOWER to mean RETURN TO THE FLOWER after singing, or else the graphics pro-gramming creates the confusion.

Fifth, the simplicity required by vocabulary, syntactic, and semantic restraints allows only the simplest of actions to be written and performed. There is very little ability to provide any type of plot structure. Thus stories are actually relatively unrelated collections of single-sentence events rather than narratives that follow a well-defined story structure (called "story grammars" by text-processing researchers such as Rumel-hart, 1977). A student's attempt to add AND THEY LIVED HAPPILY EVER AFTER to the end of his story was not allowed.

Such weaknesses must continue to be valid objections to the use of holistic-oriented software for the near future. Memory size limitations put caps on the linguistic sophistication of programming, even though ad-vances in artificial intelligence research (most of which are primarily con-cerned with teaching computers to understand language) have made much more complex programs possible in larger computers. *Story Machine* is itself composed in a high-level programming language called Forth, and represents a significant step forward in this area.

Do such limitations destroy the possibility of effective use of holistic software in the classroom? Classroom experience shows that it depends upon how much the teacher values integrated language instruction (as opposed to drill work) and how much individual attention the teacher or aide is able to devote to students.

Language-experience software may be of greater practical value with older students who are more familiar with the computer and better able to deal with vagaries of software behavior on their own.

A program specifically designed to integrate reading and writing is *Story Maker*, another story creation program. It is the product of a re-search project sponsored by Bolt, Beranek, and Newman, a Boston think tank, and the National Institute of Education. *Story Maker* provides a series of strategies to be used by students to construct their own stories. While largely a writing task, the actual original purpose of the program dealt with reading by allowing students to read and discuss stories created by classmates (Rubin and Gentner, 1982). A variety of options are available that either increase or decrease the complexity of the procedure, which involves students in choosing story portions to form a unified narrative.

In one exercise, "The Haunted House," students are presented with a purpose: WRITE A STORY IN WHICH LACE MEETS CAT-WOMAN. The story begins with, LACE OPENED THE FRONT DOOR AND. . . . A series of optional story components are then presented:

1. SAW THE JOKER
2. SLIPPED INTO WHAT LOOKED LIKE A BIG BOWL OF SPAGHETTI
3. STEPPED ON A MOUSE

When the child chooses one component, it is added to the beginning of the story: LACE OPENED THE FRONT DOOR AND STEPPED ON A MOUSE. Another series of components is then presented. The child chooses the components that will eventually lead to fulfillment of the computer-generated purpose, that of the main character Lace meeting Catwoman. Each component choice limits later choices. If the child ignores the correct choice, she is inextricably forced down a path that does not allow fulfillment of the story purpose. When the student is finished with the story, the computer informs her that the purpose was not met and gives her another chance to write the story. As the children become familiar with the structure of the choices (a tree diagram of the various choice options is accessible from disk), they learn the consequences of their choices and become aware of the inherent structure of narrative prose.

In a wonderfully creative manner that sometimes puzzles teachers unused to the method, the software authors place emphasis upon exploration and discovery of story structure rather than upon whether choices are correct or incorrect. Children are encouraged to examine all choices and to construct several different stories based on the same theme. The authors arrange this approach by leaving no clues as to the "correct" choice in the first series of options. As a result, the children usually spend some time exploring various story options that cannot lead to fulfillment of the story purpose. This exploration of the mazelike story options leads to insights about how stories are constructed and organized into coherent patterns.

Once finished, students are able to print out their stories to share with other students. Another option included on the disk, called *Story Maker Maker*, allows students to create their own story choices and place them in memory for future users.

Rubin and Gentner (1982) suggest that *Story Maker* helps achieve the following goals related to student conceptualizations about high-level characteristics of narrative prose:

A. Provides an active language experience that allows children to construct stories easily.

B. Demonstrates to children the consequences of choosing different ways for a story to proceed.

C. Avoids the problem of overemphasis on skills unrelated to the major purpose of the program, such as spelling and handwriting.

Alan Lesgold (Malone and Levin, 1984) has indicated that this function of the computer enables it to act as an "intellectual prosthesis." Well-designed software can enable students to exercise cognitively advanced subskills before they completely control all the lower-level mechanical skills. The computer supports the mechanical details while children are left to deal with the more challenging functions of story creation.

D. Provides a real audience for children's writing and opportunities for children to work together on story creation.

E. Creates the opportunity to compare stories with different structures.

F. Motivates by guaranteeing success.

As with *Story Machine,* this program does not have the neat format of a drill exercise. The possibilities for exploration and play all involve important aspects of story structure, however.

4. Might the child choose this reading material on his own if given the chance? Holistic instruction focuses on long-range effects of instruction. Rather than zeroing in on what the child is learning today, teachers must also be concerned about developing a love for language, a desire to read and write. Drills do little to inspire such motivation. Of most value is software that allows students choice of topics for reading, just as student choice of reading material is a key component of such techniques as Barbe and Abbott's (1975) "personalized reading" or Fader and McNeil's (1968) "hooked on books."

5. Is there provision for some form of feedback to the teacher to indicate how well the process is going? By their very nature, many integrative activities do not lend themselves to the kind of management system that keeps track of subskill growth. Feedback may sometimes be available in the form of completed composition work. In many cases, however, the teacher will have little idea of a student's progress without provision for teacher-student conferences. In *Story Maker,* for instance, the final product (the completed story) tells little about the conceptualizations that have taken place during story construction. A meeting with the teacher to discuss the experience, to allow the student the opportunity and guidance to explicitly formulate and express these conceptualizations, is invaluable. It can be a learning experience for the student and a diagnostic tool for the teacher. Since much holistic software requires close teacher supervision during use, observations made during this supervision can be used as one basis for discussion during the teacher-student conference.

The Subskill Approach: The Components of Comprehension

The mechanics of computerized subskill practice are considered in greater detail in Chapter 6.

1. Is the subskill objective important to the reading process? *MicroSystem 80 Critical Reading* is a comprehensive program that attempts to teach students the skill of critical reading. While the skill itself is an important higher-level comprehension tool, the actual approach to instruction has been criticized (EPIE Institute, 1983). Students are taught logic rules such as the use of *or* in sentences to make inferences, then given practice on multiple-choice reading exercises using the rule:

```
Jane is articulate or conniving.
She won her case in front of the
      Court of Appeals.
(d) Jane is conniving.
True   False   Unsure
```

Does such instruction actually increase reading comprehension ability, or does it rather teach logic rules without much transfer to actual reading experiences? Application of logic rules is certainly important to critical reading, but whether the isolated teaching of such logic rules will do very much to increase comprehension is doubtful.

2. Are requisite subskills taught in a developmental sequence? Studies of children's summarizing skills have given great insight into the enormous complexity of the seemingly simple "find the main idea" skill. Brown, Campione, and Day (1981) examined the research to suggest that there are several abilities essential to summarization. Readers must be able to delete repetitive or trivial information. Fifth graders were found to be able to do this with 90% accuracy. Readers must substitute a general term for a more specific list of items or actions. For example, the word "pet" might be substituted for a list such as "cats, dogs, gerbils, and goldfish." Students from the fifth grade on gradually develop this sophistication, with college students performing very well. Development of the ability to choose the topic sentence also occurred gradually.

The most difficult ability involved invention of the reader's own topic sentence when no such sentence was given in the text. This ability was applied successfully only occasionally by secondary students, and only about half the time by four-year college students.

If finding the main idea is actually composed of such subabilities, each must be taught before students can be expected to perform. One program designed to give students practice in finding the main idea is the comprehension game *Getting the Main Idea*, written at two elementary school levels (2.0–3.5, 3.5–5.0).

The program simulates a board game in which students roll dice by pressing a key to have the computer generate the results. The students then move the appropriate number of spaces on the game board displayed on the monitor. The size of the monitor limits some of the graphic effects, since only a small portion of the game board is displayed at any one time. Each player must visit 26 "cities," each illustrated by a picture, before arriving back home. The first player to finish wins.

On the game board are "story spaces" in black. When a player lands on one of these, the monitor displays a paragraph. The player reads the paragraph, then chooses a main idea sentence from the three possible choices given. Accurate answers speed the players on their way.

While the attractive graphics and the game format combine to make this an enjoyable activity for small groups (up to six) of youngsters, it is the teacher's responsibility to be sure that this type of activity fits the developmental sequence of reading instruction. The game assumes that children have the skills prerequisite to finding the main idea. Practice is given in the final higher-level skill, not in its components.

3. Do the exercises clearly deal with the targeted skill?   Does each exercise clearly differentiate the comprehension processes specific to the targeted subskill from other similar skills? Practice exercises that do not clearly require use of the behavior being studied are confusing to students. This lack of clarity is of particular concern in the area of comprehension, where even researchers are unclear as to the delineations of the varied subskills.

When training children to draw conclusions, for instance, do the exercises included in the program require that particular skill, as opposed to the many other similar comprehension subskills, such as making an inference or making a judgment? If the program does not clearly differentiate between these varied skills, children will become confused when they later encounter materials designed to teach the other skills.

4. Is the presentation in an interesting and effective format?   If the activity is a game, does it add to or detract from the overall objective? If graphics are included, do they add to or detract from the objective? Good teachers know that practice work need not be boring. The extra effort needed to turn a dull, lifeless drill into an adventure is often considerable, however. In terms of programming, such extra effort may involve hundreds of hours of additional programming time for the addition of a game component or graphics presentations.

The use of graphics in educational software is still a matter for debate. "There seems to be no disagreement that the most important sense for learning is the visual sense, perhaps because of the rich complexity of information that can be gathered visually" (Bork, 1981, p. 27). Graphics are used for two basic purposes: to provide information (as in graphs, charts, illustrations) and to motivate and stimulate.

Computer enthusiasts are especially addicted to graphic displays, it seems. Each new video game on the market is judged largely according to how realistic and effective (or simply unique) are its graphics. The introduction of *Dragon's Lair* in the arcades, the first major game integrating videodisc technology for interactive game playing, resulted in fantastic popularity and huge demands for the game machines.

The results of this graphics worship are most evident in reviews of software in such general computing magazines as *Creative Computing* and *Popular Computing.* One reviewer extolled the value of *Rocky's Boots*, for example, a colorful program designed to teach logic through examples of electric circuitry, because the electrical flow was pictured as a moving red current, making "the abstract more concrete." The reviewer appeared to suggest that the program was a valuable educational tool simply because of its graphic display. No attention was paid to any important educational questions, such as the value of teaching young children about electrical circuits, whether the logic of electrical circuitry would transfer to other applications of logic in the child's thinking, or whether the program would actually succeed in the classroom.

Such tunnel vision makes many reviews of educational software useless. John Victor, president of Program Design, Inc., has labeled software created under these misguided principles "fluffware": "Fluffware is a supposedly educational program with little actual educational content, but very strong computer graphics . . . [which] serve to lure the parents to get them to buy the products" (Victor, 1983, p. 10).

Today's technological limitations also combine to present problems for graphic presentations. High-resolution graphics require a great deal of memory space. As a result, the lack of variety often kills the long-term effectiveness of the program. In the vocabulary drill program *Tank Tactics*, for example, an "enemy" tank fires a word part out of its cannon. The student must choose the affix that matches and command the appropriate "friendly" tank to return fire. While this is an interesting variation on the typical multiple-choice drill, the motivational value of the unvarying graphics display wears thin in a short time.

An alternative to repeatedly presenting a single graphics display, which can be kept in the computer's memory and instantly drawn on the monitor, is to offer multiple displays. *Getting the Main Idea*, for example, draws a simple high-resolution picture for each city the students visit in an imaginary trip around the world. Since computer memory is limited, however, the pictures must be stored on disk and accessed whenever needed. This requires several seconds each time. Although the students don't mind at first, the wait required while the computer draws a picture of a palm tree for the sixth time, when the sixth student has just landed in Miami, wears on the nerves.

Reinking (1984b) described a session in which two fifth grade students played a computer game designed to develop comprehension skills. During the 20-minute game, each student read only six passages of about four sentences each. The remaining time was spent in off-task aspects of the game. Since time on task is important to development of any skill, Reinking noted his doubt that this game did much for the students' comprehension.

5. Does the program branch for individualization? Computer *branching* involves individualization of instructional presentation. The learning activities are presented differently to different students, meeting the individual needs of each. Branching can be carried out in a number of ways.

6. Does the program aid the teacher in diagnostic/prescriptive classroom management? The task of skill management, keeping track of student progress in the various subskills of reading, consumes great amounts of time. Properly designed computer drill programs can take care of this arduous task automatically.

Comprehension Power, a general-comprehension-development drill program, presents reading selections in one of two optional formats. The student may elect to read the selection paragraph by paragraph or to develop reading speed by line-by-line presentation at set reading rates. Each selection is followed by ten to 20 multiple-choice comprehension questions.

The strength of the courseware lies in the management system. Each lesson's results are automatically analyzed into a detailed record of achievement, broken down in some 25 subskills in general categories of literal understanding, interpretation, analysis, evaluation, and appreciation. By use of the teacher management system, the instructor can monitor these subskills for several classes of students by either displaying class charts on the monitor or printing them out.

7. Is comprehension taught, rather than simply tested? Most comprehension software makes no attempt to instruct students. Authors assume that children learn by doing, that comprehension cannot be taught by direct instruction. This assumption is sometimes glossed over by describing software as using the "inductive approach." In this way, courseware developers parallel actual classroom practice, as Durkin (1978–1979) discovered in a research study which found that teachers spent less than 1% of reading lesson time in helping students understand or work out the meaning of text.

Drills that yield only "correct–incorrect" feedback do not teach. They are designed to enhance performance speed and automaticity. *Getting the Main Idea, Comprehension Power,* and most other comprehension-development programs tell students only whether they are right or wrong. For those students who do not yet know how to perform the required skills, this can be a frustrating and useless experience.

CONFERENCING PROCEDURES

Effective teacher-student conferences are essential in providing feedback and opportunity for expression when engaged in holistic language activities that do not lend themselves to more mechanical forms of monitoring. Such conferences are too often unplanned jumbles of unrelated comments. Arbur (1976) suggests that the following pattern be followed:

1. Engagement
2. Problem exploration
3. Problem identification
4. Agreement to work on the problem together
5. Task assignment
6. Solution
7. Termination

Informal conferences should be planned to achieve the following purposes:

Assess progress

Give recognition and praise for progress, attitude, perseverance, or other personal factors

Allow for discussion of personal problems that may affect learning

Analyze skill strengths and weaknesses

Make referrals, in terms of supplemental or optional work to meet needs or interests

The teacher's own competence in an interview rests largely upon being organized and having a good idea as to topics for discussion. Familiarity with the student's needs and achievement is important. Use of a filing system for maintaining up-to-date information on each student's skill development and achievement aids in providing guidance and structure during the conference.

9

SOFTWARE: STUDY SKILLS AND CONTENT AREA

In this chapter we turn our attention from the learning of language skills to the employment of those skills in learning content area material. The "content areas" are such subjects as mathematics, sciences, social studies, vocational studies, and literature. Whereas teachers in the language skill areas are primarily concerned with their students "learning to read and write," in the content areas teachers are concerned with the obverse. Their students "read and write to learn."

This chapter is divided into three sections. The first deals with software designed to teach techniques of content area language skills. The second deals with using language skills to elaborate on content area software, in particular simulation games. The third discusses software designed to develop specific study skills.

LANGUAGE IN THE CONTENT AREAS

Harold Herber, a leading researcher in content area reading, describes two types of content area teachers (1978). The first is the *assumptive* teacher. Assumptive teachers *assume* that students have the ability to deal with learning materials used in the classroom. They assume that students know how to learn from text in an efficient manner. They assume that students are able to apply learning strategies in their particular subject areas.

Prescriptive teachers, on the other hand, make no such assumptions. Instead they evaluate students on their abilities to function in the subject areas. Are they able to read the text? Do they know effective strategies for learning the course content? Can they organize and learn the large amounts of factual and conceptual material covered during the year? If not, prescriptive teachers adjust their approaches to the course. Perhaps a lecture on cell development will include some pointers on how to take organized notes. Perhaps a supplemental book on world economics will be used as an aid for students having trouble with the text. Perhaps some particular attention will be paid to word problem-solving strategies during review of math homework.

If students are to learn subject matter effectively and efficiently, they must be able to apply concepts to that subject matter which are often thought by teachers to be the domain of the reading teacher or the English teacher. Experience shows, however, that unless such language and study skills concepts are the concern of every teacher, there will be little transfer between subjects. While in principle a skill such as finding the main idea is the same no matter what the subject area, in practice there is a great deal of difference between finding main ideas in readings from English class and from science class. Materials in each content area have radically different structures and emphases. Literary readings in English class require different strategies from those needed for the expository readings used in science or social studies. Exact reading with close attention to the details and symbols of mathematics is different from reading of history books where major trends and concepts are of primary concern. Vocational emphases upon "how to do it" deal with ability to follow directions, which is of less importance in academic subjects.

Two general principles of content area language skill instruction are applicable to software designed for that purpose.

Integration of Language Skill Development with Instructional Content

Teaching reading, writing, and study skills out of the context of content learning experiences is less valuable than weaving that skill development into the learning of meaningful material. A series of isolated drill exercises in finding main ideas is not meaningful to students or to content teachers. Of far more value would be a program designed to teach recognition of main ideas while reading about the African tribal cultures under study in social studies class.

How to Read in the Content Areas: Science, Social Studies, Literature, Mathematics (4 disks) suffers from such a weakness. A series of unrelated readings are offered to the students. Each is followed by a series of questions designed to determine main ideas, to make inferences, to build vocabulary, and so forth. The program cannot be easily integrated into a content area unit or course. It is instead a general comprehension development drill exercise, with topics drawn from the specified subject areas. No subject-area-specific skills are targeted.

For example, look at the following frame:

```
3. In paragraph four (4) the
   story tells that . . .
```

> "Dr. Edward Kasner, an American
> mathematician, was the first to
> introduce the term googol. His
> nine-year-old nephew invented the
> name googol."
>
> What does the word <u>his</u> mean?

This question deals with pronoun reference. The only relation to mathematics reading is the general topic, which is about large numbers (the *googol* is a term for the number represented by 1 with 100 zeroes after it).

As a sidelight involving the general quality of programming, note the lack of clarity in the response demand. Just how does the student answer? "Dr. Kasner's" is counted as a wrong answer. "Belonging to him" is also wrong. The correct answer, according to the program, is "Dr. Edward Kasner"—which does not even show the possessive qualities included in the meaning of *his*.

Activities like this are designed more for reading teachers than for content teachers because they are actually no more than ordinary reading drills—useful in reading class but not in mathematics.

Certainly software producers will have difficulty satisfying this criterion. Such specificity limits sales potential in a market where it pays to produce materials that are applicable to a wide variety of uses. Teachers rarely see printed material adapted to specific content area topics. It is unlikely that such computer software will soon be available.

Teaching Skills That Are Important to the Content Area Targeted

A math teacher is less interested in traditional main idea skills than a social studies teacher. Following directions is important to vocational and science lab teachers, but less so to English teachers. Text organizational structures vary widely between content areas.

Materials designed for the teaching of reading in the sciences should aim specifically for those skills important to reading in the sciences. Science teachers see little sense in dealing with more general reading skills.

SIMULATION GAMES

One type of software that is of particular interest to content area teachers and rich in potential for language development is the simulation.

The television show *Star Trek* was canceled by the NBC network in 1969. Disappointed "trekkies" soon found refuge in reruns and in the popular series of paperbacks based on the show. More recently, movies have been released featuring the gallant crew of the *United Star Ship Enterprise*.

In the midst of all this, however, the *Enterprise* was engaged in exploits of an entirely different nature from those depicted in the print, television, and celluloid media. The computer game *Star Trek* was born in the late 1960s and soon was on the main computer of every college campus.

Why did so many college students spend long hours zapping Klingons and commanding Federation space fleets? The answer seems to have something to do with personal involvement.

Reading and watching television are often relatively passive activities. Unfortunately, few readers become strongly emotionally involved in their reading. The book world, whatever that may be, seems removed from reality. Readers distance themselves from events and information in books—a problem that English and reading teachers continually attempt to overcome.

Television, according to McLuhan (1964), involves viewers in a more personal, active way than reading does. McLuhan suggested that print was dead and that video and pictures were the media of the future. While this idea was enthusiastically received for a time, its popularity soon ran its course as people recognized that a technical society generates more and more print, rather than less. But McLuhan did have a valid point: Television involves our children in personal and emotional ways more than print does.

The computer program *Star Trek* went a step further than the television program. Rather than simply reading what someone else had written, or viewing what someone else had filmed, the computer program offered the chance actually to *be* captain of the *U.S.S. Enterprise.* Anyone who wanted could be the commander of the starship that stood between Earth and alien menace. Photon torpedoes flew at your command; fleets attacked or retreated at the touch of a button. The computer became the link between the 20th and 24th centuries.

Star Trek's educational value was somewhat dubious, of course, but this program served as a forerunner to a host of popular computer programs called *simulations.*

A simulation is a model of a world. The world can be real or imaginary. It can be placed in the past, present, or future. The variety of worlds that can be modeled is unlimited. Users are allowed a glimpse into an otherwise inaccessible learning environment—the life of a fish in the ecological cycle of *O'Dell Lake,* for example, or the adventures of a pioneer on the *Oregon Trail.* Computer simulations have a long history of use in science and business. Practice in flying the Space Shuttle was modeled by astronauts long before the first launch occurred. Control room operators at nuclear power plants have been trained using computer simulations for years.

Each simulation is based upon components called *variables.* A variable is a factor that varies from situation to situation. In *Lemonade Stand,* students operate a roadside stand selling lemonade. The program has three user-dependent variables. That is, there are three ever-changing factors that are under the user's control. The user must decide how much to spend on advertising, the number of glasses to make every morning, and the amount to charge for each glass. The computer then generates a sales total based on a formula involving each of the three variables. By trial and error, students try to determine the exact parameters of the formula, which is hidden within the programming, to arrive at the optimal arrangement of the variables.

Nonelectronic simulation games have often been used by teachers to provide vicarious experiences that are valuable to students. High school seniors have engaged in pseudomarriages to provide a chance to deal with interpersonal and financial problems. Classroom businesses have been formed to exhibit the free enterprise system. Such activities have been used as tools to bring home the importance of otherwise theoretical concepts of life and the marketplace.

While certainly of value, such simulation activities have serious drawbacks, and most teachers use them to a very limited extent. They present great demands on teacher time and energy to set up, and the class time spent in carrying out the activities can be considerable, especially when the concepts can be verbally conveyed to the students (albeit in a much less meaningful way) in a few minutes of lecture.

Computer simulations, while not designed to replace such classroom activities completely, offer many of the same advantages and some others in addition.

Why Use Computer Simulations?

1. Simulations provide students with experiences that are difficult to obtain, given the present educational situation. A field trip designed to investigate ecology can take several days or even longer if the discovery method is used. *O'Dell Lake* provides a discovery-oriented investigation of the relationships between various types of underwater plants and fishes, as well as the animals that inhabit the lakeside. The student is placed in the role of a particular type of fish and must decide whether to flee intruders, attack or eat them, or ignore them. The consequence of making a mistake can be dramatic.

Laboratory experiments of a dangerous or expensive nature are also obtainable through simulation. It's far better to have a meltdown occur on the computer screen during training exercises than to have inexperienced operators cause one in real life. *Three Mile Island* can give advanced secondary students the opportunity to operate a nuclear reactor of their own.

The advantages of these simulations for the purposes of content area teachers are clear. Simulations also have use in reading instruction, for the development of background knowledge. Reading involves an interaction between print and the reader's knowledge structures, called schemata by cognitive psychologists (Steffensen, Joag-Dev, and Anderson, 1979). Simulations provide an inexpensive method of developing and personalizing these schemata and thereby provide success in related reading tasks.

2. Thorndike (1917) pointed out the close relationship between reading and reasoning. Simulations develop intuitive and analytical think-

ing. Success in a simulation depends largely upon ability to foresee and solve the problems to be encountered. If on one occasion failure to spend money on medical supplies leads to their wagon train dying of the plague in *Oregon Trail,* next time students will plan for this problem. The whole conception of the marketplace, the American free enterprise system, is rather dry when a teacher's lecture presentation is being memorized. It becomes an involving experience when students control the reins of their own businesses in *Lemonade Stand.*

3. Simulations provide experiences impossible to obtain in real life. The days of the *Oregon Trail* or *Hammurabi* are long gone, but an understanding of the problems encountered by American pioneers or ancient civilizations can benefit our students in both a practical and historical sense.

4. Simulations are motivational. Just as *Star Trek* led thousands of computer buffs to spend their nights zapping fleets of attacking Klingon battle cruisers, student motivation in simulation games is high. Even "dull" subjects like history and economics come alive when participation in events is possible. Students enjoy *doing* things. They use their background knowledge and decision-making abilities to effect results on the computer screen, a contrast to children's lack of influence over most daily real-life affairs.

5. Simulations fit well into the classroom environment. They do not demand a great deal of teacher time, nor are they messy. They convey important concepts to the students with a minimum of classroom disruption.

Can Simulations Encourage Language Learning?

Content area teachers in the sciences and social sciences readily appreciate the value of simulation software for their instructional purposes. Simulation activities are also of value to language development.

The development of background knowledge is of foremost importance. Cognitive psychologists emphasize the importance of the mind's knowledge structures, or schemata, to reading. Reading involves an interaction between the printed page and the reader's background knowledge (Rumelhart, 1977). Readers from different cultural backgrounds, for example, understand and misunderstand stories based on the inferences they make. These inferences are in turn based on their own past experiences (Steffensen, Joag-Dev, and Anderson, 1979).

Poorer readers, especially those from disadvantaged social backgrounds, encounter very real problems in school reading. These are at least in part due to their lack of concepts that are familiar to the typical middle-class student. Without background knowledge, comprehension suffers, for the reader cannot bring information that is presupposed by the author to bear on the text. This factor may partially explain the rapid decline in urban reading achievement scores in the intermediate grades, where comprehension, rather than mere word recognition, becomes the important factor.

Simulations afford an inexpensive method of providing some amount of background experience. An actual visit to a forest lake to observe the food-chain cycle may be optimal, but no school district can afford many such trips for children. A simulation can work to develop background schemata and thereby provide success in reading about similar topics.

If we can improve our students' reasoning abilities, we can improve their reading. Indeed, some reading theorists have suggested that our concept of *literal-level* reading is faulty. They argue that all reading is carried out at the inferential-thinking level. In an analysis of results of the National Assessment of Educational Progress, Petrosky (1982) reported that students did very well in answering multiple-choice questions about reading passages. When asked to think through their answers and explain and defend them, however, pitifully few students were able to function at all. Only 5% of the answers in the section dealing with "explaining responses to written works" were acceptable. While our success in teaching lower-level reading skills is clear (Micklos, 1980), reading teachers now need to turn their attention to development of higher-level skills.

Finally, many simulation activities require a lot of reading. Some, like *O'Dell Lake,* require prior reading and study so that the student can differentiate prey and predators. Others, like *Hammurabi,* place large amounts of text on the screen, all of which must be read and comprehended in order to function well as ruler of ancient Sumeria. Like many types of computer activities, directions are often fairly extensive. Unpleasant results—such as starving to death in *Hammurabi* or melting down a nuclear reactor core in *Three Mile Island*—dramatically illustrate to students the importance of reading and following directions carefully.

Choosing Simulation Software

Simulations are unique among types of educational software. Several key factors must be considered before purchase (Balajthy, 1984b).

How valuable are the concepts taught? Publishers of educational software simulations sometimes take no thought for the actual content of their games. *Snooper Troops,* for example, is a highly rated series of mystery simulations. Students seek clues to solve the mystery, piecing together the evidence until they arrive at the solution to the puzzle. The programs are entertaining. They require thought and analytical problem solving, but they do not teach any facts or concepts worth knowing. Choose software that teaches as well as entertains.

Does the simulation involve significant language activities? Simulations offer a variety of ways to use language. Children can engage in language behaviors through reading instructions or reading text on the screen. They can work cooperatively to play the game, using speaking and listening skills. They can express their commands in written form by typing.

There appears to be an unfortunate trend toward less text and more graphics in simulations. The best-seller *Castle Wolfenstein,* a World War II adventure game in which the player is an Allied soldier imprisoned in a Nazi castle, has set a pattern for games in which text is almost completely eliminated in favor of high-resolution diagrams.

Can related printed reading materials be used effectively to supplement the computer activity? Publishers should include bibliographies of articles, stories, and books related to topics covered in the simulation. These games are not educational in isolation. Their true value lies in being used in conjunction with class discussion and supplemental readings and research.

Does the publisher supply appropriate supplemental teaching aids? Teacher's guides can provide valuable ideas for enhancing instructional use of the program. Ditto worksheets can save teacher time in carrying the vocabulary and concept development several steps beyond the simulation itself. A summary of the inner workings of the simulation can help teachers comprehensively understand the activity without spending hours investigating every detail of the program.

The Minnesota Educational Computing Consortium (MECC), a state-funded organization that promotes instructional computer use, typically provides rich documentation to accompany its varied simulations. Its 20-page teacher's guide to *Voyageur* (1981) includes a summary of the program and two major objectives:

1. To study the development of the fur trade by its parts:
    the influence of geography,
    the presence of fur-bearing animals,
    the human participants,
    the market for furs.
2. To study in detail a part of the fur trade through simulating the experience of the voyageur:
    by controlling variables (the quantities of goods needed to survive a journey by canoe),
    by making decisions to affect the outcome.

The teacher's guide goes on to give background information on the North American fur trade of the 18th and 19th centuries, a map, a six-day lesson plan, bibliographic references, and several ready-to-duplicate research study guides, with an answer key. Sample frames give a synopsis and explanation of the simulation's operation.

Are the number of variables appropriate to the age group of your students? A simulation's difficulty rests largely in the number of variables a student must manipulate in order to determine the satisfactory solution. *Lemonade Stand,* for example, uses three user-controlled variables (price, advertising, raw materials). It seems appropriate for upper elementary students. Older students are able to deal with larger numbers of variables. Younger students may want to use the program *Sell Apples,* which offers only one user-controlled variable (price) to teach similar economic concepts.

Are there any random variables? Some programs occasionally will throw in a surprise for the user. Most days in *Lemonade Stand* are sunny, but every once in a while the rain comes. The weather affects sales, and students must adjust to those effects. You never know when a plague might strike along the *Oregon Trail,* so your wagon train had better bring along plenty of medical supplies. All popular games involve mixtures of skill and luck. Simulations should be no exception.

Be sure that the game is not all random chance, however. *Furs,* a simulation of the French Canadian fur trade, offers little opportunity for skill. The student decides how many mink, beaver, ermine, and fox skins to carry. Then the computer generates sales results that do not depend upon the decisions made. The activity is little more than a game of chance.

Does the program employ graphics?   If a student makes a wrong decision in *O'Dell Lake* and decides not to swim away from another fish that considers him to be lunch, the graphics make the mistake very clear. Newer versions of *Oregon Trail* display the wagon train's slow progress westward on a map of the western United States.

Is there an unacceptable level of violence?   The *adventure game* is one type of simulation. Many of these deal with sword and sorcery fantasies in which evil magicians and dragons are hacked apart by valiant elves and other heroes. Others center on war gaming, with accompanying troop movements, military strategy, and battles. The educational value of such software is minimal.

Using Simulations in the Classroom

Simulation activities are most productive when carried out by a group of students working together to make decisions. Groups allow for exchanges of ideas, debate, interpersonal development, and increased involvement in general. They also allow more students access to the limited computer time available to most classes.

Even fairly simple simulations involve keeping track of several variables during the course of the game. A sophisticated simulation might automatically record results, but this is a case where more is actually less. Students will learn more effectively by keeping track of their own decisions and the results. Each group should appoint a recorder to make note of findings, amounts of supplies available, money on hand, and so forth.

Many simulations involve some elementary arithmetic. Another student in the group may be equipped with a hand calculator to speed up these calculations.

Perhaps the most crucial decision on the part of the teacher, once the software has been chosen and purchased, involves presentation to the class and classroom management. In other words, how can the simulation be carried out most efficiently?

Computer-assisted instruction experts often advise that the teacher demonstrate the program to the whole class, explaining the purpose and walking them through a section of the program so that they will gain an understanding of the instructions. This is just another example of how content area teachers fall into the habit of deemphasizing the students' need to read.

A number of reading options exist. In many programs the directions are included in the introductory comments and can be read on the screen. A preferable method, given the lack of computer time and students' propensity to skip over the directions in order to get to the "good stuff," is to duplicate directions for student perusal before they begin work at the computer.

It is often necessary to rewrite the directions. Most available programs have been constructed by programmers who are unaware of such writing issues as clarity and readability. Posting the instructions or a summary of the important commands near the machine is also helpful.

Since the small group will be working on the program while other groups within the classroom are engaged in teacher-led activities, it helps to have a student consultant to whom the group can go for advice and help. The time spent training such consultants is well worth the effort. Otherwise there will be a string of constant interruptions of the teacher as each small group begins to get acquainted with the program. Post the names of the student software consultants on the bulletin board.

Presimulation activities. The simulation lesson may be organized in much the same way as a directed reading activity, with developmental exercises preceding and following the computer activity. A discussion of the technical vocabulary relevant to *Lemonade Stand,* for instance, may include the concepts of *assets* and *deficits.* While most of the simulations designed for elementary students avoid using many technical words, it can be helpful to provide them to students before the activity so that group discussion can be more precise. These new terms will then be added to the students' permanent vocabulary as they are used on a daily basis.

Hansen (1981) emphasized the need to engage students in two types of activities prior to reading: personalization of relevant themes and prediction of outcomes. A similar approach can be used to introduce children to simulation activities. Organize class discussion around such questions as, "Have you ever been in a situation in which . . . ?" or, "What do you think would happen if . . . ?" As you help children review their background knowledge before engaging in the activity, learning will be enhanced.

Students will benefit most from the activity if they have already read a story or completed research on the subject involved. *O'Dell Lake* is a meaningless exercise without an understanding of ecology and of the food chain. Prior readings about various fishes and lakeshore animals help make the exercise a learning experience rather than a mere game. It has been years since the Three Mile Island crisis. Rather than waiting for the next meltdown crisis to make the *Three Mile Island* simulation relevant to your students, have them read some old newsmagazine articles on the incident.

Simulations present an ideal opportunity for individualized or small-group research assignments culminating in whole-class discussions and presentations. Students can research a variety of topics related to Mesopotamia in preparation for the game *Sumer*, where they will guide the ancient kingdom in an economics exercise.

Improve efficiency of the research by providing one or two learning stations. Students rotate between spending time at the computer and at research stations. For *Fur Trader* or *Voyageur* students might research encyclopedia articles and books about the old French Canadian fur trade. Another learning center might include artwork, music, and literature concerning the society of Old Montreal, Quebec, and the other French Canadian colonies.

During-simulation activities. Carefully planned worksheets like those in the accompanying figures can be used to structure students' data collection and thinking.

Figure 9–1 presents a worksheet designed for use with the simulation *Lemonade Stand.* Players start at Turn 1 with $2.00 in assets. They must take note of the weather, which may be sunny or rainy and will affect sales. They must also note the price per glass of the raw materials for their product. Then they decide on the number of glasses to make and the number of advertising signs to construct. Costs of raw materials add up to the total expenses. Players must also decide on the amount to charge per glass.

The computer then generates results of the day's sales and prints the number sold. Gross income and net profits and losses are computed. The final column lists total assets at the end of the turn.

Players determine a strategy for the next turn and describe it briefly in the blank provided. Perhaps more signs will be made or a lower price charged for each glass of lemonade. Decisions are again recorded. After the computer generates results, conclusions based on the new strategy are drawn and recorded. Figure 9–2 shows a completed worksheet.

These worksheets present great opportunities for discussion, providing concrete evidence to back up assertions.

Lemonade Stand and other similar programs also offer the opportunity for developing graph skills. Figure 9–3 presents a graph of results for one student's exploration on the computer, with sample accompanying questions and problems. Such worksheet assignments lead to a rich array of graphing activities that can vary from the very simple to the extremely complex.

Oregon Trail lends itself to the maintenance of a log (see Figures 9–4

LEMONADE STAND

Players' Names: Game No.:

                                         Date:

A	B	C	D	E (C+D)	F	G (F#.15)	H (E+G)	I	J	K (IxJ)	L (K-H)	M (M+L)

TURN NO.	WEATHER	COST PER GLASS	GLASSES MADE # Total Cost	SIGNS MADE # Total Cost	TOTAL EXPENSES	PRICE PER GLASS	RESULTS # Income Sold	PROFIT/ LOSS	TOTAL ASSETS

START									$2.00

1											

##

2											

STRATEGY: CONCLUSION:

##

3											

STRATEGY: CONCLUSION:

##

4											

STRATEGY: CONCLUSION:

FIGURE 9–1. *Lemonade Stand* study guide

and 9–5) in which are recorded events and supply inventories. Initial decisions about supplies are made before logging on, to save computer time. A detailed log of events, and their effects on supplies, aids in follow-up discussion and analysis. Without such a record, it is hard to recall just when the medical supplies began running short, or when the wagon train should have stopped to hunt food.

Postsimulation activities. Writing and discussion activities help students focus on the discoveries they have made during the game. Students must be guided to think back about what their own thinking processes have been and the problem-solving methods they used to play the game. Brown, Campione, and Day (1981) suggest that summary-writing activities be used to develop this analytical *metacognitive* ability (that is, thinking about your own thinking processes).

Teachers should place emphasis in summary writing upon the students' recall of their own thinking processes during specific events in the simulation. They may be led to make *what if?* conjectures such as, "What if we had spent more money on farmland during the third round of *Hammurabi?*" or, "What if we had charged less for our lemonade in *Lemonade Stand?*" Teachers should also guide students to recognize cause-and-

FIGURE 9–2. Completed sample *Lemonade Stand* study guide

LEMONADE STAND

Players' Names: Game No.:

                                   Date:

A	B	C	D	E (C+D)	F	G (F+.15)	H (E+G)	I	J	K (IxJ)	L (K-H)	M (M+L)
TURN NO.	WEATHER	COST PER GLASS	GLASSES MADE # Total Cost	SIGNS MADE # Total Cost		TOTAL EXPENSES	PRICE PER GLASS		RESULTS # Income Sold		PROFIT/ LOSS	TOTAL ASSETS
START												$2.00
1	Sun	.02	50 /.00	6 .90		1.90	.10		50 5.00		+3.10	5.10
2	Sun	.02	75 /.50	7 /.05		2.55	.10		59 5.90		+3.35	8.45

STRATEGY: *Increase number of glasses + advertising*   CONCLUSION:

| 3 | Sun | .04 | 75 3.00 | 10 /.50 | | 4.50 | .10 | | 59 5.90 | | 1.40 | 9.85 |

STRATEGY: *Increase advertising*   CONCLUSION: *Increasing advertising doesn't help*

| 4 | Sun | .04 | 75 3.00 | 7 /.05 | | 4.05 | .08 | | 68 5.44 | | 1.39 | 11.24 |

STRATEGY: *Decrease price*   CONCLUSION: *Raises sales, but profit is lower than in Turn 2*

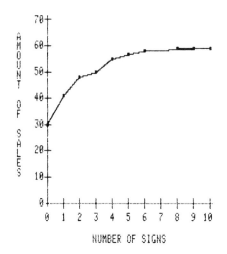

NUMBER OF SIGNS

THE ACCOMPANYING GRAPH PLOTS SALES IN "LEMONADE STAND" FOR SUNNY DAYS
WHEN THE PRICE CHARGED IS 10 CENTS PER GLASS.

1. What is the maximum number of glasses that can be sold each day at
.10 per glass?

2. If I make 8 signs on a sunny day and want to charge .10 per glass,
how many glasses should I make for maximum profit?

3. To figure out maximum profit possible for each different amount of
signs, do the following (example is for 3 signs):

    a. Multiply Amount of Sales Times Price to determine INCOME.
       50 * .10 = $5.00
    b. Multiply Number of Signs times .15 to determine COST OF
       ADVERTISING.
       3 * .15 = .45
    c. Multiply Cost of Materials Per Glass times Number of Glasses
       Made (that is, Amount of Sales) to determine COST OF
       MATERIALS.
       50 * .05 = 2.50
    d. Add COST OF ADVERTISING and COST OF MATERIALS to determine
       TOTAL EXPENSES.
       .45 * 2.50 = 2.95
    e. Subtract TOTAL EXPENSES from INCOME to determine PROFITS.
       5.00 - 2.95 = 2.05

4. Make a chart of maximum profits by amount of advertising, based on
sunny weather, a price of .10 per glass, and cost to you for materials
of .05 per glass. Determine the most efficient number of signs to
make based on these conditions.

5. Play LEMONADE to chart the same results, but on hot and dry days.

FIGURE 9–3. *Lemonade Stand* graph-reading exercise

OREGON TRAIL

Players' Names: _____   Game No.: _____

Date: _____

READY TO GO: How good a shot are you?
    Oxen ($200-300) :   1 - Ace marksman
    Food   :   2 - Good shot
    Ammo ($1=50 shots):   3 - Fairly fair
    Clothing   :   4 - Need practice
    Miscellaneous   :   5 - Shaky knees

****

1847	MILEAGE	FOOD	BULLETS	CLOTHING	MISC.	CASH	EVENTS
APR. 12							
APR. 26							
MAY 10							
MAY 24							
JUN 7							
JUN 21							
JUL 5							
JUL 19							
AUG 2							
AUG 16							
AUG 31							
SEP 13							
SEP 27							
OCT 11							
OCT 25							
NOV 8							
NOV 22							
DEC 20							

FIGURE 9-4. *Oregon Trail* player's log

effect relationships. "Hammurabi's people starved to death because we didn't plant enough seed."

Students can then write a letter of advice to future users, detailing their findings and making suggestions on how to play the game most effectively.

FIGURE 9–5. Completed sample *Oregon Trail* player's log

OREGON TRAIL

Players' Names: Game No.:

                                                   Date:

READY TO GO:		How good a shot are you?
Oxen ($200-300)	: 250	1 - Ace marksman
Food	: 100	2 - Good shot
Ammo ($1=50 shots):	10	③ - Fairly fair
Clothing	: 100	4 - Need practice
Miscellaneous	: 75	5 - Shaky knees
	535	

1847	MILEAGE	FOOD	BULLETS	CLOTHING	MISC.	CASH	EVENTS
APR. 12	168	119	451	92	75	165	Wild animals
APR. 26	379	101	451	92	75	165	
MAY 10	588	83	451	92	70	165	Illness
MAY 24	743	105	430	92	66	165	Riders / Daughter broke arm
JUN 7	941	87	430	92	58	165	Wagon breaks down
JUN 21	1077	58	130	92	48	165	Riders / Indians help find food / Blizzard
JUL 5	1283	40	130	92	48	165	
JUL 19	1446	79	106	92	43	165	Hunt / Bit by snake
AUG 2	1653	42	60	82	43	165	Riders / Wild animals Stop at fort for food
AUG 16	1747	32	93	82	33	105	($50), bullets ($10) Unsafe water / Blizzard
AUG 31	1911	70	81	82	33	105	Hunt / Cold weather Stop at fort for
SEP 13		22	81	62	60	65	Arrive at Oregon City / Misc. ($40)
SEP 27							
OCT 11							
OCT 25							
NOV 8							
NOV 22							
DEC 20							

Challenge students to develop their own variations or improvements on the simulation. What would they change? How would they make it simpler or more complex?

Discussion should also focus on the differences between the simulation and the reality. No simulation can be completely accurate. Simulations are actually simplifications of reality. Real life is far more complex. Students should be able to list some of these complexities. Perhaps they can suggest how the simulation could be modified to reflect the additional factors.

Pose hypothetical problems for the students to work on and discuss. In many cases not all students will face exactly the same situations while engaging in the simulation. By constructing a worksheet that poses a particular problem—perhaps one that you encountered as you previewed the game—you can focus the entire class's attention.

GENERAL STUDY SKILLS SOFTWARE

Reading Rate Improvement

Some schools include rate training in their developmental reading programs, but it is often ignored. Research shows that speed of reading levels off at about the sixth or seventh grade. Most adults read between 200 and 300 words per minute.

For the most part, of course, it would appear to be better to be a faster reader than a slower one. There are exceptional circumstances. In mathematics and science, for example, the faster the reading speed, the less the reader tends to understand. In literature, true appreciation and personal involvement are probably not to be gained by rushing through the experience. Mortimer Adler, known for his advocacy of reading the "great books" of Western civilization, has been quoted as saying, "In the case of good books, the point is not to see how many of them you can get through, but rather how many of them can get through you."

Reading teachers emphasize flexibility in reading rather than speeded reading. Students should know when to speed up and when to slow down. Harris (1968) noted that most readers have very rigid rates of reading, approaching all reading tasks with the same speed.

While excessive speed can be detrimental to comprehension, improvement in reading rate is certainly desirable for most older readers. A variety of mechanical devices have been used to improve rate. *Tachistoscopes* flash images of letters, words, or phrases for short periods of time to improve visual skills. A variety of accelerating devices force readers to read material at preset rates. The Controlled Reader (Educational Developmental Laboratories) presents stories line by line at rates of speed controlled by the reader.

These gadgets often have motivating value, but they have not been shown to be superior to speed-reading programs that do not employ mechanical means. There is no reason to believe that the computer will offer any distinct advantages over mechanical devices, especially since software designed to teach speed-reading simply mimics the action of mechanical devices. Some comprehension programs offer an optional speed component. *Comprehension Power*, for example, allows either the teacher or student to command presentation of reading selections at rates varying from 50 to 650 words per minute.

For many years, teachers thought that rapidly displaying words and phrases by using a flashing device called a tachistoscope was the key to improving reading speed. Miles Tinker (1967), one of the foremost authorities on speeded reading and eye movement research, in his review of the research on mechanical reading devices, concluded, "The tachistoscope is without value for increasing speed of reading" (p. 3), and condemned the employment of eye-movement training methods for the purpose of increasing reading ability. Apparently Silicon Valley Systems chose to ignore such well-established research findings, for their *Rapid Reader* is a program that turns the computer into a tachistoscopic flashing device.

In *Rapid Reader* students choose to flash words, word pairs, phrases, or sentences on the computer monitor at rates of speed ranging from 50 to 2,700 words per minute. The program developers regrettably constructed the phrases and sentences out of words randomly chosen from text files. Speed reading meaningless sentences such as THE BALD CAT WHISPERED CAREFULLY or WHEN THAT BAD MAN WIGGLED HAPPILY TO AN AUDIENCE, SHE WAITED wears thin after about the fifth sentence.

Reference Skills

Remote data base research.   One of the important contributions made by the computer to research has been the establishment of computerized data bases. In virtually every field from science to law to education, computer users can now use their machines to communicate with data bases across the world by telephone lines. These data bases enable users to carry out searches on relevant topics.

The School Practices Information Network, for instance, is managed by Scott, Foresman publishers. SPIN gives access to a variety of educational data bases, including the Educational Resource Information Center (ERIC). If a teacher wants a list of references on reading and microcomputers, those two descriptors can be entered, and the data base computer will search its file for appropriate entries.

Several public data bases are available for more general purposes. CompuServe (5000 Arlington Center Boulevard, P.O. Box 20212, Columbus, Ohio) and The Source (1616 Anderson Road, McLean, Virginia 22102) are two of the largest. These data bases can be used for general research and for a wide range of other services, including shopping and electronic mail.

Your school's computer is connected to a data base by means of telephone lines. The *peripheral* (that is, added onto the computer) device that allows the micro to send and receive messages over the phone is called a *modem*. The modem converts electronic signals from your computer to transmit them over the phone lines. They are reconverted to electronic computer code by a modem at the other end.

Few computers have built-in modems. Two types may be purchased. *Acoustic couplers,* in which the telephone handset is inserted in the modem itself, are increasingly outnumbered by *direct connect modems,* which do not require a telephone. Instead, they are plugged directly into a phone jack.

One remote data base useful for students is Magazine Index, which can be accessed through several services. Also available in microform, this index is a bibliography of popular magazines and journals usually available in school or community libraries.

Library skills have been taught to students for many years. Now computer data bases need to be added to the list of reference skills that students should know about.

Data base management programs. Did you know that New Jersey is a leading manufacturer of industrial chemicals? Did you know that Tom, Susan, and Samantha all live on Green Street?

Data base software is an invaluable tool for school or classroom management (see Chapter 20 for a more detailed explanation of data bases). It can also be used for instructional purposes in the content areas. These programs are electronic filing cabinets that categorize, sort, store, and retrieve information according to your commands. In using data base systems, students additionally gain experience with a valuable tool for career education, since data base management systems are widely used by businesses and government.

In what ways can you use data base programs in your classroom? Jackson (1983) suggests that social studies teachers start off with an informal sociological study of their classes. Set up a data base with fields such as STUDENT NAME, BROTHER'S NAME, SISTER'S NAME, PET, and FAVORITE FOOD. Lists of all students who have brothers can be printed out, or all students who enjoy pizza. Students can discuss what it's like to have a brother or sister or how cats are different from dogs. Jackson reports that the children enjoyed seeing their names in print and learning about their classmates.

The skill we call *classification* is a key to learning many content topics. Categorization of various rocks into igneous, metamorphic, and sedimentary, for example, helps students learn more about the mineral kingdom. Classification of historical events according to time and place may lead to better understanding of the flow of history and interrelationships among events. Classification of various diseases according to symptoms and treatment can aid in integrative recall of these facts.

The establishment of a classroom data base can be as simple as the class project described above, or it can be a massive research effort by groups or the entire class. A history project may involve teams of students researching and filing world events, with different teams for different countries or continents. Follow-up study and discussion could focus on interrelationships of events. Students might be amazed at the number of military interventions undertaken by the United States in the past 40 years of so-called peace, for example. A science teacher might want to add to the world events data base by having students research scientific developments and their origins.

The list of possible topics for such data base construction and research is endless. Various careers could be explored. International customs could be listed. Similarities and differences between microscopic plants and animals could be included, or at the other end of the size scale, between different kinds of dinosaurs. Community or school surveys on a variety of issues would give students valuable experiences in first-hand research.

The key to use of this data base research involves teacher direction. Students do not have the sophistication to set up the data base themselves in a manner that will lead toward a meaningful learning experience, nor can it be assumed that students have sufficient research skills to obtain the necessary information. With proper direction students can be guided through a discovery-oriented learning experience that reveals much about both the content topic and the way in which research is carried out. A sample format for a data file on the various states in the United States is presented in Figure 9–6.

FIGURE 9–6.   State data base format

```
                    UNITED STATES DATA BASE


    STATE:

      CAPITAL:

      POPULATION:

      LAND AREA:


    MAJOR INDUSTRIES:


    MAJOR AGRICULTURE:


    TOURIST ATTRACTIONS:


    STATE FLOWER:

    STATE BIRD:


    ENTERED UNION:
```

Test-Taking Skills

Every year almost half a million American young people face a three-hour rite of passage called the Scholastic Aptitude Test. With their futures on the line in this test, these young people form the target market for some of the best-selling computer software: SAT preparatory programs.

Many high schools, responding to the pressure from parents, offer SAT courses that some hope will miraculously make up for years of inattention to educational quality.

The fact of the matter is that gains from such preparatory lessons are rather slim. Educational Testing Service, producers of the SAT, estimates that a six-week intensive course will raise scores by only 20 or 30 points on the test (which has a maximum score of 800 and a minimum score of 200). Consider for a moment the vast number of words in the English language that may be used on an SAT verbal test. What is the chance that, in a course lasting only several weeks, an increase in vocabulary knowledge can be made to significantly improve a verbal aptitude score? Not much. Experienced instructors of SAT preparation courses avoid having their students memorize lists of vocabulary words, since there is a strong likelihood that not a single word from the memorized list will appear on the test.

The benefit of an SAT preparation course lies in exposure to the format of the test. There are certain established procedures for answering analogies, which many students do not have the leisure or desire to figure out on their own. There are also recommended procedures for answering the other types of problems on the SAT. It is practice to make the student more "test wise," as opposed to improving reading ability or vocabulary knowledge, that is the main benefit of SAT prep courses.

Those students who know their stuff but tend to do poorly on tests because of a lack of understanding of the question-answering procedures or because of stress, can be helped to improve dramatically. Those who do poorly because they actually are weak in vocabulary or reading will not be helped.

Courseware publishers have been quick to capitalize on the national paranoia concerning the SATs. A wide variety of software packages for SAT preparation are available, some of them costing more than $1,000. The motivational value of computerized instruction stands these publishers in good stead. Most of the packages on the market actually offer very little more than the books for SAT preparation, except that the problems appear on a computer screen instead of on a printed page. It takes a highly motivated individual to spend more than a few hours with one of those thick, forbidding SAT prep books filled with small print. The computer looks much more inviting.

MicroSystem 80 College Entrance Examination Preparation presents both verbal and mathematics tutorials. The instructional modules include quizzes and, something that is supremely important with material of this sort, feedback on correct answers and definitions. Any program that does not explain *why* your answer was wrong is useless. Clear explanations are most important when dealing with analogies, verbal problems that many people find confusing.

Some programs, such as Krell's *College Board SAT,* rely on rapid, continuous presentation of questions, with immediate and brief feedback but without the in-depth learning provided by Borg-Warner's *MicroSystem 80* program. Students often prefer this rapid-fire type of program as faster moving, even though it is more superficial. It is also a closer replication of the actual timed testing session.

Be careful that the program you choose actually does what it claims to do. Some publishers have apparently succumbed to the lure of financial gains to be made in the SAT preparation market. *PSAT and SAT Word Attack Skills* is actually a limited vocabulary development program rather than a full SAT preparation course, despite its name. It teaches affixes, then presents the sample words in antonym and synonym exercises.

An SAT package should cover the full spectrum of SAT item types. *Improving College Admission Scores* offers sections on fill-ins, opposites, analogies, reading comprehension, grammar and usage, and sentence correction. There should also be a large store of items from which the computer can choose, since long-term study is required for significant improvement.

Keep in mind that practice should also be carried out on printed test samples. The actual test, after all, will not be on a computer monitor. Experience in a testing situation as close as possible to the real one is invaluable.

Analogies are often used in vocabulary and cognitive assessment tests. Students who are familiar with techniques used in solving analogies and who have practiced to speed their work on these word problems have a tremendous advantage. *Wordrace* provides analogy work in game format. Students race the clock to solve the problems and win points for success. The program disk comes with several files of analogies ready for student practice, but teachers can also use a utility option to add their own choice of analogies to the program.

Study Aids

A number of programs are available to aid in vocabulary or rote memorization tasks. A user loads *Vocabulary Prompter* and creates a data file by typing in vocabulary words and their definitions, or English words and their French equivalents. The computer program then randomly selects from its file and quizzes the user on the items.

E-Z Learner is a more sophisticated *flash card* program for self-study. The user types in questions and answers that are saved on disk. Several options are available. In the "electronic study card" mode, each question is displayed, followed by its answer. The learner determines whether or not he knew the answer, then types C for correct or W for wrong. The "type-in response" mode requires that answers be typed. Exact answers are required, so this mode is best carried out using multiple-choice, true-false, or one-word-answer questions.

Questions may be presented in order or randomized. If questions are presented in order, learners are able to customize branching so that if a particular question is answered correctly, a certain number of related questions will be skipped.

Files of questions may be edited, updated, or merged at any time. The program is capable of handling an unlimited number of files.

10
WORD PROCESSING FOR WRITING INSTRUCTION

The Greek Stoic philosopher Epictetus once wrote, "If you want to be a writer, write." Contemporary reading and language arts teachers recognize the value of frequent exposure to the writing act, and many today make such self-imposed rules as, "My students will write—at least a little—every single school day."

The teaching of writing is about to undergo a change more dramatic than any since our far distant ancestors first developed the alphabet, paper, and writing instruments. The revolution to come (and it has already occurred in many business offices) will involve word processing, a computer operation that is redefining our concepts of writing. As Joseph Deken argues in his book *The Electronic Cottage*, "Far from eliminating the writing of ordinary prose and poetry, the growth of computer languages bids well to make this writing easier to produce, evaluate, polish, and present" (1981, p. 299).

After introducing word processors and making suggestions for choosing one, this chapter describes a number of ideas for managing classroom word processing and teaching your students how to use one. We then turn our attention to some major issues involved in writing instruction and to just how word processing technology addresses these issues. The first issue involves analysis of the writing process into prewriting, writing, and postwriting phases. The second issue has to do with automatic feedback about compositions which the computer can provide to students. Chapter 11 will continue our discussion of the word processor with descriptions of a wide variety of activities.

WHAT IS A WORD PROCESSOR?

A word processing (WP) program allows the computer to function as a typewriter. Some WPs used in offices are *dedicated* computers. They are computers designed for only one function, word processing. For general-purpose microcomputers like those used in classrooms, the WP is a program stored on diskette. The program allows text to be typed into the computer, then printed out using a peripheral printer. The computer's usefulness in the classroom or in the home is thereby increased dramatically. Anything a typewriter can do, a micro with WP and printer can do.

The story only begins here. The WP offers far more advantages than a typewriter. For starters, the WP features *wrap-around* typing. That is, the typist never has to make a carriage return. Each time a line is filled, the WP automatically wraps the line around, placing any incomplete words at the beginning of the next line.

In addition, anything that is typed can be stored on a diskette in what is called a *file*—a collection of words, sentences, and paragraphs encoded magnetically on the diskette. The file can be retrieved, edited, or printed at any time. A composition stored today can be recalled from storage and printed out tomorrow or, for that matter, next year. Retyping has become a thing of the past.

Another dramatic potential of the WP involves its text-editing capabilities. No longer does a paper have to be erased or retyped to correct errors or make changes. The WP enables the following revisions to be accomplished with the mere touch of one or two appropriate keys.

1. Elimination of letters, words, or larger sections of text.
2. Insertion of letters, words, or larger sections at any point within the text.
3. Correction of misspelled or mistyped words.
4. Insertion of blank lines (for example, between paragraphs).
5. Automatic centering of headings and titles.

Also, the WP offers unique text-formatting features. Regardless of whether it is done before, during, or after typing, the user can order single or double spacing, adjustment of margins, right justification (that is, vertical alignment of the right margin), automatic pagination, a print stop after every page (so that individual sheets of paper or ditto/mimeograph masters can be inserted in the printer after each page is printed), single or multiple copies, and other features as well.

Finally, many WP systems have extra capabilities that go beyond dealing with pages of prose text. Some allow the user to type in a form letter, then have the computer "fill in the blanks" with names, addresses, and other variable information (see Chapter 20 for detailed discussion). Others offer adjunct programs to check for spelling or grammatical errors. Many provide the capability, if a consistent spelling error is found during proofreading, to perform a *global search and replace*—that is, to order the computer to search for all the similar errors and automatically correct them.

WP programs for personal computers are available at prices ranging from free (with the purchase of the microcomputer for which it was designed) to several hundred dollars. The price depends largely on the number of functions available. A powerful program like *WordStar* offers a host of specialized functions important to business offices. It costs hundreds of dollars. Less expensive WPs such as *Screen Writer II*, *Word Handler*, and *SCRIPSIT* generally go for less than $200 each and more than satisfy the demands of home or classroom use. *Bank Street Writer* is a stripped-down version of a WP adapted for children's use by elimination of many adult-oriented WP capabilities and priced at well under $100.

EVALUATING WORD PROCESSORS

The publication of *Bank Street Writer* in 1983 was an important turning point in the application of WP technology to the classroom. Previously, teachers working with WPs and children had been beset by obstacles which only the most dedicated could overcome. One obstacle was price of software. *Bank Street* was published at $35.00 per disk, more than affordable. Another obstacle was training of students. Documentation for existing WPs was written for adults and had to be adapted for children's use. Essentially the entire manual had to be simplified and rewritten, an arduous task. Actual hands-on training was laborious and time-consuming, for individual attention was required to instruct each student. A third problem was complexity of the adult WPs. The more functions available, the more complicated is a WP's operation.

Bank Street Writer addressed all three concerns and quickly became the standard by which other classroom WPs were judged. *Bank Street Writer* did have serious shortcomings, and many teachers still preferred the more challenging adult WPs to it, but *Bank Street* was an important first step in development of classroom WPs. Its publication was quickly followed by production of several other simplified children's WPs, such as Milton Bradley's *Word Processor*.

Personal evaluation of complex software such as WPs is difficult, since each requires hours to learn. No one can try out seven or eight different WPs. In choosing, consult evaluation sources to narrow down your choice to two or three at most, then check each for yourself. Computing magazines frequently publish up-to-date charts that compare various WP capabilities (for example, Heintz, 1982). The WP characteristics discussed below must be considered.

Number of Functions

The original version of *Bank Street Writer* lacked many capabilities that adults would demand of a WP. It would not underline, for instance. The maximum length of its files was limited. It did not offer an 80-column screen page. That is, when the manuscript appeared on the monitor screen, the letters were printed so large that each line was much shorter than the average line that would be printed on a standard 8½ by 11 inch sheet of paper. Most adults would demand a WP in which "what you see is what you get" once the writing has been printed on paper. The first important issue facing each teacher is deciding which functions will be important to the children in his or her classroom. For high school business students, a more complex word processor, which better demonstrates the functions they will be using in business offices, may be required. For children employing the WP for technologically undemanding tasks like writing compositions, the *Bank Street Writer*'s capabilities are sufficient.

Ease of Use

The number of functions available in a WP must be balanced against its ease of use. The more functions, the more complex is the WP. Prepublication advertising for *Bank Street* had suggested that it would be easier for children to use than adult WPs. Actual examination of the WP showed that it was easier to learn than most WPs not because of innovative new approaches, but because it has eliminated many functions normally present in adult WPs. Teachers had previously met this challenge by simply not teaching students unnecessary functions. If students don't need to underline, don't teach them the underlining commands. Direct their attention to the most important commands.

Many teachers are attracted to *Bank Street Writer* because of its command menu displayed at the top of the monitor screen. If the user wishes to delete a portion of text, a cursor is moved to DELETE and a series of printed commands explains how to proceed. In practice this procedure is only minimally easier than keeping a file card with the necessary commands posted next to the computer for quick student reference.

New developments in word processors add somewhat to their ease of use, though WPs on the "cutting edge" of technology are usually extremely expensive. *Cursor control* has always been a problem. The cursor is the blinking dot on the monitor screen that signals the point in the text to which the computer's attention is directed. Usually it is at the end of the text, moving along as the writer types in letters. As the writer presses a letter key, that letter appears under the cursor and the cursor moves rightward to the next space. If the writer wishes to erase a word, the cursor must first be moved to that word. Almost every text-editing operation requires cursor movement.

Traditionally this has been carried out with key presses. In *Word Handler*, for instance, an ARROW key (← or →) must be pressed to indicate whether the cursor should be moved forward or backward. Then the CONTROL key must be depressed and L pressed repeatedly to move the cursor to the line desired. Then the forward arrow key must be pressed to move the cursor to the appropriate spot on the line. Needless to say, this operation takes a little time to learn and is time consuming, especially when large numbers of revisions must be made.

Screen Writer II allows use of a joystick, the control device used in video games, to move the cursor. Toggle the joystick forward and the cursor moves up. Toggle it right and the cursor moves to the right. Some newer model computers such as the Apple Macintosh have a *mouse,* a small hand-held box that is rolled across a flat desktop to move the cursor. Roll the mouse forward and the cursor moves up the screen page. Advanced models such as the Hewlett-Packard microcomputer allow users to simply touch the appropriate point on the monitor screen with a pen and the cursor immediately shifts to that point.

Each new technological advance contributes to ease of learning and use. Busch (1983) predicts a day in the not-too-distant future when word processors will automatically check spelling against an unabridged dictionary, use color-coded symbols for editing tasks, and allow voice input. "I'm 35 years old," he notes. "I believe that by the time I retire, my word processing terminal will be able to carry on my career without me for at least several more years. If it works quietly enough, I may not even notice" (p. 135).

Provision for Training

The two great advantages of the *Bank Street Writer* are its price and its training materials. Each diskette is double-sided. Flip the disk over and insert it in the disk drive, and students are able to engage in a tutorial that leads them through actual explanation and practice of the various commands. A printed student manual written at a fifth grade level also provides detailed explanations of each procedure.

The importance of these training materials cannot be overemphasized. The two factors that are most discouraging to teachers and students during implementation of word processing in the classroom are lack of typing ability (see Chapter 16) and the amount of time and effort needed to teach students how to use the processor proficiently. A prepared, comprehensive training program that can be used independently by students is invaluable—if not absolutely required—for widespread use of word processing in classrooms.

Guidelines for Using a Word Processor

1. Don't try to teach too much too soon. Movement of text blocks and global search and replace techniques are cute, but their importance is minimal. It is often just as easy to retype a short section as it is to move it. Teach the basics.

2. If a complex WP is used, rewrite and simplify important parts of the manual. WP manuals are written for secretaries or professionals and are often highly confusing even to them. Even second and third graders, however, can be taught the few simple commands necessary to do the basics of word processing: cursor location, inserting, and deleting. Students require only entry of prose text and simple editing, not the many extra features built into most WPs. See Figure 10–1 as an example.

3. Monitor quality is important. In order to avoid eyestrain and fatigue during lengthy WP sessions, a clear monitor image without glare is invaluable.

```
    If you need to add a word at some spot within a paragraph, move
the cursor to the spot by--

    1.  To go forwards:  Hold down the CTRL key and press
        L till you come to the right line.
    2.  To go backwards:  Press the <-- key, then hold down
        the CTRL key and press L till you come to the right
        line.

    Press the --> key till the cursor reaches the spot where you
want to start.

    Press the CTRL key and I.  Type your word or words.

    Press the --> key when you are finished.
```

FIGURE 10-1. Insertion procedure using *Word Handler*

4. Become familiar with the WP before using it in the classroom. You'll only confuse yourself and your students if you introduce it before knowing it well.

A corollary: Administrators who wish their students to benefit from modern technology must commit the organizational and financial resources necessary. Schools that spend thousands of dollars on hardware and allot nothing for teacher training are extremely shortsighted.

5. Students profit from some typing skills when using a WP, but it is so easy to correct errors that even those who "hunt and peck" will be able to use it. A self-instructional software program for teaching typing would be a valuable addition to your software library if you use a WP in the classroom.

6. Only one person at a time can actually type at the keyboard, but many activities can be structured so as to allow two additional "advisers" to work with the central user. Moffett and Wagner (1983) have described this "sharing" process as central to writing instruction. Research shows the power of cooperative learning.

Working in groups helps make writing an interactive activity in much the same fashion as speaking. In speaking, children receive immediate feedback from others, making them aware of the need for clarity and for expressing their ideas so that they can be understood by others. The ability to sit back and review one's writing from the perspective of others requires an objective, uninvolved viewpoint, a feat which even older students find difficult to achieve (Bridwell, 1980). The group process provides objective, interactive feedback that is extremely helpful to revision and provides the writer with experience in objectively criticizing others' writings as well.

Daiute (1983) argues that the group process enhances the subtle sense of audience given by the computer itself. The computer "seems like an audience, thus stimulating the writer to take a reader's point of view" (p. 141).

7. The neatness of the final printed copy can be a great ego boost to younger and lower-ability students whose papers are often blotched and messy.

This professional appearance may, however, lead to a phenomenon called *smokescreen revision* by M. Schwartz (1983). Some students assume that insignificant changes such as spelling corrections, together with a neatly typed format, make a meaningful composition. Appearance is not the same as reality. A neatly printed copy may well camouflage poor content, organization, and mechanics.

8. Children (and adults) are usually unpracticed at composing and typing simultaneously. Cognitive overload results, frustration occurs, and the pace is very slow. Teachers can get around this problem by having children write on paper first, then type into the WP. Revision can occur while typing.

The ultimate goal, however, is composition at the keyboard.

9. If you have only one micro in the classroom, rotate students who will use it. That is, Group 1 uses the WP for the first composition, Group 2 for the second, and so on.

10. Micros that do not yield both capitals and lowercase letters are inexcusable in educational settings. The old Apple II, for instance, will print only capitals unless it has a minor hardware modification or unless special software modifications such as that in *Word Handler* are available. It is certainly worth the extra cost to make the modifications.

11. Engberg (1983) notes that the function of the teacher during word processing changes from that of final critic to that of editor and mentor. The WP offers the potential of cooperation not only between students but between teacher and students as well. As the teacher circulates to observe student progress, weaknesses can be observed and discussed while work is still on the screen, before it has been printed out on paper. Teacher and student work together to overcome writing obstacles while the writing is still in progress.

The cooperative give and take in such a session can be an invaluable learning experience. Too few children see the composing or editing processes actually modeled for them. That is, teachers often seem to "magically" arrive at a correct mechanical revision or a revised wording. The students only see and hear the result, not the process (Rubin, 1980). By sitting down with a student and analyzing a problem, verbalizing each step of the solution to demonstrate the thinking involved as the revision is made, teachers can communicate the essence of the writing process.

12. The WP offers great advantages but also makes great demands. For effective use of the WP, the school must make a commitment to its use. In a limited research study designed to test the effectiveness of the WP in improving college students' writing, Collier (1983) examined videotapes of results and found few advantages of the WP over normal handwriting in improving quality of composition. His four subjects had received only two sessions of training and practice on the WP, an apparently insufficient time allotment for effective use. Collier notes, "I saw after viewing only a few minutes of the videotapes that the attention shifts needed when a writer is manipulating the keyboard for operations other

than simple typing interrupted continuous concentration on the text itself" (p. 153).

If composition by computer is to become as natural an act for children as composition by handwriting, they must be allowed sufficient time to develop proficiency with the keyboard and with the specific WP commands. If students already have some basic knowledge of the keyboard, a good guideline seems to be to allot three sessions a week of 30 minutes each during the first month of use and at least once a week thereafter. Any less time on task leads to a frustrating amount of memory loss between sessions.

A little arithmetic will show that any teacher with only one micro has a tough scheduling job if he or she is to teach the WP to all students. The only workable method seems to be that of teaching the class in alternating groups of six to eight. During October Group 1 might be given intensive practice. In November, Group 2 gets the intensive practice, and Group 1 is allowed to work on the computers once a week. In December, Group 3 is trained, and Groups 1 and 2 use the computer once a week, and so forth.

INTRODUCING THE WORD PROCESSOR

If the entire class will use the word processor, whole-class instruction in its use is certainly most efficient. The ideal situation would place the teacher at the front of a computer laboratory room with large-screen monitors for demonstration purposes and one or two children sitting behind each computer. In any case, the key principle should be *as much "hands-on" activity as possible.* One doesn't learn to word process by listening to a lecture. One learns by doing it.

Adult word processors do not have accompanying documentation or tutorials that would be suitable for use with children. Teachers must do the planning and carry out instruction themselves. This may seem forbidding, but many teachers report success in such endeavors, rejecting the prepared teaching materials available for such programs as *Bank Street Writer* in favor of the harder-to-teach but more powerful WPs.

INSTRUCTIONAL TECHNIQUES

The most powerful use of any software is the use for which it was designed. While the WP can be used for many applications in the language arts, these uses do not always take advantage of the program's full potential.

As a tool for practice in writing, however, the WP's usefulness is unparalleled. Writing theorists have long advised that the key to fluent writing is to write as much as possible. The key to exact writing is to revise repeatedly.

The WP was designed for revision. As a matter of fact, some office efficiency studies have shown that WPs do not reduce the time a business devotes to correspondence (Kepner, 1983). Time saved by the WP is spent revising and rewording so that documents are "perfect" (Marcus and Blau, 1983). Secretaries and students plunge into the editing task with a vigor never seen when using pen or typewriter. Individual words can be erased, inserted, or moved. Whole chunks of text can be reorganized with the touch of a few buttons. Editing features eliminate the drudgery involved in rewriting drafts of manuscripts, and the writer obtains a perfect printed copy of the entire paper within seconds of completing the revision.

Ideally, the writer simultaneously composes and types, backspacing to correct immediately recognizable errors. With appropriate facilities (that is, sufficient microcomputers for students involved in writing) the habit of composing/typing can develop to replace that of composing/writing. Complaints of inability to think and type into a micro at the same time arise at first, but with some practice students adapt to the new system. As with any worthwhile skill, this ability develops slowly and with some frustration, but it saves time and energy in the long run. Undoubtedly, within ten years the process of sitting before a micro to compose will seem natural to us all, as the WP becomes a part of everyday life.

Basic Methodology

The writing experience can be analyzed into three stages.

Prewriting. The writer determines a need for writing. This need can be practical (writing a letter) or for simple personal satisfaction (describing a meaningful experience). Prewriting also includes the thoughts involved in forming some organized plan of attack for carrying out the writing process. This might include making mental notes, writing a purpose statement or summary, or drawing up an outline.

Writing. The first draft, written quickly with relatively little concern for fine points of spelling, grammar, or punctuation, develops the major ideas to be included in the paper. The writer is concerned to expand upon the *macrostructure* (Kintsch and van Dijk, 1978)—the organization of general ideas—developed during prewriting. The central task at this stage is to write as many ideas as possible.

Contemporary models of writing often emphasize this stage of the process to the exclusion of the first. The traditional approach has been to follow an outline strictly, to write down what is already known. Writing theorists today suggest that this stage—the construction of the first draft—must be the discovery stage, a time in which the writer learns as he records. Some would even label this process a "prewriting" stage, since emphasis is on learning and self-discovery rather than the mechanics of exact writing. The widespread requirements for students to maintain ungraded journals and engage in free writing are based upon this reconceptualization of the writing process.

Postwriting.   Now the writer turns attention to the *microstructure*—the details needed to fine-tune the paper. Concepts presented in the first draft are examined for clarity and sufficient elaboration. Additional information and examples are added if necessary to make ideas more concrete. Relationships between these ideas are made explicit by use of signal words. Finally, the text is checked for spelling errors, grammatical problems, and punctuation.

Such has been the advice of writing instructors. The time problems involved in extensive rewriting or retyping have eliminated the actual implementation of this instructional model of writing. Neither teachers nor students are convinced that the benefits of the revision process are worth the dull, time-consuming mechanics of repeated rewriting. Students are often terrified of even beginning to put their thoughts down on paper because of the work and time involved in making corrections (Shaughnessy, 1977).

Now, however, the WP systems available for microcomputers promise to help realize the advantages offered in this three-stage model. Rewriting and revising are allowed to be the cognitive processes they should be, rather than being dominated by the mechanical aspects of actually putting letters and words down on paper. Students learn to approach their writing errors from a different point of view, by struggling to understand what causes problem phrases, sentences, or paragraphs. L. Schwartz (1983) has found a parallel between the problem-solving strategies developed by his students using WPs and the metacognitive strategies Papert (1980) has found in teaching LOGO programming to children. Writers become *debuggers,* epistemologists who analyze their own thinking and writing for a better understanding of language and of mind. Writing is far more complex than programming, so that the two skills are not exactly analogous. "The real equivalency is in the process of learning to see mistakes as a challenge and then struggling to fix them" (L. Schwartz, 1983, p. 35).

The following lesson plan offers a suggested standard sequence of activities. Parts of this sequence may be carried out using pen and paper to save computer time if facilities are limited.

1. Student develops a purpose statement for the writing experience.
2. An informal outline of the composition, one major idea for each projected paragraph, is typed using the WP and printed for reference.
3. Student examines and revises outline for logical order and fulfillment of the purpose statement. Consultation may be held with the teacher or peer advisers for their input.
4. Using the revised outline as a guide, the student composes the first draft, entering and saving the draft in a file. Little or no attention is paid to mistypings, grammar, spelling, punctuation, or other mechanical aspects of writing. The main purpose is to get the ideas into the file.
5. Close examination of this first draft will reveal shortcomings. The student revises and refines, adding and subtracting to make the points

clear. Mechanical changes are made at this point. This step will require more time on task than needed to write the first draft.

6. The teacher or student consultants examine the revised text. Each loads the composition onto a terminal (the draft completed in step 5 remains intact in the file on diskette) and types in comments or suggested revisions. These consultative revisions are then saved onto diskette.

7. The writer examines the consultants' comments and suggestions, incorporating worthwhile revisions into the draft. This final draft is then saved onto the student's personal diskette and, if desired, made available to the class for reading and other activities on a diskette to which all students have access.

AUTOMATIC FEEDBACK

WPs do not provide feedback concerning the quality of writing. The teacher or students must read the composition and suggest improvements.

Several forms of software are available that will automatically analyze text and provide students with suggestions on weaknesses and possible revisions. The most popular is the *spelling checker,* which analyzes words and compares them to an internal dictionary of correct spellings. Other software packages check for certain grammar errors.

Teachers often react negatively to such devices on the assumption that they remove the necessity of learning to spell or of learning correct grammar. In fact, demands are placed upon the writer even when such software is used. A spelling checker, for example, cannot determine whether a word is actually misspelled. It simply reports whether a particular target group of letters is in its internal dictionary. The writer must make the final determination. In other words, these checking devices do not do all the work. They make suggestions but leave it up to the writer to make the final decisions.

In addition, error-checking programs help students learn a step-by-step approach to revising, concentrating on one problem area at a time. If the student realizes that spelling and grammar will be analyzed later on, he or she is free to concentrate on composing. Focusing on the task at hand makes greater success more likely because demands on limited cognitive capacity and attention are not overly taxing.

Spelling Checkers

Spelling-checker software has built-in dictionaries of correctly spelled words. The text file created by a word processor is analyzed by the spelling checker. Each word in the file is compared with the internal dictionary to find a match. If no word in the dictionary matches the spelling of the target word, the target word is reported as a possible misspelling.

There are limitations on spelling checkers that place the burden of knowledge on the user. Consider the following sentence:

```
THE JONESES CONSULTED A LOCALE NUMISMATIST TO FIND WEATHER
THERE UNCLE'S STAMP COLLECTION WAS VALUBLE.
```

A spelling checker would find certain errors and would not find others. Spelling checkers cannot determine whether words are used correctly. *Numismatists* are coin collectors, not stamp experts, but the spelling checker would not recognize this definitional error. It might well identify *numismatist* as an error, however, for only the more frequent words in the English language are included in the checker's dictionary. *Joneses* would also be identified, since few proper names are in the dictionary. Of course *locale*, *weather*, and *there* would not be identified as improper spellings, since the computer would find a match for each in its dictionary. *Valuble* would be correctly identified as a misspelling, and the user would be offered the option of replacing it with the correction.

Internal dictionaries vary in size, depending on the word processor. *Sensible Speller IV* has a dictionary with 80,000 words. Each user is able to build upon the original dictionary with a personal dictionary composed of words he or she typically uses, of trade names and other proper nouns, jargon or technical terms, abbreviations, and so forth. When a word such as *numismatist* is singled out as a possible misspelling, the user is given the option of adding that word to the dictionary. A single key press stores the word on disk, and future uses of it will be recognized as correctly spelled.

Grammar Checkers

Spelling checkers are rather routine and mechanical to use. Grammar checkers offer a good deal more in terms of writing improvement. They analyze aspects of the composition for certain types of weaknesses much as a teacher might do when correcting compositions. The revision is left up to the user, though possible variations might be suggested. Grammar checkers offer useful feedback and provide a real learning experience in composition.

Grammatik uses advice offered in a variety of style manuals to analyze documents. It will search out such problems as use of archaic words, capitalization errors, missing end quotation marks, and repeated words (*the the*). It will also spot some redundancies, such as *joins together*, as well as common grammatical errors like *must of* instead of *must have*. It can check for sexist terms like *businessman* or *chairman*.

A final report from *Grammatik* includes total number of words in the document, the average word and sentence lengths (an actual readability analysis would be handier), number of short sentences (few than 14 words) and of long sentences (more than 30 words), and a variety of other data.

Thesaurus Software

Use of the thesaurus can easily lead to stilted writing and incorrectly used words by students who try to replace familiar words with the unfamiliar. Traditionally, however, teachers have found that, used with restraint, the thesaurus can be a valuable reference tool. Thesaurus programs offer computerized versions.

In *Thesaurus*, you type in the word for which you are asking synonyms, and the computer lists several. If you type the sentence in which you'll be using the word, the sentence will be printed several times, each time with a different synonym.

In addition to costing many times the price of a *Roget's Thesaurus*, this computer version is far less efficient. In order to use it, the WP file being written must be saved to disk, the *Thesaurus* disk booted, and the target word typed in. Then you must wait a few seconds while the computer searches its memory for synonyms. Then the WP must be rebooted, the file loaded, and the new synonym inserted in its correct location. This takes far longer than looking the synonym up in a book thesaurus. In addition, *Thesaurus* has only about half the synonyms to be found in *Roget's*.

11

WORD PROCESSING
ACTIVITIES

Word processing can be used for a host of writing activities, only a few of which can be described here. Practically any writing activity imaginable lends itself to use of the word processor. Go to texts on writing instruction, read their ideas, and let your imagination be the guide to construction of your own exercises.

The first two sections of this chapter discuss two important activities in which the word processor (WP) can play a major role, the language experience approach and journalism studies. The chapter concludes with short descriptions of many more WP activities.

LANGUAGE EXPERIENCE APPROACH

Allen (1976) has argued that the teacher's major role when dealing with beginning readers is to help them internalize key principles about language. The conceptualization of these principles is the hallmark of the Language Experience Approach, a system of teaching that combines speaking, reading, and writing in a variety of integrated activities. Allen and Allen's (1966) classic lines describe the LEA's principles as follows:

> What I can think about, I can talk about.
> What I can say, I can write (or someone can write about).
> What I write, I can read.
> I can read what others write for me to read. (p. 6)

The LEA, in its various formats, can be used with children of all ages, but beginning readers benefit most from extensive use. There are five basic steps:

1. The teacher finds an idea—for example, an event, object, or anything in the child's experiential background through which the child can learn more about her world.

2. The student (or the whole class) dictates a story about the chosen idea to the teacher, who records it on paper. The teacher rereads the story aloud to check for accuracy.

3. The story is printed on paper for the child to read.

4. The teacher reads the story, then the story is read in unison by the teacher and student. The teacher points to every word as it is read.

5. Follow-up activities, based upon words in the story, elaborate on generalizable comprehension and word-recognition skills needed to read it successfully.

The WP can be a tool for the teacher throughout the LEA process. The time-consuming task of transcribing the story as the student reads, then typing it on a paper or ditto master, has vanished. Now the teacher simply types in the story as the student verbalizes, saves it in a file for future use, and immediately prints as many copies as needed.

Should the teacher wish to check on individual students' abilities to read the words in the story, she can simply pull out the story file from diskette storage, rename it to identify the particular student and date (for example, ZOO STORY, JOHN 10/21), and have the child read on the monitor. If desired, the cursor can be used as a pointer, though a pencil is more convenient (if not quite as technologically impressive). Some word processors allow unknown words to be underlined with the press of a button or two. The story, annotated to identify words the child was unable to recognize, can then be saved for review at a later date.

Word Banks

Teachers have long recognized that records of words (called *word banks*) that the student knows on sight are invaluable when teaching beginning reading. Such records, kept in notebooks or on file cards, offer immense satisfaction to the children as their lists grow longer and longer. The words can be used in a variety of word-recognition activities related to the Language Experience Approach. Creative writing exercises can be based upon sentence construction from words in the word bank. When a word not in the bank is required, the child is taught to write and spell it.

A computerized version of file cards can be stored as a list on diskette, accessed by the word processor when needed, and modified as often as necessary. New words can be added to the end of the list or inserted in alphabetical order. The child can print out the list whenever required, perhaps retaining an up-to-date version printed on a notebook page for easy reference.

For older children who are developing a meaning vocabulary, store the words in conjunction with other useful information, such as definition and pronunciation guides.

A whole-class vocabulary file can be constructed as well. Research on vocabulary learning has consistently indicated that repeated exposure to a word is necessary to learn it, in both similar and different contexts (Manzo and Sherk, 1972; Beck et al., 1982). Study of a limited number of words in depth increases vocabulary to a greater extent than learning a large number of words superficially.

As an activity to help students elaborate their vocabulary learning, a file can be created for each word studied. To provide a variety of contextual usages, students are assigned to write meaningful sentences using each word. The students with the best examples enter their sentences in the appropriate file. Other students who have trouble with the word are able to load that file to examine correct usage.

JOURNALISM STUDIES

Some years back the popular television show "Lou Grant" ran several episodes highlighting the joys and frustrations involved in the introduction of word processors to newspaper reporting and publishing. The word processor is a fine tool for classroom or school newspapers, as well. The simplicity of revising makes the editor's task neat and efficient. Monahan and Scoland (1983) report that "the ease with which our students are able to make revisions, coupled with their desire to get extra time on the computer, seem to combine to encourage the types of revisions that advisors have always attempted to foster with threats and innuendo" (p. 28).

Training of student reporters and editors in the use of the WP should be well-organized and thorough. Elementary classrooms may find a simple WP to be satisfactory. A more sophisticated WP will enable complex print layouts to be formatted. For example, text can be printed in columns of any desired width. A right-justification command can align text along both margins for very professional-looking copy.

Special printing hardware, such as the PKASO printer interface, allows dot matrix printers to use different sizes of type for headlines and newspaper titles and to incorporate them in the word processor article files (see Figure 11–1). Other software, like the *Graphics Magician,* enables printers to use a variety of different typefaces for printing headlines, which can then be cut-and-pasted into the main body of text (see Figure 11–2). Simple diagrams and illustrations can be constructed using graphics tablets and software, then printed for insertion in the newspaper.

Newspaper pages may be printed on mimeograph masters, then duplicated. For larger projects, the pages may be laid out and a single copy printed, then sent to a print shop ready for photocopying and printing. The WP eliminates the need for setting type.

GENERAL IDEAS FOR THE CLASSROOM

1. Correct and annotate students' papers on the computer monitor by inserting appropriate diacritical entries. For example, if a student wrote, "The night fought the dragon he won the battle," the teacher's

CAFETERIA
FOOD
TO CHANGE

New Food Service
Comes to Central

Mr. Robert Allen, principal
of Central Junior High School,
reported that the Evansville
Board of Education had signed
a contract with Van Allen Food
Services. Van Allen will
begin providing food to the
CJHS cafeteria next week.

A representative of Van
Allen told reporters that the
quality of food would continue
to be "excellent." The
company does plan to closely
analyze student preferences,
however, to prepare menus
which are more popular than
those used previously.

FIGURE 11–1. Word processor news article

annotations would be, "The night—sp—fought the dragon—run-on—he won the battle."

2. Instead of annotating (as above), make a list of number and kinds of errors and file it on the student's diskette. The student must then check the list and find and correct each error.

3. Have students rewrite each other's papers (or sample papers provided by the teacher) to make improvements. This task lends itself well to group work for the planning of revision strategies.

4. Provide a file of compositions written from a particular point of view, such as "Our Town Is Ugly" or "School Should Be Held during the Summer." Assign students the task of editing the composition so as to change its basic argument: "Our Town Is Beautiful" or "No School during the Summer!"

5. Take a student's composition file (or a sample composition you provide) and delete particular key aspects such as the signal words that provide cohesion, the pronouns, or the prepositions. The class task is to reconstruct the composition by reinserting appropriate words. Compare results in class discussion.

6. When assigning group research reports, each student participant may type his section of the report and save it on the group diskette. As students in the group review the various sections written by their co-workers, they can revise or insert additional information obtained in their own research.

7. Set up a computerized mail service in which students write notes to one another via the WP, storing the notes on disk in files labeled TO JANET or TO CLASS. Children respond enthusiastically and actually would rather write these notes and check the Class Mail Diskette daily than talk to one another. If two or more children desire some degree of privacy, a separate diskette accessible only to them can be made available. *Bank Street Writer* provides a password system that restricts access to particular files to those students who know the correct password, another option to provide privacy.

The teacher may also leave messages, such as, "TO MARK: Remember, your shark project is due next week. If you're having problems, see me today!—Mrs. Sampson."

8. A class story construction project involves each student in the task of telling a story. The teacher provides a first sentence or phrase: "As I looked down the street . . . ." Then students take turns adding sentences (or paragraphs) to the story using the word processor. This technique is particularly useful for helping students become at ease in creative writing activities. As they see how the story develops, they recognize parallels between the group story and stories they may write as individuals.

The final result should be printed, read aloud, and displayed. An adaptation of this method could provide a story starter and have each individual student expand on it to create a complete story. Compare the results in class discussion.

9. Using the "fill-in-the-blanks" capability of the WP for standardized forms, children can write their own holiday greetings to friends and relatives, personalizing the greetings by inserting names of the recipients.

FIGURE 11–2. Headlines by *Graphics Magician*

New Courses Offered

May 19, 1986   **June Grads**

Prom Day Approaches

Art Exhibit

FUTURE CHOICES

FACULTY SHOW

If the classroom has a graphics tablet, computer graphics may be used to spice up the appearance.

10. Construct a classroom newspaper or yearbook from the best files. With most word processors, filed stories, compositions, and poems would have to be printed individually, then pasted together to form a booklet, which could be photocopied or duplicated using a Thermofax machine. With a little work and planning, the same page could be repeatedly sent through a printer, once for each article, with margins set so that no article would be printed on top of another. This page could then be photocopied or Thermofaxed.

11. In early May, as the summer break approaches and students (and teachers) begin thinking of their upcoming vacation plans, create a form fill-in letter requesting travel information. Students who plan to travel can use the form (Figure 11–3) to send to local and state chambers of commerce, national park offices, and tourist agencies for information. These assignments make good, practical use of library reference skills as students consult travel guides such as *Mobil* and *Fodor's* for addresses.

Use your school for the return address so all students can see the

FIGURE 11–3. Form letter requesting travel information

```
                                Arlington School
                                17 Bethany Road
                                Arlington, Ohio 33333
                                (Date)


(Name of Addressee)
(Address line 1)
(Address line 2)
(Address line 3)


Dear Sir:

    My family and I will be traveling to (State) during the
month of (Month of trip) this year.  We are interested in
obtaining information about (Name of place).  We would like to
know about interesting places to visit, as well as dining and
sleeping accommodations.

    Please send this information to the above address, care of
myself.  Thank you.

                                Yours,



                                (Your Name)
```

results. Tell school secretaries to expect the return mail so that it will be forwarded correctly to you.

12. Start a class project to develop a file of form letters of all different types, to be accessed when needed. Keep in mind that creating form letters is possible even if your WP does not have the form fill-in capability. Students simply use normal editing techniques to delete and insert as necessary. WPs can usually insert in two ways, either by *replacement*, in which new words automatically erase and replace old words, or normal *insertion*, in which the old words are maintained as new words are typed to replace them, then must be deleted in normal fashion by delete commands. Students just beginning to use the WP often find this second method the easiest to start using.

Form letter files can include several different styles for each of the following (see Figure 11–3):

Get well letters to sick classmates
Thank you notes
Party invitations
Personalized letters of reminder to parents about PTA meetings
Birthday greetings
Requests for information

13. Set up a composition exchange with another classroom using a compatible word processor. Send disks with interesting compositions back and forth for reading and editing. This is a particularly interesting activity if the classes are in different schools or even in different states. One school in Alaska reportedly mails stories about whale hunting and salmon fishing to a school in California, which returns stories about surfing and the latest television shows.

Educational computer user groups are the natural sources for finding other teachers interested in a diskette pen-pal arrangement. When attending computer workshops at professional conferences, establish contacts for such projects.

If you send diskettes through the mail, wrap them securely and provide stiff cardboard backing. Prepared diskette mailers may be purchased at computer stores or through mail order. Label clearly, "Magnetic Media—Do Not Expose to Electrical Fields," for careful postal service handling.

14. Have students write compositions with purposefully inserted errors: "This composition has four run-on sentences. See if you can find and correct them."

15. Your students are hard at work, writing their compositions. As you look around the room, you note that Steven hasn't gotten very far. He's written only one or two sentences and looks tense and frustrated with himself. He's got writer's block and is frozen, seemingly unable to put his thoughts down in print.

Students like Steven suffer a breakdown in expressive communication when it comes to writing their thoughts. Often they have not been able to personally conceptualize and apply the parallels between oral communication and written communication. At other times they have developed a perfectionist approach to their writing. Their first drafts are filled with so many self-corrections that progress is brought to a halt and paragraphs have no internal coherence.

Steven needs to be freed to create. "The computer has proved to be a destroyer of writing blocks" (Daiute, 1983, p. 143). Ease of revision can remove much fear of making errors and the frustration of false starts.

One standard practice in dealing with such students is to place little or no emphasis on English mechanics during the writing of the first draft. Another technique designed to take the student's attention away from the actual print and place it on the ideas to be expressed is writing without ink. Students are given a blank sheet of paper with a piece of carbon paper and another blank sheet underneath. They use a pen without ink to write their compositions. Since they cannot read what they've written, they are encouraged to write freely without mechanical concerns. All creative thought can be devoted to the actual ideas to be expressed, leaving revision for later.

The electronic equivalent of writing without ink is simply to turn off the monitor or adjust brightness and contrast controls so that text is not visible. On most computers, the monitor can be switched off while the computer is still operational, leaving students to stare at a blank screen. As they compose their first drafts, the mechanical problems involved in editing are eliminated. Students' concerns are simply to type the ideas as they come, in a natural sequence without concern for transitions, spelling, punctuation, or grammar.

Practice with this method may help overcome one of the problems some students develop when using the WP. This particular problem arises because of the ease of editing on a WP. That is, some students find that the coherence and flow of ideas are impeded by frequent editing regressions to correct minor problems. A poor typist, for example, who makes several errors on each line will find that the flow of composition is broken up by each correction. Ordinarily, if using a typewriter to compose, such a writer ought to ignore these petty errors, leaving them for later revision. Revision is so simple on the WP that the writer might break up her train of thought repeatedly for the second or two needed to make each correction. Students need to be wary of falling into this trap.

Marcus and Blau (1983) report that this "invisible writing" helped students concentrate attention on their thoughts rather than on premature editing that interferes with the composing process. One student summed up the experience like this:

> When I do visible writing, I tend to look back on what I've written and it slows my thoughts down, and I tend to lose track of what I had in my head. With invisible writing. I . . . think there's a sort of anticipation. I find I'm

wondering what I'm writing and I look forward to seeing what's on my paper. (p. 13)

Younger children enjoy invisible writing and take to it readily, looking upon it as a kind of game. They respond particularly well to editing after the invisible composing experience, recognizing the clear need for it better than in normally written first drafts.

16. Do not hesitate to print out the entire composition for the final revising pass. Writers need to skim their text to maintain control over the evolution of ideas (Perl, 1980). A major limitation of WPs is that only a small portion of any composition can be displayed on the monitor screen at any given point. This limitation is a problem especially at the very end of the writing process, when the writer needs to look over the composition as a whole to establish whether he has achieved an overall unity of idea structures. By printing out the entire composition for a final pass, the writer can get a feel for the overall structure much better than flipping line by line through the composition on the screen.

Frequent printouts are also necessary during the writing and editing of lengthy works (longer than eight pages), allowing easier cross-referencing between sections of the paper.

17. Encourage experimentation in writing, a dynamic approach to writing. Since revisions are made so easily with a WP, this is usually a natural outcome of computer use, but experience shows that it is not necessarily so. Donald Graves (1983) has warned that seeing neatly printed drafts may make children even less likely to revise, since words typed are more final and official than handwritten words.

Experimentation in which students try one revision, reject it, try another, and so forth is encouraged by two factors, one depending upon the software and the other upon the teacher. Students are much more willing to make changes if the word processor allows those changes to be easily rejected and the text restored to its original form. Many WPs have the functions UNERASE and UNMOVE, though few are so easy to use as *Bank Street Writer*'s provisions. When a student erases a word or sentence, then on reflection decides that the erasure was not effective, an immediate command to UNERASE brings back the deleted text. If a block of text is moved and examination shows that the move was ill-advised, the UNMOVE command reinserts the text in its original location. Such options make it easy for students to try out new arrangements.

The teacher factor is even more critical. Proper modeling of the experimental, dynamic approach to writing must be carried out by the teacher. Using whole-class demonstrations with large monitors or several monitors chained together by cable, teachers can revise sample compositions, simulating the experimental revision process. Move a block of text, and allow students to take a look at it, discuss the efficacy of the move, and decide whether or not to make the move permanent. Show students the thought processes involved. Don't be afraid to make mistakes—

perhaps even be sure that you make them! Students will not develop a conceptualization of text as fluid unless teachers demonstrate it.

18. A major advantage of the WP for writing improvement is that the writer's attention may be focused on one type of revision during each pass through the manuscript. If a child has a problem with both run-on sentences and subject-verb agreement, the first revising pass might focus attention on checking whether basic sentence structure is correct. The second pass through the paper might involve checking each sentence for matching subjects and verbs. Then spelling can be checked. While much the same procedure can be carried out with pen and paper, the corrections become so confusing after one or two passes that the paper can hardly be read. A WP automatically reformats as corrections are made.

Research has indicated that errors in writing are often attributable to short-term memory limitations (Daiute, 1983). As writers plan and produce long sentences or paragraphs, the wording and ideas in initial phrases or sentences fade out in memory. Writers, especially those without skills developed to the point of automaticity, have trouble keeping track of what is happening as they weave together spelling, grammar, and meaning in their compositions. By focusing on a single skill or a single step in the writing process at a time, they reduce the cognitive load on memory and are better able to deal with the complex task.

19. Collier (1983) has observed that inexperienced writers often assume that writing is based upon principles identical to those that control speech. If text is altered, students act as if its retrieval were impossible. Therefore, they are reluctant to revise.

This barrier may be easily overcome by storing all drafts and revisions on disk. This operation usually involves an extra step in WP operations, as most WPs automatically erase the original file when a revised file is stored. Often users are required to use a COPY function to make a second copy of the original file, then make revisions in this second file. When the revised file is saved, both it and the original are available from disk.

Sophisticated WPs like *WordStar* automatically create a *backup* file—a copy of the original—whenever the writer accesses the original file. Other WPs, such as *Screen Writer II*, allow users to specify different names for the *input file* (the original file) and the *output file* (the new revised file), thereby creating a backup.

20. The contemporary emphasis on revision naturally leads to maintenance of a classroom policy that compositions be revised and that copies of each revision be kept for teacher and peer examination. In addition, teachers must come to view writing as process rather than product if they are to communicate that attitude to their students. That is, too often feedback to the writer comes only in the form of teacher comments *after* the assignment has been completed. This procedure fosters the idea that focus in writing must be on the end product.

To shift this focus to the actual process of writing, teachers must become involved in the writing process. Do not wait until the last draft has been written to provide input. Structure writing assignments so that teacher and peer comments are continuous during the whole time of writing and revision (Graves, 1983).

21. Volunteer parents or students from typing classes can help younger students type their compositions into the word processor. The most time-consuming part of the WP experience for students who do not know how to type is actual entry of the first draft. Some teachers avoid this frustration by having their students handwrite the first draft and submit it to a typist for input into a WP file. Then the students use the WP to revise.

12

OTHER ACTIVITIES FOR WRITING AND READING

The microcomputer's greatest potential for influencing the teaching of language arts lies in its ability to edit text. Word processors are already in widespread use in classrooms as teachers recognize their capabilities for revolutionizing students' conceptions of the revising process. Certainly if there is one piece of software that every classroom should have, it is a word processor.

The computer's contribution to the teaching of writing need not be limited to word processing. The creative teacher can make use of microcomputers for writing instruction and practice in a wide variety of ways, from exercises on the most elemental levels of mechanics to the construction of essays and creative works. The computer offers the possibility of establishing an individualized experience in learning to write that may someday become almost as natural as learning to speak. Children learn oral language by listening to others speak, practicing, and receiving feedback. Microcomputers already possess limited capacities to provide such feedback during writing experiences, checking for spelling and some grammatical and usage errors.

> We take for granted that there should be a gap between the spoken and written language. Children learn to speak as babies without formal instruction. But the written language comes later, if at all, and seems to require deliberate professional teaching. But why should this be so? Is writing really harder than speaking? I believe not and that the computer will close the gap. (Papert, 1980, p. 157)

Our first topic is the controversial issue of instruction and practice in language mechanics such as grammar and punctuation. We then consider a broad range of imaginative applications of the computer to writing, varying from programs that help students write compositions and poems to activities in which students use the computer to "publish" their written creations. The final section of this chapter describes software available for spelling instruction.

PRACTICE ON LANGUAGE MECHANICS

The ability of the computer to supply practice exercises lends itself to grammar instruction. There are already enough software programs on the market to replace the traditional grammar workbooks in a classroom. Program objectives range from teaching the parts of speech to sentence diagramming to sentence combining. At their best these offer the same advantages of computerized exercises discussed in other chapters, with instant feedback, individualized rate of presentation, the possibility of branching, record keeping, and motivational value.

A question that each teacher should face is, "Given the potential for computerizing grammar drills, should I go ahead with it?" In too many classrooms writing instruction has very little to do with actual writing. Instead, children are drilled on meaningless grammar activities.

Few types of drill are so far removed from their ultimate objective as grammar drills. In reading comprehension drills, at least the students read something. In vocabulary drills, students are exposed to words and their meanings. In grammar drill, however, where the ultimate goal is to improve students' writing, students *do not write*. Instead they are subjected to identification of parts of speech or recognition of errors in sentences contrived by a textbook author. As a result, few grammar skills transfer from the drill activity to meaningful writing tasks. As long ago as 1963, a National Council of Teachers of English report noted the following:

> In view of the widespread agreement of research studies based upon many types of students and teachers, the conclusion can be stated in strong and unqualified terms: the teaching of formal grammar has a negligible, or, because it usually displaces some instruction and practice in actual composition, even a harmful effect on the improvement of writing. (Braddock, Lloyd-Jones, and Schoerr, 1963, pp. 37–38)

Some guidelines to follow when choosing software for practice in mechanics of writing are these:

1. Teach for transfer. The teacher must control the practice program, not vice versa. When grammar instruction is seen as an end in itself, there will be little improvement in the ultimate goal—writing itself. Every practice activity should be directly related to a writing activity, or else students will see no application of the rules involved. The teacher's role is central here, for computer software development is not yet at the point where this transfer can be made automatically.

2. Be sure the tutorial instruction is not on a higher level than the usage skill being taught. Language is a complex subject. Explanations of grammatical rules and concepts can quite easily become so contorted that

students may be able to perform the activity without being able to understand the instructions.

Teachers should provide the bulk of initial instruction and reinforcement in mechanical usage themselves. The computer can be used for follow-up reinforcement to develop automaticity and speed of performance.

3. Tutorial instruction should use more than one approach to explaining concepts. The complexities of English language mechanics cannot be clearly communicated to all students in the same way. Some students conceptualize a grammar rule through one approach, and others through another. For example, in addition to defining and giving samples of adverbs, software ought to state that most adverbs end in *-ly*. The *and, but, nor* rhyme may be helpful in teaching conjunctions. Throw your whole teaching arsenal at the youngsters and hope that at least one technique works for every child.

4. Tutorial instruction should be clear, though clarity is hard to come by in language skill areas. Consider, for example, the traditional definition of a sentence: "A sentence is a complete thought." Perhaps philosophers have some understanding of just what is "a complete thought," but sixth graders certainly do not. One program designed to teach the parts of speech defines a pronoun as a word that "relates a noun or pronoun to another word in the sentence," then defines a conjunction as a word that "joins words or groups of words together." These are ambiguous differentiations.

5. Demand *response-specific error checking.* In grammar exercises, students exhibit patterns of incorrect responses based upon their lack of knowledge and skill. Each type of error should be handled in a different way. Consider the following frame from *Grammar Mastery:*

```
            TELEPHONE ANSWERING
        Fred just bought a machine that
        answers the phone.  Now, when
          Fred goes out, the machine
             records messages from
              everybody who calls.


        What's the correct pronoun?
```

Yes, the range of possible responses is infinite. A student could type in HIPPOPOTAMUS or IGNEOUS ROCK. Computers cannot possibly be programmed to respond differently to every possible input. But the range of *likely* responses is very small, namely, pronouns. Computers *can* be programmed to recognize the type of pronoun error made and respond specifically to that type of error.

So if our user Carlos inputs HIM, the computer recognizes that he has made a case error, substituting an objective pronoun for a subjective: YOU NEED A SUBJECT PRONOUN. If Carlos types in SHE, the computer notes the gender error: FRED IS A MAN, NOT A WOMAN. Response-specific error checking diagnoses and teaches as it drills.

A wide variety of traditional grammar tutorials are available in computer versions. Some deal with only a single skill. An increasing number of large publishers are putting out very comprehensive large-scale programs.

Grammar Mastery is a comprehensive grammar tutorial series designed for students of English as a second language (ESL) and English as a foreign language (EFL). It is also largely appropriate for native English speakers. Three levels (beginning, low intermediate, and intermediate) contain six diskettes each (see Figure 12–1). The publisher of *Grammar*

FIGURE 12–1. *Grammar Mastery* scope and sequence

```
Series A

    Verbs

    Nouns and Pronouns

    Verbs

    Prepositions and Two-Word Verbs

    Adjectives and Adverbs

Series B

    Yes/No Questions

    Modal Auxiliaries

    Expressions of Quantity

    Pronouns and Relative Clauses

    Comparatives and Superlatives

    Present Perfect

Series C

    Past Perfect

    Past Modals

    Passives

    Noun Clauses

    Conditional Sentences

    Infinitives and Gerunds
```

Mastery, Regents/ALA, also puts out *Essential Idioms in English*, which gives elementary and middle school students an opportunity to deal with idiomatic expressions.

Teachers will find it easy to construct their own grammar drills. A simple linear program like the one below can be adapted to many grammar skills. (More sophisticated examples of quiz programs are in Appendix A.)

```
10 PRINT "SALLY WENT TO THE STORE."
20 INPUT "WHAT IS THE SUBJECT?"; A$
30 IF A$ = "SALLY" THEN PRINT "GOOD!": GOTO 50
40 PRINT "NO.  THE CORRECT ANSWER IS 'SALLY'."
```

Line 50 would present another sentence as in line 10, and so forth. As many sentences may be added to this program as desired.

BEYOND DRILL AND PRACTICE

In an earlier chapter we made a disparaging comment about the phrase "beyond drill and practice," which has become a cliché at computers-in-education conferences. Nevertheless, it seems appropriate here, for teachers should involve students in meaningful communication experiences. Computer tutorials and drills can be invaluable for freeing the teacher for the more difficult tasks in teaching composition—giving feedback on writings to students. But use grammar practice as little as possible. Athey (1983) has noted, "The common root, and hence the reason for the interdependence among the four aspects of language (*that is, reading, writing, listening and speaking*), lies in the search for meaning" (p. 197). There are few if any software grammar drill programs that maintain the dignity and meaningfulness of the writing process.

We do not have to conclude, however, that the computer's only use for writing instruction involves word processing for the writing of whole compositions. Computers can be used by the imaginative teacher in a variety of ways that teach and give practice in writing with meaning.

Gimmicky Games for Communication

At first glance, gimmicky communication games may seem to have only marginal justification for use in the classroom. As a matter of fact, I've given them some second glances as well, and most just didn't come up to my standards for classroom activities. However, they have been acclaimed by so many teachers that I think I might be missing something. Press (1976) labels them the "exploration and play mode for computer assisted learning" (p. 202). They *are* fun. They *do* involve communication. They are what I call "gee whiz" activities: "Gee whiz! Look what I can do with a computer!"

The computer as conversationalist. Have you ever wondered what it would be like to carry on a conversation with a computer like HAL in *2001, A Space Odyssey?* In the mid-1960s, Joseph Weizenbaum developed a program called *Eliza* that was designed to simulate the role of a psychotherapist. The "patient" types in a portion of the conversation, then the computer responds to that input. The conversation attempts to follow Carl Rogers's approach to psychotherapy, in which the computer "doctor" draws out the patient's thoughts by reflecting his statements back to him. Weizenbaum offered the following as a sample of a typical conversation. User responses are in italics.

"Patient": *Men are all alike.*
"Doctor": In what way?
They're always bugging us about something or other.
Can you think of a specific example?
Well, my boyfriend made me come here.
Your boyfriend made you come here.
He says I'm depressed much of the time.
I am sorry to hear you are depressed.
It's true. I am unhappy.
Do you think coming here will help you not to be unhappy? (1976, pp. 3–4)

. . . and so forth. Several variations of *Eliza* are available, including some in the public domain. The reaction of people using *Eliza* programs is shocking. They become genuinely emotionally involved and freely divulge quite personal secrets. The computer's response seems uncannily human and sympathetic.

While *Eliza* might fool people into believing that computer programmers have reached the stage where the computer can understand and respond intelligently to human speech, this is not at all true. The Rogerian form of therapy employed, in which the computer is simply rephrasing and repeating what has been typed in by the user or is drawing from a file of ambiguous stock comments, is suited to such exchanges.

Eliza does, however, uniquely (at least to this point in the history of software development) illustrate just how complex are our language processes, both in what the program can do and in what it cannot do. It can also provide the basis for some serious discussions about communication with other people, dealing with what we say and what we mean when we say it.

Finally it offers a rich resource for thought and discussion of our responses to the computer. As the computer becomes an integral part of our lives, what will our reactions be?

The fact that individuals bind themselves with strong emotional ties to machines ought not in itself to be surprising. The instruments man uses become, after all, extensions of his body. Most importantly, man must, in order to operate his instruments skillfully, internalize aspects of them in the form of kinesthetic and perceptual habits. In that sense at least, his instruments become literally part of him and modify him, and thus alter the basis of his affective relationship to himself. One would expect man to cathect more intensely to instruments that couple directly to his own intellectual, cognitive, and emotive functions than to machines that merely extend the power of his muscles. (Weizenbaum, 1976, p. 9)

Several other programs offer a less sophisticated approach to conversation with computers. *Hello* involves the user in a conversation with a computer psychologist, as in *Eliza*, but in this case the program does not understand natural language. The user enters responses to questions posed in a multiple-choice format. This program can be easily modified by teachers with some knowledge of BASIC to fit any age group.

```
     SAY, PAUL, I CAN SOLVE ALL KINDS OF
     PROBLEMS.  WHAT KIND OF PROBLEMS DO
   YOU HAVE (ANSWER FRIENDS, HEALTH, MONEY,
                  OR JOB)?
                   Money
        SORRY, PAUL, I'M BROKE TOO.
   WHY DON'T YOU SELL ENCYCLOPEDIAS OR
   MARRY SOMEONE RICH OR STOP EATING
   SO YOU WON'T NEED SO MUCH MONEY?
```

In *Dr. Z*, another spoof of Rogerian therapy in which the therapist never makes a value judgment, the computer generates randomly chosen questions to ask: WHY ARE YOU HERE? DO YOU FEEL COMFORTABLE WITH THIS FEELING? DO YOU THINK THIS IS REASONABLE IN THE LIGHT OF YOUR INTERESTS? *Dr. Z* is far simpler (and more limited) than *Eliza* and can be easily typed into a computer (Ahl, 1977). Ahl noted that such programs can be used in the classroom as a focus for discussion of the roles of spoken and written language in communication, as well as the importance of nonverbal "body language" such as facial expressions and body movements.

The computer as tutee.   Children enjoy turning the educational tables on computers by using programs in which they can teach computers rather than the opposite. In *Animals* the computer starts off with a very limited knowledge, and the students teach it about characteristics of animals. The program begins with the child thinking of an animal. The computer tries to guess which animal it is. Since at the beginning of the program the computer is only familiar with one animal, the program asks how the student's animals are different from the one it knows about. As the program advances, the computer collects a greater and greater store of knowledge about animals, hierarchically storing this information in memory in a networking pattern that simulates information storage in the human brain.

After having described several animals to the computer, a student might carry on the following conversation:

```
Computer: DOES IT LIVE IN THE WATER?
Student: N
IS IT VERY TALL?
N
DOES IT LIVE IN AFRICA?
Y
DOES IT HAVE HORNS?
N
IS THE ANIMAL YOU'RE THINKING OF A LION?
```

Here the computer makes its guess, basing the guess on process of elimination. If correct, the computer beeps and prints I GOT IT RIGHT!! If not, it asks,

```
ALL RIGHT.  I GIVE UP.  WHAT
ANIMAL WERE YOU THINKING OF?
Leopard
PLEASE TYPE A QUESTION THAT WOULD
DISTINGUISH BETWEEN A LION AND A LEOPARD.
Does it have spots?
WHAT WOULD THE CORRECT ANSWER FOR LEOPARD BE?
Y
```

In the future, the computer knows about leopards and can include them in the guessing game.

Students engage in a good deal of writing as they communicate their answers to the computer. This program is particularly beneficial to children who are having problems in school because it provides a successful experience that is often hard for such children to come by. That is, they are the teachers, with a particularly dumb student, the computer. As the computer asks questions to refine its newfound knowledge, students are able to answer because the questions are versions of their own input.

Animals is only one of a series of public domain programs identical except for the topics in which the computer must be tutored. A commercial version of *Animals* is included in *Mix and Match*.

The computer as adversary. *Abuse* is a program in which the student attempts to create more effective insults than the computer can deliver. Some teachers report that this program generates a great deal of enthusiasm and that a good deal of reading and writing goes on.

Some teachers might be concerned that this program would encourage a habit of insulting others that is all too prevalent, especially among poorer students for whom mockery reflects low self-concepts. *Abuse* has no place in my classroom.

Readability Analysis of Writing

Several readability formulas have been computerized. Passages are typed into the computer and automatically analyzed, and then a grade-level report is issued. Their most frequent use is as teacher tools in the evaluation of written material. Readability formulas can also be used to help students evaluate their own writing.

Teachers of writing try to communicate an awareness of audience to their students. That is, writers should keep their target audiences in mind as they write, using a style and difficulty level appropriate to that audience. Readability software can aid students in analyzing the approximate levels of their writing. For example, if students are engaging in a creative writing assignment to construct short stories for younger children, the grade level of each story can be determined by using the readability formula.

Evaluation of student compositions by readability formulas can be motivational as well. Since everyone writes at a lower level than he or she reads, results of the analysis are always lower than the student's actual grade level. A tenth grader, for example, would typically find his writing to be at about the seventh or eighth grade level. By glossing over the actual explanation for this phenomenon, teachers with a mildly devious bent can provide students with some incentive for increasing the sophistication of their writing style.

Mad-Lib Activities

Mad-Libs are published in paperback form by Price, Stern, and Sloan Publishers. Children enjoy playing them in pairs, with one child asking another for words representing various parts of speech. Then each word is inserted into a fill-in-the-blanks paragraph to form a nonsense story. The same process can be carried out by the computer. A simple adaptation is listed in Appendix A, the program *Favorite Words*.

```
HI.  WHAT'S YOUR NAME?
TOM
HELLO, TOM.  NAME A FAVORITE ADJECTIVE.
BLUE
OK.  NAME A FAVORITE NOUN.
DOG
HAVE YOU EVER SEEN A BLUE DOG?
```

There is no "right answer" to these questions. Instead the young child finds amusement with nonsense responses, controlling the computer's production. Just as with Mad-Lib books, the program is unable to determine whether the child has accurately supplied parts of speech. Instead, the child's ear provides feedback: Does it "sound right," even if it is nonsensical in meaning?

Lengthier programs of Mad-Lib-like activities are available in the public domain, in print (Press, 1976), and on commercially prepared disks. They are easy, though a bit time consuming, to construct on your own.

Poetry Generators

A poetry generator is a program that leads students through the process of simple poetry writing in step-by-step fashion. Many different styles of poems lend themselves to this mechanical procedure. Teachers find that these methods of encouraging youngsters to write their own poetry are personally relevant introductions to the study of poetic language. Poetry can be terrifying at first. Students who commit their thoughts to paper experience firsthand the problems of rhyme, meter, and other aspects of poetry. The skilled teacher of poetry encourages progress by careful guidance and by convincing students that their creative works are successful (Freeman, 1983).

This approach to poetry has been popularized among teachers by Kenneth Koch's books *Wishes, Lies, and Dreams* (1970) and *Rose, Where Did You Get That Red?* (1974). The goal is to provide students with successful initial experiences in writing poetry, without the pressure that typically accompanies first attempts to deal with language forms that are strange and ambiguous. Koch used highly structured procedures. "I don't mean to say the idea wrote the poems: the children did. The idea helped them to find that they could do it, by giving them a form that would give their poem unity and that was easy and natural for them to use" (1970, p. 7).

The "wish poem" is one example. Students simply construct a series of sentences that begin with "I wish . . . ." Put them together and, presto, you've got a poem.

Poetry-generating programs are actually very simple. First the program explains the form of poetry under study and gives a few examples of poems written in that form. Then the student is asked to develop lines according to the appropriate format. For example,

```
COMPLETE THIS SENTENCE:
        I WISH ...
```

The student might type in, THAT I COULD GO TO THE MOON; THAT THERE WAS PEACE ON EARTH; THAT I WAS A SPACEMAN.

The computer then arranges those lines into a poetic structure:

```
I WISH THAT I COULD GO TO THE MOON.
I WISH THAT THERE WAS PEACE ON EARTH.
  I WISH THAT I WAS A SPACEMAN.
```

This repetition format gives the children an easy way of dividing their poems into lines. It also fits in nicely with children's repetitive manner of speaking. Press (1976) lists a wish poem generator that can be typed into the computer.

The actual programming techniques involved in poetry generators are quite simple. Words and lines are entered by the students and stored in computer memory as *variable strings.* When all the necessary information has been entered, the strings are rearranged into the appropriate arrangements and printed onto the screen or on paper.

Poetry generators can deal with a wide variety of highly structured poetic forms, including diamanté and haiku. *Terquain,* listed in Appendix A, is a simple program that guides students through the writing of terquains. A terquain is a three-line poem.

```
                  WORK
      HOMEWORK, HOUSEWORK, CLASSWORK
                   YUK
                      --Sam, Grade 5
```

The first line gives the topic. The second line has two or three words to describe it. The third line shows some feelings about the subject.

```
                SUMMER
         BEACH, BOATS, BOYS
              VACATION
                    --Erica, Grade 8
```

Terquain prints poems on the screen. If you have a printer, you might want to add a few lines to print the poem in hard copy. Another idea is to devote *Class Anthology,* another program listed in Appendix A and discussed below, to terquains or to whichever form of poetry students are writing.

Teachers who are familiar with BASIC can easily alter *Terquain* to deal with wish poems and haiku. A similar listed program, *Write a Cinquain* (Pfluger, 1983), leads students through writing an adaptation of the five-line cinquain poem. Students write a noun on the first line, two adjectives describing it on the second, and three participles on the third. (TYPE A VERB THAT ENDS IN "ING," SUCH AS JUMPING OR SINGING. USE AN EXCITING WORD.) The fourth line contains a short phrase describing the subject, and the last line gives a noun that means the same thing, or nearly so, as the topic.

Sam, the fifth grader whose terquain is listed above, amplified it to create a cinquain, with a little help from the thesaurus.

```
                  WORK
          HOMEWORK, CLASSWORK
     SICKENING, SADDENING, SMARTENING
              HATE TO DO IT
                  LABOR
```

Pfluger suggests having children write poems about themselves, what they think they really are, how other people see them, and how they would like others to see them. Teachers might read volunteers' poems aloud, without mentioning the names, and have the class guess who wrote each poem.

```
                    LORRAINE
               HAPPY, AMBITIOUS
          CLIMBING, RACING, WINNING
            SOARS ABOVE THE CLOUDS
                     EAGLE
                                --grade 8
```

Terquains and cinquains offer an ideal opportunity to spin off a short adjunct lesson on parts of speech. Less able students may need help in this area.

Stephen Marcus (1983), the developer of *Compupoem,* noted that these poetry generators are best considered as prewriting instruments. They provide the means of producing rapid and copious first drafts, which can then be rewritten and refined, either on the screen through use of the poetry program or on paper. "The fact that students can easily produce first drafts proves to be a significant factor for those who find writing difficult, and especially for those who do not have the faintest idea how to write a poem" (p. 10).

Class Archives

Children love to see their writing in print. After completing a creative writing unit, many teachers type and reproduce a booklet of their students' creations. Constructing an electronic version of this class anthology can be an exciting project. Seeing your poem on ditto paper is not half as exciting as seeing it on the computer screen.

Class Anthology (See Appendix A) provides the building blocks for construction of an anthology of student-written poetry or prose. The program consists of little more than PRINT statements to print out the poems on the monitor screen. Even students who are rank beginners at BASIC programming can handle this simple task.

After Susan (grade 5) wrote her cinquain using the *Write a Cinquain* poetry generator, she printed it out on the classroom printer. Then she took the *Class Anthology* disk, booted it, and was presented with the menu page presented by the subprogram.

```
                CLASS ANTHOLOGY
               TABLE OF CONTENTS
                   ROOM 113
```

Directions: Choose one of the chapters of poems listed below. Type RUN X, then press ⟨RETURN⟩ (where X is the letter listed to the left of the chapter title).

```
A. HAIKU
B. TERQUAIN
C. CINQUAIN
D. CINQUAIN: HOLIDAYS
E. WISH POEMS
F. "ATTACK OF THE CUCUMBERS" (STORY)
M. INSTRUCTIONS FOR ADDING NEW POEMS
```

Susan already knew how to add a new poem, so she didn't bother to read the instructions. She typed LOAD C and pressed RETURN. After the disk drive came to a halt, she typed LIST. The program listing, filled with the commands to print dozens of poems written earlier, flashed by. The last lines of the program finally registered on the screen.

```
487 PRINT "              BY MARK ARMINIAN"
488 INPUT "PRESS ANY KEY TO GO ON.";A$
489 GET A$
```

Since prior poems had used up the first 489 lines, Susan decided to start her poem on line 490. She typed the following:

```
490 HOME
```

This commanded the Apple computer to clear the screen so her new poem could be printed.

```
491 PRINT "         HORSE"
492 PRINT "    BEAUTIFUL, STRONG"
493 PRINT "RUNNING, JUMPING, RACING"
494 PRINT " GALLOPS ALONG THE TRAIL"
495 PRINT "         FRIEND"
496 PRINT "              --BY SUSAN KIERA"
```

These lines of commands would create the poem on the screen, each set of words within quotes being printed on a separate line.

```
497 INPUT "PRESS ANY KEY TO GO ON.";A$
498 GET A$
```

This would print the PRESS ANY KEY message at the bottom of Susan's poem and allow the user to either keep Susan's words on the screen or to press a key to go on to the next poem, if there was one.

Susan then typed SAVE C (remember, C is the program name for the anthology of cinquain poems) and was finished. Her poem had been added to the class collection.

Composition Starters

The hardest step in any writing assignment is the first—actually getting started. Composition starters are programs designed to take students in a step-by-step fashion through the stages of choosing a topic, gathering important data, and organizing subtopics to form a unified composition. The students do the work. The program simply provides the organizing principles upon which the work is based.

Composition starters serve two valuable purposes. The first is the obvious purpose of helping students get started on a writing assignment. The second is more important, however: These programs serve as models of the composition process, demonstrating key principles of heuristics involved in the prewriting stage of composition. Rather than serving as a crutch for students to lean on, a well-planned composition-starter program provides a paradigm that will develop students' independence in writing. Hugh Burns (1983), developer of *Aristotle's Topics*, calls this process a duet, "A duet of language and thoughts, thoughts and language" (p. 7), in which generalized patterns of questions from the teacher (in this case, the computer) lead students through analysis of the chosen topic.

The following conversation between computer and student is part of one high schooler's session with *Aristotle's Topics*. It has been edited and abbreviated.

```
WOULD YOU BRIEFLY DESCRIBE THE PURPOSE
OF YOUR PAPER BY COMPLETING THIS STATEMENT:
THE PURPOSE OF THIS PAPER IS TO . . .
DESCRIBE WHAT LOYALTY IS.
WHAT ARE THE GOOD CONSEQUENCES OF
LOYALTY?
FRIENDSHIP, HELP, LOYALTY IN RETURN.
BY GEORGE, PAUL,
GOOD ONE.  WRITE A LITTLE MORE PLEASE.
LOYALTY IS NEEDED TO KEEP FRIENDS.
ANYTHING ELSE?
NO
DOES PUBLIC OPINION ABOUT
LOYALTY
DIFFER FROM PRIVATE OPINION?
YES
AHHH, SHORT AND SWEET.  NOW TELL ME WHY?
IN OTHER WORDS, ELABORATE A LITTLE.
PUBLICLY, PEOPLE SAY THAT WE MUST ALWAYS
BE LOYAL.
OKAY.
DO YOU WISH TO NARROW OR CHANGE YOUR SUBJECT?
(MAYBE REVISE THE WAY IT SOUNDS IN THOSE
QUESTIONS?)
YES
```

```
GOOD FOR YOU, PAUL.
NOT EVERY WRITER NARROWS OR CHANGES HIS OR
HER TOPIC THIS EARLY IN THE INVENTION
PROCESS.
PLEASE TYPE IN YOUR NEW SUBJECT.
```

Burns suggests that a computer program can imitate the subroutines involved in prewriting in a variety of ways. The program can be designed to do the following things:

1. Ask the question
2. Clarify the question
3. Define the question
4. Call attention to the composition's purpose
5. Purposefully distract to provide time for thought
6. Rephrase the question
7. Create metaphors
8. Offer research suggestions
9. Print a copy of the dialogue for later evaluation

Research at the college level on a composition starter indicated that students using it had more ideas about their topics than control-group students who brainstormed their topics without computer help (Burns, 1983). Perhaps one of the most exciting results from the study was that students reported that the best answers to the questions often occurred *after* the computer session, indicating that they were stimulated to continue thinking about their topics.

School Electronic Mail Systems

Everyone loves to receive mail. The newness of electronic mail systems adds even more to this enjoyment, and computer *bulletin boards* have sprouted across the country.

A bulletin board is a service operated with the use of a central computer to allow persons to send messages to one another. If User A wishes to send a message to User B, User A types a message into the central computer, often using a modem to enable his own computer to communicate with the central computer over telephone lines. The message is stored in a disk file, usually on a *hard disk* capable of storing much more information than the smaller floppy disks used in most microcomputers. The disk file with the message is stored under User B's name.

When User B checks into the central computer, he scans the listing of messages for any bearing his name, then orders the computer to display them.

Bulletin board services enjoy great popularity. There are hundreds in existence, most operated by computer hobbyists who enjoy providing this service to other hobbyists. Some local computer user groups operate bulletin boards for their own members to send messages to one another. Many of the bulletin boards store public domain programs on disk as well so that users can copy the programs to their own computers over the phone.

No one loves to receive mail more than children. Teachers can operate a simple bulletin board service in their own classrooms or schools. Children send and receive electronic messages. A variety of methods can be used to set up such a bulletin board.

The most efficient method is to use a networked linkage between computers in the classroom or school. Networks are discussed in Chapter 13. A good networking system offers bulletin board software that can be used to store and retrieve messages. The central network is a great convenience, as each microcomputer hooked into the network will be capable of directly accessing the central storage device, usually a large disk with great amounts of memory, which retains the message files.

Microcomputers in many businesses are already tied into networks. Employees can communicate memos and office mail instantaneously through electronic circuits. In ten years or so many schools may have the same facilities tying together their classrooms into a unified net.

Much the same effect can be obtained less expensively with microcomputers that are not linked together, as shown in the following example:

At 11:30 Susan put down her reader and walked back to the computer table at the rear of the classroom. Tom saw her coming and knew that his computer time was up, so he saved the composition he was editing onto his disk and made way for Susan to get started.

Susan leafed through the box of diskettes stored next to the computer and found the one with her name on it. She inserted it into the disk drive and checked the catalog. It read,

```
FROM BETTY
FROM ARLENE
WEEK'S ASSIGNMENT.
```

She loaded and quickly read the two personal messages. Betty wanted to remind her of the party on Saturday. Arlene needed to know whether Susan's father could drive them both to Girl Scouts on Thursday. Susan found Arlene's disk in the box of diskettes and wrote a confirmation, storing it under the file name FROM SUSAN. She reloaded her own disk and erased both messages, then looked at her teacher's message stored under WEEK'S ASSIGNMENT.

"Susan—Complete Lessons 3 to 5 on the Cloze Exercise Program. If you have any problems, see Mark for help. He did this assignment last week. Mrs. Aravian."

Susan was just about to load the cloze exercise disk when she remembered that Mrs. Aravian had asked the class to look at some poems written by children in the fourth grade class across the hall. She found the disk that had been sent from the fourth graders and loaded several of the poems. One about trees was particularly good. After copying it onto her own disk for future reference, she settled down into her exercise.

The electronic mail system described in Mrs. Aravian's class is awkward, involving a great deal of shuffling between disks, since the system has no permanent central memory unit. It is highly motivational, however. Students will be more than happy to send message after message to one another, preferring it even over speaking to one another in class (just as passing notes during class is invariably preferable). The system is far from perfect, but teachers find it to be worth the effort to maintain.

Encourage children to use the mail system to share compositions and creative writings. Such a setup can even be used for peer editing of compositions, as files stored on disk can be changed using the word processor.

Electronic Mailbox, printed in Appendix A, is a simple version of a classroom electronic mail system. Children can type short messages to one another and store them in the computer's memory. A variety of creative activities can be carried out using this program. On one day children can bring in jokes and fill each mailbox with a different joke or riddle. On another day you can fill the mailbox with brainteasers for students to solve. During holidays children can send greetings to one another, electronic valentines, Christmas/Chanukah cards, or June "See You in September" farewells.

Writing Student Manuals

"How can I delete this file?" "I turned on the computer and nothing happens!" "The program just stopped and won't do a thing!" The constant barrage of questions and problems soon wears on most teachers. They begin to wonder whether it's all worth it. Sure, the computer is a great tool, but sometimes it seems to be too much trouble.

One partial solution is to provide manuals designed to explain frequently encountered problems, written at the children's level, but design of such manuals takes time.

Instead, have your students do the work. The activity will give them valuable experience in the reading/writing skills involved in following directions. They will be writing for a specific audience. The purpose is clear, and the feedback will be too. If directions are ambiguous or unsatisfactory in other ways, the writers will soon hear about it. Here are some ideas:

1. Choose a standard-size manual for ease of storage. Unlined 5 by 8 inch file cards are a handy size and readily available. Your manuals should be small, since table space is often limited in computer work areas.
2. Punch holes in the top or side of the cards through which metal rings or loops of string can be inserted. These manuals will lie flat, and pages can be flipped over to the back of the book so that less table space is used.

3. Make plenty of extra blank pages and keep them handy. Student authors should be responsible for keeping the manuals up to date, carrying out revisions when mistakes are found. Rewriting of the manuals should be an ongoing process, as newer and better ways of expressing the directions are developed.
4. Provide covers of colored poster board. This makes it easier to close the book to its cover when finished. If the manuals are long and involved, poster board dividers may be placed between the sections.
5. Print with felt-tipped pens. Manuals must be attractive and neat. A design can be drawn on the cover.
6. Use round paper reinforcements to strengthen the punched holes, right from the start. This will help keep pages from falling out later and getting lost.
7. Stand the manuals up on a shelf or hang them from hooks through their metal rings. They should be readily accessible.

Insist that students consult the manuals first before asking you a question. If a student does ask a question about an issue discussed in one of the manuals, refer him to that manual. Remember, following directions is a valuable skill and needs to be practiced. Teachers are often too quick to lift this responsibility from the students' shoulders, thereby increasing student dependence upon the teacher. Foster independence by helping students get into the habit of reading the directions *before* all else fails.

Manuals should be written on a variety of topics and may be coded by cover color. Green covers may contain information on use of hardware, blue on vocabulary exercises, red on word processing, and brown on programming.

Choose-Your-Own-Ending Stories

Choose-your-own-ending stories are popular with children, giving them a sense of control and involvement otherwise lacking in fiction. In a sense they create their own story lines by choosing from lists of options provided by authors. These books are a simple form of interactive fiction, for the reader has a degree of control over the plot.

Your Choice (see Appendix A) presents a very simple program outline for an activity in which students employ simple programming skills to write their own electronic choose-your-own-ending stories. This activity is set up so that students need to know very little programming. Only a few basic principles have to be followed, once the teacher has typed the program outline and saved it on a master disk. Student authors then copy the program onto their own disks and create the story using the master outline.

Step 1. Type the title of your story on line 20 using a PRINT statement:

```
20 PRINT "THE KLARNON ATTACK ON EARTH"
```

Step 2.   Type the authors' names on line 30 using a PRINT statement.

```
30 PRINT "BY ANDREW ADAMS AND STEVEN SERVIDSKI"
```

Step 3.   Use PRINT statements to write the first screen page of the story on the even numbered lines 102 to 140.

```
102 PRINT "    IN THE YEAR 2050 OUR STARSHIP"
104 PRINT "WAS PATROLLING IN THE DELTA QUADRANT"
106 PRINT "OF THE GALAXY.  MR. ROCK, SECOND"
108 PRINT "OFFICER, SPOTTED AN ENEMY KLARNON"
110 PRINT "FLEET APPROACHING EARTH."
```

First, the number of letters and spaces in each PRINT line must not exceed the number of characters allowable on the screen. Apple II's, for example, allow 40 characters to be printed on one line. If the PRINT line has more than 40, there will be a wrap-around problem; that is, part of the line will be split off and printed below the first part.

Second, print only on even-numbered lines. If in the future you wish to modify the program (for example, to provide double spacing for easier reading), modifications can be made on the odd-numbered lines.

Third, the number of lines to be printed on each page must not exceed the page height. Apple II's allow 23 lines to be displayed on a screen page. If you try to squeeze in 24, the top line will disappear off the top of the screen. Space must be left for the program options to be printed at the bottom of the page. By printing on even-numbered lines between 102 and 140, the screen page will include a maximum of 20 text lines, with room for three extra lines at the bottom to be used if necessary.

Step 4.   Think of three options for readers to choose for their next plot element. Insert brief descriptions in lines 155, 160, and 165. Remember, the total number of characters within the quotes must not exceed the screen width allowable by your computer, or else there will be a wrap-around problem.

```
155 PRINT "PRESS 'A' TO DESTROY THE KLARNONS."
160 PRINT "PRESS 'B' TO RETREAT TO EARTH."
165 PRINT "PRESS 'C' TO HIDE IN THE ASTEROIDS."
```

Step 5.   Repeat Step 3 for each of the three options. Option A would be provided in PRINT statements between lines 202 and 240, option B between 302 and 340, and option C between 402 and 440. Each of the three options would in turn offer three more options.

By the end of this program, students would have constructed a total of 13 screen pages ordered in the hierarchy listed in Figure 12–2. While this may appear to be complicated, the actual writing of the program can be easily understood by students who have an introductory knowledge of

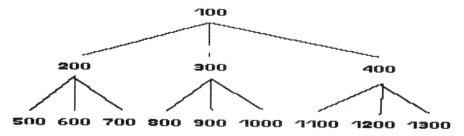

FIGURE 12–2. Choose-your-own-ending program structure

BASIC programming. The most difficult part of it is to be sure that no PRINT statement includes more than the appropriate number of characters and spaces. Care in counting is all that's required.

Teachers or students may want to modify this program. One suggested modification for older students is to allow for longer options. Several screen pages can be provided for each optional story section. Another modification is to provide for linkages between the branches of the story structure. Perhaps two different options provided by the first choice can lead to the same ending. In addition, there is no limit to the complexity and length of the story. Some students may even write stories so complex that they must be stored in separate files on disk because of computer memory limitations!

Once programmed and saved on disk, these stories can be read and shared for years to come.

SPELLING SOFTWARE

Children quickly realize that in some ways the computer is a very dumb device. Make a simple typing mistake, like spelling your name Mxry, and the computer may well call you Mxry for the remainder of the program. If the computer asks, "In which state were the battles of Lexington and Concord fought?" and you type in "Masachusetts," you are wrong. No ifs, ands, or buts—wrong.

By its very nature, use of computers encourages exactness by showing how important spelling is to communication. Computers simply do not recognize the *intent* of a message. They recognize the *content*. And if that content is inexact, communication fails.

A variety of programs are available that purport to teach spelling. The fact of the matter is that we really do not know what makes a good speller. Some people seem to learn, and some do not. A few generalizations can be made, however. Exposure to a great deal of printed material probably improves spelling. Teaching all the incredibly complicated rules of English spelling is probably useless. If spelling is to be improved, a good deal of time (60 to 75 minutes per week) should be devoted to it in the classroom (Fitzsimmons and Loomer, 1978). Especially with older students, a diagnostic approach to spelling is most efficient. That is, target the words that each student has problems with.

Most spelling software differs only in the form in which the student is told what word must be spelled. Each should include a printed listing of the spelling words used, for teacher reference. Some programs include teacher utility packages so that the teacher may create his or her own personal spelling lists.

Word Scrambler Super Speller flashes the target word on the screen. Students must then type the word correctly. If the spelling is incorrect, the word must be respelled five times with the word shown on the screen and once without. Whether this tests spelling or quickness of visual perception of the flashed word is questionable. An additional option flashes the word with letters scrambled. *Spelling Quiz1* (see Appendix A) is a simpler spelling program with some similar features. Teachers can type it into their computer.

Spelling Bee and Reading Primer has two spelling programs on its disk. One is a tutorial in which a picture appears on the screen and the word representing that picture is flashed. The student must respell the word. Of course this form of problem presentation is limited to words that can be clearly portrayed pictorially. In the drill program, only the picture appears. No misspelled word is allowed to appear on the screen as the student types, an important feature. If misspelled words appear in spelling programs, an undesirable lasting impression may be made on the student.

Wordwatch succumbs to this critical error in program design. One of its subprograms, *Hide n' Spell*, displays four words on the screen. Students must choose which is misspelled. Remember when *you* used to be a good speller, before you started reading youngsters' compositions and learned their mistakes?

Comprehensive spelling programs are also available, with a scope wide enough to replace the traditional classroom spelling curriculum. *Fundamental Spelling Words in Context* is a set of six disks that teaches 5,280 spelling words for grades 1 to 8. Words are flashed on the screen. Then a contextual sentence appears with a blank to be filled in by the spelling word. It is unclear whether giving the context particularly helps spelling. It may even divert attention from the objective. *Fundamental Spelling* also recycles incorrectly spelled words at the end of each lesson for reinforcement.

Spelling Strategy emphasizes the visualization of words. For some strange reason, words are first presented three letters at a time. It would make more sense to divide the words according to syllables. Once the word has been visualized, students spell it backward, drawing upon their memory of the visualized word image. *Spelling Quiz2* (see Appendix A) also requires visualization and reverse spelling and can be typed into the computer by teachers.

13

THE MICROCOMPUTER READING LAB

As microcomputers were first introduced in educational settings, most schools considered themselves lucky if they had one microcomputer to devote to reading instruction. Rapidly declining costs soon made it more feasible to assemble a bank of micros in the reading lab for development and remediation. During the introductory years of the electronic calculator in the early 1970s, prices declined 55% each year. If microcomputer developments follow that course, quality micros will be available for $100 within five years. Just as many reading labs today have a wall of carrels with reading machines, the far more flexible micros will come to occupy a place of central importance in reading instruction.

This chapter discusses microcomputer laboratories, though most of the issues are just as applicable to classrooms with only one or two micros. Centralization of microcomputers within a school or within a subject-area department offers many advantages over placing individual micros in separate classrooms. Their use and care can be supervised more efficiently. Only one software library has to be established and monitored. With proper scheduling, each micro can be kept in use most of the time.

Proper research and planning is important for a successful micro lab, especially because of the tremendous financial investments involved. A little money spent to provide expert consultants can result in a great deal of money saved in hardware costs. In the *Book of the World's Worst Decisions*, David Frost (1983) recounted the story of the Nigerian government's 1974 Third National Plan, a massive effort to make Nigeria one of the world's most developed nations. Planners ordered 20 million tons of cement to build new roads and buildings.

As freighters laden with cement arrived at Lagos, the government planners realized that the docks were capable of handling only a couple of thousand tons a day. Working every day, it would have taken 27 years to unload the ships waiting at one point off the Nigerian coast with one-third of the world's entire supply of cement hardening in their holds. Don't make problems for yourself. Plan first.

ORGANIZATION FOR INSTRUCTION

What factors need to be taken into consideration when planning a microcomputer reading lab? A four-step plan of action would include the following:

1. Determination of resources
2. Goal planning
3. Implementation
4. Ongoing evaluation

After discussion of these four steps, several special concerns about microcomputer labs will be singled out for elaboration. The first concern is organizing your classroom around a "networking system" in which all computers are linked together. The second is the problem of providing "backup" copies of software for continuity of instruction in the event your disks are damaged or lost. The third concern—one often ignored—is maintaining your computers in good condition. Finally, we will deal briefly with a number of other matters important to smooth operation of a lab.

Determination of Resources

A reading supervisor in charge of developing a new curriculum has two basic resources to consider, people and money. Both are vitally necessary for any educational change—appropriately trained teachers and aides must have the time to develop and implement the curriculum, and they must have the money to purchase necessary materials and supplies. Before leaping off into the unknown, supervisors should have realistic ideas of just what they have to work with.

First and foremost, teachers must be willing to devote their energies to learning about microcomputer instruction. They need to be enthusiastic and convinced of the effectiveness of their tasks. Not all teachers are particularly optimistic about technology in education. Not all teachers are willing to change their tried and true teaching methodologies, nor are all teachers able to devote the time necessary to learn the ins and outs of the varied software programs that would be available in a full lab setting. If the faculty is not ready and able to do the job, there is not much sense in even trying to organize a micro program on a large scale. Keep in mind the disastrous consequences of the "open experience" programs of the late 1960s, when unprepared faculty were dumped en masse into instructional settings foreign to them both in terms of procedures and philosophies. If training is necessary, often the district or regional educational offices will be able to provide competent, experienced teacher trainers. If not, local college education departments may be of help—many are now instituting graduate courses in "microcomputers in reading and language arts." More general courses in micros and education may be less useful, concentrating on programming instruction rather than on use of the computer to teach skill or content subjects. Another source of training may be the local computer store. Radio Shack, the maker of the TRS–80, has led the way among computer distributors and manufacturers, making available free training classes to educators. Apple has also developed an introductory multimedia program, which is available through its area offices.

The most important issue to keep in mind when dealing with the introduction of any dramatically new instructional technique is depth of training. Giving teachers a one-day workshop on use of microcomputers might be worse than nothing. Without time to fiddle around with the things, to run a few sample programs, and in general to become comfortable with them, most people (teachers included) are understandably intimidated. After all, it wasn't very long ago that computers were the exclusive domain of the hermit-like creatures who crawled around university computer center basements at all hours of the night. Novices need time and patience, and—since it is hardly fair to expect teachers to bear the burden of this additional training themselves—monetary compensation for their time.

Despite criticism of the American tendency to "throw money at problems" in an attempt to solve them, it's surprising how little can be accomplished without the stuff. Money, while it does not automatically solve problems, is needed both for materials and for faculty. Without proper financial planning, a micro lab can turn into a white elephant. Coburn et al. (1982) describes the bitter disappointment of students who, expecting to use the new micros purchased by the school and featured in the local newspapers, find that the school has made no provisions for software purchases or for repair of the machines when they break down.

Hardware and software purchasing issues have been discussed earlier in this book, but planning for the purchase of materials is only the first step of financial forethought. Arrangements must also be made for these costs:

1. Periodic preventive maintenance
2. Repairs
3. Replacement of damaged software
4. Future purchase of software
5. Replacement of outdated or worn out hardware

Trusting to luck to keep such expenses at bay will not do. While microcomputers are surprisingly durable—having few moving parts to break down—the inevitable will eventually occur. To have thousands of dollars in hardware sitting unusable in a closet because no one has the hundred dollars necessary for repair is wasteful in the extreme.

Where is the money to come from? The fact of the matter is that the availability of grant money for computer education has been much overstated in the press. Pennsylvania, for example, allotted $800,000 for computer education, an impressive and well-publicized figure, but try dividing that amount by the number of schools in the state. You come out with only a few hundred dollars for each—hardly enough to matter much. Unless the nation makes a strong commitment to technological education, a doubtful possibility in light of recent conservative trends, the financial support for microcomputers must come from the local district and be backed by local tax dollars. The PTA's cake sale won't go very far in buying what is needed.

This is not to say that districts or individual teachers should overlook the possibility of acquiring grant money to fund their programs. Most computer manufacturers support foundations that provide money and hardware for educational purposes. Your grant application must be unique and quite innovative for serious consideration, however. Apple Corporation is not going to supply Mrs. Jones with five micros for her remedial reading class. After all, there are thousands of equally deserving "Mrs. Joneses" out there. Mrs. Jones will first have to demonstrate that she will use the Apples in a creative fashion, demonstrating a new and exciting use (and, therefore, one more potential market) for the Apple.

Goal Planning

Goals are developed to meet specific needs. What target group will benefit from the reading computer lab? What are their needs? This preliminary diagnosis is vital—irreversible policy and purchasing decisions must be made *before* the beginning of the program. You won't be able to switch microcomputer models once you've begun instruction, nor will you be able to buy all new software.

Consider each of the following issues:

Age level of students.   Materials should be age-appropriate, neither too childish nor too adult. The easy availability of Hi-Lo (high interest, low level—for older remedial readers) materials in print far exceeds present Hi-Lo software. Publishers are still trying to catch up with demands for quality programs for the large developmental reading audience. It will be some time before much is available for the smaller cohort of older remedials.

Range of ability levels of students.   One of the key principles (Heilman, 1977) of reading instruction involves giving youngsters reading material with which they can succeed and be challenged (that is, at their instructional level). Be prepared to spend a good deal of money on developing a software library that meets the range of these ability levels. Some experts on computers in education are recommending that schools budget twice as much for software as they plan to spend on hardware. While this recommendation might be somewhat exaggerated, a reading lab with the flexibility to meet all students' needs will need a great variety of software.

Skill needs of students.   A preliminary survey of skill needs of representative students will enable your software evaluators to target their attention to the most valuable materials. Another factor to be determined involves the integration of microcomputer instruction with standard printed materials. Software should complement, not duplicate, books, workbooks, and other printed materials with which students will be working.

Interests of students.   As was pointed out rather forcefully to one well-meaning teacher, *Vocabulary Baseball* is a motivational flop with students of English as a second language, unless they happen to come from a baseball mecca such as Puerto Rico or Japan.

Keep in mind that the greater are the ranges of age, ability, skill needs, and interests among your students, the more money you will need to budget for software purchase.

Philosophy of reading instruction.   A reading lab designed to emphasize holistic instruction—the interrelationship of the varied language arts in meaningful contexts—will of necessity be arranged differently from a lab centered on subskill development. Some subskill proponents are already envisioning a future in which each student can be plugged into his or her micro station to drill, drill, drill on the tremendous variety of phonics skills. A microcomputer lab, with all stations connected by cable to the teacher's monitor "master" computer and with the computer itself regularly reporting on progress and adapting instruction to diagnosed needs, lends itself to the purpose of the massive subskill management systems such as the Wisconsin Design, the Prescriptive Reading Inventory, and others.

On the other hand, those teachers whose educational philosophies demand a more open holistic approach that integrates all the language arts of reading, writing, listening, and speaking will require a more flexible reading lab construction, with an increased ability to vary types of microcomputer programs applicable to those varied areas. A networking system that limits this flexibility would be inappropriate.

Teacher functions.   If the teacher is to be more than a software librarian and security guard, some attention must be paid to relieving him or her of the pressure of those functions. Networking systems can provide such relief by doing away with the need for separate diskettes for each station. Network 2, for example, allows the word processor *SCRIPSIT* to be accessed by each student directly from the teacher's own disk drives, rather than requiring a separate disk for each student.

Management of instruction.   If monitoring of student progress and systematization of instruction are important concerns, software that provides such services should be selected. A little more money paid for programs that incorporate management systems may save hundreds of hours of teacher time over the long run.

Number of students and scheduling.   While some software lends itself to grouping two or three students on a single computer at the same time, other software is amenable only to individual use. Class size must be adjusted accordingly, and scheduling should be realistic.

Service to the school beyond language arts. To be cost effective, the school's computers should be kept smoking—in use as much as possible. Can content area courses use the micro lab as a resource room during the reading specialist's free period? Will students be allowed to come in early or stay late in order to work on the computer? Would the local adult school be interested in using the lab for computer courses in the evening and on weekends in return for some financial reimbursement? Is a teacher willing to sponsor a school-wide computer club? Such varied uses help justify the expense and make district boards of education more willing to spend the necessary money.

Implementation

The key to beginning any new project in education is realism. The reading teacher in charge of a micro lab needs to be realistic about the many factors involved, both curricular factors and teacher/student factors. Too many micro labs have been started with wide-eyed optimism about effects of microcomputer instruction on achievement, or about teacher or student enthusiasm for the project. Unconsidered assumptions about the lab (for example, projections of major achievement gains or expectations that teachers and students will be so enthusiastic that the lab will practically "run itself") lead to bitter disappointment.

Unless you have had prior experience in curriculum implementation (of any type—not necessarily only in microcomputers), it is best to start small and gradually work into a major program. It's also important to have someone to whom you can go for advice—whether it be the high school computer supervisor, a local college or university, a computer enthusiast on the faculty, or a paid outside consultant. The formation of a community advisory group made up of parents and other interested members of your community might be invaluable.

Ongoing Evaluation

Finally, plans must be made for continuing evaluation of the effectiveness of the microlab. No educational curriculum works flawlessly the first time it is put into operation. Provision for evaluation and for implementation of changes should be planned in advance.

SPECIAL CONCERNS

Networking

Imagine the poor reading teacher, tossing and turning in bed, in the midst of a nightmare. Hordes of raving floppy disks are pouring out of the walls, attacking in maddened waves! Hundreds—no, thousands!—of 5¼-inch plastic circles are overwhelming the defenses! A scream of panic is heard: "Oh, help! They're all over me!" She awakens to find herself in her micro reading lab—and the nightmare is true! Dozens of diskettes are lying all over—demanding a time-consuming, laborious organizational system that is enough to tax the sanity of anyone who lacks the single-minded dedication of a full-time librarian.

Don't panic. A solution, though as yet very imperfect, is at hand. Imagine again:

Students enter the micro reading lab and immediately key into the classroom's central message system on their terminals. Each student has a computer-generated note specifying the day's assignments or options. Perhaps the note includes a short personal admonition or word of encouragement from the teacher as well.

John sees that he has an electronic mail "letter" from Paul, his friend in another class. "Can you look over my article on 'Motocross' for the next issue of the reading center's newspaper? I think it needs some editing. File B605. Thanx." John keys into the file, which is stored on an open account (that is, no secret password needed) on the lab's central storage disk, makes a few spelling and grammar changes, then orders the corrected file to be stored in Paul's private account.

John then looks at the note from his teacher. "You've been doing very well the past few weeks, John. How about we move you up to the Blue Level in your comprehension program? Start with Lesson 3—Inferential Strategies." He keys in the proper commands and starts work on the reading lesson.

Later that period, his teacher Mrs. Jones, sitting behind her own micro, asks the computer for a progress report on the students. She sees that several students have been having trouble with their lessons on finding main ideas, so she breaks into their programs to ask if they would like some help. Karen indicates she wants to keep trying on her own for now, but Mike and Sally ask for a conference.

Mrs. Jones suggests that they meet in the back of the room in three minutes. She goes to her file cabinet and pulls out some activities on making inferences, then notices a flashing signal on her monitor. John has run into some trouble and is asking for help. She types in that she will be with him in ten minutes or so—Why doesn't he check with Randy, who is working on the same thing?

And so on. There are no worries about managing dozens of pieces of software, because all software is immediately accessible to each student on a central disk storage system. Supervision and the checking of student progress can be handled without the teacher's ever moving from behind her own computer. All computers in the classroom are interconnected so as to provide instant communication between students and teacher.

The possibilities in such a setup are almost endless. Students might be able to hook up with other schools over telephone lines, or with national educational computing services. Rather than working as isolated individuals at separate terminals, students can work together on research or writing projects. An on-line class newspaper, with articles changing daily, can be accessible to all students.

Is this a futuristic dream? No. Your micro lab can be run in such a manner, if you so desire. To date, however, there are significant complications and disadvantages to this *networking* system. Decisions to network your classroom must be made strategically.

What is networking?

A *network* is a system in which microcomputers are interconnected by wires. The term has come to be used for a wide variety of such systems (Watt, 1983).

Local and remote.   Local networks are interconnected within the same classroom or building. Remote networks connect machines that are separated geographically, usually through telephone lines. Local networks are of most interest to classroom teachers. There are two types:

1. Resource-sharing networks: A number of micros are hooked up to the same peripherals, such as printers or disk drives.
2. Communication networks: In addition to resource sharing, users are able to communicate to one another, either live or by way of messages stored on a central disk (also called "electronic mail").

Resource-sharing networks.   Master-slave resource-sharing networks are the simplest, the cheapest, and the most limited. In the TRS–80 Network 3, for example, up to 16 "slave" micros can be connected to a "master" micro equipped with a controller and special software. Only the master has to have disk drives, a considerable savings in hardware costs. Software is accessed through the master computer, loaded into the memory of each slave, and used by the student.

The major disadvantage of such a system is its inability to run different software at the same time. Students may only access whatever is in the master computer. If the master contains a phonics program with three lessons, for example, students may access any of the three lessons, but no student using the system is able to use a word processing program: Choice must be made from the phonics program. This limitation defeats the very concept of individualization, for each student in the class must be doing more or less the same thing, though different rates of progress are allowed to some extent.

This problem may be solved by equipping all computers with disk drives or cassette recorders. Each micro may then be used as a slave— hooked into the master computer's program—or as an independent micro station, using software in its own disk drive. Of course, when this system is used, the financial advantages of the master-slave system are eliminated.

Another disadvantage of the master-slave system is that not all software lends itself to its use. For example, any software that reaccesses the disk (that is, goes back to the disk for more information, thereby replacing whatever had been in the computer's memory) is unusable unless modified by the publisher. Since much of the more sophisticated educational software is of this variety, a very real limitation is imposed.

The only real advantage of such a system lies in whole-class instructional methodologies. If the teacher decides that every student on each micro will be working on the same software, a master-slave system in which the software has to be loaded into only one computer is a lot easier to handle than going around to every disk drive and individually booting the same disk over and over.

The rationale of having every student do the same thing in the name of computerized individualization is questionable. Such systems are only justifiable in reading if all students in the class are at the same level, have the same reading skill needs, and have similar interests, a rather unlikely circumstance. There are exceptions to this general rule. One example could be writing centers in which all students will be using a word processing program for composition. The word processor must, however, be specially modified for network use, a factor that eliminates most processors from consideration. Network 3 allows a special version of the word processor *SCRIPSIT* to be used.

Communication networks. The communication network represents a major step beyond resource sharing, though some limitations still exist. One is cost. The Corvus Omninet system, for example, costs more than $3,000, but it eliminates the need for all but one or two disk drives with its hard-disk software storage system. With a system of ten or more Apples, a Corvus *hard-disk* system costs less than purchasing a floppy disk drive for each Apple (Daniel Watt, 1983).

Hard-disk (often called *Winchester*) systems consist of an aluminum disk coated with a magnetic recording medium, encased in its own unit. The read/write head of the disk drive is encased in a sealed housing with the disk so that damaging dust or smoke particles cannot enter. A 5¼-inch Winchester drive may hold 5 million bytes or more of programs and data—enough room for a very healthy collection of reading software. Bigger systems are also available.

In theory, then, a Winchester drive system can support a number of micros, each of which can access any of the software programs stored on the hard disk. Students can work independently, choosing whatever programs they have been assigned. Systems such as Corvus Omninet allow students to send and receive electronic mail messages, as well.

In practice there are some problems with hard-disk technology. As yet, its appeal to schools has been limited because of its expense. As a result, most manufacturers of hard disks are not equipped to supply schools with necessary support services. In addition, there are serious technical quirks that suggest that anyone choosing to use such a system must be knowledgeable about computer hardware (The, 1983). Schools interested in such technology should deal only with manufacturers who are specializing in educational applications.

Software Connections, for example, has been developing a software program called *Classroom Monitor* for the Corvus Omninet system. The program allows teachers to send short messages (less than 40 characters) to individual students, interrupting the student at work. (This feature is not available in simpler electronic mail systems, where the student must first check his "mail box" to determine whether any messages have been left for him.) Teachers can also use their own computer console to covertly observe the students at work.

The most serious limitation of hard-disk systems involves the limited availability of software. Most educational software is "copy protected," eliminating the possibility of moving the program from the diskette sold by the software publisher to your own hard-disk storage system. Publishers do not want software to be copied illegally, so computer programmers incorporate sophisticated protection devices into their software in order to make such copying (called making a *backup* if done legally, and *software piracy* if illegally) difficult or impossible (see section on backups later in this chapter).

While at present there is no way around this dilemma, innovative software companies are already working on the problem. Unicom of Providence, Rhode Island, for instance, is adapting copy-protected software to the Corvus Omninet system for Apple computers. The procedure is quite complex, with legal arrangements to be negotiated between Unicom and the software producers, an unprotected copy of the program added to the Unicom network, then protection resupplied so the program cannot be copied by users.

Once a school system contracts with Unicom, it is locked into the Unicom system for the long term. Only Unicom-modified software can be used on the system, so that the school is severely limited in terms of instructional flexibility. Any school engaging with such a supplier must be dedicated to the software provided by that supplier before contracting.

Networking is a technological development toward which microcomputer instruction is moving, because of the benefits of interaction among computers, vast storage capabilities that allow many programs to be accessible from a single disk system, and convenience of software management. For the next several years, it appears that the technology is not sufficiently advanced for useful application in reading and language arts micro labs, since flexibility in terms of software choice is severely impaired and the cost of an effective system is high. As networking systems increase in sophistication and suitability, the following checklist will be useful for evaluation purposes:

1. Does the system allow different students to work on different software at the same time? If not, are you willing to center your instruction on a single software program at a time in a large-group approach to microcomputer instruction?

2. Is the system easier to use than a system in which each micro station has its own cassette recorder or disk drive? That is, would the lab's overall efficiency be increased enough to compensate for increased costs?

3. Does the software you want to use (or might want to use in the future) work on the system?

4. How much storage space does the central storage unit (usually a hard-disk drive) have? Is this sufficient for your needs, present and future?

5. Does the system allow messages to be sent from student micros to the teacher's micro, and vice versa? If it does, will you use that capability enough to justify its expense? (It might be easier, and perhaps more "human," simply to walk over to the student's desk and hold a short conversation.)

6. Does the system allow the teacher to look in on a student's work, unbeknownst to the student? If so, will you use that capability? (Some teachers and students might dislike the "Big Brother" aspect of such monitoring. Also, much the same result can be obtained simply by walking around the room and observing the students at work.)

7. Does the system provide security devices to prohibit a student from tampering with another student's files, or with the instructional software stored on the central storage unit, or with your grade management system?

8. Is there an electronic mail system in which students and teachers can write notes to one another? Such a system works well as a motivational device, though its actual usefulness as compared with sending paper notes is somewhat debatable.

Backup!

Someone has said that the three rules of computing are:

1. Backup!
2. Backup!
3. Backup!

It seems that everyone has to learn the hard way, by accidentally erasing a file of data or damaging a disk of word processing files. Sooner or later the inevitable will happen. Something you have spent hours or days working on is irretrievably lost.

The solution is to create *backups*—second and even third copies of programs or files. Many users make two backup copies, one on a disk stored separately from the first copy and one *hard-copy* version (printed on paper). Some materials might be important enough to have three or more backups.

Backups of instructional software are just as essential. Children find a multitude of ways to damage disks accidentally—and some might even be inclined to intentional sabotage. Fingerprints on the exposed section of the disk, writing in pen or pencil with a disk below the paper, dropping the disk onto a dusty floor, losing it—the list of possibilities can go on and on.

What will you do if your one copy of the central instructional program for your classroom is ruined? If you have a backup or two stored away, it's no problem. If not, you could be in for a wait of weeks while the software publisher mails you a replacement or a wait of months while you wait for your school to provide money to purchase a replacement.

The solution: Insist on backups. Publishers handle this matter in different ways, some of which are completely unsatisfactory. For example, some insist that you mail your copy back to them and wait until they get around to returning a new copy. Meanwhile, your computers sit idle. This might be satisfactory for the less important software in your classroom but certainly not for any programs you use on a daily basis. Other publishers make no provisions at all for damaged disks—you have to buy a new one at the original price.

More reasonable methods include making available extra backup copies at nominal cost (that is, about the price of a blank disk). Keep at least two on hand. Make sure that you can purchase these backups at any time. Some publishers require that you purchase the extras immediately after the initial purchase, but this procedure is of no help to you a year later when both your backups have been ruined.

Fortunately, some publishers are realizing that it is unreasonable to *copy protect* their materials. Copy protection involves incorporating programming tricks into the software that make it impossible for the user to copy the software using standard copying techniques. Publishers copy protect their software because they do not want people who have not paid for it to use it. Such software piracy is widespread. Popular programs like *VisiCalc* are estimated to have more illegal pirated copies floating around than legally purchased programs, so the fear of piracy is legitimate. Special copying programs like *Locksmith*, *Nibbles Away*, and *Copy II* are specially designed to defeat copy protection schemes so that virtually any program in existence can be duplicated.

While software pirates often justify their copying by pointing to exorbitant software prices and to the importance of maintaining backups, schools need to be careful about using illegal materials. Software copying is just as illegal as photocopying copyrighted materials, and software publishers are said to be willing to sue institutions and individuals engaging in the practice. A much better practice is to insist that publishers from whom you purchase materials follow these guidelines:

1. A single school should have to pay full price for a piece of software only once for each classroom in which it will be used. If the same software will be used in several classrooms within the school, very sizable discounts (or very reasonable prices) should be available.

2. If a disk is damaged, the software must be *immediately* replaceable. That is, backup copies purchased at minimal cost must be available in the school. At no time should a school be forced to wait for replacement copies to arrive by mail or to buy replacement software at full price.

A fair statement of the mutual rights and responsibilities of schools and publishers has been developed by the International Reading Association Computer Technology and Reading Committee (1984). Schools have the responsibility to avoid cheating publishers. Publishers have the responsibility to develop reasonable pricing and consumer policies. The committee's concluding statement sums up potential results of the present antagonistic relationship between computer-using teachers and software publishers: "Without mutual trust and cooperation on this important issue both parties will suffer and, ultimately, so will the learner" (p. 82).

Maintenance

Computers are like automobiles in that preventive maintenance goes a long way toward reducing breakdowns. Here are some important considerations in the use and care of your computers:

1. Dust causes damage. Dust of any kind—chalk dust, road dust, smoke—will damage your computer and your disks. Use a transparency projector or white marker board rather than a blackboard, if possible. At any rate, keep machines and disks covered when they are not in use. Some people use electrostatic air cleaners, especially if they smoke. This should not be a problem in a school micro lab, of course.

2. Carpeting sometimes creates static electricity, which may affect your computer's operation or even erase diskettes when they are touched. If this is a problem, check with your computer store for remedies.

3. Install fans in computers to avoid overheating. Some brands are more susceptible than others, but if you plan to use your micros for continuous periods of time (as you should!), look into purchasing individual fans to be installed in each. Some brands are sold with built-in fans.

4. If your computer is the type that can be opened up to expose the inside works (such as Apple and Franklin), and if you start fooling around with the inside components while the power is on, *the world will end!* (Translation from computer jargon to ordinary English: You might electrocute yourself or, more likely, destroy the main board of the computer.)

5. The more you move your computer around, the greater the chance for damage, especially to mechanical parts in disk drives and printers. Purchase movable work stations to roll the micros from classroom to classroom. Keep the original cardboard containers, with foam padding, to use for transportation outside the building. Special cases for transportation of computers are available for purchase.

6. If power surges are a problem in your area, surge protection devices are necessary to guard your computers and software.

7. Make arrangements with a local computer servicing center (preferably the store where you purchased the micros) for prompt repairs.

If something goes wrong:

1. Read the manual *first.* Try to figure out the problem yourself before bothering someone else for advice.

2. Check all the connections. Make sure everything is plugged in and that outlets are working.

3. If your computer's internal workings are accessible, push down with moderate firmness on each of the chips and internal boards. *Make sure the power is off!*

4. If your computer's workings are accessible, clean the gold-colored contacts on internal boards with a pencil eraser. *Make sure the power is off!*

5. Diagnose by process of elimination. For example, if you can't get your printer to work, the problem could be in the software, the computer, the interface (connection) between computer and printer, your commands

to the printer, or the printer itself. Try each out in turn with alternate equipment, software, or commands.

6. Check with your in-building or school system experts.
7. Call your computer store or software publisher for advice.

Other Uses for the Computer Center

A room full of thousands of dollars of computer equipment should not be left idle at any time, day or evening, expecially not in these days when there is such a great demand for training in and use of computers.

While the primary use of a reading and language arts micro lab would, of course, be instruction in related areas, a variety of possible uses can fill those hours when the lab is not being used for its primary purpose.

A. During school hours
   1. School secretarial work (for example, mailing lists, data base records)
   2. Administrative work (scheduling)
   3. Faculty work (word processing of handouts, tests; grading records)
   4. Computer literacy training—usually in BASIC, the native language of most micros. The more flexible, more expensive micros also make such languages as LOGO (for younger students) and Pascal (for secondary students) available.
   5. Computer graphics work for art classes
   6. Simulation game experiences for content area classes (science, health, social studies)
B. Before and after school
   1. Computer club
   2. Supplementary computing courses
   3. Supervised free laboratory use
   4. School newspaper editing
   5. Faculty use (to encourage computer literacy among teachers and administrators)
C. Evenings and weekends
   1. Special tutorial use (by remedial reading or special education groups)
   2. Adult school courses in computer literacy or word processing
   3. Loans of hardware and software to teachers to encourage their learning about computers

Other General Matters

Here are some tips that will make for a smooth daily operation of your lab:

1. First and foremost, train teachers. To achieve success in any curricular change, teachers must be motivated and comfortable with the

change. Noncredit in-service courses should be offered using district staff or outside consultants. Advantage may be taken of credit courses offered by local colleges and universities. Released time may be provided for attendance at workshops and conferences. Short after-school miniworkshops may be provided for teachers who are not interested in a more comprehensive course. For those teachers who are interested in advanced study, training in programming or in the use of authoring systems may be provided.

2. Keep teachers informed about what is available in the micro lab. If you have a skill program that is just right for remediating sentence-writing difficulties at the seventh grade level, your seventh grade teachers should know about it so that they can refer students appropriately.

3. Provide a schedule on the outside door of your center. Mark those times when the center is in use for classes. Allow teachers and students to sign up for times when the center is open for supervised free use.

4. Keep track of your students' progress. Use the available class management systems as aids, but keep in mind that such systems are cumbersome for some purposes. Use charts and checklists which can be easier to keep up to date. Books on individualizing reading instruction offer many suggestions for management (for example, Mueser, 1981; Morrow, 1982).

5. Develop an organized filing system for software, with appropriate security measures (such as a locked cabinet). A student sign-out sheet should be used to help keep students responsible for the condition of software they use. Color-coded adhesive labels will quickly identify diskettes and documentation. For example, use blue labels for vocabulary programs, red for students' personal word processing text files, and yellow for games.

6. Train a group of computer lab assistants. These assistants can provide help to beginners and relieve the teachers of much of the non-instructional burden. They need not always be your "best" students—as long as they are responsible and willing to spend time learning how to use the hardware and software.

7. Install at least half your computers on movable desks so that they can be rolled into other classrooms when needed. Keep one or two large-screen color monitors available for large-group demonstrations.

14

THE CLASSROOM MICROCOMPUTER STATION

Once upon a time there was a scuba diver who wished to search the ocean floor for sunken treasure. He donned his gear, dove into the water and began his search. Soon he encountered a flounder, who greeted him, "Hello, friend. What are you seeking?"

"I am looking for sunken treasure," replied the diver.

"For a small sum I'll give you these fins to speed your search," the flounder offered. The diver gladly paid the price and sped off on his way, twice as fast with the new fins.

He soon came across a crab. "Where are you going?" the crab questioned.

"To seek hidden treasure," answered the diver.

"I've got an underwater motor scooter here," the crab explained. "For a reasonable price I'll let you use it to go four times as fast as with those fins."

The diver considered for a short time, then paid the price and sped off four times as fast, still searching for his treasure. Soon he came across a shark. The shark asked him what he was doing, and he replied as before.

"Well," the shark nodded. "I know a shortcut that will lead you to your fortune almost immediately. I'll show it to you for free!" The diver gladly thanked him, happy to find a shortcut to save time.

"It's right this way," the shark smiled and pointed to his wide-open mouth. The diver scooted right in and was never heard from again.

The moral of this story: If you don't know where you're going, you're likely to get there faster than you expected.

(With my apologies to my first scuba diving instructor, who might— or might not—have adapted this story from Robert Mager, 1962.)

The first section of this chapter briefly outlines the process of curricular change within the classroom. We then deal with a common question: "How can 30 students use one microcomputer?" Finally, some practical ideas are offered for beginning to incorporate microcomputer instruction into the normal classroom curriculum.

CURRICULUM CHANGE IN THE CLASSROOM

Too many curricular changes have taken place in our schools without administrators or teachers having a clear picture of where they are going. Educators need to remember that technology is not the hidden treasure we seek. Computers will not solve our educational problems in and of themselves. They are simply tools that can help achieve preestablished goals if used with a clear understanding of theory and research.

The classroom teacher, when considering adding a microcomputer to her reading or language arts curriculum, needs to first reconsider the curriculum itself in order to determine which needs the computer will fill. What are the strengths and weaknesses? Which areas of instruction are well-served by existing materials and methods? Which areas need shoring up, additional or different materials and methods to meet students' needs?

Some time ago there was a great deal of interest in "teacher burnout," a loss of professional enthusiasm caused by several factors related to stress. Although the fad of interest in the topic was itself soon "burned out," the problem still exists today. Many teachers have lost the dream, have seen their interest in teaching wane with the years. Teaching has become an unchallenging cycle of mundane daily activities, devoid of long-range goals and the accompanying satisfaction in their achievement.

The excitement of curricular innovation is one path out of burnout. Each year should bring a new round of self-evaluation, a new series of objectives to be met before June. "A good teacher makes the difference," to paraphrase the National Education Association's slogan, and good teachers are always looking for new challenges to improve their instruction.

Figure 14–1 illustrates a simple three-stage analysis of the classroom reading program to be carried out prior to installing a micro in the classroom.

First, what existing curricula need refinement? Which units did not quite come up to par last year? Which lessons simply did not hold students' interest or did not meet with success? What materials leave something to be desired?

Second, what did I miss last year? Are there skill areas that we simply did not cover? Did students demonstrate some weaknesses last year in areas that were not part of the existing curriculum? Have there been innovative developments in the reading field? Did I come across some good new ideas at a conference last year, or is there new software designed to meet previously unrecognized needs of my students?

Third, how can I further individualize instruction in my class this year? What aspects of whole-class instruction can be modified for indi-

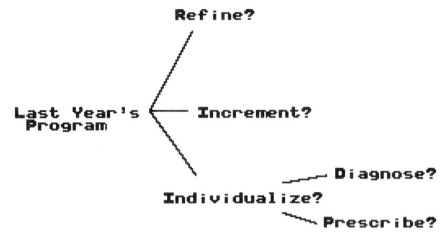

FIGURE 14–1. Three-stage curriculum analysis

vidualized work? What skills do a few of the students seem to lack each year? What interest areas can be investigated to increase motivation? How can I better diagnose these needs to provide more accurate prescription?

A skills checklist can serve to target curriculum analysis. Many such checklists are available. Figure 14–2 suggests some areas of concern. More detailed "scope and sequence" lists are readily available in teacher manuals of basal reading series, in curriculum reports (Gengler, 1972; New York City Bureau of Curriculum Development, 1968), and in many reading and language arts texts (for example, Barbe and Abbott, 1975).

Only *after* this analysis is the classroom teacher ready to begin making plans to incorporate the microcomputer into instruction.

INCORPORATION INTO THE CLASSROOM

Deciding how to use the computer in the classroom reading and language arts program depends largely on the availability of software in specific skill areas. The abundance of word processing programs suggests that a natural role for the computer lies in the teaching and practice of writing skills. Some word processors are specifically designed for ease of use rather than for the complexity desired in business applications. The word processor is one of the most powerful uses of the microcomputer, and serious consideration should be given to reorienting most writing activities around its use.

The language skills of listening and speaking, on the other hand, do not readily lend themselves to microcomputer activities. Instead, the teacher might guide students to use these skills as they work together on and react to a wide variety of micro applications, such as simulation activities, language and problem-solving games, and whole-class lessons. The key here, as in all of language instruction, is to skillfully weave together the varied language arts, capitalizing on the primary benefits of each.

The use of software instructional programs for direct teaching of language skills heavily depends on availability of such programs. Ninety-five percent of larger courseware packages are for arithmetic. Major emphases of instructional software are on skill development and lower-level

FIGURE 14–2. Evaluation of classroom curriculum

Topic	Priority for Improvement				Type of Change			
	1	2	3	OK	R	I	D	P
Word Recognition								
Sight words								
Phonics								
Structural Analysis								
Dictionary								
Vocabulary								
Meaning								
Multiple meanings								
Technical terms								
Comprehension								
Literal								
Inferential								
Critical								
Appreciation								
Study Skills								
Reorganization								
Location								
Rate								

recall (EPIE Institute, 1981). Wedman (1983) examined software catalogs to analyze trends in reading software. She found that publishers emphasize lower-level drill and practice exercises rather than skills requiring more sophisticated responses. Her classification and tabulation of existing software is charted in Figure 14–3.

In the light of this very practical consideration, it would appear that teachers will find a wealth of material for lower-level skills drills. Forty percent of reading programs are designed to teach phonics and structural analysis. If you include dictionary work and general vocabulary improvement programs in this subtotal, 78% of the programs would fall into the lower-level category. Rubin's (1983) survey of language arts programs con-

FIGURE 14–3.   Reading software availability (Wedman, 1983)

```
Word Recognition

        Sight words              6

        Phonics                 72

        Structural Analysis     28

        Context                  8

        Dictionary              29

Comprehension

        Vocabulary              68

        Literal                 19

        Interpretive             8

        Applicative              0

Study Skills

        Organizing               5

        Maps, Charts, Graphs     5

        Resources                1

        Following Directions     0

        Rate                     4

Recreational                     0

                              _____

                               253
```

firmed Wedman's findings. Only 21 of the 317 programs analyzed by Rubin required students to read and understand connected text. Teachers will clearly need to do some hard searching if they are to find programs that do more than the least imaginative word-recognition workbooks.

Similarly, of the 27 comprehension programs, 19 (that is, 70%) are at the literal, factual level. The need for additional instruction at this level is doubtful. A large body of research, including Guszak's well-known 1967 research study, has indicated that the vast majority of teacher and basal series questions (about 80%) are aimed at that level of comprehension. Further emphasis on the literal level is simply not needed. Indeed, it may well be harmful.

Blachowicz (1978–1979), for example, has found that middle-grade students are less likely to make inferences than younger students. The great emphasis upon lower-level recall in many classrooms fixates students at these literal levels of comprehension. Teachers must pay more attention to higher levels of comprehension and will find that instruction and practice in these areas positively affect student performance in reading (Hansen, 1981). Some reading researchers suggest that the more inferences children make during reading, the better their comprehension will be (Omanson, Warren, and Trabasso, 1978). Pearson and Johnson (1978) actually define comprehension as inferencing: "Comprehension is building bridges between the new and the known" (p. 24).

With the severe budget restraints on the educational system, it seems likely that children's lack of access to microcomputers will be one of the major problems facing teachers who wish to take advantage of the new technology. Melmed (1982) estimated that in order to provide every child in the country's public schools with only 30 minutes of microcomputer time each day, it will be necessary for the schools to have 4 million micros. There are about 52,000 computer units (micros and terminals connected to larger remote computers) in the schools today. To arrive at the necessary quantity by 1995, the number of micros in the schools will have to increase by 50% each year.

Some simple arithmetic will help bring these figures home to the individual classroom. With one micro and 30 children, the computer must be in operation three full hours a day if each child is to spend one-half hour with it each week. Thirty minutes a week is not a very impressive figure when considering the time necessary to word process a composition or read a short story.

MAKING THE MOST USE OF THE MICRO

1. Make a commitment to using the micro. This might seem obvious, but experience has shown that many teachers greatly restrict access to their classroom micro. Students are only allowed to work on it when "nothing important" is going on in class. Unless there is a commitment to individualized instruction on the part of the teacher, whole-class activities will take up all instructional time, and the micro will gather dust in a corner.

2. Arrange a user schedule. In the name of fair play, each child should have his or her share of time on the computer. It is easy enough to arrange the schedule so that students who are particularly in need of instruction can have a bit more than the average.

By scheduling in advance, the teacher is making a commitment to use of the micro (and to individualization) and is able to organize instruction so as to make it effective and manageable. As part of the schedule, the children should be told just what they are supposed to do with their time.

Schedule in the following manner:

a. Arrange your weekly lesson plans first. Determine when you will have whole-class activities, what your small-group activities will be, and which students will be working on their own. When these plans are clearly laid out, the micro user schedule can be built to fit in.

b. Construct the micro user schedule (see Figure 14–4). First, consider each of the whole-class activities. Which, if any, students would profit more from individualized micro instruction than from the particular whole-class activity? Second, schedule the remaining students so that they will not miss their small-group activities. If you find that there is no time to schedule all students because of the great number of large-group activities which, in your judgment, cannot be missed, perhaps you should reconsider your commitment to individualized instruction.

Be sure to leave some unscheduled time slots so that last-minute changes and additions can be accommodated. Post the schedule on a bulletin board in order that students may know that they should complete any preliminary work (for example, looking over the instructions to courseware) before starting work on the computer.

All this work just to incorporate microcomputer instruction in my class? Is it worth it? Please note: Such scheduling is not "just" to use the micro. Why not simultaneously schedule children to use the writing corner, a learning activity packet, the word-identification learning center, or any of a number of activities designed to meet their needs as individuals? The micro should be *only one of many* individualized programs within the master teacher's classroom. Remember, the micro is a tool to be used for individualization and is certainly worth the effort if such individualization is your curricular goal.

3. Make use of the micro for whole-class or small-group instruction, if appropriate. While drill programs are best completed individually, many instructional programs can be used with groups of students, thereby encouraging discussion and interchange of ideas. *Hammurabi* and other simulation games, for example, work well with groups of students. A word-processed composition may be proofed and improved. Game exercises such as *Quizit* may be played between the two halves of the class. Edupro has developed their Microgroup series of programs specifically for use with several students at a time. Two groups of several players each compete to solve word puzzles in *Team-Work*, for example.

Large-group use of the micro can certainly be so overdone that it

	M	T	W	R	F
BEFORE SCHOOL					
9:00– 9:30					
9:30– 10:00					
10:00– 10:30					
10:30– 11:00					
11:00– 11:30					
11:30– 12:00					
12:00– 12:30					
12:30– 1:00					
1:00– 1:30					
1:30– 2:00					
2:00– 2:30					
2:30– 3:00					
AFTER SCHOOL					

FIGURE 14–4. Microcomputer user schedule

defeats the basic purpose of the classroom micro, to individualize. Occasional large-group activities can be beneficial. It helps to have access to a large-screen monitor for the purpose. Usually one or two such monitors per school is sufficient. Another option is to hook up two or more smaller monitors to the same computer by using monitor wires with multiple extensions.

Many teachers have noticed that children work together as teams more on computer-centered tasks than when they work at more traditional activities. Children frequently consult their peers for advice and feedback and identify certain other children as resources to whom they can go for help. To some extent this increased peer interaction may be due to the new and technical nature of computers. The central factor in encouraging such interaction must be the teacher, however, who can recognize and capitalize upon the benefits of such academic-oriented interaction occurring in spontaneous and natural ways.

A number of research studies point to the benefits of students cooperating with each other in instructional settings. Frase and Schwartz (1975), for example, found that when pairs of students question each other during reading, retention is improved.

A summary analysis (called a "metaanalysis") of some 122 research studies on the effects of cooperative learning found that it improved children's academic abilities and interpersonal relationships (Johnson et al., 1981) better than competitive learning tasks.

Novice computer users often have serious, time-wasting problems of a low-level, mechanical variety. They may forget to press RETURN after typing an answer, or they may make a typing error or forget the important difference between the letter O and the number 0. When children work together, others can spot these errors immediately, and the cognitive task at hand remains uninterrupted by the petty details of computer workings.

4. Use microcomputer activities to structure peer tutoring experiences. By combining the interactive benefits of microcomputer instruction with the well-researched effects of peer and cross-age tutoring, the best of both can be obtained. Peer tutoring is a widely used method for providing individualized instruction. It is based on a philosophy similar to Comenius's often-quoted adage that "He who teaches others teaches himself." Comenius added, "If a student wishes to make progress, he should arrange to give lessons daily in the subjects which he is studying, even if he has to hire his students."

Research on student tutoring indicates that the tutors learn as much as, if not more than, the tutees (Hassinger and Via, 1969; Melaragno, 1976; King, 1982). Peer tutoring has also been shown to improve self-concept (Mason, 1976) and attitude toward school (Kokovich and Matthews, 1971).

Use of the microcomputer eliminates much of the training necessary for an effective peer-tutoring program. The software provides the center for instruction, while the peer tutor acts to explain the processes involved.

Using a team composed of one better and one poorer student to work on *Getting the Main Idea,* a comprehension drill program that lacks feedback as to just *why* selected answers are correct or incorrect, makes up for the courseware's weaknesses. Interaction between the students makes clear the rationale behind answer choices. The better student is provided with the opportunity to analyze and explain his or her comprehension processes, and the poorer student is given an explanation, not simply an indication of accuracy or inaccuracy.

A peer tutoring program should be well planned. Some general principles developed over years of research with peer tutors include the following applications to using microcomputers in the classroom:

a. As with any instructional technique, enthusiasm and commitment on the part of the teacher are definite prerequisites.

b. Pupils who serve as the tutors should be trained in tutoring skills and techniques using software, with an emphasis upon the importance of their responsibilities and upon teacher support (King, 1982). One of the most effective training techniques is for the teacher to model instructional techniques using the software in a simulated lesson.

c. Tutors should be familiar with the materials they are using. They should understand how to run the software and have already completed the lessons.

d. Microcomputers allow informal tutoring techniques to be employed because of the immediate feedback provided by the software. The tutor does not need to know "all the answers," since they will be provided by the program. An understanding of the skills involved is necessary, however, in order to avoid "exchanging ignorance."

e. Close supervision on the part of the teacher is important in order to determine when modifications to instructional assignments need to be made (Melaragno, 1976).

f. An interesting class project might involve cross-age tutoring, in which younger students are brought into the class for microcomputer tutorial work with your older students. An older class of poorer readers might "adopt" a younger class (Wheeler, 1983).

g. Peer pairs will enjoy using teacher utility software to construct tests, cloze exercises, crossword puzzles, and the like for each other. The teacher might be able to use the results of such projects with future classes.

h. As much as possible, arrange group work so that peers have opportunities both to give and to receive help.

i. Rather than use peer interaction to introduce new concepts, peer tutoring works better in practice, mastery, and drill sessions, just those areas for which there is a great deal of software.

For more information and materials on tutoring, see the following works:

DeRosier, Cynthia. *You and Your Charge: A Brief Handbook for High School Tutors Working under the Waianae Model Cities Tutorial Plan* (ERIC ED 056 011). Waianae, Ill.: Leeward Community College, 1971.

FRY, EDWARD B. *The Emergency Reading Teacher's Manual.* Highland Park, N.J.: Jamestown, 1971.
RAUCH, SIDNEY J. *Handbook for the Volunteer Tutor.* Newark, Del.: International Reading Association, 1969.
WEINSTEIN, GERALD, ET AL. *Youth Tutoring Youth. A Manual for Trainers. For the Tutor. Tutoring Tricks and Tips. You're the Tutor* (ERIC ED 063 543). New York: National Commission on Resources for Youth, 1970.

5. Every software program has a different set of instructions. In most cases these instructions can be typed out on ditto sheets or file cards, where they can be read without consuming precious microcomputer time. Let students read instructions before they get to the micro.

6. In using the word processor for composition, much computer time can be saved by having students write out their works in longhand, type them into the computer, then proofread and revise a printed copy. This procedure defeats much of the usefulness of the word processor, since on-line composition and correction of mistakes are two of its great benefits. If you have no choice, however, it makes sense to cut out these aspects of the computerized composition process.

7. Make computers available before and after school, and during lunch hours. Many students would be more than willing to give up free time for an additional chance to work on the computer. Providing such an opportunity would involve a whole-school effort in which the micros could be rolled on carts to a central location with a teacher or aide to supervise.

8. Use computer lessons in conjunction with more traditional teaching methods and materials. Let each method elaborate upon the other, reinforcing and expanding the concepts or skills taught. Modla (1984) has incorporated a *Fact-Opinion Exercise* into a major unit centered on the theme of teddy bears. Second graders are taught to differentiate facts from fantasy and opinion in study of factual information about the history of teddy bears and in the reading of such imaginative works as *Winnie the Pooh.*

9. Use the computer only for those activities in which it offers a real advantage over nonelectronic teaching methods.

FITTING THE MICRO INTO YOUR CLASSROOM

The following ideas ought to be considered as you begin using the micro in your classroom:

1. Don't try to do too much. With only one micro for 30 students, the teacher's expectations in terms of the scope of instruction should be realistic. Do you hope to use the micro for arithmetic, social studies, science, health, reading, writing, and classroom management? A more realistic picture might include only one or two of those content and skill areas. As a matter of fact, it is best to limit your expectations even

if you plan to use the micro for only reading and language arts instruction.

The possibility of overdoing it is an especially important consideration if you hope to use one of the more comprehensive courseware packages such as Radio Shack's *Computer Assisted Reading Development (CARD)* program with pretests, posttests, and a variety of sentence skill lessons, or if you plan to let all students make use of word processing software for writing experiences. Both require many hours of computer time for each student. In addition, the use of a word processor requires advance preparations involved in teaching students the rudiments of typing and of how to use the processor.

2. Introduce new materials gradually. If you throw out all your software to the students at once, you will confuse them and confuse yourself. Every package has a different set of instructions. It's hard to keep them all straight. Maintain a sense of control over the confusion by a controlled rate of introduction.

3. Individualize gradually. Singer and Donlan (1980) point out that students should not be thrown into independent work without first having been prepared for independence. They suggest a repeated process in which the teacher introduces each new methodology with whole-class work, tightly planned and managed. As time goes by, students are introduced to more and more small-group work and independent activities in which they learn to function without continuous teacher direction. Doubtless some students will proceed more rapidly than others. Avoid the problems associated with the "assumptive" teacher (Herber, 1978), the teacher who assumes that all students are equally capable of doing all kinds of work.

4. Be familiar with your materials. Your students' time is wasted if your assignments are inappropriate to their skill needs or ability levels. Similarly, be familiar with the procedures involved in running the software. If a student cannot access the appropriate lesson because of your mistakes in dealing with the courseware's management system, valuable instructional time is wasted. Keep notes on each software system so that it takes only a few seconds to find that "Control I" accesses the management system in *Sentence Combining*, but that "Shift 911" is necessary to use the teacher utility in *Customized Alphabet Drill*.

5. Most software designed for children beyond the primary years requires some basic knowledge of the computer. Students need to know, for instance, that the RETURN key is often a signal to the computer to present the next screen page of information or to enter requested information. It is most efficient to present this information to the entire class in a large-group activity.

There are some simple instructional programs designed to introduce new users to simple keyboarding. *Apple Keyboard*, from the manufacturers of the Apple, introduces such critical keyboard concepts as the functions of the RESET, ESCAPE, and CONTROL keys. Run through such a program with your whole class in order to avoid later confusion and time-consuming individual explanations.

6. Insist that students consult written instructions before interrupting you for help. When you do explain, do so by explaining how your student could have found the answer from the instructions rather than simply answering the question. In other words, encourage independence and exactness in following directions.

7. Develop a system of peer experts for each piece of software and for the hardware. These may be drawn from the list of students who have already successfully used certain software, or who have shown a particular interest and ability in using micros. Some computer experts suggest using "gifted" students as peer experts. Don't fall into this elitist trap. It doesn't take an IQ of over 130 (or whatever your district's "gifted" cutoff score may be) to serve perfectly well in this function. The important issues are ability in dealing with the particular software and willingness to take on the responsibilities, not the score on some test.

Post a list of each piece of software, with an accompanying list of those students who are familiar with it. Students should be instructed to ask one of the peer experts before coming to the teacher. They should also be asked to choose a student who is not deeply engaged in another activity, if possible.

8. Fluorescent lights and sunlight create glare on monitor screens. Arrange the monitor so that it does not reflect light sources. A cardboard or plastic hood extending several inches from the top of the monitor is often helpful in cutting overhead glare. Glareproof monitor screens are also available for purchase.

9. Make plans to deal with noise. While teachers who use small groups and individualized methodologies must of necessity tolerate a higher noise level than more traditional "raise your hand if you have something to say" teachers, computer noise can easily reach the point of the ridiculous. Imagine your student successfully completing an exercise to the tune of "The Entertainer" or starting a baseball reading game with "The Star-Spangled Banner." Many software programs allow the sound effects to be turned off. Make sure the programs you buy have such a feature, if sound effects are included.

Another noise problem arises from the printer, a vital and often-used peripheral for reading and writing instruction. Some printers are so loud that one popular writer about computers has joked that next-door neighbors could commit justifiable homicide if the printer were used at night. One solution is to require that any printing be carried out only at certain specified times during the day. Another solution is to purchase a silent thermal printer. Still another, less convenient solution is to require students to carry their disks to a central computer room or office to use another computer to print out their material.

15

BUT I DON'T HAVE ANY SOFTWARE . . .

You've turned to this chapter first, right? Your school's PTA bought the darn computer a month ago, but there's no software at all. What can you do?

Frankly, I'd give the computer to a math teacher and have him teach programming. A computer without software is more trouble than it's worth. The ideas presented in this chapter work best to supplement an existing software collection.

In the effort to present their schools as keeping up with the times, many administrators have sensed the need to purchase a microcomputer for their students. "Schools are in the grip of a computer mania. . . . The influx of microcomputers in education has grown from a mere trickle to a torrent, engulfing teachers and administrators in a flood of confused expectations and unfulfilled promises" (Watt, 1983, p. 83). Part of the confusion has resulted in money being spent to purchase hardware with no budgeting for the software to put this hardware to use.

So what can you do if you have no software? Not much. In fact you might as well not bother to even consider using the computer for reading or language arts instruction. Wait until appropriate funds can be gathered to buy software in large enough quantities to make the amount of time you spend learning to use the computer worthwhile.

Then why include this chapter in the book? Well, there are a few things you can do to locate free programs or to construct your own, but these options are definitely "second bests." They are best used to supplement a solid library of commercially prepared software rather than to stand alone. The disadvantages of each outweigh the advantages as far as the average teacher is concerned. Rather than spending your time on these projects, your hours might better be spent working on a part-time job at McDonald's and using the money to buy software for your youngsters. But they rate some consideration.

RAISE MONEY FOR SOFTWARE

Since many people are concerned today about introducing computer technology into the schools, there may be sources of income in your community. This text is not a fund-raising treatise, but some sources might include the PTA; local businesses; local, state, or federal grants; special appeals to the board of education; and community service organizations.

If only the army had to hold a bake sale to buy. . . .

PUBLIC DOMAIN SOFTWARE

A great deal of *public domain* software is floating around, especially for the computers that grabbed the fancy of computer enthusiasts early on in the micro revolution. The Apple is the best example. Public domain programs are programs that are not copyrighted. Writers of these programs have donated them to the public.

This donation process is usually carried out through a user group. Suppose a computer user has a personal need for a particular type of program. For example, a teacher wants to have a program to quiz students on cause-and-effect relationships. The teacher then writes the program and types it into a computer. The program might then be donated to a user group, which puts it into a disk library. Other users are allowed to copy and use the program for free (or for a minimal donation to cover copying costs). Other user groups copy the program and make it available to their members. Sooner or later, the program is available throughout the country.

This informal network of distribution often makes it impossible to determine the original sources or authors of programs. Even some programs that are copyrighted may be circulating unbeknownst to their users or copiers.

The one big advantage to public domain programs is that they are free. Teachers need to be wary of their many disadvantages, however. First, if the program was really excellent, the programmer would not have donated it to the public domain. He or she would have sold it to a software publisher. Second, these programs are written by amateurs, lacking the ability and time necessary for successful programming. Third, relatively few teachers have begun programming, especially outside of the mathematics and computer sciences. There are precious few reading or language arts instructional programs available.

Fourth, many public domain programs are insufficiently debugged. That is, they may not work properly. Fifth, they often include gross spelling and grammatical errors, again evidence of the lack of time and care used in the construction. Is that enough? Clearly, these programs are not the answer to all school needs. There are some useful programs available, but the teacher who counts on free software will be sorely disappointed.

Interestingly, some commercial software is based on older programs that are in the public domain. *Sumer* is based on a public domain program called *Hammurabi*. *Oregon* has high-resolution graphics added, but it is essentially the same as the public domain program often called *Oregon Trail*.

One common type of public domain software that may be of interest to teachers is the electronic board game (see Chapter 18). Teachers of the gifted are particularly interested in gamelike activities that stimulate analytical and creative skills. Since these same skills are also often of interest to computer buffs, amateur programmers have developed a wide variety of thinking games.

Your local computer user group will direct you to sources of public domain software in education. The magazine *Educational Computer* runs a regular column, "Free and Inexpensive Software," which reviews public domain software.

USER GROUPS

Computer users have banded together across the country to form user groups. Most meet monthly to exchange knowledge, to bring their problems to others who might know the answers, and to demonstrate hardware and software. While user groups are oriented heavily toward technical applications of computers, many of the larger organizations have begun special-interest groups for education.

It is through the user group that most people gain access to public domain programs. Many groups have large libraries of programs collected from across the country. These disks are available at cost.

Some local and state professional education groups have begun microcomputer committees which function as user groups. The New Jersey Reading Association and Virginia State Reading Association, for example, have both begun projects to collect public domain programs and distribute them to members. Information may be obtained from such organizations, which might be affiliates of the National Council of Teachers of English (1111 Kenyon Road, Urbana, Illinois 61801) or the International Reading Association (800 Barksdale Road, Box 8139, Newark, Delaware 19714).

PRINTED PROGRAMS

A wide variety of programs are available in printed form, ready to be typed into the computer and saved to disk. Some computer magazines include one or two such programs in each issue. Many books of printed programs are available in your local bookstore.

A first step might be to check whether someone has already typed the program and donated it to public domain sources. If so, a great deal of work can be saved, especially with longer programs. In addition, some journals make their printed programs available in disk format at low prices.

While most computer enthusiasts go through the stage of searching out printed programs, this procedure wears thin very quickly. The disadvantages far outweigh the one advantage, price.

First, your typing skills are probably less than perfect. Every one of your typing errors will create problems with the program, and programs are far more difficult to proofread than text. You will need to run the program repeatedly to *debug* it—to spot the errors and correct them.

Second, the program listed in the magazine or book will inevitably contain errors. Some of these errors may be corrected in later issues of the magazine, so it is necessary to search those issues before beginning to type. Unless you have good knowledge of the programming language, you will not be able to debug these errors.

This method is almost useless for those who do not know BASIC, unless someone who does know programming is available for consultation. If you are in the process of learning BASIC, however, this is one of the best methods to learn: Type in someone else's program to spot the techniques and procedures used.

Third, it takes a great deal of time just to type a complex program. As mentioned before, your time might be better spent working at McDonald's and paying for the software. After typing, of course, the debugging often runs into many additional hours.

Fourth, because of space limitations, printed programs are often simplistic. In addition, they frequently require a great deal of editing. For example, text might be displayed in a single-spaced format irritating to the eye. Modifications are up to you.

Fifth, also because of space limitations, programs may be user-unfriendly and may lack internal directions, user control over speed of presentation, and so forth. These problems can be a major disadvantage in any case, but especially if children are to use the program. The book *Apple Backpack* (Kamin and Waite, 1982) presents excellent suggestions for modifying programs to make them user-friendly on the Apple computer. The modifications are listed in Applesoft BASIC and must be adapted for other computers.

Sixth, related to the problem mentioned just above, programs are written in one version of BASIC and must be adapted for other computers. This is a complex process, involving knowledge of both versions of BASIC. For example, the command to clear the screen of print is CLS for the TRS–80 and HOME for the Apple. This is one of the simplest changes necessary. Others are much more complex.

In a valuable "how-to" article, Stewart (1983) suggests that the following guidelines be followed when considering the task of translating a program to a different form of BASIC:

1. Screen graphics presentations of drawings, charts, or patterns vary widely in technique from computer to computer, making translation

difficult or impossible. Sometimes the graphics part of the program can simply be eliminated.

2. Machine language subroutines (recognized by such commands as USE or CALL) and keywords that directly address computer hardware (PEEK, POKE) are not directly translatable.
3. The program should be short, less than 100 lines, to be manageable.
4. Documentation should be available to let you know how the program should be run when finished.

Appendix A lists several programs. Other books that include programs appropriate for the classroom can be obtained in your public library or bookstore. Try these:

LIPSCOMB, SUSAN DRAKE, AND MARGARET ANN ZUANICH. *BASIC Fun: Computer Games, Puzzles, and Problems Children Can Write.* New York: Avon, 1982.

ORWIG, GARY W., AND WILLIAM S. HODGES. *The Computer Tutor: Learning Activities for Homes and Schools.* Boston: Little, Brown, 1982.

The following book presents a valuable introduction to the process of typing listed programs and includes several simple programs designed for language arts instruction.

DICKSON, WAYNE, AND MIKE RAYMOND. *Language Arts Computer Book.* Reston, Va.: Reston Publishing, 1984.

CONSTRUCT YOUR OWN PROGRAMS

You've already read the story of my initial addiction to hacking. I was saved from the clutches of total micromania before turning into one of those unwashed, unkempt, mildly deranged addicts who wander the basements of university computer centers. The fact of the matter is, however, that if I follow a reasonable schedule of working hours, I do not have time both to teach and to compose very many software programs. Even simple courseware requires far more time than most beginners would suspect.

Some teachers have found an intense sense of self-satisfaction in constructing their own programs for their classrooms. Most teachers do not have the hundreds of hours available for such a task, nor do they have the interest in this area. One generally accepted estimate is that 200 hours of programming time are necessary to yield one hour of computer instruction, not including the months of work necessary to learn programming.

The majority of reading and language arts teachers will never learn to program for the same reason that so few people ever really learn a foreign language. Learning a language is not difficult (after all, three-year-olds do it), but it takes commitment and time that few are willing to give. Similarly, learning to program is not difficult, but it takes time that few teachers have.

So educational programming will continue to be pursued by professionals and by "enthusiasts"—teachers who have taken to computers as a spare-time hobby. If you don't have the time or willingness to program, you can still do just fine with micros by using commercial software or programs that your colleagues have written. If all teachers diverted their attention from their own specialties to programming, the schooling of our youngsters would undoubtedly suffer.

One reason to get involved in writing or typing in your own programs is that your students will know that *you* did it. A few personalized touches here or there can arouse tremendous enthusiasm. Construct a title frame with your school name on it.

```
SYNONYM MATCHING
MRS. MAREUN'S FIFTH GRADE CLASS
ARLETH SCHOOL
```

If there is a story, use your students as characters (or use your own name and those of other teachers and administrators in the school to avoid having to update names every year). You might want to have students use computer graphics to draw a picture of the school for the title frame. Children love any attempt to personalize the program.

Make use of secondary school facilities for developing programs. A partnership between the secondary computer teachers and other district personnel may lead to using high school students who are enrolled in computer courses to construct programs designed by teachers. Such a program would offer double benefits. First, the school district would benefit from the availability of improved courseware, and, second, the computer students themselves would be involved in construction of a relevant program rather than the artificial assignments typical of computer courses.

If you are interested in doing your own programming, here are some suggestions:

1. Get access to a micro. Don't worry about the make or model. If you move to a different brand of micro, the adjustment in what you learned will be very minor. Every micro uses the programming system of commands called BASIC (for Beginner's All-purpose Symbolic Instruction Code). There are only minor differences in the different versions of BASIC used for the various brands of computers.

Keep in mind a financial rule of thumb: Don't buy a micro if you can get one from someone else. You will need to spend a great deal of time, so a few minutes allowed here and there won't do. Perhaps friends or neighbors might let you use theirs, but a better bet is to check around your school system. Keep in mind that any supervisor or teacher who has micros will be reluctant to share them for fear of irresponsibility on the part of users, so use flattery, cajolery, pestering, bribes, social pressure, threats—anything so long as you can get access to the micro whenever you want to use it. If you are attending graduate school, your college may have a microcomputer room that is open to students.

If all else fails, consider buying a micro. Again, if your sole goal is to learn BASIC, any kind will do, the cheaper the better. Remember, the ultimate goal is to have the school purchase the expensive, more permanent models.

Several models of microcomputers are available for under $100. They have very serious limitations (and should not be considered if you have long-range goals for your computer or want to do word processing), but cheapness is a virtue. These models can be hooked up to your television set as a monitor, and they can use inexpensive cassette tape recorders to store programs. Some versions can also be used to play video games, an added attraction (or disadvantage, depending on your attitude toward the games) for those with children.

2. Begin learning BASIC. In order to develop software, it is necessary to use certain commands to order the computer to do what you want it to. The system of commands most useful in dealing with micros is called BASIC. It was developed during the 1960s at Dartmouth College and was designed as a language for beginners. It includes a limited number of commands, and a learner can begin simple programming almost immediately.

Depending upon your own learning style, it is possible to begin BASIC in several ways. Many people like to have new ideas explained to them, apparently preferring a personal approach to learning. Some computer shops offer short, informal sessions as free introductions to BASIC. Many school systems have also begun to offer their teachers in-service seminars on computerized instruction. These informal sessions start the beginner off, but a continued commitment to self-instruction and practice is necessary to achieve any reasonable level of proficiency.

Some prefer to learn with more structured conditions and feel more committed to learning when under traditional academic pressure. Colleges offer courses in BASIC, often in combination with a general introduction to computers. Be aware, however, that many introductory computer courses assume a certain level of higher mathematical ability, and that programming exercises and examples are directed to mathematical problem solving and ignore the concerns of educators. Classroom teachers will profit by searching for a course that caters to their particular needs.

My own preference has been for the free-wheeling pace of self-instruction. A plethora of instruction manuals are available. Choose one that is designed to be used with the micro model to which you have access, since it will take into account the idiosyncrasies of the particular machine. It is useful to have a second, backup manual should your first book fail to explain certain concepts to your satisfaction.

Choose books that have plenty of sample problems and sample computer programs, with the answers and verbal or visual descriptions of how the program should run. Some manuals simply list sample programs and follow them with statements like, "See what happens." Such books are useless unless you have a micro in front of you. Once you are hooked on computers, you will find it amusing and profitable to work on the book even when your micro isn't available.

Tutorial software designed to teach BASIC is available, but it is too expensive to purchase for your own one-time use.

3. Start writing your own reading and language arts program as soon as the inspiration strikes. BASIC is best learned through actual practice in writing programs, so don't wait until you've learned every facet of the language.

The inspiration for my first program came upon me some time ago as I was studying a chapter on an aspect of programming called *variable strings*. In brief, strings allow the programmer to intersperse preselected words, sentences, and phrases with words that are typed into the computer by the user. "I can write a program like *Mad-Libs*," I concluded, and promptly did so. Users were asked to type humorous nouns, adjectives, and so forth into the computer. The program then directed the computer to insert those words into a story and printed the results.

As I learned more about BASIC, I went back to the program and improved it until it gradually grew into a quite respectable and enjoyable activity. Meanwhile, as new ideas occurred to me, I began writing other programs. A beginner's knowledge of BASIC tends to limit programming ideas to those that are possible to complete. With more experience, one can start with ideas that are educationally valid and important, then write programs based on those ideas. In the meantime, however, the tail (your knowledge of programming) will tend to wag the dog (your knowledge of quality reading and language arts instruction).

If you are interested in writing your own programs, one of the best methods of improving your understanding of programming as applied to educational software (as opposed to the mathematical and business programs with which you probably learned BASIC) is to work through someone else's printed programs, such as those in Appendix A or in educational computing magazines.

4. Put the horse before the cart. As your ability to manipulate BASIC matures, develop an appropriate procedure for developing software, beginning with the most important question to ask when designing any instructional system: "What abilities or skills does the child need?" Process analysis and instructional goals yield an appropriate starting point. The second question to ask, "How may these abilities best be taught?" proceeds to instructional techniques. Reading and language theory suggest answers to both these questions.

Only after our knowledge of reading and language acquisition has been taken into account can we ask the question, "How can I design microcomputer software to implement these sound educational practices?" In other words, the teacher carries out software designs based on an understanding of successful teaching of reading. The simple fact that a computer is involved will not suddenly confer justification on such doubtful practices as massive isolated skill drills, for example.

A good place to continue one's study of educational programming is in the large body of research and theory completed on mainframe applications. "The potential use of computers in education has only recently gained visibility throughout the educational community, and it is easy for beginners to assume that they are stepping into a new field" (Walker and Hess, 1984). The fact of the matter is that computer-assisted instruction has a long history of special grant-funded projects designed to research curricular effectiveness of computers. Mason, Blanchard, and Daniel's (1983) book is a richly annotated reference to projects dealing with reading instruction.

16

TYPING AND COMMUNICATING TO THE COMPUTER

TYPING

Fads come and go in our educational system, but few times in the past have been as manic as the late 1960s and early 1970s when it seemed that dozens of fads ran through the schools, disappearing almost as fast as they came.

One such fad involved teaching typewriting skills to elementary age students in order to improve their language abilities. Dozens of articles were published in educational journals and magazines detailing research and practice in using typewriters to teach composition or reading. While results were often positive, the cost and effort involved in incorporating typing into the curriculum prohibited many teachers from using the method.

The introduction of microcomputers into the society at large must bring new life to this former fad. As the novice views a microcomputer, the most formidable sight is the keyboard, a set of keys that looks remarkably like the keyboard of a typewriter. As a matter of fact, the two keyboards are almost identical, except for a few extra function keys on the computer. Ability to use a typewriter is a major advantage when working with computers, as cognitive capacity can be dedicated to conceptual matters rather than to the mechanics of punching keys. A major stumbling block to using word processors for teaching writing is the students' lack of typing ability.

Formal typing instruction offers major advantages in a number of ways. Accuracy and speed in using both typewriters and computers is far better than the self-taught "hunt and peck" routines which even many computer experts employ today. By learning the correct methods from the start, students avoid the frustrations involved in unlearning such old habits as improper finger movements and looking at the keyboard. Once they've become somewhat facile in using two fingers to type, few people are motivated enough to spend time learning how to do it the right way.

In addition, typing skill is a valuable tool in the job market, and not only for secretaries. In our "information society," anyone who needs to communicate to others benefits from the speed and professional-looking results of typing. Finally, typing can be highly motivational for students, enabling them to turn out compositions and other written work that have the surface appearance of adult material. Hall has made the following observation:

> If the hand writing of letters is a problem for some students, maybe going completely to typing with some type of word processing format would help with the competency of writing compositions? This might be a way to bypass some psychomotor restrictions and lead to more students writing compositions. (1981, p. 16)

The first section of this chapter deals with the relationship of typing to language arts instruction. Suggestions on how to teach typing are then followed by two hardware issues: the layout and the construction of computer keyboards. We will then look at some new alternatives to using the traditional typewriter keyboard to communicate to the computer, including voice recognition, touch-sensitive screens, simplified keyboards, light pens, "mice," and character-recognition devices.

Typing and Language Arts

While much of the literature of the past has extolled the benefits of teaching typing in conjunction with language arts, a close look at most articles concerned with this issue shows that there was precious little direct connection between typing activities and language arts development. Most such programs were actually formal typing classes with little or no attention paid to integrating the various language arts. Teachers assumed that language development would occur incidentally as students were instructed.

To some extent, this assumption is justified. Typewriting has been shown to improve reading, writing, grammar, punctuation, and spelling (Kaake, 1983). For instance, Campbell (1973) worked with learning disabled students between seven and ten years of age. One group completed exercises in standard fashion, using handwriting. A second group used typewriters in "hunt and peck" fashion to answer exercises and do writing work. This second group displayed significant gains in reading ability over the first.

Campbell suggested a number of reasons for the gains, all of which are important advantages of typing. First, the task of typing is simpler than handwriting at beginning stages. In typing, all the child has to do is to point. Handwriting demands that a great deal of attention be paid to producing the shape of the letter. As a result, students with poor psychomotor development find learning to read and write easier on the typewriter. Second, the "hunt and peck" routine provides exploratory activities and increased exposure to the visual cues important to letter and word recognition. Finally, typing is less threatening and more responsive than handwriting, leading to more positive attitudes about learning to read and write.

Despite these findings, it is unwise to leave learning of language skills to incidental learning. If teachers are to be justified in using valuable instructional time to teach formal typing skills to their elementary students, these skills must be integrated with meaningful language activities far more thoroughly than in most earlier applications. Rather than using language development as a rationalization for the teaching of typing, typing should be used as one method for the teaching of language skills.

Typing drills are essential to the development of touch-typing skills. Students usually begin with the "home keys" of ASDF and JKL-semicolon, drill until the placement of fingers is well established, then move on to the other keys one by one. Emphasis is placed upon good typing habits such as posture (to avoid muscle fatigue during long sessions at the keyboard) and avoidance of looking at the keys.

The "key" to integrating typing skills with language arts is the rapid movement from emphasis upon the motor tasks involved in finger movement to the use of meaningful language. Typing of isolated words can begin as soon as the students have learned the home keys, with words composed of those seven letters. Teach vowels early so that many words can be formed.

When all the letters have been learned, students can begin to use the keyboard for a wide variety of communication activities. Most typing teachers insist that students not be given work that requires use of keys beyond those which have already been taught, as this will force the student to search the keyboard, a poor habit (and one difficult to break) in learning to touch-type.

Once the keys have been learned, students can engage in a variety of language activities. Poems, stories, and compositions written in class or at home can be typed, then photocopied and incorporated in a class anthology. Articles can be "cut and pasted" and duplicated to form a class or school newspaper. Kaake (1983) suggests that students be allowed freedom to complete work related to their personal interests, such as copying material from favorite books, listing frequently misspelled words, and typing personal notes and letters.

Another story construction idea involves a familiar cooperative writing technique applied to typing, that of "musical typewriters." Each student in a small group begins a story on his particular typewriter by writing a single sentence. Students in the group then switch, and each adds another sentence to the story on the new typewriter. They switch again and again until the stories are complete. With microcomputer word processors, rather than moving disks from one machine to another with the accompanying necessity of reloading the file, have the students switch seats.

Teaching Typing Skills

Teaching typing as part of the whole language arts curriculum requires a major shift of emphasis on the part of the teacher. It is time consuming, cutting into an elementary curriculum already chock full of important skills and concepts. In addition, it requires a commitment of money for equipment and accompanying repair costs.

How soon can children begin learning to type? Preschoolers often take piano lessons. If their hands can span a piano keyboard, they can span a computer keyboard as well (Dacus and Dacus, 1983).

If implemented in the elementary school, typing instruction is best carried out separately from the central classroom experience. While typing on a computer keyboard is far less noisy than using standard typewriters, so that typing drill need not be isolated in a classroom off by itself as in the past, the teaching of typing is a highly structured experience, especially in its beginning stages. Carefully sequenced drills and activities are absolutely necessary. If the teacher is unable or unwilling to spend the time to teach the right way, it is probably best to let the children hunt and peck at the keyboard and wait for a later time when attention may be devoted to proper instruction.

Since learning to type is a highly mechanical procedure involving repetitive drill and practice, initial teacher-led instruction is most efficiently carried out in large groups. The individualization important to more cognitively oriented skills such as reading and arithmetic is unnecessary, though the typing teacher must be aware of individual needs to some degree, of course. As a result, typing instruction is best done outside the regular classroom, in a course specifically designed to teach the skill, held in a room with many typing stations. In these days when only one or two micros are available in each classroom, it is the school's responsibility, therefore, and not the individual teacher's, to provide for organized instruction in this area.

Typing and the classroom teacher. Without adequate equipment for whole-class instruction, the classroom teacher is unprepared to deal with typing skills and is probably wisest to let students hunt and peck as best they can. Make-do alternatives such as using paper keyboards or labeling student's fingernails with felt-tipped markers (Switzer, 1979) for simulated drills are frustrating and ineffective in the long run. While some teachers report that children can become proficient after as little as three hours at the keyboard (Suttles, 1983), and it is certainly true that three hours of instruction are better than none, the levels of proficiency are minimal.

Attention must be paid, however, to the setup of the computer keyboard, to such keyboarding skills as use of the CONTROL, ESCAPE, and RETURN keys. Without knowledge of these, even the most user-friendly programs are not understandable to students.

Teachers can use ditto copies of the keyboard, with some or all of the labels missing, to familiarize students with the keyboard layout by having them fill in the missing labels. A whole-class project to construct a giant keyboard on the classroom wall can be amusing and informative. The "keys" can be constructed from cardboard or small boxes (such as shoeboxes) and from plastic hamburger cartons from the local fast food outlet. Some teachers have taught kindergartners the keyboard layout by constructing a giant vinyl or cardboard keyboard-on-the-floor, before introducing actual typing. Children may hop, skip, slither, or jump to the keys. The top row of keys represents birds in the sky, and children "fly" to them with arms spread wide. The other rows, from top down, represent the rabbits (hopping), humans (walking), and worms (slithering).

Each computer manufacturer makes available an introductory tutorial program explaining the functions of the various special-function keys. Apple, for instance, offers a motivational program called *Apple Keyboard*, which simultaneously teaches the keyboard layout and some of the capabilities of the computer. Users are given simple tasks to complete and are monitored closely by the computer to insure understanding. Most similar programs are designed for older users, however. Teachers would need to provide their own amplified introductions for younger elementary students, with appropriate repetition and reinforcement.

Some frequently used programs require manipulation of special groups of keys to achieve functions. *Bank Street Writer*, for example, uses the I, J, K, M keys to move the cursor up, left, right, and down. A simple device to save younger children the frustration involved in remembering these commands is to mark the appropriate keys with directional arrows on self-adhering labels. Some readiness programs designed to teach directionality, such as *Juggle's Rainbow* or the drawing activity in *Early Games for Young Children*, require students to punch keys in certain sections of the keyboard. For instance, in response to the prompt ABOVE in *Juggle's Rainbow*, students must press a key in the upper two rows of the keyboard. Children move a cursor to draw lines in *Early Games* by punching keys on the right of the keyboard to move right, on the bottom to go down, and so forth. Teachers may insert a strip of cardboard between the appropriate rows as a help to students.

Another way to aid students is to color-code typewriter keys with adhesive labels. With a word processor, for example, the D key may be used to delete a character. Put a red label on the front of the D key (not on its top—the letter D should be in sight) and another on a file card next to the word DELETE. Use different colors for other commands. Keep the card posted near your computer for quick reference.

Elaborate keyboarding tutorials are also available on diskette. These programs offer a series of typing lessons, with accompanying drill and practice exercises. The more comprehensive programs are complete typing courses in and of themselves. They are not, however, designed for younger elementary students. They also require a great deal of self-discipline and self-motivation, as typing drills are tedious.

A variety of less comprehensive typing drill and practice programs exist and may be more appropriate to the classroom. *Typing Tutor II*, for

THIS LESSON HAS TWO PURPOSES —

(1) PRACTICING THE HOME KEYS IN

SIMPLE COMBINATIONS

(2) STRETCHING FOR G AND H.

REMEMBER TO RETURN YOUR INDEX FINGER

TO ITS HOME KEY (F OR J) AFTER YOU

STRETCH FOR G OR H.

FIGURE 16–1. Sample frame from *MasterType*

instance, gives practice exercises of randomly generated letters. Lessons start with the home keys, and as the typist improves, more letters and other characters are added to the assignments. The program keeps track of keys learned and speed of production of each, forming exercises geared to individual needs. In constructing the exercises of random combinations of letters, however, students do not deal with meaningful language nor even with actual words.

MasterType, a speed-typing program in arcade video game format, offers very brief lessons on typing skills (see Figure 16–1) and displays letters and words at varying difficulty levels for typing. The typist must race to type the words before a fleet of attacking alien spacecraft destroys his own defensive energy fields. Each word successfully typed destroys an enemy spaceship. If the attacking ships get through twice in the same quadrant, the typist's ship is destroyed, and the lesson starts over.

Results are reported in terms of score in the game, average speed, and number of mistakes. The typist is also given a summary conclusion such as, "Your score is not bad," or, "Your score could use some improvement; keep working on this lesson." The program automatically diagnoses results and directs the typist to continue with the same lesson or go on. *MasterType* also provides the capability to construct lessons composed of words of the user's choice.

The QWERTY Issue

When typewriters were first developed, one of the major problems was jamming of keys. Speedy typists would type so fast that the first key struck would not have time to reset itself before the second key was hit. As a result, the traditional keyboard layout (often called the QWERTY keyboard, for the six left-hand keys immediately above the home key row) was developed by Christopher Sholes, a Milwaukee inventor, in 1873, largely to slow down typing. That is, keys that were hit the most frequently were placed in relatively out-of-the-way places so that the speed of typing would not be so great as to jam the keys.

Electronic developments have made such a procedure unnecessary today, since no typist can outrun the speed of an electronic typewriter or a video monitor. A number of optional keyboard layouts have been designed to improve typing speed, the most popular of which is the Dvorak keyboard, designed 50 years ago by a University of Washington professor. Research indicates that typing speeds can be increased 100% by using the Dvorak layout, which is designed for efficiency rather than for slowing down the rate of typing. The most frequently used keys (A, O, E, U, I, D, H, T, N, S) are placed in the home row.

The "QWERTY phenomenon" (Papert, 1980) has hindered the implementation of these new keyboards, however. Papert explains that the older technology has become entrenched in our society, since virtually all typists are familiar with the older keyboard layout and are resistant to change. No microcomputer today uses the newer layouts as its primary keyboard pattern, though it is relatively simple to make the modification. It is possible to readjust several of the more sophisticated word processors (such as *Screen Writer* II) so that they will use any layout desired. A typist can simply reassign the key functions to the style desired, and the word processor will follow the new layout.

Many advocates of the new keyboards are fanatical in their devotion and bitter in their denunciation of typing teachers who continue to teach the QWERTY style. At the moment, however, typewriters using the Dvorak keyboard are rare. A typist trained in Dvorak methods would be limited to the few machines that use the new layout. This unfortunate situation seems well-nigh unchangeable for the foreseeable future, since our society has no mechanism for "official" change in this area. Until such a mechanism takes effect, children must be taught to use the traditional keyboard structure.

Keyboard Quality

For anyone interested in spending a lot of time typing on a computer, two hardware factors are essential. The first is the quality of the monitor screen. High resolution is a requirement. Try it for yourself. Type for a couple of hours at a low-resolution screen. Then switch to a high-resolution one. You'll be convinced.

The second factor is the quality of the keyboard. There are several types. The least expensive is the *membrane keyboard*, which does not have actual keys. A layer of plastic covers contacts. It is nice for young children who may spill things on the computer, but unacceptable for other uses. *Chiclet* keys are square and flat, and they are a significant step up from membrane keyboards. For large amounts of typing, however, nothing will do short of a standard typewriter keyboard with well-shaped keys approximating the style and feel of the IBM Selectric typewriter.

Again, type for a couple of hours at a cheaper computer console, then try a quality keyboard. You'll appreciate the difference.

Ideas for Typing Instruction

1. Order printed cardboard keyboards for practice drills. Computer Practice Keyboard Company (616 9th Street, Union City, NJ 07087) makes versions for several different microcomputer models. It's not difficult to make your own on a ditto master and run off copies for your students.
2. Record your oral presentation of typing drills on cassette tapes for future use.
3. Use spelling and vocabulary words for targets during drills.
4. For one type of class drill, write a single phrase on the chalkboard. The prize goes to the child who types the most copies of the phrase in the allotted time.
5. When scoring student typing work, score separately for speed and accuracy. Don't use a composite score. This procedure improves quality of feedback to students, indicating which skill needs further concentration.

ALTERNATIVES TO TYPING

Voice Recognition

One of the highlights of Walt Disney World's EPCOT Center is the sophisticated computer exhibits, featuring voice-recognition devices and touch-sensitive screens. One game, for example, involves a *Pacman*-like activity, with a central figure wending its way through mazes. The game player directs movement by commands spoken aloud: *up, down, right,* and *left.* These games are both an indication of things to come and a demonstration of the severe limits of voice-recognition devices.

Voice recognition will play an invaluable role in teaching reading and writing in a natural way, basing learning upon children's already well-developed oral language skills. Imagine a preschool youngster seated in front of a microcomputer equipped with microphone and voice-recognition device. As he recounts his recent experiences at the zoo, the words and sentences—perhaps even some pictures—appear automatically on the screen. The process neatly integrates oral language with composing and reading one's compositions in an electronic version of the language experience approach. Such devices may well revolutionize the teaching of beginning reading.

This futuristic picture is still far off, however. Present-day voice-recognition devices are extremely limited. Even the Disney World state-of-the-art machines have vocabularies of only a few words, and even those are not always recognized reliably. The most difficult problem is word segmentation, recognition of the boundaries between words. Attempts to program computers to separate words during connected oral discourse demonstrate the incredible complexity of this featural conceptualization about language toward which reading teachers must guide their readiness-level youngsters. A word is not a discrete unit, except as we conceptualize its discreteness in terms of our linguistic awareness. Sophisticated speech-recognition devices today use the vast memory capabilities of large mainframe computers. Even then speakers are required to speak in isolated word units, with 100 millisecond pauses between each word. The most advanced systems are capable of recognizing fewer than 300 words with 97% accuracy (Gould, Conti, and Hovanyecz, 1983).

Simpler speech-recognition devices are now available for use in the classroom.

Scott Instruments produces the VET voice-recognition console, a peripheral device to be attached to the microcomputer. The console, called a Voice Entry Terminal, allows sounds to be analyzed and stored as electronic signal patterns. Students can speak to the computer and be understood, within strict limits.

Scott's *VBLS* (Voice-Based Learning System) *Authoring System* enables teachers to construct their own courseware to make use of the VET. The teacher is requested to TYPE QUESTION NO. 1. She might type in the following:

```
WHICH WORD IS MISSING?
      THE ___ BARKS.
  DIG   DAG   DOG   DUG
```

After she has typed the question, which will later be presented to the students exactly as typed, the teacher is requested to pronounce the correct answer. She speaks into a microphone, "Dog," and types the word. The computer asks her to repeat the pronunciation of "dog" several times. The VET takes these several oral inputs and "averages" their voice patterns to synthesize a pattern range that it will consider correct when spoken by the students.

When the child begins the lesson, he is first presented with a series of key words to pronounce repeatedly. The computer must learn to recognize new voice patterns each time a new child begins the program. As a result, simple responses that are consistent throughout the program are most reliably recognized (for example, A, B, C, D, yes, no, true, false). After this oral input session, the actual instructional program begins and the child is able to dictate his answers orally.

The VET is sophisticated, considering the primitive state of the art in microcomputer voice recognition. Numerous recognition errors invariably occur, however. In addition, extraneous noise cannot be completely accounted for. Another child shouting on the other side of the room may cause an input that will be counted as an error. Voice recognition is not yet nearly precise enough for speech articulation therapeutic purposes, though the future trend will lead in that direction.

Voice recognition will have an important role to play in education. The most rapid advances may well come in the area of special education, where governmental agencies are most willing to spend the large amounts of money necessary to provide each child with these expensive devices. Voice recognition might allow a paraplegic to "type," for example, though this is as yet well in the future. It is already within the capability of microcomputers to govern common household appliances. "Oven," spoken aloud, might turn on the oven, or "Lights on" activate the house lights. Since such a device is used by only one person, the necessity of reregistering voice patterns for various users is eliminated.

Touch-Sensitive Screens

Another of the sophisticated information-processing devices on display at EPCOT is the touch-sensitive video screen. Information booths display pictures and diagrams on video monitors. All the visitor has to do if she wants further information about restaurants is touch the picture of food on the screen. The computer is programmed to recognize the touch and responds by providing the information.

Virtually no microcomputer software is now available for this technology, as touch-sensitive screens are expensive and not yet widely available. Experimental work using mainframes has demonstrated the effectiveness of this simple input device, especially with preschool children. All the child has to do is point to the correct answer on the screen, and the computer will register the result. The next few years will see a dramatic increase in use of this hardware, especially in readiness and beginning reading activities.

Simplified Keyboards

A variety of electronic learning devices are on the market that make use of simple keyboards. Arithmetic activities, for example, might use a keyboard with only the numerical and math function (for example, +, *, and =) keys. Multiple-choice programs might have only four keys, one for each of the answer options. Younger children find such keyboards far less formidable than the standard typewriter layout.

Light Pens

A *light pen* is a pen-shaped device connected to the computer by a wire. The user communicates to the computer by simply pressing the pen against an appropriate spot on the monitor screen. The pen allows standard microcomputer hardware to function almost as if it were equipped with touch-sensitive monitor screens.

Let us suppose the monitor display looks like Figure 16–2. This is a *menu page*, which typically would list numbers next to each lesson on the menu. The kindergartner might press the 1 key to be presented with an exercise of fill-in problems such as

_ J K

or the 5 key for a multiple-choice problem like

A : b   c   a   e

Notice there are no numbers on the screen display in Figure 16–2. All the child needs to do is use the light pen to touch the little box next to the

FIGURE 16–2. Monitor display for a light pen

exercise of his choice, and the computer will understand that input. The light pen speeds up simple input to the computer, especially for children who have problems with keyboarding.

How does this work? The monitor screen presentation appears to be static, a solid display. In actuality the display is formed by a single rapidly moving dot of light. This dot sweeps across the entire screen, turning on and off as it goes, to form images on the screen. It starts at the upper-left corner and sweeps toward the right, then drops a line (there are hundreds of such lines on the screen) and makes another right sweep. The dot traverses the entire screen 60 times each second, so rapidly that we perceive the screen as static.

The light pen operates by detecting the monitor's dot of light as it passes. The computer is able to make a precise determination of the light pen's placement horizontally by subtracting the time from the last *horizontal sync* signal (that is, the signal from the computer to the monitor to start another rightward horizontal sweep) from the instant the dot passes the pen's point. The computer determines vertical placement of the pen by counting the number of horizontal sync signals since the last *vertical sync* signal (that is, the signal from the computer to the monitor to start over at the top-left of the screen).

At any rate, the computer is able to place the pen with quite a bit of precision. Light pens offer benefits particularly for those students unfamiliar with use of the keyboard. Software must be programmed specially for light pen input, however. Many courseware publishers whose programs are designed for use of the light pen also offer an optional command at the beginning of each program so that it can be used in classrooms that do not have the devices. At the beginning of the program, the user is asked, ARE YOU USING A LIGHT PEN? (Y/N). If not, keyboard input is accepted and the monitor displays are adjusted accordingly.

The Mouse

A *mouse* is a small box-shaped device connected by cable to the computer. It is designed for ease of cursor movement. The user simply rolls the mouse along the desktop. Forward motions move the cursor up the screen, rightward motions move it to the right, and so forth.

Character-Recognition Devices

One more input device designed to overcome the problems of typing is the character-recognition device, which allows the user to print his input using a stylus. Personal Penpad, for example, is a book-size peripheral device for the IBM PC, with a 15½-inch square screen. The user is able to print block letters one at a time on the screen with a ballpoint pen cartridge fitted to a stylus. The printed characters appear immediately on the computer's video monitor.

Personal Penpad, unlike many earlier character-recognition devices, does not recognize the printed character by pressure of the stylus on the tablet surface. Instead, the hand movements involved in constructing the letters are recognized, making it possible for the computer to recognize different sizes of print. If the character is so badly formed as to be unrecognizable, a question mark appears on the video terminal. Personal Penpad also recognizes Arabic numerals and some special characters.

The usefulness of such devices is limited at present, since they are not compatible with much of the hardware and software available to educators. The next few years will see many new applications, again reducing the demands of keyboarding skills upon computer users. Children and adults will be able to print their compositions or answers to questions.

In addition, think of the implications of such a device for development of handwriting skills. Instantaneous feedback for production of letters and words could greatly speed attainment of this skill.

17

TEACHER
UTILITIES

In an effort to insure that every student is taught every required skill and all content matter, the educational establishment has divided the delivery of instructional material along lines of demarcation determined by skill and content area. The teaching of expository writing, for example, is the domain of the English teacher, not the social studies teacher. Vocabulary development is to be handled during the reading period, not the writing. Arithmetic skills are employed only during mathematics lessons, not in science.

There are excellent reasons for such categorization of learning experiences. The basic rationale is that learning should be organized for effectiveness and efficiency. Organization, whether in the army, the factory, or the school, is the result of analyzing superordinate tasks into their smallest components and dealing with each component in turn.

Somewhere along the line, however, integration must occur. If the army is doing its "thing" while the air force merrily goes along its own path, the two will be shooting at one another instead of the enemy. If the pieces don't fit at the end of the assembly line, the product is useless. If students are not able to put together all of what they have learned into coherent patterns of meaning, they will be unable to apply their learning in real-world tasks. Much of the criticism of today's schools may be the result of just such inability to combine and transfer skills to new situations. Students who can read and write just fine in school find it difficult to follow even the simplest directions on the job, where no teacher is there to administer a multiple-choice test.

Many of the most important advances in education in the past 40 years have resulted from attempts to systematize education. Complex skills management systems attempt to cover every conceivable skill in their target areas. Creation of basal reading systems costs publishers millions of dollars as they try to meet every conceivable objective.

Despite these costly endeavors of educational experts, most teachers remain dissatisfied with the classroom materials provided to them. The materials somehow just don't meet the needs of their classes. As a result, few teachers depend solely upon the comprehensive instructional systems. A huge market exists in materials to supplement the larger systems.

One problem with the use of these supplemental workbooks, texts, and other materials is lack of integration. They are not correlated to one another or to the central basal or skills management system used in the classroom. Vocabulary words taught in the workbooks have little or nothing to do with the story just read in the basal. Writing exercises in the grammar text are not at all related to the experiences of students on their latest field trip. Spelling instruction is divorced from both writing and reading work.

The answer to these problems involves the teacher, who must provide the integration necessary for meaningful learning. Teacher-constructed materials require great amounts of time to prepare, however, and it takes a teacher years before any significant amount of such materials can be accumulated. In these days of such tremendous teacher mobility—of yearly movement between grades, between schools, and between school systems—one year's material development might well be useless the next year, and the teacher would be forced to start from scratch once again.

Computers offer an answer to some of these problems. Software known as *teacher utilities* aids teachers in many ways in the construction of materials specifically designed for their classrooms. Supplemental exercises in the form of crossword puzzles can be constructed dealing with the particular vocabulary words under study this week. A cloze exercise can be created from the story just read. A computerized drill exercise dealing with any skill or content can be constructed with no knowledge of programming skills, almost as simply as just typing the questions into the computer.

Utility software varies in complexity. Some packages require little more than following explicit directions to type in such material as vocabulary words and their definitions. Other packages are quite complex, enabling the teacher to perform a wide variety of tasks, but requiring time-consuming efforts to learn and use. Program-writing systems such as *PILOT*, for example, are virtual computer languages, though specifically designed to meet the needs of teachers.

SUPPLEMENTAL EXERCISE UTILITIES

Did you ever wish that the find-a-word puzzles in your filing cabinet matched the vocabulary words in the stories your children were reading? Or, do you find that cloze exercises based on your children's social studies textbook are so time consuming to construct that you use only the multiple-choice questions provided in the teacher's manual?

The computer can generate find-a-words, cloze exercises, crossword puzzles, and a variety of other exercises automatically. All the teacher has to do is type in the raw information.

Find-a-Word Puzzles

Figure 17–1 illustrates a find-a-word puzzle generated by *Puzzler*. The program guides the teacher with explicit instructions to type in the desired list of words. It then arranges the puzzle automatically and prints out the finished product. If a ditto master is used in the printer, the teacher can run off sufficient copies for the whole class in a matter of minutes.

Several options are sometimes available in this type of utility. One important option involves use of definitions as clues to the words. The instructional value of a find-a-word in which the actual words to be found are printed at the bottom of the puzzle is questionable. A far more valuable activity is to use word definitions as clues. *Puzzler* offers both options. The program also prints out an answer key for the teacher.

Hartley Courseware's *Wordsearch* is another find-a-word construction utility. Purchasers should check for desired options. *Wordsearch*, for example, does not allow definitions to be used as clues. Quality of final printed output of these programs may also be a concern, as the spacing of letters in vertical and horizontal positions may vary disconcertingly.

Puzzles created by most of these utilities are designed to be printed out and duplicated for students. Students do not work out the puzzles on the computer. A program with the same title as the Hartley program described above, *Wordsearch*, is a part of Encyclopaedia Britannica's *Wordwright* series of vocabulary programs. It is an on-line find-a-word activity in which students move a cursor to find and identify hidden words.

Crossword Puzzles

As with find-a-words, several utilities are available for the construction of crossword puzzles. Teachers are requested to type in each of the desired words with its clue or definition. The computer does the arranging, then prints out the result. Quality of printed copy varies considerably between programs, with different techniques used to form the puzzle graphics.

MECC's *Crossword* is one such utility. *Crossword Magic* allows teachers either to print the puzzles or to have students solve them on the screen. Another program entitled *Crossword*, part of Encyclopaedia Britannica's *Wordsearch* series, can only be used on screen. Students move a cursor to the first space in a word, then request clues in the form of definitions, etymology, and sample sentences. When the word is correctly guessed, the letters appear in the blanks.

Cloze Exercises

The cloze procedure was first developed by Wilson Taylor in 1953. Since then it has been used widely in classrooms as both a teaching and testing device. The procedure is actually rather obvious. Words are de-

NAME .... TEACHER ....

CLASS .... DATE ....

COMPUTERS

```
P T Q P N C F E F R N P T T L F T J K J G D K Q Y M M T R
E U E Q R J V C N U M X R U X Q X I O X F R U F L H J Z Q
M G Y V G I S N F R G U K H P V C X F X O N Q K A L I A P
G O F M F S N E B W R R K Z R N T X U W L J G E M Q U Y P
O I P B K S N T P W J U A I B G I M T M F V V D X C Y U Y
K O G K G D U M E G X E M P M J S E I H U T B E F O E A J
S L X K Q U T O P R Y F T L H J N H H T M C F R U Y H R I
C N B E I F H A P A C S T Z G I X R P I P U O L F P P Q Z
Z S A K T K G I G F U I T H W I C H T A Q T I M S Y P Q C
E R K B S R W T U U O L D R C U I S H E I Z I I A Y V M D
U Q P V C T D T U P T U O F Q Z R G I N K Q Q B M D Y I U
B S O Z T W W S J Y Q Z H W M Q B O O Y V B A W C C Y T N
A K T I T E J T Y F V U F Y Y Z D M Z I H Y I D M M W U P
S F F S C O O J A K V A R Q R P I E F N U S X I T Q B H E
I B V B F M G B F J X V I K X U S Q J W S V D S O W E V M
C G P A A U A B X Q G W C A A G V H S V W P G K K X B K M
S D D F D W D N V M R G Z X X T S B L J C J P D D N X X V
X I J D D T W E L T F M E D O J X H U T L F O W O F B F V
E K M K D T P G J B L C W O C J I K K I L E B H W G W P N
X G K U M J E G I G N V B F N Z E W K B T X X C L M D E H
U H A R E T U P M O C O R C I M N W N E F P X R W L W G P
```

1. BEGINNER'S PROGRAMMING LANGUAGE
2. START UP A PROGRAM
3. OBJECT WHICH STORES DATA
4. PICTURES
5. MAKE DATA AVAILABLE TO COMPUTER
6. A SMALL COMPUTING SYSTEM
7. TELEVISION SET
8. LINKED COMPUTER SYSTEMS
9. RECEIVE DATA FROM COMPUTER
10. MAKES HARD COPY

FIGURE 17–1. *Puzzler* find-a-word

leted from a text passage and replaced with blank spaces. Students must use their context skills to determine the words that belong in the blanks. Heavy demands are placed upon students' comprehension and vocabulary skills, and a good deal of reasoning ability is required as well.

Teachers use cloze instruction in a variety of ways. Selective deletion patterns reinforce use of particular types of words. For example, deletion of pronouns gives practice in pronoun reference. Deletion of connectives such as *in addition to this* or *however* gives practice in use of text-organization strategies. More often, children complete random deletion exercises in which every fifth or every tenth word is deleted for practice in context recognition.

Teachers have also found cloze testing to be a valuable tool for matching students to textbooks. Children answer a cloze exercise based on a textbook passage. The teacher scores for exact replacement. If the student has scored between 44 and 57% correct (Bormuth, 1967), the book is at the instructional level in reading difficulty. If lower, the book is beyond the student's capabilities.

Cloze exercises leave the first and last sentences of the passage intact. Deleted words are replaced by blanks of equal length. At least 50 blanks are required for acceptable reliability. Every fifth word is deleted for narrative (story-like) passages and every tenth word for exposition.

Software is available to aid teachers in this time-consuming task. The *Cloze Test* automatically constructs a cloze exercise from passages typed and saved on disk. Students read the passage as many times as desired, then fill in the blanks by typing their answers. The computer immediately scores the results and can print out a copy of the results, including the incorrect answers.

Teachers find that cloze exercises based on high-interest passages are very motivational. A tennis player can complete a passage about court strategies, a vocational student can work on a passage about auto mechanics, and so forth.

TEACHER UTILITY OPTIONS

Recognizing that their practice programs are often unsuited to the needs of specific classrooms, software publishers are increasingly providing teacher utility options in their materials. After all, of what real use is a vocabulary drill that uses words that are not in the basal reader or in the supplemental vocabulary development workbooks? Why buy a spelling program that teaches words other than those taught in the classroom's spelling books? Teacher utility options allow teachers to adapt software to their own needs so that the material drilled fits in neatly with the overall classroom curriculum.

Crossword and *Wordsearch*, both described above, have teacher utility options. Instead of using the built-in lists of words and definitions, teachers can modify the program so that it uses words of their own choice. These modifications require no programming skills but rather can be carried out by following instructions that amount to little more than sequenced commands to type in the desired material. Once the material is typed, it is stored on the disk and available whenever needed to be used over and over again.

With the increasing availability of such programs, teachers are well advised not to purchase any vocabulary program that does not have this option. The issue should rather be the quality of the respective utility options. Some, for example, severely limit the number of lessons a teacher can store on disk. If only four lessons can be stored on disk, the teacher must either buy several copies of the same program (an unsatisfactory option in terms of finances) or continually be erasing material from old lessons and typing in new material (unsatisfactory in terms of teacher time).

Utility options allow the teaching of a variety of skills using any words desired. *Word Division* teaches structural analysis skills. Students must position a marker between meaningful word parts to divide the word. *Fragmentation* is a similar game in which word parts must be moved across the screen, matching them to form words. *Wordmate* deals with compound words. *Word Families* teaches initial and final consonant and medial vowel recognition. *Word Attack* builds vocabulary skills through definitions and example sentences. *Antonyms/Synonyms* requires students to supply antonyms or synonyms for words in sentences. Each of these programs has a teacher-utility optional component.

Comprehension drill programs are less suited to use of utility programs, since the time required for teachers to type stories and questions is much greater than that needed for isolated words and definitions. In addition, comprehension exercises involving the reading of stories and factual material function much better than isolated vocabulary drill exercises as programs that stand alone, not requiring close integration with other classroom materials.

TEST AND DRILL MAKERS

The use of the computer to administer testlike exercises is generally called "drill and practice." Much computer-assisted instruction has been built around drill and practice routines based on the same instructional principles as programmed learning. So many instructional programs, especially in the content areas, are of this variety that many educators have complained that computers are little more than overly expensive "electronic flash cards."

While drill and practice may be overused, not only in CAI but in the more traditional classroom as well, few deny that such routines are inescapably a part of education, providing the necessary reinforcement for learning skills and content material. A variety of teacher utilities is available for simplified construction of electronic drill and test materials. All the actual programming is complete. The teacher needs only to type in the questions and answers. Highly complex drill and practice programs, including graphics and tutorial instruction, can be constructed using "authoring languages," discussed later in this chapter. Most teachers will be satisfied with the simpler quiz-construction utilities.

The "flash card" program *E-Z Learner* is described in Chapter 9. A teacher can use *E-Z Learner* to construct drill exercises on virtually any topic or skill imaginable. Questions are presented in either random order or in a prearranged sequence.

THE WORD PROCESSOR AS TEACHER UTILITY

If the teacher has a choice of only one program to use on the classroom computer, it should be a word processor. Chapters 10 and 11 discuss instructional uses of the word processor, and Chapter 20 gives ideas on using it as a management tool. It is the most flexible and powerful instructional device available for language arts development. In addition to its value as a teaching and management tool, the word processor offers an unlimited world of possibilities to aid the teacher in construction of materials.

Many exercises created with the word processor can be implemented in two ways. The exercise can be printed out, duplicated, and completed by the students on paper, or students can use a copied word processor file of the exercise stored on disk and complete the work using the word processor, storing the final copy back on the disk. The first two ideas presented below illustrate each procedure in detail, with advantages and disadvantages.

Anomalous Insertions

Tierney and Pearson (1981) note that some students exhibit a tendency to be "too reader-based"; that is, they depend too much on their own background knowledge and familiarity with a topic, thereby not paying enough attention to the actual text. (The opposite tendency, to be "too text-based," would involve too much concentration on the author's words, with very little use of background knowledge to aid learning and interpretation.) One strategy to encourage careful reading is to have students underline words or sentences that do not fit the reading passage.

Construction of such exercises on word processors is simple enough. A teacher could choose a reading selection at the students' instructional level and type it into a file. If the selection might be used for other purposes, it should be saved onto disk and a backup copy of the file made. (The instructional manual of the word processing software gives instructions on how to do this. Commands for each word processor differ. In *Word Handler*, for example, the user need only type in the command BACKUP and assign a name to the new file.) Contextually inappropriate words and sentences could then be inserted randomly into the backup file; this revised version could be saved onto disk; and a copy could be printed out on a ditto master for duplication. Both the original unmutilated version and the exercise would be available for later use at any time.

Cloze and Maze

While special utility programs that construct cloze exercises are available, teachers can also use the word processor for this function. First, the passage should be typed into the computer and saved onto disk. A backup copy of the file should be made. Word deletions could then be made in the backup copy according to the desired cloze application. In general, every fifth word is deleted in narrative prose and every tenth in expository. A "maze" procedure, in which the student is offered three word choices for each blank (a correct choice, a word that is the proper part of speech but does not make sense in the context, and a word that makes sense in the context but belongs to the wrong grammatical class), or a listing of the word choices at the bottom of the exercise helps students who may have difficulty with cloze.

Deleting after typing a passage is quite a bit easier than deleting during typing. Deletions can be performed in several ways, depending upon which is the most efficient method for the word processor being used. In *Screen Writer II,* for example, switching to the "change mode" of text insertion allows letters to be replaced with blanks by pressing the space bar when the cursor is positioned over the letters. It is easier to position the cursor in front of the word to be deleted, type in the desired number of spaces, then use the delete keys to erase the word in *Word Handler* and *Bank Street Writer.*

Students find using the word processor to complete exercises and to print out finished products to be an exciting experience. In a cloze exercise, students would first read the entire passage to get a general idea of its contents. Then, starting at the beginning, they would move the cursor to the first blank and type in their answer. After all the blanks have been filled in, the exercise could be either saved on disk for later teacher inspection or printed on paper.

This procedure, while a motivating and valuable experience for the student, places a number of demands on the teacher. First, it is important to keep a separate backup disk with a copy of the cloze exercise on it in case the student's copy is destroyed. Second, as many copies must be made of the exercise on disk as there are students to complete it. While making one or two copies is simple enough, the process of making 30 is long and tedious. If students are sufficiently familiar with the computer system, they might be able to make their own copies off the teacher's master diskette. Third, for security reasons it is best to have separate file disks for each student. *Bank Street Writer* attempts to overcome this need with the use of student passwords in order to gain entry to files. While helpful, this does not avert the problem of one student physically damaging the disk and thereby destroying other students' files. Fourth, teachers must ask themselves whether the benefits of using a word processor to complete exercises that could be completed almost as well on paper outweigh the costs of tying up the limited number of computers available.

Scrambled Text

Sentences with component words in scrambled order or paragraphs with sentences in scrambled order can be presented. The students' task is to use the "block movement" capability of the word processor to rearrange the sentences and paragraphs. Block movement commands usually involve marking the beginning of the "block" (the words or sentences) with one key command, marking the end of the block with another, and a final command to move the block to the desired new location. Word processors automatically move the designated block, reformatting the margins so that a perfect revision results from these few simple commands.

Punctuation

The teacher supplies a paragraph or passage with all punctuation missing. Students insert the punctuation as necessary.

Transitional Statements

The teacher provides two apparently unrelated statements. The student's task is to move the cursor between the statements and provide transitional middle statements, as in the following example:

Tom stared sleepily at the paperwork on his desk.
The governor stepped into the meeting. "Sorry I'm late," he murmured.

Transition: He had been up late the night before to hear Governor Mackenzie deliver a campaign speech. Mackenzie was slow getting started that morning as well.

AUTHORING PROGRAMS

The final type of teacher utility to be discussed is the most complicated and can be described only briefly here. Program-writing systems, known as "authoring programs," are designed to help teachers write instructional courseware. Complexity varies tremendously. PILOT, the most well-known authoring program, comes in a variety of versions and is almost as complex as an actual programming language. The more powerful and flexible the authoring system, the more complicated it is to use.

Simpler program-writing systems lead you through a step-by-step series of questions. First, you might be requested to type in a question you want asked. Then you type in the correct answer(s). You tell the computer what feedback you want to give the student for correct and incorrect responses and the number of tries allowed for each question. After all the information has been given, the computer automatically constructs the program.

18
COMPUTER GAMES IN THE CLASSROOM

For better or for worse, the computer has become associated in the public mind with gaming. This nonthreatening aspect of computer usage is actually advantageous to the integration of computers into our personal lives and occupations. Most games are simple to operate. By giving users a sense of control over a device which is perceived as mysterious and impossibly complex, games reduce so-called computer phobia.

> They represent a way to transform the most formidable and complicated powers of computers, barely understood by highly trained specialists, into something everyone can enjoy; computational power transformed into human tools of skill; mathematics into method—immediately understood because it is made visual. Video games . . . may well be the first step, . . . making computers available as insightful tools for non-computer people to use to elevate the collective human condition. (Mueller, 1984, pp. 262, 264)

Teachers make use of games in a wide variety of ways, even though most games have more to do with entertainment than with education. Teachers must be concerned about both the *skills* developed by particular games and the *attitudes* conveyed to the players.

This chapter is organized according to the major genres of computer games. One very popular kind of game is the *interactive text game*, a general category that includes educational simulations, fantasy role playing, and strategy games. Arcade *video games* are as well known as pinball these days. In addition, many strategy board games have been computerized. The incorporation of computer games as integral components of educational practice courseware is considered at the end of the chapter.

INTERACTIVE TEXT GAMES

You are armed with a broadsword and axe. A length of rope hangs from your belt, and you carry a lantern in your left hand. To the east is a room called the Ogre's Cave. To the west lies the Hidden Valley. You can climb back up the stairway to return the way you came. What is your decision? You type E and raise your sword against the huge ogre bearing down on you . . . .

Interactive text games are called by a variety of designations, including *adventure games, participatory novels, simulations,* and *interactive fiction.* The player becomes an active participant in a simulated world. In the popular *Zork* fantasy game series, for example, the adventurer passes through a kingdom of caverns and buildings in which lie treasures and dangers. The goal is to collect as many treasures as possible and return to safety with them. For each treasure, however, the adventurer must deal with the accompanying dangers. Attacks from ogres, ghouls, and various similar entities are encountered at practically every turn.

The adventurer participates by typing sets of commands into the computer. E, NW, and S are recognized by the software's dictionary as being commands to move in specific directions. PICK UP THE LANTERN or ATTACK THE WOLF are recognized as action commands. If the adventurer types in a command that the software dictionary does not recognize, because of either vocabulary or syntactic constraints, the screen displays DO NOT UNDERSTAND. Players soon learn the basics of the command language by such feedback.

These games have achieved enormous popularity with computer users. No longer must the sword and sorcery fan simply read about someone else's imagined adventures. Now she can engage in the adventures, through the narrative structures imposed by the software author. The user is challenged, both by the adventures built into the story and by the problems involved in communicating one's intentions in a form the computer will understand.

Each game offers hours of activity. Each entry into the simulated world is a unique adventure. If in one attempt to solve the murder in *Deadline,* you fail to interview a key suspect, the next time may turn up some important clues. "Look man. I'm not going to tell you I loved him, right?"

Do these games have educational value? Your answer to this question will depend largely upon what you consider "education" to be. They do offer advantages:

1. They are motivational. Children and adults find such interaction with text to be fascinating, especially if they have already developed an interest in the genre depicted.
2. They offer receptive language. There is reading involved, often a great deal of it. Each move into a separate underground room in *Zork* is accompanied by a short but vivid description.
3. They require expressive language. The player must communicate his intentions to the computer. Doing so often requires a great flexibility of vocabulary or syntax. If the software does not understand a particular

word or grammatical expression, a synonym or rephrasing must be tried.

4. They can promote interpersonal involvement and speaking and listening skills. Most games are designed to be played by only one player, but groups of students can cooperate to guide the adventurer's actions. Discussion skills can be honed as students exchange opinions about the possibilities involved in strategic planning. One unique feature of *Wizardry* is its multiplayer design. Several players can cooperate in the adventure, each playing a different character.

5. They can be enhanced with a wide variety of educationally sound elaborations. Students can write "book reports" outlining the adventures in the story. A fantasy game like *Zork* or *Wizardry* can be used as an introduction to the genre of fantasy fiction. Students can be encouraged to construct their own sword and sorcery or mystery adventures in creative writing exercises.

6. They involve data management. In *Zork,* a detailed map must be maintained in order to find one's way back home through the Underground Kingdom. Fantasy adventures lend themselves to learning and practice of mapping skills. Mysteries involve keeping track of clues. Practically every interactive text game requires some form of data-management skills.

7. They require problem solving and encourage creative and strategic approaches. Success depends upon knowledge and use of the game rules in critical situations.

Putting all these justifications into perspective, however, it would seem inappropriate to devote great amounts of classroom computer time to hacking away at evil magicians or dreadful trolls. Most adventures require many hours of playing time. Unless teachers are dealing with students who have motivational problems far greater than those of the average student, simulation activities in which students can learn important content through engagement are more appropriate for schools.

These adventures will have continued and increasing appeal to young people. As with television and the movies, teachers should plan to capitalize on their popularity with an eye toward achieving educationally meaningful goals.

Although it is not possible to construct an exact classification system for these interactive text games, most fall neatly into the following categories:

Simulation Games

The term *simulation games* can be used both as a synonym for *interactive text games* and as a subcategory of them. All interactive text games simulate a world, whatever that world may be.

The term *simulation game* is usually used to designate games with a clearly developed educational purpose. They are attempts to copy reality, and they emphasize empirical discovery-oriented learning. Players must put together information by experimenting with the environment in order to control events. In *Lemonade Stand,* players deal with the concepts of supply and demand as they attempt to operate a successful business. *President Elect* simulates a political election campaign. Players act as campaign strategists during a national election and make decisions as to allotment of advertising funds and concentration of campaign efforts.

Simulation games can play an important role in content area instruction. They are discussed in detail in Chapter 9.

Fantasy Games

Also called *sword and sorcery* games, these involve the player in worlds like those of the popular fiction genre of the same name. These games are direct descendants of *Dungeons and Dragons*, the popular role-playing board game in which participants play the role of mythic characters involved in a dangerous quest. *Zork,* described above, is an example. These games exercise the imagination as the player meets trolls, goblins, evil magicians, and so forth.

Dungeons and Dragons is in turn derived largely from the world view portrayed in J. R. R. Tolkien's *The Hobbit* and *The Lord of the Rings.* Tolkien created a magical world of Middle Earth, in which mankind coexisted with mythical creatures and fought an archetypal battle against the forces of evil. While critics may charge that Tolkien's world was simplistic in its dichotomy between the forces of light and darkness, readers for half a century have found *The Lord of the Rings* to be a powerful, almost religious, depiction of the human condition.

Despite the high tradition of fantasy writers such as George MacDonald, C. S. Lewis, and Tolkien, modern-day fantasy fiction sometimes degenerates into a meaningless series of bloodbaths. *Dungeons and Dragons,* as well as most fantasy software, motivates by greed and violence. The creators of such games have "ignored or perverted the systematic ethical and moral views that are at the core of Tolkien's world" (Goles, 1983, p. 44). The attitude conveyed is "kill or be killed" and "rob or be robbed."

Perhaps this is too strong a denunciation for what is probably a perfectly harmless, escapist activity. It is certainly true that these games are fascinating to many people. *Wizardry,* for example, can hold the attention of players for weeks as they engage in successively higher and more complex levels of play.

Strategy Games

Strategy games reflect the interest some have in war gaming. Battle strategy board games have been available for some time. Computer strategy games simply transfer the principles of such board games to the interactive nature of the computer. In *Computer Bismarck,* for example, one player must direct British efforts to locate and destroy the *Bismarck.* The other player's goal is to guide the German battleship to safety.

Emphasis in these war games is on military strategy, on foresight and planning. Strategy games have traditionally appealed to older players.

Mystery Games

Software evaluators examining these games from an educational perspective often blithely call these *problem-solving games,* especially if the games are specifically designed for children. In the family of interactive text games, problem-solving games are perhaps one step closer to educationally relevant material than general adventure games. As with most games, however, formal educational value lies more in what teachers or parents do with the activity to provide general transfer than with the activity itself.

In a mystery game, players are presented with a problem. In *The Disappearing Dolphin (Snooper Troops Case #2)*, for example, Lily has been kidnapped in the town of Costa Villa. The player must keep track of clues, interview suspects, and collect evidence in order to find the kidnapper.

The Disappearing Dolphin is one of several *Snooper Troops* adventures, mystery games that are scaled down for children's use. They have been hailed as invaluable for development of research skills, requiring organization of data and use of that data as a basis for experimentation. Students deal with a complex problem-solving scenario in a highly motivational activity. While their initial response may be to plunge in and try to solve the mysteries through trial and error, the value of careful record keeping, mapping, and thoughtful planning becomes quickly apparent. If you need to locate a suspect and have forgotten where she lives, time is wasted. It's hard to make a necessary telephone call when you haven't noted the booth's location on your map.

While *Snooper Troops* is used by many teachers, it is actually best fitted to the home entertainment market. As with most other interactive text games, these problem-solving activities are designed more for entertainment purposes than for formal education. Schools will usually prefer to teach problem-solving in relation to specific content areas, in content-specific simulation games for example, rather than the form of problem solving used in mystery fiction.

General Adventure Games

The list of categories of interactive text games could probably be extended to almost as long a list as genres of popular fact and fiction. Even biblical events have been turned into programs. In *Castle Wolfenstein*, you are an Allied soldier trapped in a Nazi-held castle prison. The game is primarily graphic in character, with little text. Another graphic simulation is *Olympic Decathlon*. Players engage in simulations of athletic events that require consideration of momentum, vectors, and ballistics.

Galactic Revolution portrays a science fiction struggle for interplanetary power that teaches concepts about political administration of complex societies.

ARCADE VIDEO GAMES

Everyone is aware of arcade games these days. These games generally require rapid, almost reflexive responses and a good sense of spatial arrangement and directionality, though the motor skills practiced may have little transfer to any other fine motor activities. Some involve elements of thought and strategy. A well-organized systematic approach to *Pacman*, for example, greatly increases chances of winning. Thinking skills involved have been exaggerated by the press, however. Most such games depend mainly upon quick reflexes to shoot or capture various types of objects, as in *Space Invaders* where rows of attacking aliens must be shot down.

Arcade games have been both criticized and praised, with lack of perspective from both sides.

Criticisms

Violence. One major criticism of video games is that they supposedly communicate the attitude that violence is an appropriate response to confrontations. Reference is often made to the Dallas teenager who was shot and killed after an argument over an arcade game or to a particularly repulsive game in which the aim is to run over pedestrians with your car. "Children do take the latent content seriously and can be affected adversely by the images provided. It is possible, therefore, that children will imitate the models of aggression implemented in educational software and in home video games" (Cacha, 1983, p. 8). Both Quisenberry (1978) and Stein et al. (1981) have indicated negative effects of television violence upon children. Arcade games may well have similar effects.

No child will be influenced to go out and kill someone by playing *Space Invaders.* But it is also true that "the violence in the educational software is in contradiction to both the values and the educational goals of our society, which are stated so specifically in many curriculum bulletins published by state education departments and local school districts" (Cacha, 1983, p. 9).

Unsocial behavior. Arcade games "tend to involve the player with the computer in a one-on-one, antisocial, intense relationship. Important human traits such as cooperation, communication with other humans, creativity, and analysis of alternative strategies tend to be de-emphasized, often quite strongly. . . . Arcade 'junkies' become in a sense addicted . . ." (Goles, 1983, p. 42). Such criticisms have actually led some communities to pass laws limiting arcade game play.

Such attacks suggest more about the attacker's attitude toward children in general than toward arcade games in particular. Some people disapprove of practically everything youngsters do, whether it be going to horror movies, playing pool, dancing, or reading comic books. Look inside an arcade parlor at a shopping mall some time. You'll find a great deal of very social behavior going on.

Male orientation. There's no doubt but that males are more interested in video games than females. *Pacman* has been cited as innovative because of its relative lack of violence and its cute lead character. Lots of women enjoy playing it. Some feminist critics of video games suggest that the violence is a subtle form of sexism (Yakal, 1983).

Advantages

Discovery.　Educational researchers and theorists such as Dewey and Piaget have long claimed that important learning occurs during seemingly aimless play. Play involves children in a spontaneous form of research and hypothesizing about their world.

Motivational value.　The video game business generates billions of dollars each year, achieving such popularity in 1982 that video games even earned what must be the ultimate triumph, a cover story in *Time* magazine.

Imagination.　Arcade games exercise the imagination. You are in charge of America's antimissile defense system as you shoot down enemy ICBMs in *Missile Defense.* You are piloting the fighter ship in *Zaxxon* and *Hadron.*

Games of all sorts involve much the same kind of "suspension of disbelief" required for reading of literature. The player enters "an imagined world, one in which the 'rules of the game' make sense within their own context but differ from the laws governing causality and relationship in the real world" (Goles, 1982, p. 12).

Fine motor coordination.　Any adult who has tried these arcade games understands the need for developing appropriate hand-eye coordination and spatial sense to succeed in zapping alien battle cruisers or shooting down approaching caterpillars. One could legitimately question whether these skills transfer to other, more important coordination activities. Many times the skills developed on one game do not even have much transfer to another game!

Strategy and problem solving.　Video games do involve strategic planning. As you run the final gauntlet to destroy the *Death Star,* the crosshairs of your laser must be aimed slightly ahead of oncoming TI fighters, but directly on top of enemy gun turrets. If you miss, your X-wing fighter must not be trapped against the valley rim by enemy fire. Each video game requires that the player use trial-and-error methods to work out the most effective strategies. Many games offer successively more difficult *levels of play* with different strategies so that the game remains a challenge through long hours of activity.

Classroom Uses

Perhaps the theoretical praises and criticisms ultimately miss the point. Computer video games are here to stay, though the period of tremendous faddish popularity has passed. What can be done with entertainment video games in the classroom?

Video games used as rewards.   Teachers have used video game playing as rewards for work completed, following in the behavioral tradition of providing concrete positive reinforcement for desired learning behaviors. Generally a contractual system is worked out with the students so that a certain number of lessons completed, for example, will earn a specified amount of playing time.

This reinforcement technique is anathema to some teachers, who assume that learning should be its own reward. Yet research on similar behavioral reinforcement procedures has found positive results. With hard-to-motivate students who, through repeated frustration and failure, have not developed the internal motivation optimal for a love of learning, such external motivators may be all that is left for teachers to use.

Writing manuals.   Video games can be used as the central focus of language experience activities in a variety of ways. One idea that students receive enthusiastically is to write manuals for play. Several such manuals have already been published and are available in bookstores. General computing magazines often contain articles that can be used as samples (for example, Ahl and Staples, 1984). These can serve as models for the manual constructed by your class. Properly organized, the writing and "publication" of this classroom product can be an experience in organizing information and research, in cooperative planning, and in writing to be read. This manual can be an ongoing project, as well, since new video games and revisions of older formats are constantly appearing.

Include the following:

Table of contents

Introduction with explanation of format

Description of the fantasy upon which the game is based. For example, *Death Star* is based upon Luke Skywalker's attack upon the Imperial fleet in the movie *Star Wars*. This story should be written in creative style.

Rules for playing the game. One version may present the rules in text paragraphs. A card-sized reference key may list important commands.

Hints and strategies for improved game playing.

Rating system for evaluating the game, comparing it to others of similar and different types.

The hints and strategies section will be the central focus, especially for the extremely complex games appealing to youngsters (and adults!) these days. *Jump Man*, a video game of the *Donkey Kong* genre with ladders, jumps, and chutes, has 30 different *boards*—action screen layouts through which the characters must move.

Students can use the following questions to provide ideas for their analysis. Strategies should be explicit and detailed, written for the complete novice as well as the expert.

Is it important to read the instructions? Why?

What option (for example, speed of play) levels should beginners choose? What about experienced arcade players?

What kinds of obstacles will be met? How can each be overcome?

What "dumb mistakes" do beginners typically make?

What are important patterns to recognize? Include diagrams or photographs taken of the monitor screen.

How can additional points be scored? Is there any way to relax for a while and pile up the points?

Are there any nasty spots? How can they be avoided?

If you need a temporary break from the action, what can you do? Are there any "safe spots"?

How can you judge how well you are doing?

Include diagrams of the various boards. Since the boards change rapidly, the best way to construct the diagrams is to take a photograph while a board is displayed on the monitor, then draw the picture from the photo. Some computers may be equipped with a special hardware printing card like the PKASO card (Interactive Structures, Inc.), which connects the computer to a printer. PKASO allows a *screen dump* to be made. That is, whatever is on the screen—whether it be text or graphics—is dumped to the printer and drawn on paper.

Make the results available to the whole school by placing a copy of the book in the school library or by allowing students to buy copies at nominal prices.

Creating games.   Dworkin and Dworkin (1983) have used game creation as a language experience for special hard-to-motivate learners. In their games seminar, students have actually developed educational video games, with the help of computer programmers funded by their project. Few teachers will be able to have the results actually programmed, but even the theoretical exercise can benefit students.

The student's task is to construct a game that is a simulated situation. If it is based on some researchable knowledge base, that research must be carried out. If the game is set on the moon, for example, the student should know something about the moon.

The game is educational in nature, designed to teach some knowledge or skill. Students are led to discover the elements of game design, including randomness, specific objectives, time limits, scoring procedures, and visual layout. A manual is written for each game and critically evaluated for clarity.

Though students will be enthusiastic about this creative activity even if the games are never actually programmed, the ultimate achievement for a student would be to see the game in operation on the screen. High school computer teachers in your district might be willing to have these game plans programmed as part of their students' assigned course work.

Creative fantasies.   Look at advertisements for arcade software in computer magazines. Do they picture excited youngsters pounding away at keyboards or jamming joysticks? No. They picture heroic adventurers blasting laser bolts at hideous aliens, or they warn, "The Zapok attack on Earth has begun. Only YOU stand between Earth and utter annihilation!" Publishers recognize that the selling power of a game is improved by the fantasy upon which it is based. That momentary suspension of disbelief in which *you* are the hero makes stylized action on the screen come alive in your mind.

Video games provide rich ground for developing creative fantasies, with all the accompanying creative writing skills of setting, character development, and plot design.

Children can choose a game and write their own fantasy stories based roughly on the game's design, or they can elaborate on the brief fantasy already provided by the publisher.

Learning-to-learn strategies.   Psychological researchers in the 1980s have given much attention to so-called *metacognitive* strategies. Cognition involves learning. *Meta*cognition involves *learning to learn.*

School learning comes naturally to most teachers, and the concepts underlying learning to learn may be a bit hard for some to understand. However, many students have not developed a natural, automatic repertoire of learning strategies. Some may not even clearly recognize when they do not understand what they are learning or reading.

Thomas Anderson (1980) gives an example of metacognition in what he calls the "click–clunk theory of learning." Have you ever been reading and suddenly realized that you really understood what the author was talking about—you felt the concepts click home? Anderson calls this the automatic "click of comprehension." On the other hand, have you ever suddenly realized that you had no idea whatsoever what the author was talking about? This realization is the "clunk of comprehension failure."

Many of our students do not have this automatic monitoring system of judging comprehension success or failure. They may not even realize when they do not understand what they've just read. Their problem is not necessarily in cognition—in learning—but in metacognition—in learning to learn.

The research in effectiveness of learning-to-learn instruction is ambiguous. We are simply not sure that metacognition can be taught, and we are completely uncertain as to *how* it can be taught. Perhaps one crucial starting point is to guide students to analyze and monitor their own learning processes. Awareness of the problem may be a major step toward its solution. If students can think about their own thinking, they may be able to adapt it to specific circumstances of learning.

Stowbridge and Kugel (1983) have used computer games as the focus of a learning-to-learn activity that can be readily adapted to many classrooms. The games used were not arcade games per se but were simpler activities drawn from public domain software. The central activity revolved around learning how to play the games. In one game, *NGuess,* the computer picks a number from one to 100, and the user must guess it in as few tries as possible. The computer gives clues as to whether the guess is too high or too low. Students were told to learn to play correctly and to develop an effective strategy. As they engaged in this learning, they were asked to keep detailed notes of their thinking, recording successes and failures. Little or no teacher help was provided. Entries in their logs might look like this:

The computer typed WHAT IS YOUR STUDENT ID? I looked at my instruction sheet and typed 501. I waited for a while.

The computer did not do anything. Then I remembered to type RETURN.

Students spent one class period learning to play the game. The next period was spent discussing their learning. Both problems and strategies were explained. Teachers guided discussion. They also categorized problems on the board, dividing them into four groups: computer operational, understanding the instructions, following instructions, and strategic.

The discussion is central to this experience, and teachers need to think through their own thinking processes before attempting to facilitate such an exchange. It is also important to realize that a variety of thinking methods may be used to approach the problem. As a matter of fact, that is the key to this whole experience: To give students a repertoire of thinking styles for problem-solving.

Some students may approach *NGuess* in terms of spatial images, thinking of a number line from one to 100, and successively dividing the number line in half with each guess. Other students seemed to use no rational strategy, simply guessing at random. Still others would use only one strategy. It never occurred to them to try another. They seemed to conclude that either they had not worked hard enough on their chosen strategy or that it would not work and therefore there was no solution to the problem.

After using several games and elaborating on the strategic approaches through discussion, a three-step paradigm, or recipe, was developed for problem solving. First, gather all the information you can and compare the situation to other similar situations it may resemble. Second, list the options. What can be done? Third, try out each option. If one doesn't work, try altering it. If it still does not work, go on to the next option.

Stowbridge and Kugel also note that teaching problem solving in game playing will not automatically transfer to problem solving in math or social studies. Students should be led through direct applications of these thinking strategies in their content subjects.

STRATEGY BOARD GAMES GONE COMPUTER

What were the first microcomputer games? Well, long before advances in programming and data storage made simulation adventures available, and before color monitors and graphics capabilities made video games available, there were microcomputer games called *Chess, Backgammon, Checkers, Poker,* and so forth. All of these older games are still around, often at very reasonable prices. Newer versions with programming improvements and souped-up graphics are also for sale. *Sargon III,* an update of the *Sargon* chess program, allows a player to choose levels of difficulty, to review sequences of play, to stop the game and save it to disk for a later time, and even to print out the current gameboard on paper.

O'Brien (1983) calls these programs "software of the second-and-a-half kind." Software of the first kind, according to Watt (1982) is drill and practice. Software of the second kind uses innovative methods, such as using word processing to learn writing. Software of the third kind uses computers to provide experiences impossible without them. Turtle LOGO geometric exercises are one example.

Software of the second-and-a-half kind provides educational experiences that are possible to have without computers but are rarely provided in classrooms. Among its educational goals is the development of higher-level thinking skills, skills ignored by schools that emphasize "back to basics."

These games lend themselves to the same kinds of activities as other games, such as writing manuals and performing metacognitive analysis. Island Software distributes a number of board-games-gone-computer under the trade name *Mindstretcher Series.* Favorites with teachers of the gifted for the problem-solving components involved in each, these include an electronic version of Rubik's Cube (*Rubik*). Another, *Jigsaw Puzzle,* presents a high-resolution picture such as Whistler's *Mother* and divides it into 24 pieces. As the player places each piece in a possible position, the computer signals with a buzz whether the placement is right or wrong. Visual memory of the pictures is tested and improved as children play.

Many electronic versions of board and card games are available for free in the public domain. Chapter 15 describes some. These rarely have the finished qualities of published games, but children may not even notice such faults in their excitement as they play to learn.

Here are some ideas for using electronic board games in the classroom:

1. Discuss winning strategies.
2. Hold tournaments—with the winners appointed as class consultants on those particular games.
3. Have students design and construct board games or card decks to match the computer activity and give opportunity to practice at home. Decorate and cover the materials with clear contact paper.
4. Have students do research on the history of their games. In *Candles,* for instance, children blow out numbers of candles in an attempt to be the one who blows out the last candle. *Candles* is a variation of nim, created in 1902 by Charles Boulton of Harvard University. Games of the nim family share in common the taking away of items by players in turns.
5. Discuss competition and its role in society and among peers.

6. Deal with any mathematical principles involved in playing the game. In poker, for instance, what is the chance of drawing a flush when you already have three hearts?

7. Have students work in teams to increase cooperation and give opportunities for speaking and listening.

8. How can the game be improved? Students may make suggestions that, if carried out by program modification, can improve the game's quality. Public domain programs can be changed by a teacher with knowledge of the particular programming language. Have students construct letters to publishers about the suggested improvements.

VIDEO GAME DRILL AND PRACTICE

The use of video games for motivational purposes in providing drill and practice is widespread, as publishers race each other to see who can develop the most exciting game and most dramatic graphics for teaching subject-verb agreement or sight-word identification or whatever.

The questions that follow deal only with the gaming aspect of computer drill, not with the content of the drill itself.

Is the Game in Good Taste?

Does it contain too much violence? Do the graphics portray images inappropriate to the classroom? This is often a judgment call. *Tank Tactics* has tanks shooting at one another. *Verb Viper* has a dragon-like creature swallowing subject-verb pairs. Are these to be disallowed because of violence? I'd say no.

Are There Levels of Playing Difficulty?

A game's flexibility and usefulness are greatly increased if students can choose difficulty levels. In *Word Radar,* students match sight words as the exercise is timed by the circular sweep of a radar screen. At slower rates of speed, the game can be a visual perception exercise for beginning readers. At moderate speeds the game serves for reinforcement. At high rates of speed the game can be used for development of automaticity.

Do Graphics Contribute to the Activity?

Graphics should add to the effectiveness of a drill. They should not distract students so much that concentration on the actual learning is impaired.

Are Graphics Well Done?

Is the screen so cluttered that students can't make heads or tails of it? Is the artistry and coloring attractive? Are graphics in high-resolution format, as opposed to the crude, blocklike drawings of low-resolution pictures?

Is the Game Motivational?

Almost every game is motivational for the first ten minutes. If the activity lasts only ten minutes for each student, that is all well and good. If students are expected to stick with the activity for greater lengths of time, the game needs a good deal more staying power.

Keep in mind that a variety of games are necessary to suit individual differences ideally. Levin (1982) noted research indicating that even the most popular video arcade game was considered so by only 17% of children surveyed. Thomas W. Malone (1981) of the Xerox Palo Alto Research Center has investigated the relationships of games, learning, and motivation by varying features of computer games played by the subjects. His results indicated that three features are especially important to a game's motivational appeal. Players need a *challenge*. The game should present a goal and should have an uncertain outcome. Accompanying feedback on success in achieving the goal adds to the challenge. A game is enhanced by inclusion of a *fantasy* that evokes vivid mental images and emotional involvement. *Vocabulary Baseball* has the fantasy goal of winning a ball game. *Hangman* requires avoidance of a fantasy catastrophe. Finally, a good game evokes the learner's *curiosity* by presenting results that are new and surprising but not entirely incomprehensible.

Does the Game Include an Element of Luck?

Popular games traditionally include some factor of luck to add a greater sense of risk and excitement. Keep in mind, however, that if the game has a management system that evaluates students' performance, the element of luck is probably inappropriate, since students will be judged on their success or lack of it.

Does the Game Include an Element of Skill?

The skill involved can be either physical or strategic. Again, as with the element of luck, the inclusion of this element works to make a management system inappropriate. This statement is especially true for the first few times a game is played, as students are still developing a sense of timing in their responses, are learning the rules, and are testing various simple strategies.

Rather than perceiving this poor initial performance as failure, students generally react quite positively. They are challenged to keep trying to improve scores, understanding that a poor beginning is to be expected in the play of any new game. Teachers should pay little or no attention to scores received by students during the first few rounds of the game, not only on the first day it is played but on succeeding days as well. They should also realize that an improved score may not always signal improvement in learning of the targeted skill or concepts—it may be due simply to improved game playing.

Is Feedback Immediate?

Drills for automaticity of performance should provide feedback concerning the accuracy of students' responses. An ongoing score is often displayed to let them know how well they are doing. Feedback can be both visual and auditory.

Is Response Rate Appropriate?

The purpose of the game dictates the response rate. Chaffin, Maxwell, and Thompson (1982) favor a high response rate, from 30 to 100 responses a minute (button pressing, handle pulling, etc.). "Such high rates of response allow for little else—that is, the individual has no time for interfering or distracting thoughts without serious penalty. The task has the player's undivided attention" (p. 175). High response rate provides much practice for the development of automaticity of performance.

Certainly speed of response rate is an important factor to consider when determining whether students have mastered a skill. Percentage of success may be high on a word-recognition skill, for instance, but if performance is slow and tedious, has the skill been mastered?

Tom Snyder, one of the originators of the popular *Snooper Troops* detective games for children, favors greater reflection during game playing. "Even *Pacman* could be an educational game if you could freeze the action. You could get higher scores by estimating distances and speeds and analyzing possible routes, as opposed to acting totally instinctively" (Dan Watt, 1983, p. 66).

Is There a Ceiling on Success?

The player cannot win in most popular video games. As the player's ability increases, she is branched into successively higher and higher levels of play. More aliens must be destroyed, attacking spaceships fly faster, or enemy gunners shoot more accurately. Players may gain bonus points that earn them extra playing time, but in the end they lose. The computer always wins.

It would seem that such negative conditions—assured failure—would discourage players, but quite the opposite is true. They are encouraged to improve their skills continually.

Are the Rules Easy to Learn?

The more complex the game, the more teacher time will be used in explaining the directions. Older students can of course be expected to handle more challenging rules.

Are Keyboarding Manipulations Logical?

Some games require ridiculous keyboarding manipulations, such as use of the U key for upward movement, R key for rightward, and so forth. A much more logical system is to use the I, J, K, and M keys, which are arranged in a diamond shape on the keyboard, for up, left, right, and down movement, respectively. Games that allow use of either the keyboard or a joystick increase flexibility.

19

PROGRAMMING AS A LANGUAGE ACTIVITY

Newcomers to the world of computing generally have one of two radically different impressions of computer programming. Some think that after a four-hour workshop in BASIC they'll be able to sit down, zip out the successor to *Pacman,* and make millions. Others think of programming in exactly the opposite vein, associating it with such esoteric skills as neurosurgery, nuclear physics, or genetic engineering. It must take years of demanding study to master such a craft, they suggest. There is no halfway measure in these fields—either you succeed or fail. They are "awesome callings" (Crawford, 1983), meriting our deepest respect.

As Crawford points out, there are no do-it-yourself brain surgeons or nuclear hobbyists. There are, however, amateur programmers and lots of them, many of whom have never taken a single computer course. "Programmers do *not* belong in this Awesome Calling category, even though some programmers enjoy being mistakenly lumped in that group just the same" (p. 153). Once you cut through the computerese jargon that programmers use (just as every other profession or craft does), you find that learning a programming language is actually easier than learning a foreign language (though perhaps just as dull and irrelevant if you have no interest or need for it). The "secret" is simply to make provision for learning and practice time. As in learning to play the piano, practice makes perfect.

This is not a chapter on how to teach programming. Instead, our theme is that simple programming, if taught thoughtfully, can be used to enhance language instruction. The key to this involves first, preplanning and, second, direct transferance to language processes.

Sadly, much of what is in circulation these days about teaching programming to children is of the genre sometimes called "educational wisdom literature": "Gee whiz, look what you can do with a computer in the classroom." There are no theoretical underpinnings of this pedagogy.

There is no research evidence to support it. Authors of such material often have greeted computers as fascinating toys. These educators, like the ancient Athenians of St. Paul's day, spend "their time in nothing else, but either to tell, or to hear some new thing" (Acts 17:21, King James Version). At least in practice, they favor change for change's sake. Still others have vested interests in promoting the national enthusiasm for computer education.

Neither group gives substantive consideration to the important educational issues. Their justifications for teaching programming are weak, *post hoc* rationalizations. The very real problem raised by the national hue and cry in favor of teaching programming to every child is this: What are we going to delete from the curriculum in order to make room for detailed study of LOGO, BASIC, Pascal, or WHATEVER? Should we perhaps eliminate emphasis on human values? Should we spend less time on reading, writing, or arithmetic? Perhaps less time can be spent on studying our own country, or other countries. Should we water down the aesthetic curricula in the arts?

We need to ask ourselves just what is important for children to learn. But, you say, we have been asking ourselves just that question for generations. Yes, we have. And now some well-publicized enthusiasts are turning out article upon article advocating what amounts to an unconsidered trashing of the traditional curriculum in favor of teaching every child to program.

Rather than hopping on this bandwagon, teachers need to step back from the national trendiness and consider whether programming should be taught, and if so, how it should be taught.

ISSUES IN COMPUTER EDUCATION

Computer education is not a new subject area. Computers have been around for quite a while, but computer education has previously been looked upon largely as a job skill, similar to many other job skills. Some students might major in the area, developing programming ability at the college or technical school level. Many students going into technical professions might need to know a smattering of FORTRAN or BASIC, taking one or two courses in high school or college so they can do their own simple programming for research studies and other applications.

Now a cry for "computer literacy" has swept the nation, implying that it is the schools' responsibility to teach all children to program with the same priority as teaching reading and writing.

Almost every teacher will be affected by this controversy. It is important to be aware of several important issues in the computer education field that are not well-publicized in the media.

Will Programming Be Required?

If you are wondering whether computer programming will be required as a job skill, the answer is clearly no. There is not now, nor has there ever been, a widespread need for computer programmers above and beyond the normal supply. Instead there have been short-lived fads for specialists in certain areas. Experts in programming of graphics, for example, were in great demand during the video game craze.

Many people will work with computers on a daily basis. Many already do. However, the vast majority of them do not need to know any programming at all. They work with software they have purchased from publishers who employ only a few programmers. I work with computers on an almost daily basis in educational research. I do not need to know any programming to run statistical analyses. Software already exists to serve all my conceivable needs. Rather than studying programming, I should have been taking more courses in research design and statistics!

What Is Computer Literacy?

Computer literacy is not the same as computer programming.

Several years ago, this statement was not true. There were very few programs available, especially for microcomputers. If you attended a user group meeting, you would almost invariably hear a discussion of some technical point of programming. As a matter of fact, not only was programming a requirement, but construction of hardware was important as well. Many of the older microcomputers came in kit form and had to be constructed by the purchaser.

Today the microcomputer field has changed radically. There is a growing consensus that detailed knowledge of programming is unnecessary for effective use of computers. Those diehards who still advocate teaching youngsters to program do so more on the unproven assertion that "programming teaches good thinking skills" than with the argument that "they will need to know how to program in order to survive in tomorrow's society." Feurzeig, Horowitz, and Nickerson, for example, suggest the following:

> Successful programming forces one to use language precisely, to make one's assumptions specific, to anticipate exceptions to general rules, to design approaches to problems, to generate and test hypotheses (in diagnosing and finding program bugs), to recognize the difference between effectiveness and efficiency. (1982, p. 138)

So what is computer literacy? Ken Brumbaugh of the Minnesota Educational Computing Consortium suggests that the computer literate person be able to discuss

> how computers are used
> how computers do their work
> how to use a computer
> how computers affect our society (1980, p. 49)

I would add two more points, important especially to the reading and language arts teacher: how to use reference skills to find the computer information you need, and how to follow directions in teaching yourself about a computer and about its software.

Should We Teach BASIC?

If I have gone overboard in panning the teaching of programming to children, it is because the public has gone overboard in its acceptance of it. If programming has any place in the classroom (and the theme of this chapter is that it *can* have a role), it is not as an end in itself, but rather as a tool for instruction and discovery of truly important learning concepts—the content areas and the basic skills.

What computer language should be taught?

Mention the programming language BASIC to a computer programmer and his or her lips are likely to turn up in a supercilious sneer. BASIC is in ill-repute among many "computer people." Understand, after all, that BASIC (Beginner's All-Purpose Sequential Instruction Code) was not developed for the expert, but for the beginner, as its name states. It is a rather simple language, with severe limitations in comparison to more powerful languages such as Pascal.

The crucial argument against BASIC is not its simplicity, however. Its structure (or rather, lack of it) is the issue.

Alfred Bork of the University of California at Irvine has led the attack against the teaching of BASIC, chopping out an astounding number of articles on the topic over the past several years. "BASIC, because it does not lead easily to structured programming, tends to develop poor programming habits" (1982, p. 33).

To understand his criticism, look at the simple programs listed in Appendix A of this book. These programs are, for the most part, "unstructured." They are simple linear progressions. First the computer does one thing, then another, then another, until finally the end of the program is reached.

So what is the problem, you ask? They can be read easily. Their sequence of commands is easy to understand. What is wrong?

The problem arises in more complex programs, with perhaps hundreds or thousands of command lines. Unstructured programs become confused and unreadable. They eventually become impossible to understand (and therefore to improve or debug).

What is a structured program? Look at *Electronic Mailbox*, the most complex of the programs in Appendix A and the one that comes closest to the structured ideal. Rather than being a simple linear sequence, the program is actually composed of a central linear sequence in which almost all the important operations are subroutines listed toward the end of the program. To print a message, for instance, the subroutine labeled REM PRINT A MESSAGE is called up by a GOSUB command earlier in the program. To erase a message, the subroutine labeled REM ERASE A MESSAGE is called up.

To do good programming, users must structure their programs. Languages such as LOGO and Pascal require programmers to think in terms of subprocedures. BASIC does not, and as a result many BASIC programmers write muddled and unclear programs.

Do you get the impression that this issue concerns educators only at the advanced high school and college levels? You're right. Until students begin thinking in terms of a career or serious avocation in programming, teachers need not be worried about this issue. Arther Luehrmann has assumed the role of BASIC's defender. "BASIC is the common language of computing. . . . For every person who can write a LOGO or Pascal program, there are probably . . . 50 who can use BASIC" (1983, p. 24).

His argument in favor of BASIC goes like this. First, BASIC is offered on every microcomputer. Other languages can add a great deal to the cost of computers. BASIC comes free with the hardware purchase. Second, the important concern is to introduce children to programming. The subtle techniques can always be taught later on when they become important. Few fifth graders are going to write lengthy and complex programs requiring structured techniques.

For the purposes of the classroom teacher, BASIC is just fine.

BENEFITS OF PROGRAMMING FOR LANGUAGE ARTS

When I give a workshop to teachers on teaching comprehension, I usually bring along three old tennis balls and begin my lecture with a short (and very inexpert) demonstration of my juggling skills. I then give the balls to a volunteer and ask him or her to give it a try. Invariably the balls fly all over the room rather than falling into the neat juggling pattern.

The point is not to show off (though I don't mind that aspect of it). I want to give a brief analogy to comprehension processes. There are two ways to try to learn juggling. The first—a holistic approach—is to simply throw the balls up in the air and give it a shot. This method doesn't work very often.

The second way is to break the juggling act down into its discrete components. The step-by-step procedure I explain to teachers comes from the book *Juggling for the Complete Klutz* (Cassidy and Rimbeaux, 1977). First, drop the ball on the ground repeatedly. Since this is the thing you will do the most, you might as well get some practice in it. Second, toss a single ball from one hand to the other for about five or ten minutes to establish a regular motion. Third, add a second ball, and so on.

My point is to show that, just as the juggling process can be analyzed into subcomponents, so can the comprehension process be analyzed into subskills and step-by-step procedures for teaching.

How do we communicate this step-by-step approach to our students? Seymour Papert, one of the developers of the LOGO programming language (and the writer from whom I stole the juggling illustration) poses a convincing argument that training in programming can guide children to develop a repertoire of cognitive skills that are not clearly taught in most schools. He calls these skills *machine thinking*, a step-by-step approach to solving problems.

In programming, we have a problem given to us. In order to solve that problem, we must consider just what its components are, then arrange the program in the proper sequence. Then we run the program to try it out. If it doesn't work properly, we must debug the program by thinking it out line by line, procedure by procedure.

Papert and others claim that this programming style will have tremendous transfer to other skills involving cognition. Dwyer reports that experience in programming "indicates that it does make sense to talk about helping students become habitual, enthusiastic, catholic, and fluent problem-solvers. As this fluency develops, creativity will also start to appear" (1980, p. 106). Is it not, after all, just such an approach to organization that a teacher would like to see in expressive language activities? Isn't sequencing a vital skill in receptive language as well?

In addition, programming teaches the importance of precision. Sloppy programs do not work. Period. Sloppy compositions can sometimes get by. Sloppy artwork might pass. But sloppy programs die a quick death, marked only by the SYNTAX ERROR message on the screen.

And isn't precision important to language? The choice of a synonym, an aptly worded sentence, a well-organized paragraph—all these are vital to effective communication. "The act of expressing a thought is not some minor function to be handled after the thinking is done; it is part and parcel of the thinking itself" (Crawford, 1983, p. 156).

The importance of programming lies in its educational value, not its vocational value. The vocational skill of programming will not be very important to many people. The ideas and principles may be very helpful. Programming teaches a way of thinking, much the way Latin and Ancient Greek were once taught in the schools. Both languages are very mathematical in nature. Put the words and inflections in their proper order, and you've got a working proposition.

We've done away with the study of ancient languages under the assumption that these thinking skills can be taught in conjunction with more relevant content areas. Unfortunately, that does not happen in most classrooms. Students are simply not motivated to spend long hours writing and rewriting their compositions for fine tuning. Foreign languages are taught by methods that emphasize fluency and speed of communication rather than accuracy.

It may well be that exactly the same cognitive skills which Papert claims result from programming training can be taught by other methods. One thing is undeniable: For today at least, students are motivated by the interaction involved in programming computers far more than by studying Latin or writing the fifth draft of their compositions.

TEACHING PROGRAMMING IN THE CLASSROOM

Well-designed curriculum packages designed to provide teachers with lesson plans and materials to teach programming or computer literacy are now widely available.

A wide variety of books now lead readers through the various languages in tutorial fashion. Be sure that books you choose are written at the appropriate level. Quite a few books are available for children. Books should be clear and specific. When students are instructed to perform a certain task on the computer, the book should tell students exactly what was supposed to happen. Also, be aware that different hardware companies use different versions of BASIC. Make sure the book you buy is for the appropriate version. Computer manufacturers often publish texts appropriate to their machines.

Visit your local bookstore to examine the latest texts for programming instruction.

One of the best ways to learn BASIC is to use tutorial software designed for that purpose. These programs lead students through the task in an interactive fashion. Be sure that the software is not simply a book transferred to the screen, however. There should be actual practice and interaction, rather than simple page flipping. Tutorial software is particularly helpful when you have students who wish to study programming in more depth than the whole-class curriculum. Put them on their own and soon they'll know more about BASIC than you!

METHODS OF INCORPORATING PROGRAMMING
WITH LANGUAGE ARTS

Dickson and Raymond (1984) describe programming as "the third language art" (p. 109). While this description overstates the importance of programming skills, it is certainly true that programming is a form of language communication that parallels reading and writing in many ways. Teachers can capitalize on these parallels to integrate the language arts with programming instruction.

Flowcharting

An outline provides the structure for a well-organized and readable composition. In like fashion, computer programmers sometimes use an outlining technique called flowcharting to plan and structure their programs. Verbal outlines usually represent sequences of ideas. Flowcharts represent sequences of actions. By incorporating the two, teachers can communicate the importance of structure in both computer programming and verbal expression, as well as the importance of recognizing an author's structure while reading. Since flowcharting can be taught very simply or in great detail, with some adjustments it is appropriate for students of any grade level (Wepner, 1983).

As such, flowcharting can be used for exactly the same purposes as a variety of similar techniques designed to teach knowledge of text structure. Mapping, outlining, charting—all these have been used to teach students to see the organizational patterns that Geva (1981) calls "hierarchies within hierarchies." The advantage of flowcharting lies simply in its relationship to computer programming (though many programmers today no longer use it, preferring a natural-language approach instead). An important first step is teaching the various symbols to students. Start with the three basic symbols, the rectangle, the diamond, and the arrow. For an applied exercise in flowcharting, ask your students what they did before coming to school in the morning. List the events on the board:

Get out of bed
Eat breakfast
Brush teeth
Get dressed
Walk to school

Each of these events may take place in a single, linear sequence. Figure 19–1 presents a sample flowchart for the operation. The rectangles in the flowchart represent operations or events. Each separate operation is assigned to a separate rectangle. Note that, depending upon the amount

FIGURE 19–1. Flowchart of morning activities

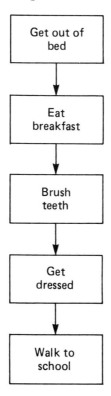

of detail necessary to your plan, each operation may in turn be broken down into a series of component operations. "Get dressed" may be analyzed into "Put on pants, Put on shirt, Put on socks," and so forth. Some prior decision must be made as to just how much detail will be included in the flowchart.

The arrows in the figure represent the direction of flow through the chart. One operation leads to another, which leads to the next, and so on.

As you list events on the chalkboard, you and your students might notice at least one or two spots where different students would choose to do different things. For example, some might need to do some chores or some homework. Others ride the bus to school. These decision points are incorporated into the diagram in Figure 19–2. The diamond shape represents decision points. One point of the diamond leads the process in a particular direction if the answer to your decision is *yes* or *true*. Another point will lead in the *no* or *false* direction. Again the process follows the arrows.

Note also that two oval shapes have been added to the diagram. Ovals with "Start" and "End" traditionally signal the beginning and the conclusion of the process.

Provide a variety of simple operations for students to sequence as individuals or in small groups. They can chart such processes as purchasing clothing, making soup or sandwiches, driving to a relative's house, or fire drill procedures. Some might want to draw up flowcharts of their favorite sports. What options are available if you're on third base and there are two outs?

As students become familiar with these basic symbols, several others can be added to enable them to construct more detailed flowcharts. Figure 19–3 presents the symbols and brief descriptions of their use.

These activities enable students to use flowcharts correctly. They also illustrate the complexity of our daily operations. Cause-and-effect relationships govern paths of action. Outside input often determines events. Minor events are all related to the main ideas. These realizations should be made explicit in the students' minds by directing their attention to them. Use questions to elicit careful analysis of organizational patterns in the diagrams. Figure 19–4 contains part of a flowchart created by Mark, a junior high schooler. The circle with a *b* inside represents the start of this section of the flowchart, a point at which the reader is the lone base runner, on second base with one out. Questions to direct analysis might include the following:

> As you run, the ball is thrown to the third baseman. Will it be close? What additional decision diamond might you place in the diagram?
>
> How might this situation be changed if there are two outs instead of one? Draw an alternate flowchart.
>
> If there is a man on first, you will be walked to third if the pitcher throws a fourth ball. Add this option to an alternate diagram.
>
> How many total steps are there if the coach signals you to run on the second pitch?

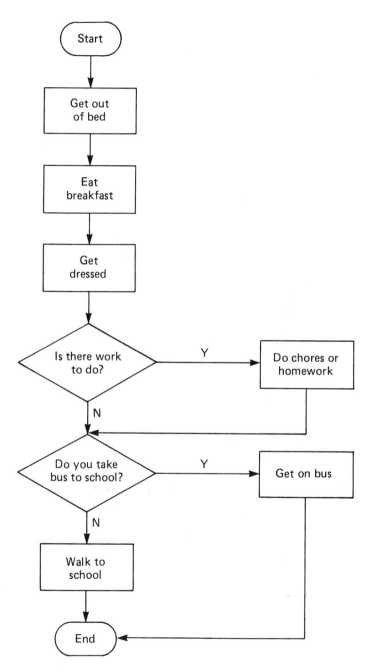

FIGURE 19–2. Flowchart of morning activities with decision points

Process symbol. An occurrence, an action, or some sequence of
events.

Arrowhead. Direction of events. May point in any direction.

Terminal symbol. Beginning or ending of a program.

Decision symbol. Represents options in the course of a program.

Input/output symbol. Information entering or leaving the system.

Connector symbol. Connects one part of a flowchart with another.
Any symbol or alphabetic character can be placed inside the
circle. For instance, connectors are used when the chart is more
than one page long, and might look like this:

Annotation symbol. To give notes or explanations.

Decision symbol. For use when more than a simple yes-no choice
is needed.

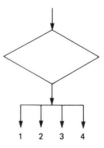

FIGURE 19-3. Flowchart symbols

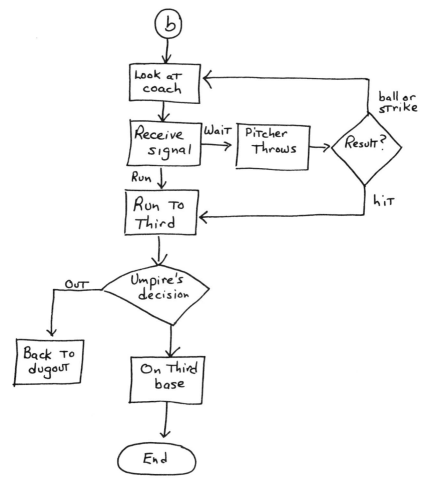

FIGURE 19–4. Mark's baseball flowchart

The count is three and two and you are still on second. How many total steps have been accomplished, according to your diagram?

Questions like these tap critical thinking and analytical skills and give the teacher some idea of how well students understand the flowcharting procedure. They also provide opportunities for small-group interaction that will encourage explicit verbalization of thinking processes. Small groups develop students' abilities to

attend closely to the words of others and to follow their meaning sequences. . . . What each participant says himself depends on what his partners have just said. . . . Transferring this attentive concentration to the printed page can be encouraged by having students talk together about a story or other text they are going to read. (Moffett and Wagner, 1983, pp. 149–150)

The next critical step involves transferring the flowcharting skills to reading and writing. For reading, begin with simple narrative paragraphs that describe events:

Albert sneered at the policeman. "I ain't done nothing," he yelled and started to walk away. The cop grabbed his shoulder and pushed him against the brick wall.
"I asked for your name," he said firmly.

Choose paragraphs carefully so as to avoid confusion. A paragraph like the one above might naturally lead to an inferential flowchart. What happens next? There are a number of options that students can predict and incorporate in their charts.

As student proficiency increases, so can the complexity of the narratives. However, a logical next step is to begin introducing simple expository text structures from the content areas for flowcharting of organizational patterns. Remember, this type of flowcharting requires attention to details. On such assignments, students are particularly motivated if that attention is directed to material that must be learned, rather than material of a general interest where attention to details is of little practical use. If students are studying different kinds of microscopic animals in science, or varying governmental structures in social studies, the time spent on flowcharts should be centered on reading selections on those topics.

Working in the opposite direction, writing assignments can be created based upon flowcharts given to students. Mark's flowchart about the baseball game could provide the structure for an instructional manual using expository prose or for a creative-writing short story. Beginning experiences with flowcharts may be based upon teacher-provided flowcharts. Later, allow students to draw up their own flowcharts and use them as outlines for a writing assignment.

Students will also benefit from creating flowcharts based upon textbook tables of contents or chapter subtitles. These give students a practical experience in the prereading skill of surveying. Before making the assignment, check carefully to see that the text or chapter has a structure that can be recognized by the students. Karlin (1975) suggests that "children work with passages whose main ideas are clearly stated before they study others with ideas that are less evident" (p. 281).

If your students are learning how to program, you might want them to construct an "adventure story" based on their flowcharts. Mark's baseball story looked something like Figure 19–5 when programmed. Notice that rectangles in the flowchart are represented by PRINT statements describing the event. The parallelogram is represented by a command to obtain outside information. The diamond decision shapes are programmed as questions requiring an INPUT decision. Depending upon the input, there are at least two paths to follow for each decision that must be made.

```
500  REM  SUBPROGRAM FOR RUNNER ON SECOND BASE WITH ONE OUT
510  PRINT "LOOK AT COACH."
520  INPUT "DOES HE SIGNAL TO WAIT OR TO RUN? (W/R)";A$
530  IF A$ = "R" THEN  GOTO 580
540  PRINT "PITCHER THROWS"
550  INPUT "IS IT A BALL, STRIKE, OR HIT? (B/S/H)";A$
560  IF A$ = "H" THEN  GOTO 580
570  GOTO 510
580  PRINT "YOU ARE RUNNING TO THIRD BASE."
590  INPUT "ARE YOU SAFE AT THIRD? (Y/N)";A$
600  IF A$ = "Y" THEN  GOTO 620
610  PRINT "YER OUT, DUMMIE!!"
620  END
```

FIGURE 19–5. Mark's listed program for baseball

Mark maintained interest in programming baseball strategies because the content was important to him. He was not wasting his time doing detailed analysis of irrelevant facts. He really wanted to learn the specifics of this content area. Academic content applications of the same methodologies might include a categorization exercise like the flowchart of microscopic animals in Figure 19–6.

Programming Parallels Language

We have seen how neatly flowcharting skills can be used to illustrate and practice reading and writing skills. Just above we saw a second-stage application of the same general principle. Flowcharting projects can be simply programmed to provide a story line or a categorization exercise.

This actual process of programming can be related to language concepts. Chan (1983) notes that a variety of skills we normally associate with comprehension are intrinsically a part of programming as well. Each line of the program plays a role in the overall operation, illustrating the relationships between main ideas and details. The program is carried out according to its sequence and organization. Understanding relationships among the various subroutines is key to understanding the program's operation. Each IF-THEN statement illustrates a comparison or contrast. An important skill in learning to program is to predict outcomes based on a reading of others' programs.

Programming parallels reading and writing in a variety of other ways as well. This parallelism is not surprising. Keep in mind that a program is actually a form of expressive language created by a human being to communicate with a machine. Both natural languages and programming languages are attempts at communication. Since our human concepts of communication are largely dependent upon our concepts of natural language, to some degree all programming languages reflect that dependency:

Programs make use of *statements*. Writers use phrases and sentences.

Programs make use of *subroutines*. Writers use paragraphs to structure their works.

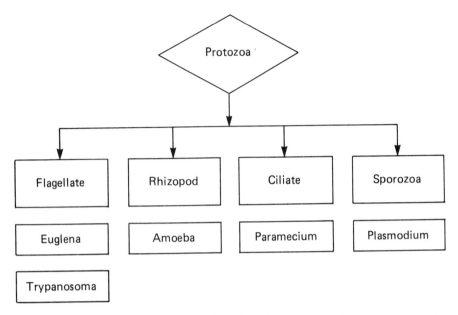

FIGURE 19–6. Microscopic animals flowchart (see *Protozoa Glossary* program in Appendix A)

Programs use punctuation marks that often parallel their use in English. Quotation marks in PRINT statements, for instance, play much the same role as in written dialogue.

IF . . . THEN commands demand the same type of logical analysis as use of *if . . . then* statements in English, or the use of *and* and *or*.

Programs use numbers to sequence their structure. Writers use connecting words such as *first, second, in addition to, as well as, because,* and *moreover*.

Computer commands have a special grammatical structure. Some models of computers, as a matter of fact, register the words SYNTAX ERROR on the screen when a grammatical error has been made. Inform students that *syntax* means *grammar*.

Spelling is crucial to communication with a computer. No misspelled word can be recognized by the computer.

Simply noting these parallels in passing will do little in the way of integrating programming and language development. The parallels must be directly taught with sufficient examples to make their application clear. Don't assume that transfer between the concepts learned in programming and concepts important to language communication will occur automatically.

Illustrating Your Programs

Drawing pictures by computer is one of our newest art forms. A complex operation, *graphics*, as it is called, requires knowledge of the computer above and beyond the knowledge of programming languages such as BASIC. Since every computer model has chosen a unique approach to graphics design, knowledge of graphics programming with one model is not highly transferable to other models.

Several types of computer graphics exist:

Text graphics. Computer artwork created simply by arranging letters, numbers, and special characters to create lines and effects of shading.

Low-resolution graphics. Computer art created by arranging blocklike shapes called *pixels* on the screen. Low-resolution artwork often looks primitive because of the limits of working with the relatively large blocks. A diagonal line, for example, would look like a staircase.

High-resolution graphics. This art is also created by the arrangement of pixels, but the high-resolution pixels are much smaller than those of low resolution. The smaller size of the pixels enables the artist to create realistic and detailed designs. The number of colors available to high-resolution graphics is usually more-limited than those available for low-resolution ones.

Many users who want the joy of creating computer art without the pain of tedious hours of programming opt to use hardware devices that can make computer drawing as easy as using pencils. These devices sense the movement of, for example, a pen across a drawing board and produce lines exactly matching those movements. If you draw a circle on the drawing board, a circle appears on the monitor screen. The graphics programming is automatically created by the hardware and can be saved onto disk and accessed at any time.

VersaWriter (Versa Computing, 3541 Old Conejo Road, Suite 104, Newbury Park, CA 91320) is a drawing board that appeals to the less artistically inclined who prefer to trace rather than draw freehand. A line drawing can be placed on the *digitizer* drawing board, a flat piece of plastic 8 by 12.5 inches in size. A stylus, connected by cable to the computer, is used to trace the design. As the tracing proceeds, the picture appears on the monitor. The lines being drawn can change color at the touch of the appropriate key. For us nonartists who can trace a good deal better than we can draw, VersaWriter is the choice for graphics work.

20

CLASSROOM MANAGEMENT

As a reading specialist, I individualized remedial curricula for 50 students. In addition to using paperback novels, newspapers, and magazines for applied reading and writing work, each student was tested in some 20 skill areas ranging from structural analysis (use of word parts) to critical reading. A prescriptive program was arranged for each student based on this diagnosis and on other factors such as attitude, interests, and age. Setting up such a curriculum was an arduous and time-consuming task, but a task I found challenging and enjoyable.

Managing the curriculum was another matter, a complex job confusing to students and teacher alike. It was mechanical and boring. Slips of paper with daily assignments floated around the classroom; charts with assignments hung on the wall; teacher and students wasted time at the beginning of every reading period figuring out what to do. And behind all this was an incredibly complex record booklet with each student's prescription in code, so filled with erasures and cross-outs from daily updatings that it was barely readable.

Imagine another situation. Mrs. Silvan arrives in her classroom early Monday morning. She turns on her microcomputer and loads the classroom management software program. DO YOU WANT A HARD COPY PRINTOUT? (Y/N), the screen reads. She presses Y. Immediately the printer zips out the latest update of her students' progress, arranged alphabetically in a list by reading group. She sees that both John and Marcia are a bit behind schedule and mentally notes that she will work with them today. Paul is almost finished with his three-day writing project. The printout suggests that he either work on a subject-verb agreement tutorial or do some free reading in his favorite area, mysteries.

DO YOU WANT TO MAKE ANY ASSIGNMENT CHANGES? (Y/N)

"Y," Mrs. Silvan replies with a touch of the key.

FOR WHICH STUDENT?
PAUL.
WHAT IS THE NEW ASSIGNMENT?
    1. SUBJECT-VERB AGREEMENT LESSON 3-C
    2. FREE READING FROM MYSTERY BOOK OF YOUR CHOICE
    3. OTHER (PLEASE SPECIFY)

Mrs. Silvan presses the 2 key. When all the new assignments have been made, Mrs. Silvan commands the computer to print out the daily assignments for each class. She posts one copy of the list near the door for students to consult as they come in. She keeps another copy for her desk.

Does this sound futuristic? It is not. Comprehensive classroom management programs similar to this are available today, helping the teacher who wishes to use an individualized curriculum to manage this task without becoming a slave to paperwork. A wide variety of *computer-managed instruction* (CMI) programs are in use in thousands of classrooms. The chapter will first discuss managerial programs specifically designed for educational purposes, then will describe more flexible *data base management* tools that can be used in a wide variety of situations.

CAI VERSUS CMI

Leiblum (1982) describes the differences between computer-assisted instruction (CAI) and computer-managed instruction (CMI) by four criteria:

1. CAI is usually instructional. CMI is usually not instructional, but rather consists of tests and/or educational management tools.
2. In CAI the computer reacts immediately to the subject. There is an ongoing interaction between the two. In CMI the results are often used in *batched* or delayed fashion. Results are printed out and kept for later reference by the teacher.
3. In CAI the benefits are directed to the students engaged in learning. In CMI the teacher benefits from the help of the computer.
4. In CAI many computer workstations are required. In CMI a single computer workstation is used, and often that workstation is available during class time for instructional purposes as well.

Management of information is at the heart of CMI, and the computer functions very well at this task. The computer's ability to store and organize data is sophisticated even at today's early stage in the development of microcomputers.

A variety of CMI programs are available to the teacher, many of which have been constructed as part of CAI software. These range from very simple progress reports that tell how many questions the student answered correctly in a grammar exercise to comprehensive systems using many diskettes and offering almost a complete K–8 curriculum. In addition, data base management software designed for general use by businesses and private individuals can be used in the classroom for management purposes.

EDUCATIONAL MANAGEMENT

Management systems designed for use by teachers are easier to use than general data base management systems. Educational systems are specifically designed for the tasks that teachers are interested in, so they make it simple to use such options.

Management systems may be divided into four categories. Most educational software available today contains management systems that fall under the category of *single programs,* composed of one or more diskettes that offer instruction and limited management in a single skill or activity, or in a small group of them. *Diagnostic/prescriptive systems* offer no instruction. Their central component is a test to be used for diagnostic purposes. The comprehensive *diagnostic/prescriptive/instructional systems* are designed to largely replace existing traditional curricula, such as that of the basal reading series. *Pure management systems* provide no instruction, but rather simply handle data. Not all programs fall neatly into one of these four categories, but this classification system works well for most purposes.

Single Programs

The *single programs* classification includes most instructional programs for use on microcomputers. The management systems are of very limited scope, relevant only to the particular skill or small group of skills taught by the program. The common drill and practice exercise in which 20 problems are presented to the student and a report offered on percentage correctly completed typifies this class of management tools. Producers of software use a wide variety of approaches to increase the effectiveness of their software through management, including the following:

Simple final report. A lesson is presented. The computer keeps track of percentage of errors and reports this information at the end of the lesson. In some cases, the computer will also report the actual problems answered incorrectly. Such a report is of value in a vocabulary lesson, for instance, where the student can be assigned additional work on words incorrectly identified.

Diagnostic final report. A more in-depth evaluation of the student's strengths and weaknesses is often appropriate. In this type of management system, the lesson's questions have been analyzed according to subskill involved. A comprehension lesson might report on ability to answer questions at varied levels, for example. The final report might include percentage of questions correct at both the literal and inferential levels. Figure 6–1 presents an example of the detailed breakdown of comprehension subskills offered by *Cloze Plus*.

Paper-and-pencil pretest and posttest. In order to save computer time, publishers may make available printed worksheets with placement tests or evaluative posttests. A student would take the pretest to determine whether the lesson was necessary or to decide on the level of difficulty at which the skill should be presented. A posttest would indicate whether the skill had been mastered. Such tests require teacher administration and grading.

Pretest with branching. Some programs begin with a short pretest to determine whether a child has already mastered the skill or to decide on the level at which the material should be presented.

Continuous monitoring with branching. The computer has the capability of continuously monitoring progress for the purpose of *branching* to a different skill, a higher or lower difficulty level, or a remedial lesson as indicated by student progress. For example, if a child scores three in a row wrong on a subject-verb agreement exercise, the computer can automatically shift to a remedial tutorial lesson.

Diagnostic/Prescriptive Systems

The *diagnostic/prescriptive* classification is limited to pure CMI programs, with no instruction involved. Students are tested, the tests are scored, and a report is computed based on the tests.

Remote computer-scored paper-and-pencil tests. Computers have been helping out in the classroom for many years. Every year standardized tests are administered to millions of students. The completed tests are then sent back to the publishers, who offer scoring services. Computers automatically score the tests and print out results for individuals, classes, schools, and entire school systems.

In-house computer-scored paper-and-pencil tests. With the purchase of hardware peripherals, schools or school systems can computer-grade their own paper-and-pencil tests, avoiding the long delays necessary when tests are sent to publishers. Many tests can be administered and graded in a very short time.

The HEI Model 121–4 is one of a number of peripheral card readers. It hooks up to the computer by cable. Students register their test answers in pen or pencil on specially printed forms, which are fed through a slot on the device. The answers are corrected immediately, and results can be stored in the computer or on disk. Software is also available for general achievement monitoring, attendance records, and grading, all based on the paper forms and their analysis in the device.

On-line testing. Tests can be presented to students as they sit at the computer. At the close of the session, tests are scored and results stored on disk for later reference by the teacher. This method has no real advantage over the in-house computer-scored paper-and-pencil testing method, especially when used for more than a few students. It uses up a great deal of computer time as well.

Diagnostic/Prescriptive/Instructional Systems

As is sometimes true of programs in the single-program classification, *diagnostic/prescriptive/instructional* programs carry the learning experience through diagnosis, prescription based on that diagnosis, and instruction based on that prescription. The key difference between the two classifications lies in the scope of their enterprise. These systems offer comprehensive diagnosis and prescription for a wide variety of skills, with the accompanying assortment of instructional programs to meet the prescribed objectives. The largest diagnostic/prescriptive/instructional systems actually replace, or come near to replacing, the traditional curriculum in the general skill area, whether it be grammar, reading, mathematics, science, or whatever.

The previous sentence overstates the actual situation at present. Consider the development of a basal reading series, for example—the series of books from which children learn to read from the preschool readiness levels right on through eighth grade. A basal series costs the publisher millions of dollars to develop. Stories must be written, or the copyrights to them purchased, lesson plans must be developed, workbooks must be constructed, and far more. Only large, established publishing firms that know they can sell their basals for use with hundreds of thousands of children are able to afford to do this.

The development of a complete software system to replace the basals would be just as major an undertaking, if not more ambitious. And the fact of the matter is that there just are not enough microcomputers out there in the classrooms to make this development financially worthwhile. As a result, when we talk about "comprehensive" diagnostic/prescriptive/instructional systems replacing existing curricula, in today's terms we are exaggerating. These comprehensive systems are more for supplementing than replacing textbooks.

Houghton Mifflin's *Microcourse: Reading* and *Microcourse: Language Arts* are two large-scale subskill-oriented systems (114 and 136 diskettes, respectively) for learners from the third to the eighth grade levels. *Microcourse: Reading* offers tutorial work with drill and practice on 330 separate skills. *Microcourse: Language Arts* deals with 440 grammar and usage skills.

Pure Management Systems

Publishers, realizing that administrators control the purse strings in school districts and can spend money on sophisticated software, have provided information-management systems designed to make their organizational and reporting tasks more efficient. These systems are similar to the general data base management tools described later in this chapter, except that these are specifically designed for educational information such as test scores, scheduling, grade records, and instructional objectives.

The Education for All Handicapped Children Act of 1975 (P.L. 94–142) has led to the development of individual education programs (IEPs) for special-education children. The amount of paperwork involved in construction of the IEPs strains the imagination. Teachers and administrators in each district must prepare hundreds of such profiles, consisting of diagnostic results and related objectives and procedures. Many IEP development software packages are on the market to aid in this task. The primary function of such software is to prepare the actual IEP document. Results of diagnostic testing are entered by the teachers. The program selects from its inventory of instructional objectives to print the final document automatically.

Special Management Tools

A wide variety of task-specific software tools have been developed for use by teachers. Some of these are useful, and it's a good idea to know what is available to meet your needs. Choose carefully, however. In some cases it is easier to do things the old way—by hand rather than by computer keyboard.

Class gradebooks. *Apple Grade Book* is a typical gradebook utility. The teacher creates a series of class rosters with student names and numbers. Then she enters grades as they become available, changing them as necessary. Grade averages are automatically calculated according to weightings specified by the teacher. That is, test grades can be weighted more heavily than quiz or homework grades. All results can be printed out at any time.

If you are the type of teacher who skims the gradebook at the end of each quarter and quickly generates a grade, these are of little help. On the other hand, if you laboriously calculate each exact grade, the computer can take a lot of work off your hands.

Readability analysis. Readability formulas are teacher tools that allow texts to be analyzed to determine their grade-level suitability. They are usually based upon two factors. First, sentence complexity is generally estimated by sentence length in number of words, longer sentences being assumed to be more complex. Second, word difficulty is generally estimated by word length in letters or syllables, longer words being assumed to be more difficult. Readability analysis by hand is a long, tedious process of counting sentences, words, and syllables. The *Fry Readability Program* automatically analyzes text as it is typed into the computer by the teacher. Three 100-word passages from a story or book must be typed. The computer then displays a chart that graphs the average readability of the passages. The results are based on Edward Fry's readability graph, the most popular readability analysis device in use today.

Remember that readability formulas are only a first step in the process of matching materials to learners. Many factors not included in the formulas influence suitability of text, including interest level, organization, use of technical terms, level of abstraction, concept load, and so forth. No examination of materials should begin and end with a readability analysis.

Advantages of CMI

Clearly the major advantage offered to teachers by CMI is the efficient use of time. Rather than spending all their time in maintaining records, teachers can leave it to the computer. Information is instantly available to the teacher, supervisors, and parents. Knowledgeable instructional decisions can be made based on up-to-the-minute information.

Bear in mind that CMI may actually increase teacher paperwork unless proper evaluation and decisions are made in advance. Individually assigning lessons in *Sentence Combining,* for example, can avoid forcing students to work on skills already mastered, but it takes longer to assign lessons to each student individually than to issue a general command for every student to do every lesson. Of course, this observation is true of all forms of individualization, not only of CMI.

Beware of several other time wasters. Some achievement reports cannot be printed out in hard copy. They must be laboriously transferred by hand from the monitor screen to the teacher's gradebook. Also, while provision of a paper-and-pencil pretest by the software publisher is better than nothing, it takes time for a teacher to correct such tests.

One critical advantage that computer management offers over traditional diagnostic/prescriptive methods is greater accuracy of subskill diagnosis. For example, do you administer diagnostic reading tests that yield detailed subscore information on a variety of reading subskills? How many test items are used to diagnose each subskill? One large city school system gives each student a criterion-referenced reading test with between three and six items for many of the subskills it tries to diagnose.

These test scores are useless for diagnosing individual students. The technical term for the problem is low *reliability,* that is, repeatability. Give a similar test the next day, and you will come up with dramatically different results for many of your students. Three items, or even six, will not give you accurate results. Statisticians suggest that 15 to 20 items are necessary for good reliability on *each* subscore! That means, for a reading test that reliably measured five skills (for example, making a judgment, finding the main idea, drawing conclusions, recognizing tone, making inferences) you would need a test with between 75 and 100 items. Such a test would take hours to administer and is impractical in most settings.

It is not impractical with ongoing computer monitoring, however. Students can learn and be diagnosed simultaneously. In *Comprehension Power,* students have several lessons to complete. Each consists of a high-interest story accompanied by interspersed questions to develop general comprehension skills. Questions are classified according to subskill involved, and the management report on each subskill adds up the results for each of the stories. By the time students have completed the lessons in *Comprehension Power*, many questions have been asked for each skill. The teacher is able to use the reliable results as an informal criterion test for diagnosis and further specific prescription. If a child has problems with main ideas, for example, supplementary work with finding-main-idea exercises can be assigned.

By the way, low diagnostic test reliability is not limited to paper-and-pencil tests. When your students are pretested with criterion-referenced tests that contain five questions for each of 32 subskills as in the *PAL Reading Curriculum*, the same reliability problem holds true. You probably would get results that were just about as accurate by flipping a coin.

GENERAL MANAGEMENT TOOLS

As stated earlier, one of the major uses of the computer in business and government is as a manager of information. Several types of information-management software are available. This software is not specially designed for educational purposes. Instead, it is appropriate for use in a wide variety of situations, ranging from home and small business use on microcomputers to international business applications on large computers capable of handling vast amounts of information.

Advantages and Disadvantages
of General-Application Software

Increased specificity means decreased flexibility. Increased flexibility means increased complexity.

Software packages designed specifically for educational purposes cannot be used for anything else. If you buy a classroom reading skill management package, it cannot be used for mathematics or social studies. If you buy a classroom management package, the school librarian cannot use it for inventory purposes. These packages are designed to be used for only one purpose, a very limiting factor.

On the other hand, packages that are designed for specific purposes are (or should be) very easy to use for those purposes. Often the user will need little or no prior training before using them. The documentation is internal, users simply answering questions posed to them on the screen: WHAT IS THE NAME OF THE CLASS? WHAT IS THE NAME OF THIS TEST? WHAT SUBSKILL IS BEING TESTED?

Software that is extremely flexible is extremely complex. In these general-application data base management packages, the computer does not automatically set up a class roster, for example. You must know enough about the software to issue the appropriate commands to have it done. However, the complexity of this command structure allows you to use this software for many different purposes.

So there is a trade-off, ease of use in return for flexibility. Most teachers will be more than happy to use the easier task-specific educational management packages, thereby avoiding the task of learning and remembering more complex command routines. Teachers who are willing to devote the several hours necessary to learning a general data base management tool, however, will find that it can be used for many activities in the classroom. Knowledge of data base software is important, as well, for understanding this important application of computer technology in our society.

Another advantage of general data base tools over education-specific packages is availability. Every microcomputer has data base software written for it. If you are having problems finding educational management software for your model, it may well be that you have no choice but to use a more general tool.

Data Base Programs

Just what is a data base program? It is an electronic filing system. Think of it as a filing cabinet, with manila folders inside. Each folder is called a *file*. You decide in advance what sorts of information will be placed inside each folder. Then you type in the contents of each folder. When you wish to retrieve information, the computer can sort it—alphabetically by name, for instance—and print it out on the screen or on paper. The information can be arranged in almost any way imaginable. If later on you wish to add or delete files, the computer will automatically do that for you as you type in the information.

Data base management software all operates on the same principles, though it varies quite a bit in terms of complexity. A home-user or teacher would not need as complex a system as a large business or college, for instance. One popular and easy-to-use data base package that can serve as an example of applications to educational purposes is called *Personal Filing System* and comes with two central components, *PFS File* and *PFS Report*.

Preplanning of your filing system is important, though it is easy to modify it at any time. Let's set up a system to handle reading information on students in our classroom: First we decide what information we want to include. We'll want the students' names and addresses, phone numbers, the results of a reading interest inventory, standardized test information from last year's achievement test, and subskill scores from a criterion-referenced reading test.

PFS File displays a blank screen, a file *page*, on the monitor. We decide that the personal information and interests should be displayed on this page, page 1, and type in the labels:

```
LAST NAME:
FIRST NAME:
STREET:
CITY:
ZIP CODE:
PHONE:
```

Page 2 will contain the test scores and interests, each labeled appropriately. Two pages is plenty for our purposes, though *PFS File* has the capability of including several more. A third page is included for unstructured notes on the student.

After saving this *file form,* we then begin typing in the information. *PFS File* displays a blank page 1 with a blinking cursor next to our first item, LAST NAME. We type in NOWICKI and press the RETURN key. Then the cursor moves to FIRST NAME. We type JOHN. The cursor moves to the next item, and so forth.

When all the information on page 1 is entered, page 2 is displayed with its labels calling for test scores. For INTERESTS we type in SPORTS, TV, TRUCKING. At COMPREHENSION we type in 6.3, a grade-level score. At VOCABULARY we enter 9.1. At MAKING A JUDGMENT we enter M, for mastery.

The third page is left for any comments. Perhaps we wish to note that MR. SARTEUR, JOHN'S TEACHER LAST YEAR, INFORMED ME THAT JOHN ENJOYS READING PLAYS MUCH MORE THAN NOVELS OR STORIES.

After storing information for John on disk, the program recycles back to page 1 for the next student's information. This process continues until all students are logged.

Once a file has been set up, we can consult any record at any time. If we want to review John's file, we can issue a simple command and it will appear on the screen or be printed out in hard copy. We can order the computer to print out the entire contents of each file on separate pages, if desired. Figure 20–1 shows John's file printed out in hard copy.

Files can be updated and corrected at any time. Simply type the student's name. The computer will search for that student's file and display the pages on the monitor. Then move the blinking cursor to the appropriate label and type in the updated information. Files can also be added for new students or deleted for students who move away. If you decide that a fourth page should be added to hold information on writing skills, it can be added to each file, and information can be typed in just as we did with the other three pages.

Another handy feature of these filing systems is their ability to sort information. For example, suppose we have a special learning module designed for lower-ability students who are interested in sports. Choose the SORT option in the filing system. Our blank form will be displayed again. This time we consult our documentation for the appropriate commands and type "<6.0" next to COMPREHENSION, indicating that we want the computer to sort out those students who have comprehension scores less than 6.0 grade level, that is, our lower-ability students. We also type ". . SPORTS . ." next to INTERESTS, indicating that the computer should sort out those students who have an interest in sports.

The computer asks for a title for the list. We type in LOWER-ABILITY SPORTS INTEREST GROUP. It then asks what information we want printed out. We know that the learning module focuses on two reading skills, finding the main idea and making inferences. It would be handy to

LAST NAME: NOWICKI

FIRST NAME: JOHN

STREET: 1190 WEST MORRIS AVE.

CITY: NEWHAMPTON

PHONE: 332-4545

INTERESTS: SPORTS, TV, TRUCKING

GATES COMPREHENSION G.E.:   6.3

GATES VOCABULARY G.E.:   9.1

JUDGMENTS: M

MAIN IDEA: R

CONCLUSIONS: R

PHONICS: M

STRUCTURE: M

CRITICAL READING: R

COMMENTS

    MR. SARTEUR, JOHN'S TEACHER LAST YEAR, INFORMED ME THAT JOHN ENJOYS

READING PLAYS MUCH MORE THAN NOVELS OR SHORT STORIES.

FIGURE 20–1. Student data base file

know just how our students perform on those skills. So we type in FIRST
NAME, LAST NAME, MAIN IDEA, and INFERENCES. The computer
will then automatically sort out students according to our specifications and
print out an alphabetized list similar to that in Figure 20–2. Such sorts can
be made in any combination of the information we put in our files, an
invaluable resource for grouping and individualizing instruction.

    This suggestion raises an important point about input of informa-
tion. Style must be preplanned and consistent for accurate sorting. That
is, if for some students you type in grade equivalent scores (for instance,

3.1, 9.5, 8.2) under the COMPREHENSION category and for others you type percentiles (34, 15, 93), the computerized sort will be confused. Also, if for one student you type FOOTBALL under the INTEREST category, then command the computer to look for students interested in SPORTS, it will not recognize football as a sport. Consistency is vital. For each file you construct, keep a page of notes to remind you of its file name, the general contents, the manner in which you entered information (for example, grade equivalents, raw scores), and your *descriptors*—the key words you use for entries (for example, SPORTS as opposed to listing individual sports, TRUCKING as opposed to TRUCKS).

Data base systems can perform a host of management functions. For special-education students, include a listing of due dates for IEP annual reviews. Each month those students with IEPs due the next month can be sorted out and listed. When data base programs are linked to a word processor, letters to parents for notification and consent can be automatically printed and mailing labels addressed.

Organization of information for the school or classroom library is another possible function of the data base program. Teachers who motivate children to read must be familiar with children's books, but how can you remember all those books you read? Some teachers keep file cards with the books and brief descriptions. The data base program can serve as an electronic file card collection, useful especially as the file grows to a considerable size. After finishing a book, enter the title, author, readability level, and descriptors into the filing system. Include descriptors of the type of book, such as romance, science fiction, and historical fiction (see Figure 20–3 for a sample entry), as well as topic and any possible bibliotherapeutic functions.

Bibliotherapy involves the use of books to help students better understand and deal with problems in their lives (Riggs, 1971). It is "a process of dynamic interaction between the personality of the reader and literature—interaction which may be utilized for personality assessment, adjustment, and growth" (Russell and Shrodes, 1950, p. 335). When a child has problems, many times it is helpful to make a tactful and careful

FIGURE 20–2. Student data base listing: lower-ability sports interest

SPORTS LOWER ABILITY INTEREST GROUP

FIRST NAME	LAST NAME	MAIN IDEA	INFERENCES
ASKOV	ERICA	R	R
DARREN	SAMUEL	M	R
EVANESKI	ANTHONY	M	M
MILLER	PAULA	R	M
VAN ALLEN	JOHN	R	R

TITLE: THE WORLD TURNED INSIDE OUT

AUTHOR (LAST NAME FIRST): RADLEY GAIL

PUBLICATION: NY: CROWN BOOKS, 1982

LOCATION: VALLEY PUBLIC LIBRARY

CALL NUMBER: YOUTH F RAD

GENRE: TEENAGE FICTION

TOPICS: DEATH, SUICIDE, FAMILY

READABILITY: 8-9

FIGURE 20-3. Book data base file

recommendation of books with characters who share those problems (Lehr, 1981). Books help us to understand ourselves, our neighbors, and our world. Teachers who familiarize themselves with children's books can help students by making such books available. The computer can aid in this by categorizing books according to bibliotherapeutic function and readability level.

By including short stories and poems in your filing system, it is easy to construct units based on particular themes or elements of literature. Simply have the computer sort for such information as a theme of NATURE or the element of FIRST PERSON NARRATOR and your reading list is generated automatically.

Construction of a file system for book reviews makes an interesting classroom project as well. Many teachers already do this in nonelectronic form.

Do your students have trouble finding interesting books for book reports, independent reading, or sustained silent reading? An adaptation of the book data base program designed for children's use is effective. When a book report is first assigned, provide a day in which children can access the data base at any time for suggestions on books in the school library. Competence in working the program is important, and data base programs are tricky, especially if the students are not using them on a day-to-day basis. Post explicit instructions or, even better, arrange to have a peer expert available to give advice.

Children must be aware of the *descriptors*, the list of possibilities. When asked to provide the topic, for example, they need to consult the list of possible topics, such as war, science fiction, romance, U.S. history, and so forth.

For example, Mark has just read the *Star Wars* books and is interested in another war story set in the future, a science fiction battle between humans and alien forces. Consulting with the peer expert, he uses the following descriptors:

Topic: war
Genre: science fiction
Setting (time): future

Several files are automatically printed for Mark, all of which are available in the school library or public library. Construction of this data base book file is an awesome undertaking for a teacher or librarian. By making this a class project—perhaps one that extends over the years as new books are added to the library— teachers can give students insight into the important career skill of data base management and use the project as a partial replacement for more traditional book report formats. As each student completes a new book, he or she adds the information on that book to the data base. If a listing for the book is already stored in the file, then the student checks the information for accuracy and appends comments on the book's quality. It won't be many months before a huge array of books are included. Figure 20–4 presents a sample file form for such reports.

FIGURE 20–4. Book report data base file

TITLE:

AUTHOR (LAST NAME FIRST):

LOCATION:

CALL NUMBER:

PUBLISHER:

DATE:

PLACE OF PUBLICATION:

GENRE:

TOPICS:

RATING:

TWO SENTENCE PRECIS:

Word Processors as Management Tools

Earlier chapters discuss use of word processors for instructional purposes (Chapters 10 and 11) and as teacher utilities (Chapter 17) in preparing instructional materials. As perhaps the most flexible software tool of them all, word processors are also useful for classroom management. As with all general-purpose tools, the flexibility of performance with a word processor must be weighed against its complexity. All the functions listed below can be carried out much more easily with special-purpose software. The reality of the school situation is, however, that few can afford to purchase a special-purpose program for every possible function. Get a word processor first, then add special-purpose software as you are able.

Gradebook. The word processor can be used as a gradebook. Figure 20–5 presents a page from such a record book, with names and grades of students for several tests. The word processor cannot add up the grades for you, but a neat, clean record will be available for updates or changes or printouts at all times. Since word processors enter information in a left-to-right direction, it is easier to enter new information at the left margin than the right. Reversing the arrangement of the typical gradebook page, and placing names at the right and grades at the left, is easiest for entry of new data.

By the way, once you've typed in your class list, make a copy of the original file and use the backup copy for grade entry. That way you will have a class list readily available in the original file that can be used for future gradebook pages and other uses.

Class skill record keeping. Much the same sort of system can be used to keep records of standardized and informal testing scores, for use in grouping and individualizing. Word processors cannot sort or alphabetize data. They can keep neat records that are easy to update. Figure 20–6 presents a sample record-book page.

Correspondence. Have you ever wished to keep in closer contact with your students' parents? Do you have standard letter formats that you must send out occasionally? Must you write individualized reports, all of which share much the same contents? This use of the word processor fits neatly into its intended use, writing and correspondence.

FIGURE 20–5. Grade book by word processor

11/23	10/21	10/14	9/7		NAME
85	86	95	80		ARMENIO, PETER
99	92	87	86		BAILES, ANTHONY
81	89	82	86		BEHREND, PAULA
72	86	100	76		CHRISTIE, KEVIN
100	97	96	99		CURLEY, EDWARD
86	54		83		DINERSTEIN, SILVIA

PHON	CONC	JUDG	MN ID	VOC	COMP	NAME
M	F	F	F	3.2	3.9	ARMENIO, PETER
F	F	F	F	3.0	3.1	BAILES, ANTHONY
M	M	M	M	3.7	4.1	BEHREND, PAULA
M	M	M	M	4.2	4.0	CHRISTIE, KEVIN
F	M	F	F	2.9	2.4	CURLEY, EDWARD
		F	M	3.1	3.8	DINERSTEIN, SILVIA

FIGURE 20–6. Student file by word processor

The key to this use of the word processor is called the *fill-in* function. The first step is to type up a master copy of your form. Figure 20–7 presents a sample master copy of a letter from a reading specialist to classroom teachers, informing them that a certain student has been scheduled for remedial reading periods and asking for any feedback on observed needs. This letter was written on the word processor *Word Handler*. Note that certain sections are enclosed by less than (<) and greater than (>) symbols. These are the "blanks" that will be filled in when you complete the form. Each word processor has its own system of command symbols, but *Word Handler* is typical.

After finishing, store the master copy on disk under a file name such as CLASSROOM TEACHER. Type the command FILL-IN. The computer will ask for a file name. Type CLASSROOM TEACHER. This indicates that you want to use the master copy that you called by that title. Then you are asked for the new file's name. This new file will comprise the actual letter you will send to Mrs. Perotti about Susan, your new remedial student. Call the name SUSAN.

The words TEACHER NAME will appear on the screen. Type "Mrs. Perotti". Then you are asked for STUDENT NAME. Type "Susan".

FIGURE 20–7. Sample fill-in letter form

```
TO:   <TEACHER NAME>
FROM: MRS. STEIN, READING SPECIALIST
RE:   STUDENT PLACEMENT IN REMEDIAL READING

One of the students in your classroom, <STUDENT NAME>, has scored
low on the district-wide achievement testing in reading.  The
score was <READING SCORE>.  As a result he/she is to be placed in
a remedial reading group three times a week.  I will get together
with you in the near future to work out a mutually convenient
schedule.

In the meantime, could you please drop me a note about two
concerns:
     1.  Do you agree with the testing assessment of a reading
problem?
     2.  If so, what specific problems have you noted in the
classroom?

Thank you for your help.
```

Then you are asked for READING SCORE. Type "3.2 grade equivalent". At this point the computer automatically constructs the letter shown in Figure 20–8. Note how lines have been altered to fit the inputs neatly into the margins. The letter is ready to be printed out in hard copy and sent to Mrs. Perotti. If before printing you wish to insert or delete anything, you may do that in the same way you would insert or delete from any word processed file. You are now ready to use the master copy to construct a letter for another student, should you so desire.

Word processing is helpful whenever there is a great amount of repeated material to be used. The bulk of the contents of clinical case studies, for example, is different for each student. However, most case studies written by one clinician follow a set format. Perhaps there is a summary of important test results at the beginning. There may be a page that presents test results in tabular form. If the case study is written for classroom teachers or parents, there are often detailed descriptions of the various tests administered. All this standard information can be filed in a master copy, saving the laborious task of typing repetitive material. Figure 20–9 presents a sample master fill-in form for a test table page to be used with *Word Handler*.

Curriculum guides, scope and sequence charts, lists of objectives and other material required by local and state educational agencies can be filed and modified without complete retyping.

A word processing file can be used to store curricular objectives for IEPs. Members of the evaluation team can then select the objectives most appropriate for the child under evaluation, deleting any irrelevant objectives from the master list. Lists of materials and methodologies can be stored as well. If used responsibly, the word processor can aid evaluation teams in concentrating on the substantive aspects of the evaluation—the education decisions—rather than the mechanical aspects of copying the objectives and strategies onto paper.

FIGURE 20–8. Final copy of fill-in letter form

```
TO:   Mrs. Perotti
FROM: MRS. STEIN, READING SPECIALIST
RE:   STUDENT PLACEMENT IN REMEDIAL READING

One of the students in your classroom, Susan, has scored low on
the district-wide achievement testing in reading.  The score was
3.2 grade equivalent.  As a result he/she is to be placed in a
remedial reading group three times a week.  I will get together
with you in the near future to work out a mutually convenient
schedule.

In the meantime, could you please drop me a note about two
concerns:
     1.  Do you agree with the testing assessment of a reading
problem?
     2.  If so, what specific problems have you noted in the
classroom?

Thank you for your help.
```

```
STUDENT NAME:    <STUDENT NAME>          GRADE:   <GRADE>
ADDRESS:    <ADDRESS LINE 1>             AGE:   <AGE>
            <ADDRESS LINE 2>             TEACHER:   <TEACHER>
            <ADDRESS LINE 3>

REPORT COMPLETED BY:    <CLINICIAN NAME>
                DATE:   <DATE OF REPORT>

STANDARDIZED TESTING

IQ (Test of General Abilities):   <IQ>
STANFORD DIAGNOSTIC READING TEST
    LITERAL COMPREHENSION:   <LITERAL COMPREHENSION>
    INFERENTIAL COMPREHENSION:   <INFERENTIAL COMPREHENSION>
    PHONICS:   <PHONICS>
    STRUCTURAL ANALYSIS:   <STRUCTURAL ANALYSIS>
    VOCABULARY:   <VOCABULARY>

INFORMAL READING INVENTORY (SILVAROLI)

INDEPENDENT LEVEL:   <INDEPENDENT LEVEL>
INSTRUCTIONAL LEVEL:   <INSTRUCTIONAL LEVEL>
FRUSTRATION LEVEL:   <FRUSTRATION LEVEL>
CAPACITY LEVEL:   <CAPACITY LEVEL>
```

FIGURE 20–9. Diagnostic report by word processor

If you plan to use your classroom word processor for this purpose, it is best to avoid purchasing simple programs designed for children. These simplified programs are designed for classroom writing of compositions and lack many of the secretarial features of the more complex word processors. Teachers have found that adult word processors such as *Apple Writer II* and *Word Handler* can be used for both instructional and management purposes.

Do you often wish that you had the time to send for free information and materials you see listed in educational journals such as *Instructor Magazine*'s "Fabulous Freebies" column? Form letters like Figure 20–10 can be a great time saver. When I read the journals in a library or resource center, I bring along a stack of envelopes to be addressed right there. I write the name or title of the item desired on the inside flap. Then when I get home I insert the address and title in the appropriate fill-in form and print it out in hard copy, ready for mailing.

Integrated Systems

With an integrated word processor and data base program, the information from the data files can be automatically inserted in letters and reports printed by the word processor. We've seen how a data base program can sort and print lists of testing data on students. Imagine the usefulness of a program that can print a letter to each student's parents, automatically addressing the letter, inserting the appropriate test results in the body of the letter, and printing mailing labels for each. A sorting

```
                              Westview School
                              Cranston Road
                              Oldtown, CC 00000
                              <DATE>

<NAME>
<ADDRESS LINE 1>
<ADDRESS LINE 2>
<ADDRESS LINE 3>


Dear Sir:

        I am a teacher at the Westview School. Please send me
<ITEM>. This will be used for educational purposes in my
classroom.
        Thank you very much for your help in this matter.


                              Yours,


                              Sally Weckennon
```

FIGURE 20–10. Sample fill-in request form

operation could arrange that different forms of the letter be sent to different parents. Students who did poorly and require remedial help would receive one version, and students who did well would receive another. All this would be carried out automatically, without the days of clerical work that would be necessary if the operation were carried out by hand.

While there are many word processors and data base programs on the market, most are discrete systems that will not work together. Care must be taken to choose integrated systems that are easy to use. *PFS Write, PFS File,* and *PFS Report* are popular programs. The first is a word processor, the second is a data base program, and the third adds to the possible data base operations. All three work together to provide integrated functions, with the data base programs feeding information to the word processor for automatic form fill-in capability (sometimes called *mail/merge* functions).

21

PRINTED MATERIALS AND COMPUTERS

Books will be obsolete. Scholars will soon be instructed through the eye. It is possible to teach every branch of human knowledge with the motion picture. Our school system will be completely changed in ten years.

—Thomas Edison, 1913

Saettler (1968) used Edison's quote above to illustrate the durability of books. It seems that almost every major technological development in this century has led to prophecies of educational revolution in which traditional components of education would fall by the wayside. Yet the classroom of today is remarkably similar to classrooms of 80 years ago. Most instruction is teacher- and book-centered.

Each teaching medium has its own advantages, and the teacher's task is to capitalize upon those specific advantages. Teacher-directed learning is ultimately flexible. A teacher can easily revise his or her presentation to fit the particular needs of the class and, by staying abreast of current developments, can update materials to fit the needs of the day.

Instructional use of computers takes advantage of their individualized interactive qualities and data-management advantages. Television and movies offer superior graphics.

Printed materials offer unparalleled advantages in terms of print display. Clarity of type is excellent. Books give the ability to skim and scan large amounts of material. A single printed page can hold many times the amount of text allowed on a computer monitor. It seems unlikely that computers will soon—if ever—retire the book from educational proceedings, though Reinking and Schreiner (1984) have shown that computer presentation of text, with appropriate computer-provided aids, can improve learning from text.

Teachers find many ways to combine use of printed text and computer materials to make use of the strong points of each.

SUPPLEMENTAL WORKSHEETS

Owing in no small part to the recognition that students have limited computer-access time, many publishers include printed worksheets with their software that elaborate on skills learned or practiced on the computer. Such worksheets are especially useful for elaborations that require little interaction and much time-consuming thinking, writing, or illustrating.

COMPUTER MAGAZINES

Show students that reading is a natural way to improve their knowledge of their hobbies and interests. So many youngsters have become interested in computers that a number of colorful magazines designed for young computer buffs are available.

DIGIT (P.O. Box 29996, San Francisco, CA 94129) offers a wide variety of articles on computer software and hardware. The magazine is written for children and has a heavy emphasis on educationally important topics, especially in the field of programming.

Even video game buffs have their own magazines. *Electronic Games* (P.O. Box 1128, Dover, NJ 07801) is a wildly illustrated source of information on the latest video offerings, with a monthly best-seller list and the rankings of top players nationwide (for example, Lance Simon of Carmichael, California—579,660 points in Atari *Asteroids*). Articles have such titles as "Everything You Ever Wanted to Know About *Miner 2049er*" and "The Challenge of *Zork*."

DRAMA AND COMPUTERS

Combine computer education with drama by using printed plays to teach computer literacy. Magazines such as *Teaching and Computers* occasionally offer dramatic plays and skits oriented to computer education. Such plays present opportunities for combining content-learning experiences with a chance for self-expression and creativity. Rotenberg (1983), for instance, has written a takeoff of Dickens's *A Christmas Carol* on the history of computers, called "A Computer Carol."

COMPUTERS AND LITERATURE

No publisher is seriously considering doing away with printed books in favor of on-line text presentation. The computer does offer the possibility of increased individualization of reading assignments, however. Several software publishers now produce computer materials designed to be used in conjunction with independent book reading assignments of popular children's literature. Pendulum Press has published a *Read-and-Review* series of disks for use with their *adapted classics* (books rewritten at an easier readability level). Pendulum's *Illustrated Classics* are written in comic book form and include *Frankenstein, The Red Badge of Courage, Tom Sawyer,* and many others. Each classic is accompanied by a student activity book with vocabulary and comprehension questions. The microcomputer program is limited, consisting of only 20 questions per book.

Pomfret House programs deal with adapted versions of classic short stories such as "The Black Cat" and "The Hound of the Baskervilles," as well as with topical materials such as UFOs and the Bermuda triangle. Illustrated filmstrips are offered as options for each. Sunburst Communications has produced *Micro Skillbuilder Sets* and *Newbery Winners* to accompany Newbery Award–winning books and other popular books for young people. *Island of the Blue Dolphins, My Side of the Mountain, Sounder,* and *The Summer of Swans* are only a few. Computer work includes a comprehension test, with chapter references given after the first incorrect response to aid students in scanning for the answer. There are also synonym and crossword puzzles for vocabulary and an out-of-order sequence of events list.

For teachers interested in encouraging student choice of reading material, these programs offer great potential. As with all software, however, they must be evaluated for quality.

1. Is there a printed summary of the book included with the teacher documentation? *Micro Skillbuilder Sets* include a two-page summary of each book.
2. Are all materials at the student's reading level? There should be a match between difficulty level of the book and of the computer materials.
3. Does the computer lesson comprise a learning experience, or is it simply a test? Both *Micro Skillbuilders* and *Read-and-Review* give hints when a question is missed to allow children to refer back to the book and scan for the answer. For instance, the monitor display may read, SEE CHAPTER 7, or, HINT: HE IS THE MAIN CHARACTER.
4. Is the teaching sequence logical? Most materials available at present are designed solely for postreading use. It would make more sense, for instance, to give vocabulary words *before* the reading rather than after.

BASIC PROGRAMS

Programs included in this appendix are described in the text. All are written in BASIC for the Apple II computer, but a teacher with minimal programming ability will find translation to the BASIC language of another computer very easy. Each of these programs has purposely been made short and simple, because complex programs are usually difficult to translate.

Consult your computer manual for information on how to type programs and save them on disk or cassette. Type carefully and proofread. Save your work frequently to avoid accidental erasure, and make backups. Further details on typing listed programs are included in Chapter 15.

Where helpful, each program is followed by a sample "run" that illustrates its procedures. User inputs and explanatory comments within the sample runs are underlined.

Spelling Quiz1 listing

```
]LIST

1  REM        SPELLING QUIZ1 BY ERNEST BALAJTHY -- SEE CHAPTER 12 FOR DESCR
   IPTION AND INSTRUCTIONS.
2  REM     TO INCREASE OR DECREASE LENGTH OF WORD FLASH, CHANGE THE '300' I
   N LINE 150 TO A HIGHER OR LOWER NUMBER.
3  REM     TO CHANGE THE LIST OF WORDS, ADD OR CHANGE ANY OF THE DATA LINE
   S.  ANY LINE NUMBERS BETWEEN THE FIRST AND LAST DATA LINES MAY BE US
   ED.
5  HOME
10  HOME
20  DATA    RECIPROCAL
30  DATA    PROCEED
40  DATA    INTERVENE
50  DATA    ASSURANCE
60  DATA    INEPTITUDE
70  DATA    INTERFERING
80  DATA    ALLIANCE
90  DATA    OBVIOUS
100  DATA    SADDENED
110  DATA    REGARDLESS
120  READ A$: REM    READ THE SPELLING WORD:NEXT L
135  VTAB 7: HTAB 5: PRINT "GET READY..."
137  VTAB 10: HTAB 3: PRINT "--->": FOR W = 1 TO 1000: NEXT W
138  VTAB 10: HTAB 9
140  PRINT A$
150  FOR W = 1 TO 300: NEXT W
160  HOME
170  INPUT "NOW SPELL THE WORD:  ";B$
180  IF B$ = A$ THEN  PRINT "RIGHT!": GOTO 250
190  PRINT "WRONG"
200  PRINT "THE CORRECT SPELLING IS ";A$;"."
210  FOR W = 1 TO 3000: NEXT W
215  PRINT "LET'S TRY AGAIN."
216  FOR W = 1 TO 1500: NEXT W
220  GOTO 135
250  GOTO 120
260  GOTO 120
```

Sample run for *Spelling Quiz1*

```
]RUN
     GET READY...
   --->
          RECIPROCAL
NOW SPELL THE WORD:    RECIPROCAL    (Note:  This word is briefly flashed.)
RIGHT!
     GET READY...
   --->
          PROCEED
NOW SPELL THE WORD:    PROCEDE
WRONG
THE CORRECT SPELLING IS PROCEED.
LET'S TRY AGAIN.
     GET READY...
   --->
          PROCEED
NOW SPELL THE WORD:   PROCEED
RIGHT!
     GET READY...
   --->
          INTERVENE
```

Your Choice listing, lines 1–386

```
]
]LIST 1-386

1    REM    YOUR CHOICE BY ERNEST BALAJTHY
2    REM    SEE CHAPTER 12 FOR DESCRIPTION AND INSTRUCTIONS.
5    HOME
10   REM    TITLE PAGE
15   VTAB 10
19   REM    MAKE A PRINT STATEMENT WITH YOUR TITLE ON LINE 20
20   PRINT "YOUR TITLE HERE"
25   VTAB 15: HTAB 10
29   REM    MAKE A PRINT STATEMENT WITH YOUR NAME ON LINE 30
30   PRINT "YOUR NAME HERE"
35   FOR W = 1 TO 3000: NEXT W
40   HOME
99   REM    WRITE THE FIRST PAGE OF YOUR STORY ON EVEN NUMBERED LINES 102 TO
            140.
145  VTAB 23: PRINT "PRESS ANY KEY TO GO ON."
148  GET A$
150  REM    OPTION PAGE.   TYPE YOUR OPTIONS IN PRINT STATEMENTS ON LINES 15
            5, 160, AND 165.
154  HOME
155  PRINT "PRESS 'A' TO ****."
160  PRINT "PRESS 'B' TO ****."
165  PRINT "PRESS 'C' TO ****."
183  GET A$
185  IF A$ = "A" GOTO 200
186  IF A$ = "B" GOTO 300
187  IF A$ = "C" GOTO 400
200  REM    WRITE THE FIRST OPTION ON EVEN NUMBERED LINES 202 TO 240
245  VTAB 23: PRINT "PRESS ANY KEY TO GO ON."
248  GET A$
250  REM    OPTION PAGE.
254  HOME
255  PRINT "PRESS 'A' TO ****."
260  PRINT "PRESS 'B' TO ****."
283  GET A$
285  IF A$ = "A" GOTO 500
286  IF A$ = "B" GOTO 600
300  REM    WRITE THE SECOND OPTION ON EVEN NUMBERED LINES 302 TO 340
345  VTAB 23: PRINT "PRESS ANY KEY TO GO ON."
348  GET A$
350  REM    OPTION PAGE
354  HOME
355  PRINT "PRESS 'A' TO ****."
360  PRINT "PRESS 'B' TO ****."
383  GET A$
385  IF A$ = "A" GOTO 700
386  IF A$ = "B" GOTO 800
```

Your Choice listing, lines 400–1,099

```
400   REM   WRITE THE THIRD OPTION ON EVEN NUMBERED LINES 402 TO 440.
445   VTAB 23: PRINT "PRESS ANY KEY TO GO ON."
448   GET A$
450   REM   OPTION PAGE
454   HOME
455   PRINT "PRESS 'A' TO ****."
460   PRINT "PRESS 'B' TO ****."
483   GET A$
485   IF A$ = "A" GOTO 900
486   IF A$ = "B" GOTO 1000
500   REM   WRITE THE FIRST OPTION ON EVEN NUMBERED LINES 502 TO 540.
599   END
600   REM   WRITE THE SECOND OPTION ON EVEN NUMBERED LINES 602 TO 640.
699   END
700   REM   WRITE THE FIRST OPTION ON EVEN NUMBERED LINES 702 TO 740.
799   END
800   REM   WRITE THE SECOND OPTION ON EVEN NUMBERED LINES 802 TO 840.
899   END
900   REM    WRITE THE SECOND OPTION ON EVEN NUMBERED LINES 902 TO 940.
999   END
1000  REM   WRITE THE SECOND OPTION ON EVEN NUMBERED LINES 1002 TO 1040.
1099  END
```

Class Anthology listing, lines 1–999

```
]
]LIST 1-999

1   REM   CLASS ANTHOLOGY BY ERNEST BALAJTHY
2   REM    SEE CHAPTER 12 FOR DESCRIPTION AND INSTRUCTIONS
100  HOME
110  INVERSE : PRINT "            CLASS ANTHOLOGY            "
120  NORMAL
130  PRINT : PRINT "                ROOM 100"
140  PRINT : PRINT "              MRS. JABLONSKI"
143  FOR W = 1 TO 3000: NEXT W
145  HOME
150  PRINT : PRINT : PRINT "      TABLE OF CONTENTS"
160  PRINT : PRINT "      A. HAIKU"
170  PRINT : PRINT "      B. TERQUAIN"
180  PRINT : PRINT "      C. CINQUAIN"
190  PRINT : PRINT "      D. CINQUAIN--HOLIDAYS"
200  PRINT : PRINT "      E. WISH POEMS"
210  PRINT : PRINT "      F. ATTACK OF THE CUCUMBERS (STORY)"
215  PRINT : PRINT "      I. INSTRUCTIONS FOR ADDITIONS"
220  PRINT : PRINT "INSTRUCTIONS:  TYPE THE LETTER OF YOUR"
230  PRINT "CHOICE."
240  GET A$
250  IF A$ = "A" THEN  GOSUB 500
260  IF A$ = "B" THEN  GOSUB 1000
270  IF A$ = "C" THEN  GOSUB 1500
280  IF A$ = "D" THEN  GOSUB 2000
290  IF A$ = "E" THEN  GOSUB 2500
300  IF A$ = "F" THEN  GOSUB 3000
305  IF A$ = "I" THEN  GOSUB 400
310  GOTO 145
400  HOME
401  PRINT "INSTRUCTIONS:"
403  PRINT "TO ADD YOUR POEM, FIND THE LAST ENTRY"
405  PRINT "LINE OF THE APPROPRIATE CHAPTER.  START"
408  PRINT "WRITING YOUR POEM ON THE NEXT LINE."
410  PRINT "USE PRINT COMMANDS FOR EACH LINE OF "
413  PRINT "YOUR POEM.  YOUR FIRST LINE SHOULD BE"
415  PRINT "'HOME' TO CLEAR THE SCREEN. THEN 'PRINT'"
418  PRINT "EACH LINE OF THE POEM.  YOUR LAST LINES"
420  PRINT "SHOULD READ"
423  PRINT "  PRINT ''PRESS ANY KEY TO GO ON.''"
425  PRINT "  GET A$"
430  PRINT : PRINT : PRINT "PRESS ANY KEY TO GO ON."
440  GET A$
499  RETURN
500  REM
501  HOME
510  REM
520  REM   HAIKU CHAPTER
530  REM
540  INVERSE
550  PRINT : PRINT : PRINT "            HAIKU CHAPTER            "
560  NORMAL
570  FOR W = 1 TO 3000: NEXT W
999  RETURN
```

Class Anthology listing, lines 1,000–3,499

```
1000  REM
1001  HOME
1010  REM
1020  REM   TERQUAIN CHAPTER
1030  REM
1040  INVERSE
1050  PRINT : PRINT : PRINT "        TERQUAIN CHAPTER        "
1060  NORMAL
1070  FOR W = 1 TO 3000: NEXT W
1499  RETURN
1999  RETURN
2499  RETURN
2999  RETURN
3499  RETURN
```

Protozoa Glossary listing, lines 1–300

```
]
]LIST 1-300

1   REM   PROTOZOA GLOSSARY PROGRAM BY ERNEST BALAJTHY.
2   REM   SEE CHAPTER 19 FOR DESCRIPTION AND INSTRUCTIONS
10  GOTO 100
40  REM   LAYOUT OF DEFINITION PAGE
41  VTAB 8: HOME
42  PRINT "                    ";A$
43  PRINT : PRINT : PRINT : PRINT B$
44  PRINT : PRINT C$
45  PRINT : PRINT D$
46  PRINT : PRINT E$
47  PRINT : PRINT F$
48  VTAB 23
49  PRINT "              PRESS ANY KEY TO GO ON."
50  GET X$
51  GOTO 100
100 HOME
101 A$ = "":B$ = "":C$ = "":D$ = "":E$ = "":F$ = ""
109 INVERSE
110 PRINT "                    PROTOZOA                    "
120 PRINT "FLAGELLATE RHIZOPOD  CILIATE   SPOROZOA"
130 NORMAL
140 PRINT "    !         !         !         !"
150 PRINT "    !         !         !         !"
160 PRINT "EUGLENA     AMOEBA PARAMECIUM PLASMODIUM"
170 PRINT "TRYPANOSOMA"
180 PRINT : PRINT : PRINT "TYPE THE NAME OF THE PROTOZOAN ABOUT"
182 PRINT "WHICH YOU WANT MORE INFORMATION"
185 INPUT A$
186 IF A$ = "FLAGELLATE" THEN  GOTO 300
187 IF A$ = "RHIZOPOD" THEN  GOTO 310
188 IF A$ = "CILIATE" THEN  GOTO 320
189 IF A$ = "SPOROZOA" THEN  GOTO 330
190 IF A$ = "EUGLENA" THEN  GOTO 340
191 IF A$ = "TRYPANOSOMA" THEN  GOTO 350
192 IF A$ = "AMOEBA" THEN  GOTO 360
193 IF A$ = "PARAMECIUM" THEN  GOTO 370
194 IF A$ = "PLASMODIUM" THEN  GOTO 380
200 GOTO 100
300 REM   FLAGELLATE PAGE
```

Protozoa Glossary listing, lines 301–389

```
301 B$ = "MOVE AROUND BY MEANS OF A WHIPLIKE"
302 C$ = "TAIL CALLED A 'FLAGELLUM.'
303  GOTO 40
310  REM  RHIZOPOD PAGE
311 B$ = "MOVE AROUND AND TRAP ORGANISMS FOR FOOD"
312 C$ = "BY PUSHING PART OF ITS JELLY-LIKE BODY"
313 D$ = "FORWARD AND THEN FLOWING INTO THAT PART."
314 E$ = "THE PUSHED OUT PART IS CALLED A"
315 F$ = "PSEUDOPOD."
319  GOTO 40
320  REM  CILIATE PAGE
321 B$ = "MOVE BY MEANS OF TINY HAIR-LIKE"
322 C$ = "STRUCTURES CALLED 'CILIA'."
329  GOTO 40
330  REM  SPOROZOA PAGE
331 B$ = "A WIDELY DIFFERING GROUP OF ANIMALS"
332 C$ = "WHICH USUALLY DO NOT MOVE EASILY."
333 D$ = "SOME TYPES CAUSE THE DISEASE CALLED"
334 E$ = "MALARIA."
339  GOTO 40
340  REM  EUGLENA PAGE
341 B$ = "EUGLENA ARE ANIMALS BUT ARE ALSO"
342 C$ = "CLOSELY RELATED TO PLANTS.  THEY"
343 D$ = "PERFORM PHOTOSYNTHESIS JUST LIKE GREEN"
344 E$ = "PLANTS."
349  GOTO 40
350  REM   TRYPANOSOMA PAGE
351 B$ = "THIS FLAGELLATE CAUSES THE DISEASE"
352 C$ = "CALLED AFRICAN SLEEPING SICKNESS."
359  GOTO 40
360  REM   AMOEBA PAGE
362 B$ = "THE AMOEBA IS THE SIMPLEST OF ALL"
363 C$ = "ANIMALS.  IT LOOKS LIKE A PIECE OF"
364 D$ = "CLEAR JELLY.  IT FLOWS AROUND ITS FOOD"
365 E$ = "TO EAT IT."
369  GOTO 40
370  REM  PARAMECIUM PAGE
371 B$ = "THE PARAMECIUM IS SHAPED LIKE A FLAT"
372 C$ = "SHOE.  IT HAS A SORT OF MOUTH AT THE"
373 D$ = "SIDE OF ITS BODY.  IT PUSHES FOOD INTO"
374 E$ = "ITS MOUTH WITH ITS TINY CILIA."
379  GOTO 40
380  REM  PLASMODIUM PAGE
381 B$ = "THE PLASMODIUM IS SHAPED LIKE A TWISTED"
382 C$ = "SPINDLE.  IT CAUSES MALARIA WHEN IT"
383 D$ = "ENTERS THE HUMAN BLOODSTREAM."
389  GOTO 40
```

Sample run for *Protozoa Glossary*

```
]RUN
                PROTOZOA
FLAGELLATE  RHIZOPOD   CILIATE   SPOROZOA
    !           !          !          !
    !           !          !          !
    !           !          !          !
EUGLENA       AMOEBA PARAMECIUM PLASMODIUM
TRYPANOSOMA


TYPE THE NAME OF THE PROTOZOAN ABOUT
WHICH YOU WANT MORE INFORMATION
?EUGLENA
                EUGLENA


EUGLENA ARE ANIMALS BUT ARE ALSO

CLOSELY RELATED TO PLANTS.   THEY

PERFORM PHOTOSYNTHESIS JUST LIKE GREEN

PLANTS.


          PRESS ANY KEY TO GO ON.
```

Electronic Mailbox listing, lines 1–190

```
]
]LIST 1-190

1    REM   ELECTRONIC MAILBOX BY ERNEST BALAJTHY
2    REM   SEE CHAPTER 12 FOR DESCRIPTION AND INSTRUCTIONS
5    HOME
7    GOTO 85
20   DIM MS$(30,100): REM   THIS WILL BE THE ARRAY WHICH CONTAINS THE LETTE
     RS' MESSAGE.
21   DIM AD$(15): REM   THIS ARRAY CONTAINS THE ADDRESSES.
25   X = 0
50   REM   START OF MESSAGE INPUT LOOP
59   HOME
60   X = X + 1
61   PRINT "TO WHOM IS THIS LETTER TO BE ADDRESSED?"
63   INPUT AD$(X)
64   PRINT : PRINT : PRINT
70   PRINT "TYPE YOUR MESSAGE.  THIS WILL BE STORED"
71   PRINT "IN MAILBOX #";X;". FOLLOW THESE RULES-"
72   PRINT "1.  DO NOT PRESS RETURN UNTIL YOUR"
73   PRINT "     MESSAGE IS COMPLETELY FINISHED."
74   PRINT "2.  MAXIMUM LENGTH IS 5 1/2 LINES."
75   PRINT "3.  DO NOT INCLUDE ANY COLONS (:) OR"
76   PRINT "     COMMAS (,)."
80   PRINT : PRINT : PRINT : INPUT MS$(X,Y)
85   HOME
90   HOME : PRINT "DO YOU WISH TO:"
91   PRINT : PRINT "     RECORD A MESSAGE?"
92   PRINT "     PRINT A MESSAGE?"
93   PRINT "     ERASE A MESSAGE?"
96   PRINT : PRINT : PRINT "THERE IS MAIL FOR:"
97   GOSUB 500
98   PRINT : PRINT : PRINT "TYPE 'R', 'P', OR 'E'.
100  GET A$
110  IF A$ = "R" THEN   GOTO 50
112  IF A$ = "P" THEN   GOTO 120
113  IF A$ = "E" GOTO 200
114  PRINT "TYPE ONLY 'R' OR 'P'."
115  GOTO 90
120  HOME : PRINT "WHICH MESSAGE DO YOU WANT TO PRINT?"
121  PRINT "TYPE THE NUMBER. ('0' RETURNS TO MENU.)"
122  GOSUB 500
130  INPUT B
139  IF B = 0 THEN   GOTO 90
140  HOME : PRINT MS$(B,Y)
142  PRINT : PRINT : PRINT "PRESS ANY KEY TO GO ON."
144  GET D$
149  REM   THIS ALLOWS MESSAGES TO BE PRINTED IN HARD COPY.  DO NOT INCLU
     DE LINES 149 - 175 IF YOU DO NOT HAVE A PRINTER.
150  PRINT : PRINT "DO YOU WANT A HARD COPY OF THIS"
155  PRINT "MESSAGE? (Y/N)"
160  GET D$
161  IF D$ = "Y" THEN   GOTO 170
165  GOTO 90
170  PRINT   CHR$ (4); CHR$ (4);"PR#1"
175  PRINT MS$(B,Y): PRINT   CHR$ (4);"PR#0"
190  GOTO 90
```

Electronic Mailbox listing, lines 200–540

```
200  REM   THIS ROUTINE DELETES MESSAGES
210  HOME : PRINT "DO YOU WISH TO DELETE A MESSAGE? (Y/N)"
212  GET D$
220  IF D$ = "N" THEN   GOTO 85
230  PRINT "WHICH MESSAGE DO YOU WISH TO DELETE?"
232  PRINT "TYPE THE NUMBER."
240  FOR C = 1 TO X
250  PRINT C;".   ";AD$(C)
260  NEXT C
270  GET E
280  PRINT "ARE YOU SURE YOU WANT TO DELETE THIS"
290  PRINT "MESSAGE? (Y/N)"
300  GET D$
310  IF D$ = "N" GOTO 85
320 MS$(E,Y) = "   "
330 AD$(E) = "   "
340  REM   THIS NEXT SECTION OF THE ROUTINE ALLOWS A REPLACEMENT MESSAGE T
     O BE PLACED IN THE ERASED MAILBOX.
350  HOME : PRINT "THE MESSAGE IN MAILBOX #";E;" HAS BEEN"
360  PRINT "ERASED.  DO YOU WISH TO WRITE A NEW"
370  PRINT "MESSAGE IN THIS MAILBOX? (Y/N)"
380  INPUT D$
390  IF D$ = "N" GOTO 85
392  HOME : PRINT "TO WHOM DO YOU WISH TO SEND A MESSAGE?"
394  INPUT AD$(E)
400  PRINT "TYPE YOUR MESSAGE.  DO NOT PRESS "
405  PRINT "<RETURN> UNTIL IT IS COMPLETELY"
410  PRINT "FINISHED."
420  INPUT MS$(E,Y)
430  GOTO 85
500  REM   THIS IS THE SUBROUTINE TO PRINT THE CATALOG OF MESSAGES.
510  FOR C = 1 TO X
520  PRINT C;".   ";AD$(C)
530  NEXT C
540  RETURN
```

Sample run for *Electronic Mailbox*

```
]RUN
DO YOU WISH TO:

    RECORD A MESSAGE?
    PRINT A MESSAGE?
    ERASE A MESSAGE?


THERE IS MAIL FOR:
1.


TYPE 'R', 'P', OR 'E'.    R
TO WHOM IS THIS LETTER TO BE ADDRESSED?
?TOM


TYPE YOUR MESSAGE.  THIS WILL BE STORED
IN MAILBOX #1. FOLLOW THESE RULES-
1.   DO NOT PRESS RETURN UNTIL YOUR
     MESSAGE IS COMPLETELY FINISHED.
2.   MAXIMUM LENGTH IS 5 1/2 LINES.
3.   DO NOT INCLUDE ANY COLONS (:) OR
     COMMAS (,).


?HI TOM--REMEMBER THAT WE HAVE A BASEBALL GAME TONIGHT.    MARK
DO YOU WISH TO:

    RECORD A MESSAGE?
    PRINT A MESSAGE?
    ERASE A MESSAGE?


THERE IS MAIL FOR:
1.   TOM


TYPE 'R', 'P', OR 'E'.  P
WHICH MESSAGE DO YOU WANT TO PRINT?
TYPE THE NUMBER. ('O' RETURNS TO MENU.)
1.   TOM
?1
HI TOM--REMEMBER THAT WE HAVE A BASEBALL GAME TONIGHT.    MARK


PRESS ANY KEY TO GO ON.
```

Terquain listing

```
]
]LIST

1    REM   TERQUAIN BY ERNEST BALAJTHY
2    REM    SEE CHAPTER 12 FOR DESCRIPTION AND INSTRUCITONS
5    HOME : GOTO 200
10   REM   PAGE MOVEMENT ROUTINE
15   VTAB 23: PRINT "PRESS ANY KEY TO GO ON."
20   GET A$
24   HOME
25   RETURN
200  VTAB 10: HTAB 8: PRINT "TERQUAINS"
210  FOR W = 1 TO 3000: NEXT W
220  HOME : PRINT "THE TERQUAIN IS A THREE LINE POEM."
225  PRINT "LET'S LOOK AT A TERQUAIN THAT WAS"
228  PRINT "WRITTEN BY MARK."
230  PRINT "         STORMS"
232  PRINT "LIGHTNING, THUNDER"
234  PRINT "         ANGER"
235  GOSUB 10
236  PRINT "THIS TYPE OF POEM IS NOT DIFFICULT TO"
238  PRINT "WRITE.  FIRST YOU CHOOSE A ONE WORD"
240  PRINT "SUBJECT. MARK CHOSE 'STORMS.'  THEN YOU"
242  PRINT "DECIDE ON TWO OR THREE WORDS TO"
244  PRINT "DESCRIBE THAT SUBJECT.  MARK DESCRIBED"
246  PRINT "'STORMS' WITH THE WORDS 'LIGHTNING,"
248  PRINT "THUNDER.'  YOUR FINAL LINE HAS ONE WORD"
250  PRINT "WHICH SHOWS SOME SORT OF FEELING ABOUT"
252  PRINT "THE SUBJECT. MARK DESCRIBED THE FEELING"
254  PRINT "OF A STORM AS LIKE 'ANGER.'"
256  GOSUB 10
258  HOME
260  PRINT "LET'S WRITE A TERQUAIN."
265  PRINT "FIRST, CHOOSE A SUBJECT"
270  INPUT A$
280  PRINT A$
285  PRINT "SECOND, CHOOSE TWO OR THREE WORDS TO"
290  PRINT "DESCRIBE THAT SUBJECT.  TYPE THE FIRST."
292  INPUT B$
294  PRINT "TYPE THE SECOND."
296  INPUT C$
298  PRINT "TYPE THE THIRD (CARRIAGE RETURN IF YOU"
300  PRINT "HAVE NO THIRD WORD."
302  INPUT D$
310  PRINT A$
320  PRINT B$;", ";C$;", ";D$
325  PRINT "FINALLY, CHOOSE A WORD THAT SHOWS"
330  PRINT "FEELING FOR THE SUBJECT.  TYPE THE WORD."
335  INPUT E$
340  PRINT A$
345  PRINT B$;", ";C$;", ";D$
350  PRINT E$
```

Sample run for *Terquain*

```
]RUN
        TERQUAINS
THE TERQUAIN IS A THREE LINE POEM.
LET'S LOOK AT A TERQUAIN THAT WAS
WRITTEN BY MARK.
        STORMS
LIGHTNING, THUNDER
        ANGER
PRESS ANY KEY TO GO ON.
THIS TYPE OF POEM IS NOT DIFFICULT TO
WRITE.  FIRST YOU CHOOSE A ONE WORD
SUBJECT. MARK CHOSE 'STORMS.'  THEN YOU
DECIDE ON TWO OR THREE WORDS TO
DESCRIBE THAT SUBJECT.  MARK DESCRIBED
'STORMS' WITH THE WORDS 'LIGHTNING,
THUNDER.'  YOUR FINAL LINE HAS ONE WORD
WHICH SHOWS SOME SORT OF FEELING ABOUT
THE SUBJECT. MARK DESCRIBED THE FEELING
OF A STORM AS LIKE 'ANGER.'
PRESS ANY KEY TO GO ON.
LET'S WRITE A TERQUAIN.
FIRST, CHOOSE A SUBJECT
?COMPUTERS
COMPUTERS
SECOND, CHOOSE TWO OR THREE WORDS TO
DESCRIBE THAT SUBJECT.  TYPE THE FIRST.
?FASCINATING
TYPE THE SECOND.
?CONFUSING
TYPE THE THIRD (CARRIAGE RETURN IF YOU
HAVE NO THIRD WORD.
?
COMPUTERS
FASCINATING, CONFUSING,
FINALLY, CHOOSE A WORD THAT SHOWS
FEELING FOR THE SUBJECT.  TYPE THE WORD.
?WOW
COMPUTERS
FASCINATING, CONFUSING,
WOW

]
```

Alphabet ID listing

```
]
]LIST

1  REM  ALPHABET ID BY ERNEST BALAJTHY
2  REM  SEE CHAPTER 5 FOR DESCRIPTION
10 REM  ALPHABET ID
20 HOME
30 DIM AL$(26)
40 FOR X = 1 TO 26:AL$(X) =  CHR$ (64 + X): NEXT X: REM  THIS DEFINES AR
   RAY AL$ AS BEING THE 26 LETTERS.
50 PRINT "DO YOU KNOW YOUR ALPHABET?"
60 PRINT "LET'S SEE."
70 PRINT "TYPE THE COMPLETE ALPHABET, PLEASE."
75 PRINT "PRESS <RETURN> AFTER EACH LETTER."
80 FOR X = 1 TO 26
90 PRINT "TYPE YOUR LETTER, THEN <RETURN>."
100 INPUT LT$
110 IF LT$ <  > AL$(X) THEN  GOSUB 600: GOTO 90
120 PRINT "GOOD JOB!"
130 NEXT X
150 PRINT "GREAT! YOU KNOW YOUR ALPHABET!"
160 END
600 PRINT "SORRY, THAT'S NOT CORRECT.  TRY AGAIN."
610 RETURN
5000 FOR X = 1 TO 26: PRINT AL$(X);: NEXT X
```

Sample run for *Alphabet ID*

```
]RUN
DO YOU KNOW YOUR ALPHABET?
LET'S SEE.
TYPE THE COMPLETE ALPHABET, PLEASE.
PRESS <RETURN> AFTER EACH LETTER.
TYPE YOUR LETTER, THEN <RETURN>.
?A
GOOD JOB!
TYPE YOUR LETTER, THEN <RETURN>.
?B
GOOD JOB!
TYPE YOUR LETTER, THEN <RETURN>.
?C
GOOD JOB!
TYPE YOUR LETTER, THEN <RETURN>.
?E
SORRY, THAT'S NOT CORRECT.  TRY AGAIN.
TYPE YOUR LETTER, THEN <RETURN>.
?D
GOOD JOB!
TYPE YOUR LETTER, THEN <RETURN>.
```

Favorite Words listing

```
]
]
]LIST

1   REM   FAVORITE WORDS BY ERNEST BALAJTHY
2   REM   DESCRIPTION AND INSTRUCTIONS IN CHAPTER 12
10  HOME
20  REM   FAVORITE WORDS
30  PRINT "HI.   WHAT IS YOUR NAME?"
40  INPUT NA$
50  PRINT "HELLO, ";NA$;".   NAME A FAVORITE"
60  PRINT "ADJECTIVE."
70  INPUT AD$
80  PRINT "OK.   NAME A FAVORITE NOUN."
90  INPUT NN$
100  PRINT "HAVE YOU EVER SEEN A "
110  PRINT AD$;" ";NN$;"?"
115  FOR W = 1 TO 3000: NEXT W
120  GOTO 50
```

Sample run for *Favorite Words*

```
]RUN
HI.   WHAT IS YOUR NAME?
?PAUL
HELLO, PAUL.   NAME A FAVORITE
ADJECTIVE.
?GREEN
OK.   NAME A FAVORITE NOUN.
?MOOSE
HAVE YOU EVER SEEN A
GREEN MOOSE?
```

Spelling Quiz2 listing

```
]
]LIST

1  REM     SPELLING QUIZ2 BY ERNEST BALAJTHY--SEE CHAPTER 12 FOR DESCRIPTI
   ON AND INSTRUCTIONS
2  REM     TO INCREASE OR DECREASE LENGTH OF WORD FLASH, CHANGE THE '300'
   IN LINE 150 TO A HIGHER OR LOWER NUMBER.
3  REM      TO CHANGE SPELLING WORDS, CHANGE OR ADD DATA LINES AT THE BEGI
   NNING OF THE PROGRAM.  ANY LINE NUMBERS BETWEEN THE FIRST AND LAST D
   ATA LINE MAY BE USED.
5  HOME
10   HOME
20   DATA     RECIPROCAL,LACORPICER
30   DATA     PROCEED,DEECORP
40   DATA     INTERVENE,ENEVRETNI
50   DATA     ASSURANCE,ECNARUSSA
60   DATA     INEPTITUDE,EDUTITPENI
70   DATA     INTERFERING,GNIREFRETNI
80   DATA     ALLIANCE,ECNAILLA
90   DATA     OBVIOUS,SUOIVBO
100    DATA     SADDENED,DENEDDAS
110    DATA     REGARDLESS,SSELDRAGER
120  READ A$: REM     READ THE SPELLING WORD:
125  READ C$: REM      READ THE ANSWER:NEXT L
135  VTAB 7: HTAB 5: PRINT "GET READY..."
137  VTAB 10: HTAB 3: PRINT "--->": FOR W = 1 TO 1000: NEXT W
138  VTAB 10: HTAB 9
140  PRINT A$
150  FOR W = 1 TO 300: NEXT W
160  HOME
170  PRINT "NOW SPELL THE WORD BACKWARDS:  "
171  INPUT B$
180  IF B$ = C$ THEN  PRINT "RIGHT!": GOTO 250
190  PRINT "WRONG"
200  PRINT "THE CORRECT SPELLING IS ";A$;"."
210  FOR W = 1 TO 3000: NEXT W
215  PRINT "LET'S TRY AGAIN."
216  FOR W = 1 TO 1500: NEXT W
220  GOTO 135
250  GOTO 120
```

Sample run for *Spelling Quiz2*

```
]RUN
    GET READY...
    --->
        RECIPROCAL  (Note:  This word is flashed.)
NOW SPELL THE WORD BACKWARDS:
?LACORPICER
RIGHT!
    GET READY...
    --->
        PROCEED
NOW SPELL THE WORD BACKWARDS:
?DECORP
WRONG
THE CORRECT SPELLING IS PROCEED.
LET'S TRY AGAIN.
    GET READY...
    --->
        PROCEED
NOW SPELL THE WORD BACKWARDS:
?DEECORP
RIGHT!
    GET READY...
    --->
        INTERVENE
NOW SPELL THE WORD BACKWARDS:
```

HARDWARE AND SOFTWARE SOURCES

SOFTWARE

Only those programs mentioned in the text are listed. Consult software directories for more detailed lists of programs available.

Abuse
Don't Ask Computer Software

Alphabet Beasts & Co.
Software Productions

Alphabet ID
Listed in Appendix A

Alphabet Keyboard
Random House

Anagram
A subprogram of *Word Plus*

Animals
Public domain

Antonyms/Synonyms
Hartley Courseware

Apple Grade Book
J&S Software

Apple Keyboard
Apple Computer

Apple Writer
Apple Computer

Aristotle's Topics
Privately published, Hugh Burns

Bank Street Writer
Scholastic

CARD
Acronym for *Computer Assisted Reading Development*

Castle Wolfenstein
Muse Software

Chambers of Vocab
Reader's Digest

Class Anthology
Listed in Appendix A

Cloze Plus
Milleken

Cloze Test
Softside

Clue In
Regents/ALA

College Board SAT
Krell

Comprehension Power
Milleken

Compupoem
South Coast Writing Project

Computer Assisted Reading Development
  Radio Shack
Computer Bismarck
  Strategic Simulations
Context Clues
  Milton Bradley
Copy II
  Central Point Software
Crossword
  MECC
Crossword
  Part of the Wordwright series
Crossword Magic
  L&S Software
Customized Alphabet Drill
  Random House
D Base II
  Ashton-Tate
Deadline
  Infocom
Delta Drawing
  Spinnaker
Disappearing Dolphin
  Part of the Snooper Troops series of
  programs
Dr. Z
  Public domain (Ahl, 1977)
Donkey Kong
  Atari
Don't Fall
  Apple Computer
Early Games for Young Children
  Counterpoint Software
Early Games Music
  Counterpoint Software
Early Learning Fun
  Texas Instruments
Electronic Mailbox
  Listed in Appendix A
Eliza
  Several versions available:
  Radio Shack
  Ahl, 1979
English Basics Part II: Concepts in Lan-
guage Arts
  Educational Activities
E-Z Learner
  Silicon Valley Systems

Facemaker
  Spinnaker
Fact-Opinion Exercise
  Public domain, by Dr. Virginia
  Modla
Father
  Ahl, 1976
Favorite Words
  Listed in Appendix A
Find
  A subprogram of Word Plus
Fragmentation
  Part of the Wordwright series
Frogger
  On-Line Systems
Fry Instant Words Program
  Jamestown
Fry Readability Program
  Jamestown
Fundamental Spelling Words in Context
  Random House
Fundamental Word Focus
  Random House
Furs
  MECC
Galactic Revolution
  Broderbund
Gertrude's Puzzles
  Learning Company
Getting the Main Idea
  Learning Well
Grammar Mastery
  Regents/ALA
Grammatik
  Aspen Software
Graphics Magician
  Penguin Software
Hadron
  Sirius
Hammurabi
  Public domain
Hello
  Public domain
  (Ahl, 1978)
Hide n' Spell
  Part of the Wordwatch program
Homonyms
  Hartley Courseware

Homonyms in Context
Random House

How to Read in the Content Areas
Educational Activities

Improving College Admission Scores
National Association of Secondary
School Principals

Jeepers Creatures
Kangaroo

Jigsaw Puzzle
Part of *Mindstretcher Series*

Juggle's Rainbow
Learning Company

Jump Man
Epyx

Kabul Spy
Learning Company

Learning Spells
Advanced Learning Technology

Lemonade Stand
Several versions available, includ-
ing some in public domain. The
MECC version is called *Sell
Lemonade.*

Letters and Numbers
Teaching Tools

LOGO
Various publishers

Magic Spells
Learning Company

MasterType
Lightning Software

Microcourse: Language Arts
Houghton Mifflin

Microcourse: Reading
Houghton Mifflin

*MicroSystem 80 College Entrance Exami-
nation Preparation*
Borg-Warner

MicroSystem 80 Critical Reading
Borg-Warner

Milton Bradley's Word Processor
Milton Bradley

Mindbenders
Midwest

Mindstretcher Series
Island Software

Missle Defense
On-Line Systems

Mix and Match
Apple

My First Alphabet
Atari

NGuess
Ahl, 1977

Nibbles Away
COMPUTER:applications

O'Dell Lake
MECC

Olympic Decathlon
Microsoft

Oregon Trail
Several versions available, including some in public domain. The
version called *Oregon* is available
from MECC.

Pacman
Atari

PAL Reading Curriculum
Universal Systems for Education

Pandemonium
Soft Images

Personal Filing System
More commonly known as *PFS*

PFS File
Software Publishing

PFS Report
Software Publishing

PFS Write
Software Publishing

Plato
Control Data

President Elect
Strategic Simulations

PSAT and SAT Word Attack Skills
Edu-Ware

Puss in Boot
Island Software

Puzzler
Tara Associates

Quizit
Regents/ALA

Rapid Reader
Silicon Valley Systems

Riddle-Me-This
  Data Command
Robot Demo
  Part of *Textalker* disk
Rocky's Boots
  Learning Company
Rubik
  Part of *Mindstretcher Series*
Sargon III
  Hayden Software
Screen Writer II
  Sierra On-Line
SCRIPSIT
  Radio Shack
SEC Demo
  Part of *Textalker* disk
Sell Apples
  MECC
Sentence Combining
  Milleken
Snake-O-Nyms
  Milleken—Edufun Division
Snooper Troops
  Spinnaker
Space Invaders
  Atari
Spelling Quiz1
  Listed in Appendix A
Spelling Quiz2
  Listed in Appendix A
Spelling Strategy
  Apple Computer
Spelling Test
  Part of *Textalker* disk
Star Trek
  Public domain; several versions
  available (Ahl, 1979). The newer
  ⟡ video game versions of similar
  name are not discussed in this
  book.
Stickybear ABC
  Weekly Reader Family Software
Stickybear Numbers
  Weekly Reader Family Software
Stickybear Opposites
  Weekly Reader Family Software
Stickybear Shapes
  Weekly Reader Family Software

Story Machine
  Spinnaker
Story Maker
  Bolt, Beranek, and Newman
Story Maker Maker
  Part of the *Story Maker* program
Sumer
  MECC
Talking Typewriter
  Part of *Textalker* disk
Tank Tactics
  Data Command
Teacher Utilities Vol. 1
  MECC
Team-Work
  Edupro
Terquain
  Listed in Appendix A
Textalker
  Accompanies Echo II Speech Syn-
  thesizer
Three Mile Island
  Muse Software
Trickster Coyote
  Reader's Digest
Typing Tutor II
  Microsoft Corporation
VBLS
  Acronym for *Voice-Based Learning
  System*
Verb Viper
  Developmental Learning Materials
VisiCalc
  Visicorp
Vocabulary Baseball
  J&S Software
Vocabulary Prompter
  Jagdstaffel
*Vocabulary Skills: Prefixes, Suffixes, and
  Rootwords*
  Milton Bradley
Voice-Based Learning System
  Scott Instruments
Voyageur
  MECC
Wizardry
  Sir-Tech

Word Attack!
Davidson & Associates

Word Division
Ahead Designs

Word Families
Hartley Courseware

Word Flip
Part of *Snake-O-Nyms*

Word Handler
Silicon Valley Systems

Word Man
Developmental Learning Materials

Wordmate
T.H.E.S.I.S.

Word Plus
OASIS Systems

Wordrace
Regents/ALA

Word Radar
Developmental Learning Materials

Word Scrambler Super Speller
Avant-Garde Creations

Wordsearch
Hartley Courseware

Wordsearch
Part of the *Wordwright* series

WordStar
Micropro

Wordwatch
Instant Software

Word Wise
TIES, Minnesota School Districts
Data Processing Joint Board

Wordwright
Encyclopaedia Britannica

Write a Cinquain
Pfluger (1983)

Zaxxon
Datasoft

Zork
Infocom

SOFTWARE AND HARDWARE MANUFACTURERS

Only companies whose software or hardware is mentioned in the text are listed.

Ahead Designs, 699 North Vulcan #88, Encinitas, CA 92024; (619) 436–4071.

Apple Computer, Inc., 10260 Bandley Dr., Cupertino, CA 95014; (408) 996–1010, (800) 538–9696.

Ashton-Tate, 3600 Wilshire Blvd., Los Angeles, CA 90010; (213) 666–4409.

Aspen Software Co., P.O. Box 339, Tijeros, NM 87059; (505) 281–1634.

Atari, Inc., 1265 Borregas Avenue, Sunnyvale, CA 94086; (800) 538–8547.

Avant-Garde Creations, Box 30160, Eugene, OR 97403; (503) 345–3043.

Bolt, Beranek, and Newman, Inc., 50 Moulton Rd., Cambridge, MA 02138; (617) 491–1850.

Borg-Warner Educational Systems, 600 W. University Dr., Arlington Heights, IL 60604; (800) 323–7577.

Broderbund Software, 1938 Fourth St., San Rafael, CA 94901; (415) 456–6424.

Burns, Hugh, U.S. Air Force Academy, Colorado Springs, CO 80840.

Central Point Software, Inc., 9700 SW Capitol Highway, Suite 100, Portland, OR 97219; (503) 244–5782.

Commodore Business Machines, Inc., 950 Rittenhouse Rd., Norristown, PA 19403; (215) 666–7950.

COMPUTER:applications Inc., 13300 SW 108 Street Circle, Miami, FL 33186; (305) 385–4277.

Control Data Publishing Co., P.O. Box 261127, San Diego, CA 92126; (800) 233–3784.

Counterpoint Software, Inc., Shelard Plaza North, Suite 140, Minneapolis, MN 55426; (612) 544–4720.

Data Command, P.O. Box 548, Kankakee, IL 60901.

Datasoft Inc., 9421 Winnetka, Chatsworth, CA 91311; (213) 701–5161.

Davidson & Associates, 6069 Groveoak Place, Suite 12, Rancho Palos Verdes, CA; (213) 378–3995.

Developmental Learning Materials, 1 DLM Park, Allen, TX 75002.

Don't Ask Computer Software, 2265 Westwood Blvd., Los Angeles, CA; (213) 477–4514.

Early Games Company Educational Software, Shelard Plaza North, Suite 140, Minneapolis, MN 55426; (612) 544–4720.

Educational Activities, Inc., P.O. Box 392, Freeport, NY 11520; (516) 223–4666.

Edupro, P.O. Box 51346, Palo Alto, CA 94303; (415) 494–2790.

Edu-Ware Services, P.O. Box 22222, Agoura, CA 91301; (213) 706–0661.

Encyclopaedia Britannica Educational Corporation, 425 N. Michigan Ave., Chicago, IL; (312) 347–7400.

Epyx/Automated Simulations, 1943 Kiell Court, Sunnyvale, CA 94086; (408) 745–0700.

Franklin Computer Corporation, 2128 Route 38, Cherry Hill, NJ 08002; (609) 482–5900.

Hartley Courseware, P.O. Box 431, Dimondale, MI 48821; (616) 942–8987.

Hayden Software, 600 Suffolk St., Lowell, MA 01853; (800) 343–1218.

Houghton Mifflin, TSC Division, Box 683, Hanover, NH 03755; (603) 448–3838.

IBM—see International Business Machines.

Infocom, 55 Wheeler St., Cambridge, MA 02138; (617) 492–1031.

Instant Software, Rt. 101 and Elm St., Peterborough, NH 03458; (603) 924–9471.

Interactive Structures, Inc., 146 Montgomery Avenue, P.O. Box 404, Bala Cynwyd, PA 19004; (215) 667–1713.

International Business Machines Corporation, P.O. Box 328, Boca Raton, FL 33432; (305) 998–6007.

Island Software, P.O. Box 300, Lake Grove, NY 11755; (516) 585–3755.

J&S Software, 140 Reid Street, Port Washington, NY 11050; (516) 944–9304.

Jagdstaffel Software, 64 Brenda Lee Dr., San Jose, CA; (408) 578–1643.

Jamestown Publishers, P.O. Box 6743, Providence, RI 02940; (401) 351–1915.

Kangaroo, Inc., 332 S. Michigan Ave., Suite 700, Chicago, IL 60604; (312) 987–9050.

Krell Software, 21 Millbrook Dr., Stony Brook, NY 11790; (516) 751–5139.

L&S Computerware, 1589 Fraser Drive, Sunnyvale, CA 94087; (408) 738–3416.

Learning Company, 545 Middlefield Rd., Suite 170, Menlo Park, CA 94025; (415) 328–5410.

Learning Well, 200 South Service Rd., Roslyn Heights, NY 11577; (800) 645–6564.

Lightning Software, P.O. Box 11725, Palo Alto, CA 94306; (415) 327–3280.

MECC—see Minnesota Educational Computing Consortium.

Micro Pro, 33 San Pablo Ave., San Rafael, CA 94903; (415) 499–1200.

Microsoft Corporation, 10700 Northup, Bellevue, WA 98004; (206) 828–8080.

Midwest Publications, P.O. Box 448, Pacific Grove, CA; (408) 375–2455.

Milleken Publishing Company, EduFun Division, 1100 Research Boulevard, St. Louis, MO 63132; (314) 991–4220.

Milton Bradley, Microcomputer Software Department, 443 Shaker Road, East Longmeadow, MA 01028.

Minnesota Educational Computing Consortium, 2520 Broadway Dr., St. Paul, MN 55113; (612) 638–0600.

Mountain Computer, Inc., 300 El Pueblo Rd., Scotts Valley, CA 95066; (408) 438–6650.

Muse Software, 347 N. Charles St., Baltimore, MD 21201; (301) 659–7212.

National Association of Secondary School Principals, 1904 Association Drive, Reston, VA 22091.

OASIS Systems, 2765 Reynard Way, San Diego, CA 92103; (714) 291–9489.

Omega MicroWare, Inc., 222 So. Riverside Plaza, Chicago, IL 60606; (312) 648–1944.

On-Line Systems, 36575 Mudge Ranch Rd., Coarsegold, CA 93614; (209) 683–6858.

Pendulum Press, Saw Mill Road, West Haven, CT 06516.

Penguin Software, 830 Fourth Ave., Geneva, IL 60134; (312) 232–1984.

Radio Shack, 400 Atrium, One Tandy Center, Fort Worth, TX 76102; (800) 433–1679.

Random House School Division, 2970 Brandywine Rd., Atlanta, GA 30341.

Reader's Digest Services, Microcomputer Software Division, Pleasantville, NY 10570.

Regents/ALA Company, Two Park Avenue, New York, NY 10016; (800) 822–8202.

Scholastic Software, Inc., P.O. Box 7501, 2931 E. McCarty St., Jefferson City, MO 65102; (212) 505–3567.

Scott, Foresman and Co., Electronic Publishing, 1900 East Lake Ave., Glenview, IL 60025; (312) 729–3000.

Scott Instruments, 1111 Willow Springs Drive, Denton, TX 76201; (817) 387–9514.

Sierra On-Line, Inc., 36575 Mudge Ranch Rd., Coarsegold, CA 93614; (209) 683–6858.

Silicon Valley Systems, 1625 El Camino Real No. 4, Belmont, CA 94002; (415) 593–4344.

Sinclair Research Limited, 50 Stamford Street, Boston, MA 02114; (617) 742–4826.

Sirius Software, out of business.

Sir-Tech Software, 6 Main Street, Ogdensburg, NY 13669; (315) 393–6633.

Soft Images, 200 Route 17, Mahwah, NJ 07430; (201) 529–1440.

Softside Software, 305 Riverside Dr., New York, NY 10025; (212) 866–8058.

Software Productions, 2357 Southway Dr., Columbus, OH 43221; (614) 486–3563.

Software Publishing Corporation, 1901 Landings Dr., Mountain View, CA 94043; (415) 962–8910.

South Coast Writing Project, University of California, Santa Barbara, CA 93106.

Spinnaker Software, 215 First St., Cambridge, MA 02142; (617) 868–4700.

Strategic Simulations, 883 Stierlin Rd., Bldg. A–200, Mountain View, CA 94043; (415) 964–1353.

Sunburst Communications, Inc., Pleasantville, NY 10570; (800) 431–1934.

Tara Associates, P.O. Box 50065, Palo Alto, CA 94303.

Teaching Tools: Microcomputer Services, P.O. Box 50065, Palo Alto, CA 94303; (415) 493–3477.

Texas Instruments, P.O. Box 402430, Dallas, TX 75240; (214) 995–6611.

T.H.E.S.I.S., P.O. Box 147, Garden City, MI 48135; (313) 595–4722.

TIES, Minnesota School Districts Data Processing Joint Board, 1925 W. County Rd., B2, St. Paul, MN 55113.

Universal Systems for Education, 2120 Academy Circle, Suite E, Colorado Springs, CO 80909; (303) 699–0438.

Versa Computing, 3541 Old Conejo Rd., Suite 104, Newbury Park, CA 91320; (805) 498–1956.

VisiCorp, 2895 Zanker Rd., San Jose, CA 95134; (408) 946–9000.

Weekly Reader Family Software, 245 Long Hill Road, Middletown, CT 06457; (800) 852–5000.

Xerox, 1341 West Mockingbird, Dallas, TX 75247; (214) 723–0111.

INFORMATION SOURCES

The following lists of resources are meant to be selective rather than comprehensive. That is, the organizations and publications that are most useful to reading and language arts teachers are listed and annotated. For more exhaustive listings, consult the following references:

COBURN, PETER, PETER KELMAN, NANCY ROBERTS, THOMAS F. F. SNYDER, DANIEL H. WATT, AND CHERYL WIENER. *Practical Guide to Computers in Education.* Reading, MA: Addison-Wesley, 1982.
WILLIS, JERRY W., D. LAMONT JOHNSON, AND PAUL N. DIXON. *Computers, Teaching, and Learning.* Beaverton, OR: Dilithium Press, 1983.

SOFTWARE EVALUATION

In addition to the following sources, almost every magazine and journal devoted to computers contains periodic evaluations of educational software. Also consult your professional journals for reviews of computer materials.

EPIE Institute, P.O. Box 620, Stony Brook, NY 11790; (516) 246–8664.

EPIE, the Educational Products Information Exchange, distributes detailed evaluations of software in file format, categorized according to subject or skill area. Evaluations are rigorous and professional, including summaries, lists of stated goals and objectives, contents, and methods. These files are continually updated and represent one of the most consistent evaluation systems available today.

MicroSIFT, Northwest Regional Educational Laboratory, 500 Lindsay Building, 300 S.W. 6th Ave., Portland, OR 97204; (503) 248–6800.

MicroSIFT, or Microcomputer Software and Information for Teachers, offers detailed reviews of software. The review process is intensive and is carried out by several educators for each piece of software.

PERIODICALS

In the fast-changing field of computers, the publishing lag time even for journals and magazines is too great for anyone to really keep up with events. At present, however, periodicals represent the best medium for keeping aware of developments. Bear in mind that, since most rely on freelance writers for their contents and on computer hardware and software manufacturers for their revenues, reviews are often of uneven quality.

General Computing Periodicals

Several general computing magazines are available that offer relatively nontechnical approaches to microcomputing. These magazines are best used for up-to-date information on hardware developments for the average home and business computer user. They are weak when it comes to educational applications.

Creative Computing, P.O. Box 789–M, Morristown, NJ 07690.

Of the nontechnical computer magazines designed for general audiences, *Creative Computing* does best with educational issues and with reviews of software for schools.

Personal Computing, P.O. Box 1408, Riverton, NJ 08077.

Popular Computing, 70 Main St., Peterborough, NH 03458.

Educational Computing Periodicals

Except where noted, educational computing periodicals cater primarily to the teacher interested in teaching programming to children. Each contains some articles of interest to teachers who wish to use computers for content area and skill applications. Software reviews are often uneven and lack detail.

Computers, Reading, and Language Arts, P.O. Box 13039, Oakland, CA 94661; (415) 339–1106.

At press time, only a few issues of this new periodical had been published. The journal is the most useful periodical for computer-using teachers in reading and language arts.

Educational Computer Magazine, P.O. Box 535, Cupertino, CA 95015.

While oriented primarily to computer programming instruction, many articles deal with more general applications.

Educational Technology, 140 Sylvan Ave., Englewood Cliffs, NJ 07632; (201) 871–4007.

Emphasis is placed on hardware developments. Most articles deal with use of computers and other technology from a theoretical point of view and have a solid background in educational media research.

Electronic Learning, Scholastic, Inc., 902 Sylvan Ave., Box 2001, Englewood Cliffs, NJ 07632.

This magazine, together with its sister publication *Teaching and Computers,* are funded and staffed with the support of the venerable Scholastic publication group. Articles are of consistently excellent quality, though reviews of software are short and vague. *Electronic Learning* caters more to the administrator than the classroom teacher.

Teaching and Computers, Scholastic, Inc., 902 Sylvan Ave., Box 2001, Englewood Cliffs, NJ 07632.

See also the review for *Electronic Learning,* its sister publication. *Teaching and Computers* is designed for the classroom teacher and presents a wealth of "how to do it" ideas for instruction. While both publications heavily emphasize programming instruction, many articles deal with issues of more general interest.

Reading and Language Arts Periodicals

Many educational journals have begun to pay serious attention to developments in computer instruction. Articles are often more professionally rigorous than those in periodicals devoted to computers. That is, these articles lack the enthusiastic naiveté so prevalent among computer educators, preferring a realistic and research-oriented approach.

Journal of Reading, International Reading Association, 800 Barksdale Rd., P.O. Box 8139, Newark, DE 19714; (302) 731–1600.

This journal, devoted to the needs of secondary, college, and adult learners, frequently offers articles on computer instruction in reading, as well as software reviews.

The Reading Teacher, International Reading Association, 800 Barksdale Rd., P.O. Box 8139, Newark, DE 19714; (302) 731–1600.

A regular column, "The Printout," has been established to deal with computers and reading. Its editor is George Mason, noted reading and computer expert from the University of Georgia. In addition, *The Reading Teacher* offers frequent software reviews and articles dealing with computer ideas for teaching reading to elementary-age students.

The Reading Instruction Journal, New Jersey Reading Association, c/o Constance V. Alongi, Editor, R.D. No. 2, Box 277, Schoolhouse Rd., Jamesburg, NJ 08831.

Bette Kindman-Koffler edits a regular column, "The Computer Forum," which deals with a wide variety of topics related to computers and reading. The column has a heavy emphasis on organization of microcomputer programs within local schools and districts. *The Reading Instruction Journal* regularly includes articles and reviews on microcomputer use in the classroom, as well.

EDUCATIONAL SOFTWARE DIRECTORIES

A good directory will give short synopses of available programs and clear topical cross-indexing. In addition, provision will be made for annual updating.

The Apple Software Directory—Education, WIDL Video, 5245 W. Diversey Ave., Chicago, IL 60639; (312) 622–9606.

This comprises the education section of *The Apple Blue Book,* one of the more popular directories of Apple software.

Swift's Directory of Educational Software, Sterling Swift Publishing Company, 1600 Fortview Rd., Austin, TX 78704; (512) 444–7570.

REFERENCES

AHL, DAVID H. 1976. *The Best of Creative Computing,* vol. 1. Morristown, N.J.: Creative Computing Press.

AHL, DAVID H. 1977. *The Best of Creative Computing,* vol. 2. Morristown, N.J.: Creative Computing Press.

AHL, DAVID H. (Ed.). 1979. *More BASIC Computer Games.* New York: Workman Publishing.

AHL, DAVID H., AND BETSY STAPLES. 1984. "'Mastering *Jumpman*." *Creative Computing* 10, no. 1 (January): 128–142.

ALLEN, ROACH VAN. 1976. *Language Experiences in Communication.* Boston: Houghton Mifflin.

ALLEN, ROACH VAN, AND CLARYCE ALLEN. 1966. *Language Experiences in Reading.* Chicago: Encyclopaedia Britannica.

ANDERSON, RICHARD C., RAYMOND W. KULHAVY, AND THOMAS ANDRE. 1976. "Feedback Procedures in Programmed Instruction." *Journal of Educational Psychology* 62, no. 2 (April): 148–156.

ANDERSON, THOMAS H. 1980. "Study Strategies and Adjunct Aids." In *Theoretical Issues in Reading Comprehension,* ed. Rand J. Spiro, Bertram C. Bruce, and William F. Brewer, pp. 483–502. Hillsdale, N.J.: Lawrence Erlbaum.

ANGELL, GEORGE W. 1949. "The Effect of Immediate Knowledge of Quiz Results and Final Examination Scores in Freshman Chemistry." *Journal of Educational Research* 42, no. 1 (January): 391–394.

ARBUR, ROSEMARIE. 1976. "The Student-Teacher Conference." Paper presented at the annual meeting of the New York State English Council, October (ED 131 490).

ASHTON-WARNER, SYLVIA. 1963. *Teacher.* New York: Simon and Schuster.

ATHEY, IRENE. 1983. "Language Development Factors Related to Reading Development." *Journal of Educational Research* 76, no. 4 (March–April): 197–203.

AULLS, MARK. 1982. *Developing Readers in Today's Elementary Schools.* Boston: Allyn and Bacon.

AUSUBEL, DAVID P. 1960. "The Use of Advance Organizers in the Learning and

Retention of Meaningful Verbal Material." *Journal of Educational Psychology* 51, no. 5 (October): 267–272.

BALAJTHY, ERNEST. 1984a. "Reinforcement and Drill by Microcomputer." *The Reading Teacher* 37, no. 6 (February): 490–494.

BALAJTHY, ERNEST. 1984b. "Computer Simulations and Reading." *The Reading Teacher* 37, no. 7 (March): 590–593.

BARBE, WALTER B. 1961. *Educator's Guide to Personalized Reading Instruction.* Englewood Cliffs, N.J.: Prentice-Hall.

BARBE, WALTER B., AND JERRY L. ABBOT. 1975. *Personalized Reading Instruction.* West Nyack, N.Y.: Parker Publishing.

BECK, ISABEL L., MARGARET G. MCKEOWN, RICHARD C. OMANSON, AND CHARLES A. PERFETTI. 1982. "The Enhancement of Reading Comprehension Through Vocabulary Instruction." Paper presented at the National Reading Conference, Clearwater, Fla., December.

BLACHOWICZ, CAMILLE L. Z. 1978–1979. "Factors Affecting Semantic Constructivity in Children's Comprehension." *Reading Research Quarterly* 14, no. 2: 165–181.

BORK, ALFRED. 1981. *Learning with Computers.* Bedford, Mass.: Digital Press.

BORK, ALFRED. 1982. "Computers and Learning: Don't Teach BASIC." *Educational Technology* 22, no. 4 (April): 33–34.

BORK, ALFRED. 1984. "Production Systems for Computer-Based Learning." In *Instructional Software: Principles and Perspectives for Design and Use,* ed. Decker F. Walker and Robert D. Hess, pp. 96–114. Belmont, Calif.: Wadsworth.

BORMUTH, JOHN R. 1967. "Comparable Cloze and Multiple-Choice Comprehension Test Scores." *Journal of Reading* 10, no. 5 (February): 291–299.

BRADDOCK, RICHARD, RICHARD LLOYD-JONES, AND LOWELL SCHOERR. 1963. *Research in Written Composition.* Urbana, Ill.: National Council of Teachers of English.

BRIDWELL, LILLIAN. 1980. "Revising Strategies in Twelfth Grade Students' Transactional Writing." *Research in the Teaching of English* 14, no. 3 (October): 197–222.

BROWN, ANN L., JOSEPH C. CAMPIONE, AND JEANNE D. DAY. 1981. "Learning to Learn: On Training Students to Learn from Text." *Educational Researcher* 10, no. 2 (February): 14–21.

BRUMBAUGH, KEN. 1980. "Computer Literacy—1985." *The Computing Teacher* 8, no. 4 (December): 49.

BURNS, HUGH. 1983. "Computer-Assisted Prewriting Activities: Harmonics for Invention." *Pipeline* 8, no. 1 (Spring): 7–9.

BUSCH, DAVID D. 1983. "Word Processing of the Future." *Interface Age* 8, no. 7 (July): 133–135.

CACHA, FRANCES B. 1983. "Glamourizing and Legitimizing Violence in Software: A Misuse of the Computer." *Educational Technology* 23, no. 3 (March): 7–9.

CAMPBELL, DOROTHY DRYSDALE. 1973. "Typewriting Contrasted with Handwriting: A Circumvention Study of Learning-Disabled Children." *The Journal of Special Education* 7, no. 2 (Summer): 155–167.

CASSIDY, JOHN, AND B. C. RIMBEAUX. 1977. *Juggling for the Complete Klutz.* Palo Alto, Calif.: Klutz Press.

CHAFFIN, JERRY D., BILL MAXWELL, AND BARBARA THOMPSON. 1982. "ARC-ED Curriculum: The Application of Video Game Formats to Educational Software." *Exceptional Children* 49, no. 2 (October): 173–178.

CHAMBERS, JACK A., AND JERRY W. SPRECHER. 1980. "Computer-Assisted Instruction: Current Trends and Critical Issues." *Communications of the ACM* 23, no. 6 (June): 332–342.

CHAN, JULIE M. T. 1983. "What Micros Do for Reading Comprehension." *The Reading Teacher* 36, no. 7 (March): 692–693.

COBURN, PETER, PETER KELMAN, NANCY ROBERTS, THOMAS F. F. SNYDER, DANIEL H. WATT, AND CHERYL WEINER. 1982. *Practical Guide to Computers in Education.* Reading, Mass.: Addison-Wesley.

COLLIER, RICHARD M. 1983. "The Word Processor and Revision Strategies." *College Composition and Communication* 34, no. 2 (May): 149–155.

CRAWFORD, CHRIS. 1983. "Why You Should Learn to Program." *Popular Computing* 2, no. 11 (September): 153–156.

CRICHTON, MICHAEL. 1983. *Electronic Life.* New York: Alfred A. Knopf.

DACUS, JUDY, AND DAVID M. DACUS. 1983. "Time Bomb in Educational Computing: Teaching Keyboarding to Young Children." *Educational Computer* 3, no. 6 (October): 50–51.

DAIUTE, COLETTE A. 1983. "The Computer as Stylus and Audience." *College Composition and Communication* 34, no. 2 (May): 134–145.

DALE, EDGAR D. 1969. *Audiovisual Methods in Teaching,* 3rd ed. New York: Holt, Rinehart, and Winston.

DAVIS, FREDERICK B. 1972. "Psychometric Research on Comprehension in Reading." *Reading Research Quarterly* 7, no. 4 (Summer): 628–678.

DEKEN, JOSEPH. 1981. *The Electronic Cottage.* New York: Morrow.

DICKSON, WAYNE, AND MIKE RAYMOND. 1984. *Language Arts Computer Book.* Reston, Va.: Reston Publishing.

DOWNING, JOHN. 1982. "Reading—Skill or Skills?" *The Reading Teacher* 35, no. 5 (February): 534–537.

DURKIN, DOLORES. 1970. "Reading Readiness." *The Reading Teacher* 23, no. 6 (March): 528–534, 564.

DURKIN, DOLORES. 1978–1979. "What Classroom Observations Reveal About Reading Comprehension Instruction." *Reading Research Quarterly* 14, no. 4: 481–533.

DURKIN, DOLORES. 1981. "Reading Comprehension Instruction in Five Basal Reader Series." *Reading Research Quarterly* 16, no. 4: 515–544.

DWORKIN, NANCY, AND YEHOASH DWORKIN. 1983. "Computers as Learners: The Center for Unique Learners and Computer Usage by Adults." Paper presented at College Reading Association, Atlanta, Ga., October.

EMIG, JANET. 1977. "Writing as Mode of Learning." *College Composition and Communication* 28, no. 2 (May): 122–128.

ENGBERG, ROBERT E. 1983. "Word Processors in the English Classroom." *Computers, Reading, and Language Arts* 1, no. 1 (Summer): 17–19.

EPIE INSTITUTE. 1981. *EPIE Materials Report 98/99m: Microcomputer Courseware/Microprocessor Games.* Stonybrook, N.Y.: EPIE Institute.

EPIE INSTITUTE. 1983. *Micro-Courseware PRO/FILE and Evaluation: Microsystem 80 Critical Reading.* Stonybrook, N.Y.: EPIE Institute.

EVANS, CHRISTOPHER. 1981. *The Making of the Micro: A History of the Computer.* New York: Van Nostrand Reinhold.

FADER, DANIEL N., AND ELTON B. MCNEIL. 1968. *Hooked on Books.* New York: Berkley.

FEURZEIG, W., P. HOROWITZ, AND R. S. NICKERSON. 1982. *Microcomputers in Education.* National Institute of Education and Ministry for the Development of Human Intelligence, Republic of Venezuela, Report No. 4798. Washington, D.C.: Department of Health, Education, and Welfare. Quoted in Donna M. DeBonis, David Joseph, and Janet Prezioso, "Education's New Alphabet: Alphanumeric, Byte, Chip," *Academic Therapy* 18, no. 2 (November): 138.

FITZSIMMONS, ROBERT J., AND BRADLEY M. LOOMBER. 1978. *Spelling: Learning and*

Instruction—Research and Practice. Iowa State Department of Public Instruction and the University of Iowa (ERIC CS 205 117).

FLESCH, RUDOLF. 1981. *Why Johnny Still Can't Read.* New York: Harper and Row.

FRASE, LAWRENCE T., AND BARRY J. SCHWARTZ. 1975. "Effect of Question Production and Answering on Prose Recall." *Journal of Educational Psychology* 67, no. 5 (October): 628–635.

FREEMAN, RUTH H. 1983. "Poetry Writing in the Upper Elementary Grades." *The Reading Teacher* 37, no. 4 (December): 238–242.

FROST, DAVID. 1983. *Book of the World's Worst Decisions.* New York: Crown.

GABEL, DAVID. 1982. "Monitors: The Better to See Your Data With." *Personal Computing* 6, no. 12 (December): 112–197.

GENGLER, CHARLES. 1972. *Oregon ASCD Curriculum Bulletin.* Salem, Oreg.: Oregon Association for Supervision and Curriculum Development.

GEVA, ESTHER. 1981. *Facilitating Reading Comprehension Through Flowcharting.* Technical Report No. 211. Urbana, Ill.: Center for the Study of Reading, University of Illinois.

GOLES, GORDON G. 1982. "Games as Teaching Tools: Effective Uses of the Child in All of Us, Part I." *Educational Computer Magazine* 2, no. 6 (November–December): 12–14.

GOLES, GORDON G. 1983. "Games as Teaching Tools: Effective Uses of the Child in All of Us, Part II." *Educational Computer Magazine* 2, no. 7 (January–February): 41–44.

GOODMAN, KENNETH. 1967. "Reading: A Psycholinguistic Guessing Game." *Journal of the Reading Specialist* 6, no. 4 (May): 126–135.

GOULD, JOHN D., JOHN CONTI, AND TODD HOVANYECZ. 1983. "Composing Letters with a Simulated Listening Typewriter." *Communications of the ACM* 26, no. 4 (April): 295–308.

GRAVES, DONALD. 1983. *Writing: Teachers and Children at Work.* New York: Heinemann.

GUSZAK, FRANK. 1967. "Teacher Questioning and Reading." *The Reading Teacher* 21, no. 3 (December): 227–234.

HALL, GENE E. 1981. "Issues Related to the Implementation of Computers in Classrooms." *The Journal of Computers in Mathematics and Science Teaching* 1, no. 2 (October): 14–19.

HANSEN, JANE. 1981. "An Inferential Comprehension Strategy for Use with Primary Grade Children." *The Reading Teacher* 34, no. 6 (March): 665–669.

HARRIS, ALBERT J. 1968. "Research on Some Aspects of Comprehension: Rate Flexibility and Study Skills." *Journal of Reading* 12, no. 3 (December): 205–210, 258–260.

HARTLEY, J. ROGER, AND, KENNETH LOVELL. 1978. "The Psychological Principles Underlying the Design of Computer-Based Instructional Systems." In *Computer-Based Science Instruction,* ed. A. Jones and H. Weinstock, pp. 115–140. Rockville, Md.: Sijthoff and Noordhoff International.

HASSINGER, JACK, AND MURRAY VIA. 1969. "How Much Does a Tutor Learn Through Teaching Reading?" *Journal of Secondary Education* 44, no. 1 (January): 42–44.

HEILMAN, ARTHUR. 1977. *Principles and Practices of Teaching Reading.* Columbus, Ohio: Charles E. Merrill.

HEINTZ, CARL. 1982. "Buyer's Guide to Word Processing Software." *Interface Age* 7, no. 12 (December): 40–58.

HERBER, HAROLD. 1978. *Teaching Reading in Content Areas,* 2nd ed. Englewood Cliffs, N.J.: Prentice-Hall.

HUCK, CHARLOTTE S. 1979. "No Wider Than the Heart Is Wide." In *Using Literature and Poetry Affectively*, ed. Jon E. Shapiro, pp. 26–36. Newark, Del.: International Reading Association.

HUEY, EDMUND BURKE. 1908. *The Psychology and Pedagogy of Reading.* New York: Macmillan.

INTERNATIONAL READING ASSOCIATION COMPUTER TECHNOLOGY AND READING COMMITTEE. 1984. "Guidelines for Educators on Using Computers in the Schools." *The Reading Teacher* 38, no. 1 (October): 80–82.

JACKSON, ROBERT. 1983. "Five Ways to Use Databases in Social Studies." *Teaching and Computers* 1, no. 3 (November/December): 16–18.

JOHNSON, DAVID W., GEOFFREY MARUYAMA, ROGER JOHNSON, DEBORAH NELSON, AND LINDA SKON. 1981. "Effects of Cooperative, Competitive, and Individualistic Goal Structures on Achievement: A Meta-Analysis." *Psychological Bulletin* 89, no. 1 (January): 47–62.

JONGSMA, EUGENE. 1980. *Cloze Instruction Research: A Second Look.* Newark, Del.: International Reading Association.

KAAKE, DIANNE M. 1983. "Teaching Elementary Age Children Touch Typing as an Aid to Language Arts Instruction." *The Reading Teacher* 36, no. 7 (March): 640–644.

KAESS, WALTER, AND DAVID ZEAMAN. 1960. "Positive and Negative Knowledge of Results on a Pressey-Type Punchboard." *Journal of Experimental Psychology* 60, no. 1 (July): 12–17.

KAMIN, S., AND M. WAITE. 1982. *Apple Backpack.* New York: McGraw-Hill.

KARLIN, ROBERT. 1975. *Teaching Elementary Reading*, 2nd ed. New York: Harcourt.

KEPNER, TERRY. 1983. "Add Luster to Your Letters." *Popular Computing* 2, no. 11 (September): 196–198.

KING, R. TOMMY. 1982. "Learning from a PAL." *The Reading Teacher* 36, no. 6 (March): 682–685.

KINTSCH, WALTER, AND TEUN A. VAN DIJK. 1978. "Toward a Model of Text Comprehension and Production." *Psychological Review* 85, no. 5 (September): 363–394.

KOCH, KENNETH. 1970. *Wishes, Lies, and Dreams.* New York: Vintage.

KOCH, KENNETH. 1974. *Rose, Where Did You Get That Red.* New York: Vintage.

KOKOVICH, ANTHONY, AND GERALD MATTHEWS. 1971. "Reading and the Self-Concept," *The National Elementary Principal* 50, no. 3 (January): 53–54.

LABERGE, DAVID, AND S. JAY SAMUELS. 1974. "Toward a Theory of Automatic Information Processing in Reading." *Cognitive Psychology* 6, no. 3 (April): 293–323.

LEHR, FRAN. 1981. "Bibliotherapy." *Journal of Reading* 25, no. 1 (October): 76–79.

LEIBLUM, MARK D. 1982. "Computer-Managed Instruction: An Explanation and Overview." *AEDS Journal* 15, no. 3 (Spring): 126–142.

LEVIN, JAMES A. 1982. "Computers in Non-School Settings: Implications for Education." *Sigcue Bulletin* 16, no. 1 (Summer): 2–15.

LUEHRMANN, ARTHUR. 1983. "Don't Feel Bad About Teaching BASIC." *Electronic Learning* 3, no. 1 (September): 23–24.

MAGER, ROBERT F. 1962. *Preparing Instructional Objectives.* Palo Alto, Calif.: Fearon.

MALONE, THOMAS W. 1981. "Toward a Theory of Intrinsically Motivating Instruction." *Cognitive Science* 5, no. 4 (October–December): 333–369.

MALONE, THOMAS W., AND JAMES LEVIN. 1984. "Microcomputers in Education: Cognitive and Social Design Principles." In *Instructional Software: Principles and Perspectives for Design and Use*, ed. Decker F. Walker and Robert D. Hess, pp. 20–37. Belmont, Calif.: Wadsworth.

Manzo, A. V., and J. K. Sherk. 1972. "Some Generalizations and Strategies for Guiding Vocabulary Learning." *Journal of Reading Behavior* 4, no. 1 (Winter): 78–79.

Marcus, Stephen. 1983. "The Muse and the Machine: A Computers and Poetry Project." *Pipeline* 8, no. 1 (Spring): 10–12.

Marcus, Stephen, and Sheridan Blau. 1983. "Not Seeing Is Believing: Invisible Writing with Computers." *Educational Technology* 23, no. 4 (April): 12–15.

Mason, Betty. 1976. "The Effect of University Student Tutors on the Self-Concepts of Elementary School Pupils." Ph.D. diss., Louisiana State University, Baton Rouge.

Mason, George E., Jay S. Blanchard, and Danny B. Daniel. 1983. *Computer Applications in Reading.* Newark, Del.: International Reading Association.

McLuhan, Marshall. 1964. *Understanding Media: The Extensions of Man.* New York: McGraw-Hill.

McWilliams, Peter A. 1983. *The Personal Computer Book.* New York: Ballantine.

MECC. 1981. *What Would You Do? Simulations in Social Studies: MECC Elementary Volume 6 Teacher's Support Booklet.* St. Paul, Minn.: Minnesota Educational Computing Consortium.

Melaragno, Ralph J. 1976. *Tutoring with Students.* Englewood Cliffs, N.J.: Educational Technology Publications.

Melmed, Arthur S. 1982. "Information Technology for U.S. Schools." *Phi Delta Kappan* 63, no. 5 (January): 308–311.

Micklos, John J., Jr. 1980. "The Facts, Please, About Reading Achievement in American Schools." *Journal of Reading* 24, no. 1 (October): 41–45.

Mikulecky, Larry. 1982. "Job Literacy: The Relationship Between School Preparation and Workplace Actuality." *Reading Research Quarterly* 17, no. 3: 400–419.

Modla, Virginia B. 1984. "Writing a Program to Reinforce Reading Skills." *Computers, Reading, and Language Arts* 1, no. 4 (Spring): 27–29.

Moffett, James, and Betty Jane Wagner. 1983. *A Student-Centered Language Arts and Reading, K–13,* 3rd ed. Boston: Houghton Mifflin.

Monahan, Brian D., and Gerald Scoland. 1983. "Using the Computer in High School Journalism." *Computers, Reading, and Language Arts* 1, no. 2 (Fall): 27–29.

Morrow, Lesley Mandel. 1982. *Organizing for Reading Instruction: An Individualized Plan.* York, Pa.: Strine.

Mueller, Robert E. 1984. "The Cultured Computer." *Creative Computing* 10, no. 1 (January): 262–264.

Mueser, Anne Marie. 1981. *Reading Aids Through the Grades.* New York: Teachers College Press.

Naisbitt, John. 1982. *Megatrends.* New York: Warner Books.

New York City Bureau of Curriculum Development. 1968. *Sequential Levels of Reading Skills, Prekindergarten–Grade 12.* New York: Bureau of Curriculum Development, Board of Education of the City of New York.

Niles, Olive S. 1968. "Comprehension Skills." In *Developing Comprehension, Including Critical Reading,* ed. Mildred A. Dawson, pp. 126–131. Newark, Del.: International Reading Association.

O'Brien, Thomas C. 1983. "Software of the Second-and-a-Half Kind." *Classroom Computer Learning* 4, no. 2 (September): 33–36.

O'Day, Edward F. 1971. *Programmed Instruction: Techniques and Trends.* New York: Appleton-Century-Crofts.

Omanson, Richard C., William H. Warren, and Tom Trabasso. 1978. "Goals,

Inferential Comprehension, and Recall of Stories by Children." *Discourse Processes* 1, no. 4 (October–December): 337–354.

ORWIG, GARY W., AND WILLIAM S. HODGES. 1982. *The Computer Tutor.* Boston: Little, Brown.

PAPERT, SEYMOUR. 1980. *Mindstorms.* New York: Basic Books.

PEARSON, P. DAVID, AND DALE D. JOHNSON. 1978. *Teaching Reading Comprehension.* New York: Holt, Rinehart, and Winston.

PERL, SONDRA. 1980. "Understanding Composing." *College Composition and Communication* 31, no. 4 (December): 363–369.

PETROSKY, ANTHONY. 1982. "Reading and Writing." Paper presented at the College Reading Association, Philadelphia, October.

PFLUGER, ELINOR. 1983. "Write a Cinquain." *Teaching and Computers* 1, no. 3 (November/December): 36–37.

POOLE, LON. 1981. *Apple II User's Guide.* Berkeley, Calif.: Osborne/McGraw-Hill.

PRESS, LARRY. 1976. "Computers in the English Curriculum." In *The Best of Creative Computing.* Vol. 1, ed. David Ahl, pp. 202–204. Morris Plains, N.J.: Creative Computing Press.

QUISENBERRY, NATHAN L. 1978. "Relationship of TV Viewing to Violence and Aggression." *Childhood Education* 55, no. 1 (October): 59–64.

REINKING, DAVID. P. 1984a. "Reading, Computers, and a New Technology of Print." Unpublished paper. New Brunswick, N.J.: Graduate School of Education, Rutgers University.

REINKING, DAVID P. 1984b. "Reading Software: Current Limitations and Future Potential." Unpublished paper. New Brunswick, N.J.: Graduate School of Education, Rutgers University.

REINKING, DAVID P., AND ROBERT SCHREINER. 1984. "The Effects of Computer-Mediated Text on Measures of Reading Comprehension and Reading Behavior." Unpublished paper. New Brunswick, N.J.: Graduate School of Education, Rutgers University.

RIGGS, CORINNE W. (Ed.). 1971. *Bibliotherapy: An Annotated Bibliography.* Newark, Del.: International Reading Association.

ROBINSON, HELEN M. 1972. "Perceptual Training—Does It Result in Reading Improvement?" In *Some Persistent Questions on Beginning Reading,* ed. Robert C. Aukerman, pp. 135–150. Newark, Del.: International Reading Association.

ROBLYER, M. D. 1982. "Courseware: A Critical Look at 'Making Best Use of the Medium.'" *Educational Technology* 22, no. 7 (July): 29–30.

ROSENSHINE, BARAK V. 1980. "Skill Hierarchies in Reading Comprehension." In *Theoretical Issues in Reading Comprehension,* ed. Rand J. Spiro, Bertram C. Bruce, and William F. Brewer, pp. 535–554. Hillsdale, N.J.: Lawrence Erlbaum.

ROSENTHAL, ROBERT, AND LENORE JACOBSON. 1968. *Pygmalion in the Classroom.* New York: Holt, Rinehart, and Winston.

ROTENBERG, LESLI. 1983. "A Computer Carol." *Teaching and Computers* 1, no. 3 (November/December): 28–31.

RUBIN, ANDEE. 1980. "Theoretical Taxonomy of the Differences Between Oral and Written Language." In *Theoretical Issues in Reading Comprehension,* ed. Rand J. Spiro, Bertram C. Bruce, and William F. Brewer, pp. 411–438. Hillsdale, N.J.: Lawrence Erlbaum.

RUBIN, ANDEE. 1983. "The Computer Confronts the Language Arts: Cans and Shoulds for Education." In *Classroom Computers and Cognitive Science,* ed. A. C. Wilkinson. New York: Academic Press.

RUBIN, ANDEE, AND DEDRE GENTNER. 1982. "An Educational Technique to Encourage Practice with High-Level Aspects of Text." Report. Cambridge, Mass.: Bolt, Beranek, and Newman.

RUMELHART, DAVID. 1977. "Understanding and Summarizing Brief Stories." In *Basic Processes in Reading: Perception and Comprehension*, ed. David LaBerge and S. Jay Samuels. Hillsdale, N.J.: Lawrence Erlbaum.

RUSSELL, DAVID H., AND CHARLES SHRODES. 1950. "Contributions of Research in Bibliotherapy to the Language Arts Program." *School Review* 57, no. 3 (February): 335–342.

SAETTLER, PAUL L. 1968. *A History of Instructional Technology*. New York: McGraw-Hill.

SAMUELS, S. JAY. 1976. "Hierarchical Subskills in the Reading Acquisition Process." In *Aspects of Reading Acquisition*, ed. John T. Guthrie. Baltimore: John Hopkins University Press.

SANDBERG-DIMENT, ERIK. 1983. "For Memory, the Cassette Is a Poor Choice." *New York Times*, March 15, p. C2.

SCHRAMM, WILBUR. 1977. *Big Media, Little Media*. Beverly Hills, Calif.: Sage.

SCHWARTZ, LAWRENCE. 1983. "Teaching Writing in the Age of the Word Processor and Personal Computer." *Educational Technology* 23, no. 6 (June): 33–35.

SCHWARTZ, MIMI. 1983. "Computers and the Teaching of Writing." *Educational Technology* 22, no. 11 (November): 27–29.

SHAUGHNESSY, MINA. 1977. *Errors and Expectations*. New York: Oxford University Press.

SHELTON, J. B., AND GLENN M. KLEIMAN. 1983. "Computers and Teaching Children to Read." *Compute!* 5, no. 10 (October): 132–136.

SHEPARD, LORRIE A., MARY LEE SMITH, AND CAROL P. VOJIR. 1983. "Characteristics of Pupils Identified as Learning Disabled." *American Educational Research Journal* 20, no. 3 (Fall): 309–331.

SINGER, HARRY, AND DAN DONLAN. 1980. *Reading and Learning from Text*. Boston: Little, Brown.

SKINNER, BURRHUS FREDERIC. 1953. *Science and Human Behavior*. New York: Macmillan.

SMITH, FRANK. 1978. *Reading Without Nonsense*. New York: Teachers College Press.

SMITH, RICHARD J., AND DALE D. JOHNSON. 1980. *Teaching Children to Read*. Reading, Mass.: Addison-Wesley.

STAPLES, BETSY. 1984. "Growing Up Literate, Part 5," *Creative Computing* 10, no. 4 (April): 64–76.

STEFFENSEN, MARGARET S., CHITRA JOAG-DEV, AND RICHARD C. ANDERSON. 1979. "A Cross-Cultural Perspective on Reading Comprehension." *Reading Research Quarterly* 15, no. 1: 10–29.

STEIN, ALETHA HUSTON-, SANDRA FOX, DOUGLAS GREER, BRUCE A. WATKINS, AND JANE WHITAKER. 1981. "The Effects of TV Action and Violence on Children's Social Behavior." *Journal of Genetic Psychology* 138, no. 2 (June): 183–191.

STEWART, GEORGE. 1983. "Translating BASIC Programs." *Popular Computing* 2, no. 9 (September): 230–236.

STOWBRIDGE, MARC D., AND PETER KUGEL. 1983. "Learning to Learn by Learning to Play." *Creative Computing* 9, no. 4 (April): 180–188.

SUTTLES, A. L. 1983. "Computers and Writing: Contemporary Research and Innovative Programs." *Computers, Reading, and Language Arts* 1, no. 1 (Summer): 33–37.

SWITZER, MARY ELLEN. 1979. "Getting Keyed Up About Language Arts." *Early Years* 10, no. 3 (November): 24–25, 64.

TAYLOR, WILSON L. 1953. "Cloze Procedure: A New Tool for Measuring Readability." *Journalism Quarterly* 30, no. 4 (Fall): 415–433.

THE, LEE. 1983. "Hard Disk Drives: Are They Worth the Price?" *Popular Computing* 2, no. 3 (January): 80–104.

THORNDIKE, EDWARD L. 1917. "Reading as Reasoning: A Study of Mistakes in Paragraph Reading." *Journal of Educational Psychology* 8, no. 6 (June): 323–332.

TIERNEY, ROBERT J., AND P. DAVID PEARSON. 1981. *Learning to Learn from Text: A Framework for Improving Classroom Practice.* Reading Education Report No. 30. Champaign, Ill.: Center for the Study of Reading, University of Illinois.

TINKER, MILES A. 1967. "Devices to Improve Speed of Reading." *The Reading Teacher* 20, no. 7 (April): 605–609.

TOVEY, DUANE R. 1976. "Improving Children's Comprehension Abilities." *The Reading Teacher* 30, no. 3 (December): 288–292.

VACCA, RICHARD T. 1980. "A Study of Holistic and Subskill Instructional Approaches to Reading Comprehension." *Journal of Reading* 23, no. 6 (March): 512–518.

VEATCH, JEANETTE. 1959. *Individualizing Your Reading Program.* New York: Putnam.

VICTOR, JOHN. 1983. Letter to the editor. *Creative Computing* 9, no. 10 (October): 10.

WALKER, DECKER F., AND ROBERT D. HESS. 1984. *Instructional Software: Principles and Perspectives for Design and Use.* Belmont, Calif.: Wadsworth.

WATT, DAN. 1983. "Games Designed for Learning." *Popular Computing* 2, no. 9 (July): 65–67.

WATT, DANIEL. 1982. "Close Encounters with Software." *Popular Computing* 1, no. 8 (August): 157–184.

WATT, DANIEL. 1983. "The Wired Classroom: A Look at Local Networking in the School." *Popular Computing* 2, no. 6 (June): 70–82.

WEDMAN, JUDY. 1983. "Reading Skills: Are the Software Scales Properly Balanced?" *Media and Methods* 19, no. 6 (February): 25–27.

WEIZENBAUM, JOSEPH. 1976. *Computer Power and Human Reason.* San Francisco: W. H. Freeman.

WEPNER, SHELLEY B. 1983. "Computer Flowcharts: Road Maps to Reading Skills." *Computers, Reading, and Language Arts* 1, no. 2 (Fall): 14–17.

WHEELER, PATRICIA M. 1983. "Matching Abilities in Cross-Age Tutoring." *Journal of Reading* 26, no. 5 (February): 404–407.

WITTROCK, M. C. 1979. "Applications of Cognitive Psychology to Education and Training." In *Cognitive and Affective Learning Strategies*, ed. Harold F. O'Neil and Charles D. Spielberger, pp. 309–317. New York: Academic Press.

YAKAL, KATHY. 1983. "Nonviolent Games." *Compute!* 5, no. 10 (October): 40–48.

INDEX

7632